The Poor Had No Lawyers

Andy Wightman is an independent researcher and writer and one of Scotland's leading authorities on landownership, land rights and land reform. Born in Dundee, he was educated at the University of Aberdeen and has worked as a stalker's ghillie, environmental scientist, and an environmental campaigner before becoming self-employed in 1993. Previous books include *Who Owns Scotland* (1996) and *Scotland: Land and Power* (1999). His research interests include land relations, governance, power, local democraacy and money. He runs the www.whoownsscotland.org.uk website and a popular blog at www.andywightman.com. He lives in Edinburgh.

Now a green msp.

The Poor Had No Lawyers

Who Owns Scotland
(And How They Got It)

Andy Wightman

BIRLINN

To Isla

This edition published in 2013 by
Birlinn Limited
West Newington House
10 Newington Road
Edinburgh
EH9 1QS

www.birlinn.co.uk

ISBN: 978 1 78027 114 9

British Library Cataloguing-in-Publication Data
A catalogue record for this book is available from the British Library

Typeset by Iolaire Typesetting, Newtonmore
Printed and bound by Grafica Veneta
www.graficaveneta.com

Contents

Figures, Tables and Plates   ix
Acknowledgements   xiii
Foreword to the 2013 edition   xvii
Foreword to the 2011 edition   xix

1 Show the People That Our Old Nobility Is Not Noble   1
  Why the land question still matters

2 Superiors and Vassals   8
  A brief discourse on terminology

3 Robert the Bruce – A Murdering Medieval Warlord   12
  The first land grab – feudal colonisation to 1500

4 To Spoil the Kirk of Christ of Her Patrimony   23
  The second land grab – the lands of the Church

5 The Palladium of Our Land Proprietors   31
  The third land grab – involving the lawyers

6 In Edinburgh They Hate Us   57
  A short excursion into the Highlands

7 A State of Possession Already Subsisting Beyond the
      Memory of Man   66
  The fourth land grab – the commonties

8 Mere Miserable Starved Caricatures of Their
      Former Greatness   74
  The fifth land grab – the burgh commons

9 I Hereby Take Possession of This Island of Rockall   88
  The sixth land grab – colonial adventures

10 Look Here, Boy, Steady On. Let's Get This
      Thing Straight   102
   Politics and the Landed Elite

11 Lord Derby, Lloyd George and John McEwen   120
   *A Tory, a Liberal and a Socialist try to find out who
      owns Scotland*

12 Who Owns Scotland?   142
   The facts

13 A Considerable Ridge of Very High and Lofty Hills   167
   The Cuillin, MacLeod and a leaky castle

14 Simple Fraudulent Misrepresentation   184
   Scotland's Crown lands

15 From Lord Leverhulme to Lord Sewel   192
   Community ownership of land

16 Those Who for Our Sake Went Down to the
      Dark River   206
   The rise of the heritage landowner

17 Tartanry, Royalty and Balmorality   219
   The rise of the hunting estate

18 I Want the Assurance That I Will Not Be Evicted   232
   Farming and the agricultural tenant

19 A Highly Unsatisfactory Guddle   249
   Crofting and the Scottish Parliament

20 Planting Forests Is a Sure Way to Grow Rich   255
   Trees are political

21 I Will Not Allow House Prices to Get Out of Control   263
   The new property-owning democracy

22 Three Score Men with Clubs and Staves   268
   The struggle to protect common land

23 All Property of a Burgh   292
   Scotland's common good

24 Let for a Penny a Year   305
   The strange case of the Edinburgh common good

25 Problems Rarely Arise with Land in Private Ownership 311
   Land Reform in the twentieth century

26 Little More Than an Instrument for Extracting Money   330
   Land tenure reform in Scotland

27 Bureaucratic Nit-picking and Fine Legal Arguments   343
   The community right to buy

28 Undermining the Whole Fabric of Scottish Family Life   359
   The law of succession

29 Their Unjust Concealing of Some Private Right   368
   Secrecy in Scottish landownership

30 We Do Not Want to Punish the Landlord   376
   Land values and land value taxation

31 A Public Park and Recreation Ground for the
      Public Behoof   390
   Finding out more about community land rights

32 The Poor Still Have No Lawyers   401
   The way forward for land reform

Notes   413
Bibliography and Further Reading   439
Appendix   449
Index   451

Figures, Tables and Plates

Figures
 1 Parishes, baronies, earldoms and lordships in early
    fifteenth-century Scotland   21
 2 Distribution of commonties   67
3a Land Register coverage – titles   123
3b Land Register coverage – area   124
 4 Areas of land registered on the Land Register 2012   125
 5 Rural land owned by Scottish Ministers and public
    bodies under their direction, 2012   147
 6 Map of the Cuillin   169
 7 Distribution of sporting estates   221
 8 The pattern of private forest ownership in Europe
    and Scotland   261
 9 Diagram showing the difference in price of an
    identical house across the UK   265
10 Rynacra Commonty, Perthshire   273
11 Example of a Search Sheet   394–395

Tables
1a Landownership in Scotland, 2012   142
1b Urban/rural landownership in Scotland breakdown,
    2012   143
1c Four broad categories of rural landownership   143
2a Concentration of private rural landownership in
    Scotland, 1872–2012   143
2b Breakdown of private rural landownership in Scotland
    for 1970, 1995 and 2012   144

3   Breakdown of private rural landownership in Scotland,
    1970–2012   145
4   Landownership by public bodies, 2012   146
5   Land owned by Scottish Natural Heritage   148
6   MoD land owned by the Secretary of State for
    Defence   149
7   The 100 largest landholdings in Scotland, 2012   154–161
8   The 50 largest offshore landholdings in Scotland,
    2012   163–165
9   Community landownership in Scotland, 2012   200–201
10 Heritage landownership in Scotland, 2012   216
11 The extent of deer forests and hunting estates,
    1883–2002   222
12 The percentage of farms that are tenanted,
    1940–2008   239
13 The recipients of the 50 largest farming subsidies,
    2000–2009   243–244
14 Timeline of land reform   312–313
15 Foreign and beneficial ownership of privately
    owned rural land in Scotland, 2012   372
16 Scottish land values and the Land Value Tax
    proposal   387
17 Council Tax v Land Value Tax   388

Plates
1   Moon deed
2   Common chest of Wittenburg of 1522 in Luther House,
    Wittenburg
3   Valuation Office (Scotland) map: 1/1250 OS sheet Perthshire
    LII.15 NE
4   Allan MacRae, Chairman of the Assynt Crofters' Trust,
    celebrating the acquisition of the North Lochinver Estate
    by the Assynt Crofters' Trust
5   Newspaper advertisement for the Cuillin
6   The First Raid on Alyth Hill
7   The Second Raid on Alyth Hill with Councillor Matt Cright-
    on cutting the fence closely observed by the Alyth Consta-
    bulary

8   Rockall as unclaimed territory. Photographed from HMS *Vidal*, 17 September 1955, the day before its formal annexation

9   Affixing the plaque annexing Rockall to the Crown, on 18 September 1955 – from left to right, Lieutenant Commander Desmond P. D. Scott, Corporal A. A. Fraser and James Fisher

10   The author and Brandy, a Highland garron, in Glen Esk

11   Kinross Town Hall and library in a state of dereliction, 2006

12   Return of Owners of Lands and Heritages, Scotland, 1872–1873

13   *Daily Mail* front page, 24 January 2003

Acknowledgements

I am indebted to the many people who, over the past thirty years, have nurtured and sustained my interest in matters to do with land and its ownership. Perhaps, perversely, I should start by thanking some of the academic staff at the University of Aberdeen's Forestry Department who, by denying that such a topic was of any relevance to the study of forestry, first got me curious about it in the early 1980s. At that time, I was fortunate also to meet and get to know some big thinkers whose application to the process of scientific enquiry was inspirational and I include among them Dr Adam Watson, Drennan Watson and the late Professor Sandy Mather, who sadly died in November 2006. Two other people I first met then have remained good friends and critical colleagues along the way, namely Graham Boyd and Robin Callander, and I thank them for their ongoing support and encouragement.

This book draws on the work of many people whom I hope I have acknowledged in the appropriate manner. In particular, I would like to thank Brian Wilson, Alan Blackshaw, Robin Callander, John MacAskill, Alastair McIntosh, Fiona Mackenzie, Allan Wilson and Jim Hunter for their assistance at various stages.

I am grateful to the staff of the Registers of Scotland and the National Archives of Scotland who have provided a wonderful service over the years. Chris Fleet, map curator at the National Library of Scotland, has also been most helpful. Anne Laird at the Registers of Scotland kindly provided the map in Figure 4. Many academics helped me by providing copies of papers I would otherwise have had to pay substantial amounts of money for (see below). Particular thanks to Anne Bivert at the Revue de l'Institut de Sociologie in Bruxelles who kindly sent me a copy of Ian Adams' paper of 1973 – a hidden gem which I had been looking for for many years.

I am indebted to Fraser MacDonald, Walla Mollison, Dr Alexander Grant, Sheila Leckie, Shona Harper and John Paul Photography for their help in providing illustrations.

The ongoing project to document landownership in Scotland (www.whoownsscotland.org.uk) has been made possible by the generous donations of many people since 2003 and by the subscribers since October 2009. I thank all of them. Noel Darlow has done a magnificent job at looking after the technical side of the website and has worked tirelessly to make the whole project feasible. Many thanks, Noel.

Thank you, Jean Urquhart and Gerry Hassan, for inviting me to Changin Scotland in Ullapool in November 2009 to give a talk on the land question which was the inspiration for setting all these thoughts down on paper. I am indebted to Hugh Andrew from Birlinn who was at the same event and who agreed to publish this book. All the staff were unfailingly helpful for which I'm most grateful. I am particularly grateful to my editor, Patricia Marshall, and to Andrew Simmons who both worked tirelessly during the production process. A special mention should be made of James Hutcheson who not only designed this book but designed my 1996 edition of *Who Owns Scotland* and John McEwen's original *Who Owns Scotland* way back in 1977!

Uncharacteristically, perhaps, I would like to put on record one source of information that has been singularly unhelpful to me and that is the academic community. I don't mean individuals, many of whom have been most supportive and have assisted me in subverting some, but not all, of the difficulties I have encountered. I mean the world of academic publishing. Over the course of writing this book, I wanted to get hold of over one hundred academic publications. These are all available on various websites but typically cost £20 each. If, on the other hand, you are employed by an academic institution, they are free. I don't understand why the fruits of academic research, much of which is paid for by government funds, should not be available for free to the public. Indeed, that is surely the point of academic research. How is the public to understand more about climate change, for example, if they have to pay £20 to read an original academic paper? Of course I could have taken out membership of a university library but I would have had to join about six different universities across Scotland to obtain what I needed.

One particular case stands out and that is the UK Data Archive run by the University of Essex. This is a repository for a wide range of social and economic data. On their website, they urge academics to share their data, explaining that:

> Publicly funded research data are produced in the public interest and their value lies in their use and re-use. When data are managed well they can be shared and re-used for scientific and educational purposes. Researchers, funding agencies and the public benefit from data sharing.[1]

When I tried to register, however, I was told that since I was not employed by an academic institution, I would have to pay £450 to register and £50 for each data set I required. Not surprisingly, I declined the offer.

This book could have contained a good deal more research if data collected with public funds were made available to the citizens who pay for them with their taxes.

Finally I would like to thank Cathy and Isla who have put up with me over a rather intensive period of writing.

Foreword to the 2013 Edition

On 5 May 2011, the Scottish National Party won an unprecedented victory in the Scottish Parliamentary election. A five-year term of office and an overall majority provides the Scottish Government with considerable freedom to undertake radical reform of Scotland's land and property regime. Since the first publication of this book in 2010, very little of substance has been done to address the topics discussed in the pages that follow.

In July 2012, the Government set up a Land Reform Review Group which has been asked to produce a Final Report in April 2014. Whether it produces anything of substance and whether (more importantly) there is the political will to introduce radical land reform remains to be seen. With a referendum on independence in 2014, political energies are focused elsewhere for the foreseeable future. Whether the situation will be any different after 2014 is, as yet, unclear.

Land relations in Scotland continue to be neglected in mainstream public policy and elite interests in landownership, land use, finance and property development continue to exert significant influence on the political establishment. The issues explored in this book are of long standing and remain to be resolved. To keep up with developments in the various debates, please go to www.andywightman.com/poor where you will find quarterly updates. Many of the references can also be found there.

In the foreword to the 2011 edition (see p. xix), I highlighted the significance of the cover image and the history of this settlement in highland Aberdeenshire. I concluded that this empty house stands as eloquent testimony to our continual failure to challenge landed power. As this 2013 edition of the book goes to press, there is no sign that this is going to change anytime soon.

Andy Wightman
Edinburgh, February 2013

Foreword to the 2011 Edition

On 5 May 2011, the Scottish National Party won an unprecedented victory in the Scottish Parliamentary election. This historic win could lead to a resolution of many of the issues discussed in this book. That remains to be seen. However, with an overall majority in the Parliament, the Scottish Government can now look forward to a five-year term of office with the freedom to undertake quite radical reform of Scotland's land and property regime if it chooses to do so.

The First Minister, Alex Salmond, has already indicated that he wishes to see the administration of the Crown property rights that comprise the Crown Estate in Scotland brought under the control of the Scottish Parliament. The SNP manifesto also contains commitments to review the Land Reform (Scotland) Act 2003 and to re-establish the Scottish Land Fund. Many of the topics discussed in this book, such as succession law, land registration, common good land and land value taxation could all now be tackled and deliver lasting public and private benefits – if the political will exists.

The issues explored in this book are of long standing and remain to be resolved. Since the book was first published in October 2010, however, some of the detailed discussion surrounding these issues has moved on. To keep up with developments in the various debates, please go to www.andywightman.com/poor, where you will find quarterly updates. Many of the references can also be found there.

It is also worth saying something about the cover photograph, which is an allegory for the argument presented in this book. The image is of Ardoch farmhouse in Glen Gairn, Aberdeenshire.* Ardoch was a clachan of some 14 houses with a shop and a school. It was also the home of my wife's great-great-great grandfather's brother, Father Lachlan McIntosh, the parish priest in Glen Gairn for 64 years until his death in 1845, aged 93. The reason that this Highland community was abandoned is directly attributable to the fact that Aberdeenshire was excluded from the provisions of the 1886 Crofting Act and therefore the residents of Ardoch were never more than a year away from eviction. The reason that the last remaining house lies empty today on a large privately owned estate is eloquent testimony to our continuing failure to challenge landed power.

Andy Wightman
Edinburgh
May 2011

* Further images of Ardoch Farmhouse can be seen at: www.jamesdyasdavidson.com

1

Show the People That Our Old Nobility Is Not Noble

Why the land question still matters

This book is inspired by a talk I gave at the Changin Scotland conference at The Ceilidh Place in Ullapool organised by Gerry Hassan and Jean Urquhart in November 2009. I had last been at this event in 2003 when I organised a 'walk and talk' event which took people into the Inverpolly National Nature Reserve where, for several hours in beautiful weather, we discussed everything from deer management, the Moine thrust and carnivorous plants to absentee landlords, capital tax exemptions and land reform.

The talk was called 'The Poor had no Lawyers' and was an attempt to synthesise much of the work I have been doing over the past ten years. The title of that talk and this book is taken from an essay by Cosmo Innes (1798–1874), who was Professor of Universal History and Greek and Roman Antiquities (a Chair that was later named Constitutional Law and History) at the University of Edinburgh from 1846 until his death – of which more later. In particular, I wanted to place contemporary concerns about land in their proper historical context since it had been evident to me for some time that, despite a high-profile debate on land issues in Scotland, there remained a dearth of historical perspective, an understandable but distorted focus on the Highlands and Islands and a worrying lack of understanding of how the law operates.

Over the past decade or so, I have met and spoken to many people from all parts of Scotland about issues to do with land. It is clear that land and its ownership in villages, towns and rural areas across Scotland remains a pressing issue of concern. A frequent topic of interest is often a very small piece of land that the community has an interest in and which people assert is common land. The origins of such beliefs are to be found in the history of Scotland's villages, estates, parishes, burghs and land law and they became the focus for my work on common good and commons in general. Some of the elements of this story deserve to be made better known and this book is a modest attempt at doing so.

The institution of landownership in Scotland evolved gradually and it evolved under the political control of landowners and their agents in the legal establishment. This was the key to its survival and to the development of the current pattern of ownership. The role of the law has historically been to serve the interest of those in power and, in Ullapool and elsewhere, it is evident that there is a hunger for greater understanding and depth to contemporary debates on land in Scotland. It was with this in mind that I felt the time was right to expose some of this to wider public scrutiny.

This book follows a number of previous ones on the topic. Callander's *A Pattern of Landownership in Scotland* was (and remains) the most scholarly account of how the *pattern* of land-ownership in Scotland emerged. My *Who Owns Scotland* in 1996 attempted to analyse the *current pattern* of landownership in Scotland. And Callander's *How Scotland Is Owned* was an *analysis of the system of land tenure* underpinning property rights in Scot-land. *The Poor Had No Lawyers* revisits Callander's classic from 1986 but goes further in focussing on the legal and political mechanisms that enabled vast areas of Scotland to be appropriated by private interests. This, in turn, leads into an analysis of who owns Scotland today and an exploration of some of the key developments in land policy over the past twenty years. The book finishes with a chapter outlining proposals for reforms to Scottish land law.

My thesis is not entirely new. Much of this story has been told before. But what I want to convey is how the theft of Scotland's commons has robbed us not only of extensive communal interests in land but of a sense of connection with place which is leading to all sorts of social and economic problems. In recent years, one of my colleagues in these matters, Alastair McIntosh, has been working assiduously on this question to show that soil and soul are vital ingredients in recovering a sense of identity and belonging. Likewise, we will benefit greatly from remembering that the struggle over land is a universal one that knows no geographic boundaries. We are all creatures who require shelter and nourishment and that comes from having a place to call home. Equally, whilst for good historical reasons land issues have become associated with the Highlands and Islands almost to the exclusion of the rest of the country, the historic struggle for land rights took place across the whole country. The womenfolk in Eyemouth defending their ancient rights, the tenant farmers in East Lothian evicted because they voted for the wrong party and the community activist in Easterhouse fighting for better housing are all part of the land reform struggle – a struggle to reform, to change, the legal and economic framework that today still constrains too many people from realising their potential.

I should stress one thing. This book is about how landed power emerged and how the legal establishment connived in this process. Consequently, it says less about how such power was exercised and thus, for example, there is little discussion about the Highland Clearances or other such events where such power was deployed. Devastating though such episodes were, they were merely a reflection of the central question posed here – who owns Scotland and how did they get it? In 1909, Tom Johnston, later to become Secretary of State for Scotland and one of Scotland's finest historians, wrote:

> Show the people that our Old Nobility is not noble, that its lands are stolen lands – stolen either by force or fraud; show people that the title-deeds are rapine, murder, massacre, cheating, or Court harlotry; dissolve the halo of divinity that surrounds the hereditary title; let the people clearly understand that our present House of Lords is composed largely of descendants of successful pirates and rogues; do these things and you shatter the Romance that keeps the nation numb and spellbound while privilege picks its pockets.[1]

Johnston's observation from 1909 got pulses racing at the time and inspired generations of land reformers. Despite this heady rhetoric, however, I was, for some years, sceptical of such claims. In an attempt to avoid being painted as just another populist land reformer, I eschewed such language. Always conscious of its power and authority, however (Johnston remains a distinguished historian), I made efforts to understand the legitimacy of such claims better and the extent to which they were true. My conclusions are that such claims are by and large true. Fraud and murder were widespread. The first Duke of Buccleuch, for example, was the illegitimate offspring of court harlotry and the Cawdor Campbells' origins are with the kidnap and forced marriage of a twelve-year-old girl. Land indeed was stolen and centuries of legal trickery ensured that it stayed that way.

Why have the implications of this not been more widely understood? It is only on close textual analysis of the best history books that anything of the magnitude of the theft is clear. Mainstream history tends to pay more attention to the narrative of history and the pace and flow of events. In this book, I have tried to show that the power behind this history is what the German writer Marianne Gronemeyer referred to as 'elegant power' which is characterised as unrecognizable, concealed and inconspicuous.[2]

Tom Johnston argued that:

> a democracy ignorant of the past is not qualified either to analyse the present or to shape the future; and so, in the interests of the high Priests of Politics and the Lordly Money-Changers of Society, great care has been taken to offer us stories of useless pageantry, chronicles of the birth and death of Kings, annals of Court intrigue and international war, while withheld from us were the real facts and narrative of moment, the loss of our ancient freedom, the rape of our common lands and the shameless and dastardly methods by which a few selected stocks snatched the patrimony of the people.[3]

In *Who Owns Scotland*, I told the apocryphal tale of a Scottish miner walking home one evening with a brace of pheasants in his pockets. He unexpectedly meets the landowner who informs him that this is his land and he had better hand over the pheasants.

'Your land, eh?' asks the miner.

'Yes,' replies the laird, 'and my pheasants.'

'And who did you get this land from?'

'Well, I inherited it from my father.'

'And who did he get it from?' the miner insists.

'His father of course. The land has been in my family for over 400 years,' the laird splutters.

'OK, so how did your family come to own this land 400 years ago?' the miner asks.

'Well . . . well . . . they fought for it!'

'Fine,' replies the miner. 'Take your jacket off and I'll fight you for it now.'[4]

What this neatly illustrates is the extent to which land rights which appear legitimate and almost sacred today are, in fact, the product of a long and none-too-wholesome history. Whilst we've moved on a bit since then, the fact is that landowners today are the beneficiaries of the nefarious deeds of their ancestors, thanks to the legitimacy afforded by a land law system that their ancestors themselves constructed. *The Poor Had No Lawyers* aims to challenge this state of affairs by taking a position (pro land reform) but basing it on an analysis that is more soundly based in factual analysis than polemical rhetoric.

In the introductory chapters of the book, I argue that there were five main land grabs in Scotland – namely, feudalisation, the appropriation of Church property, legal reforms in the seventeenth century, the division of the commonties and the nepotistic alienation of the common good wealth of the burghs of Scotland.[5] This history is brought to a conclusion by a look at the landed elite. The second part of the book is concerned with who owns Scotland in 2012 and represents a follow-up to my 1996 work of that name. Chapters 13 onward provide an analysis of various aspects of the land issue including, importantly, the land reforms of the past ten years.

If everyone was living happily, there would be no land problem. But they are not – young people can't afford houses, tenant farmers are being harassed, communities are losing common land and Scotland is still a country where a tiny few hold sway over vast swathes of country. In the space available, this book can do no more than dip into these complex areas and highlight some of the issues involved. There is no coverage at all of the question of public access, for example. In particular, my treatment of Scotland's history focuses purely on those areas of most relevance to the topic but I point to sources where a fuller account can be gleaned. Throughout the book I have also included a few additional tales of related matters from *a non domino* titles to who owns Balmoral. The Latin *a non domino* translates as 'from someone who is not the owner' and the concept is covered in detail in Chapter 22 (see pp. 278–280).

In effect, this book ranges over many of the areas of work I have been involved in over the years. I hope it stimulates you to want to know more and to engage in some of the important land rights issues in Scotland. For too long the law has been the preserve of lawyers and for too long they have served the interests of the well-to-do at the expense of the poor. Of course today there are many excellent solicitors doing very fine work in areas of public interest law and on behalf of the less well-off. The Govan Law Centre and the Environmental Law Centre, both of which have contributed outstanding service to the public, deserve special mention. Contrast these with some of the Edinburgh law firms and ask yourself who in the legal profession is going to help redress the imbalance of power implicit in Scotland's land tenure system. Who will challenge the stealthy encroachment of landed power and who will stand up for the community's land rights?

A word of warning. Much of what follows is expressed in what some might regard as rather legalistic language. I make no apology for this. For good or ill, the law surrounding land has been developed over centuries and is now quite technical. But to understand landownership in Scotland and to be able to engage with matters of who owns what rights where demands a certain level of familiarity with the law. I have provided a brief introduction to some of the concepts in Chapter 2 but a growing appreciation will only come through engagement with the issue, by locating title deeds and examining them and by reading legal decisions and textbooks. It is worth remembering that, particularly over local land issues, it is quite possible to become just as well informed if not more so than many so-called legal experts. Your strengths lie in understanding the law enough, having a detailed knowledge of a particular case and being motivated. Having said this, I should point out that I am not legally qualified. What follows are my best efforts at coming to grips with an area of law that has remained, like many other areas, the preserve of legal textbooks and journals. In particular, I apologise in advance to any of my legal friends for any arguments that fall short of the standards to which they are accustomed.

Related to this, I have found myself adopting rather more of an attitude in certain parts of this book – perhaps rather more than I had originally intended to. If this is so, it is for a good reason. As I wrote it, I became more, not less, aggrieved with the situation of which I complain – namely, the way in which the law and economy around land have been structured to benefit the haves at the expense of the have-nots. You may not agree with much of what you read. That is a good thing. Above all, I want to see a more informed level of debate about such matters and look forward to engaging with those who take a different view.

Superiors and Vassals

A brief discourse on terminology

It might appear rather academic to begin with a discussion of concepts and terms. If so, feel free to skip this chapter. However, an understanding of concepts and terms is vital to any proper analysis of land since terms such as 'feudal' have been used in a variety of ways, not all of which are accurate. This book is partly about the history of land tenure in Scotland and this can only be understood if we are clear about a number of legal concepts including land, tenure, ownership and land reform.[1]

The concept of owning land in legal terms is somewhat misleading since it is (or should be) obvious that someone cannot own land in the same way that they own a bicycle. They can lose the bicycle or take it on holiday with them but you can't do that with land. A bicycle can be replaced by buying another one (land can't). Many different types of bicycle can be made by many different people (land is not made – it's a gift of nature).

Ownership of land really means the possession of a bundle of rights over land including rights to occupy, to use, to cut peats, to cross or to fish. These rights include the important right to transfer these same rights to others. Land tenure is the legal system which defines the nature of this bundle of rights, how they relate to one another and how they are conveyed and recorded. Landownership, by contrast, is all about how the rights defined by the tenure system are possessed, what is the pattern of these rights (both now and historically) and the nature and character of those who hold these rights.

It is useful to clarify what is meant by 'land' and what by 'property'. Land is essentially any part of the surface area of Scotland out to the territorial limits and includes lochs, streets, the land under buildings and the hills, fields and forests in the countryside. It also includes the land under the surface and above the surface. In Scots law land is owned *a coelo usque ad centrum*, 'from the sky to the centre (of the earth)'. Property, on the other hand, is a term used most often to refer to the sum total of land and what is built upon it. Often, for example, we think of a house as property and a field as land. The law, however, makes no distinction – *inaedificandi solo, cedit solo*, meaning that anything which is built on the land is part of the land. In this book, I tend to use the terms interchangeably although when I come to discuss topics such as land value taxation, land is taken to exclude all improvements such as buildings or roads.

The final broad terms to be understood are those of 'heritable' and 'moveable'. Heritable property is land and all that is fixed to it and associated with it, such as rights to fish. It is often referred to in historical texts as heritage. Heritors were the landed proprietors in a parish and were responsible for the upkeep of the parish school and church. Moveable property is just about everything else and, as the word suggests, is essentially anything capable of being moved.

Until 28 November 2004, Scotland's land tenure system was feudal and thus some clarification of relevant feudal terms would be useful. Widespread confusion surrounds the topic of feudal tenure and what it means.

Feudal tenure starts from the proposition that the Crown has an ultimate ownership of all land. In feudal terms, it is called the Paramount Superior. In the early days of feudalism, the crown granted feu charters (often referred to simply as charters). These were documents that defined the precise rights and privileges being granted by the Crown (in those days mainly baronial rights to exercise justice, to receive the profits of justice in terms of fines and to administer the land including the mills, dams etc) and the feudal obligations owed to the Crown (to provide knight's service and feudal payments).

The granting of land under the feudal system is called 'feuing'. The party making the grant is the 'superior' and the person in receipt is the 'feuar'. The land itself is often referred to as the 'feu' (this being the unique bundle of rights and obligations contained in the feu charter or 'deed').

The important thing to understand is that this act created a relationship between a 'superior' (the grantor) and a 'vassal' (the individual possessing the charter). The vassal held his title conditionally and any breaching of its terms could lead to forfeiture. As the concept of actual ownership of land rather than simply the administration of justice took over and charters began to convey property rights, this relationship persisted. The charter contained terms laid down by the superior that had to be observed by the vassal. When 'subinfeudation' became possible and vassals could also in turn feu land, they too drafted charters with feudal terms in them and obligations (including the payment of feu duty and restrictions or obligation on use). Vassals then also became superiors but remained a vassal of their own superior. Thus developed the feudal pyramid whereby rights in land were shared among many levels and any holder of a feu or feu charter was free to use their land as they saw fit, subject only to the laws of the land and to the terms of their charter.

Conceptually, think of it like the armed forces. The Queen is the paramount superior, the Prime Minister is her vassal. He in turn is the superior to the Chief of the General Staff who in turn is the feudal superior of the Chiefs of the individual forces and so on down the chain of command. At each level, there is an interest below (the vassal) and an interest above (the immediate superior). Obligations flow each way. The 'owner' in conventional terms is the person at the end of the chain who has 'title' (written evidence of ownership) and, in our analogy, is the soldier. Below the owner, there can, of course, be tenants who have the right to occupy and use land for a defined period only and usually for defined purposes set out in their 'lease'.[2]

Typically in a rural situation, land and property would be owned by individuals who were the vassals of the original owners of the long-established estate that originally sold the land – land they now own. This was frequently the case in villages that were developed by large landed estates and where small plots of land had been sold as former parts of a larger property.

In towns and cities, the feudal superior was typically the descendant of the individual or organisation that originally owned and (frequently) developed the land. Thus, in Edinburgh, the original owners, such as the Heriot's Trust and Fettes Trust, of the New Town were, until recently, the feudal superiors. Elsewhere it was common to find corporate bodies, such as insurance companies, owning portfolios of superiorities. This was done as part of their investment strategy in the days when the payment of feu duties still represented a significant source of income to feudal superiors. Feuing was an important mechanism for the development of Scotland's villages, towns and cities in the days before planning laws and it allowed for the orderly development of houses and streets by imposing conditions on feuars, such as the obligation to maintain part of the street and not to use the land for tanneries, candle making, heckling houses or other such undesirable urban activities.

Land is transferred either by being inherited or by 'conveyance' which is the process of transferring title from one party to another. This usually takes the form of a 'disposition' whereby land is 'disponed' from one party to another. The disposition can be a feudal disposition, which creates a feudal relationship as defined above, or it can be an ordinary disposition. Whereas a feudal grant will create a new superior/vassal relationship, an ordinary conveyance or disposition merely substitutes a new owner for the former one. The relationships stay the same and nothing new is created – only the people involved change.

This system of tenure remained the method by which the vast majority of land was held in Scotland until its eventual abolition on 28 November 2004 under the Abolition of Feudal Tenure etc. (Scotland) Act 2000. Earlier reforms included the Land Tenure Reform (Scotland) Act 1974 which allowed vassals to redeem the feu duty payable to the superior. Contrary to popular belief, however, it did not abolish feudalism and vassals remained obliged to abide by the terms of their title in all other respects.

There continue to be important reforms to Scotland's system of land tenure in areas such as leasehold, succession, common good and land registration. These developments, together with new legislation such as the community right to buy, make it ever more important for the citizen to be well informed about how Scotland is owned. Remember that, although landowners own Scotland, they don't own the system of land law that underpins it – that belongs to all of us and it's high time it was better understood.

Robert the Bruce – A Murdering Medieval Warlord

The first land grab – feudal colonisation to 1500

After the ice retreated, groupings of peoples spread across Scotland and settled by the coast and on fertile land occupying territory which was governed by no central authority. Each tribe regulated its own affairs and, where conflict arose, combined together to assert their power. Scotland developed into a tribal society with a variety of ethnic groups, including the Gaels and the Picts, which eventually coalesced into a recognisable Scottish kingdom by the twelfth century. In the north were the Norse, in the west the Scots from Ireland, on the east some Saxon colonists and in Galloway the Picts. In the south of Scotland too were peasant proprietors, descendants of the Roman soldiers who, having retired from the army were given 4 acres of land in freehold. Feudalism was an unknown concept.

Many centuries later, the Berlin Conference of 1884–85 formalised colonial rule in Africa and its outcome, the General Act of the Berlin Conference, laid the ground rules for the conquest of that continent. The Principle of Effectivity established that European powers could only hold colonies if they possessed them. This required an active process of settlement, treaties and legal authority to be established in the lands held.

This process was little different from that which established the central authority of the Scottish state over the land of Scotland and which, over the course of many centuries, developed into the concept of landed power and authority with which this book is concerned. Just as in 1889, when Queen Victoria granted a charter to Cecil Rhodes' British South Africa Company to administer the territory from the Limpopo to Lake Tanganyika, so the monarchs of Scotland drafted and granted feudal charters to the nobility in Scotland to administer large territories across the country.

Prior to the reign of David I (1124–1153), land tenure in Scotland was based on older Celtic and Nordic traditions. David I changed all that with the systematic introduction of feudalism (although his father, Malcolm III had begun the process of replacing thanes with earls, lords and barons). Landed power begins and ends with sovereignty – the supreme or ultimate power or authority over a territory. Sovereignty is vested in the Crown which is represented by the monarch. Securing the Crown thus confers absolute power and David used this power to impose the alien feudal tenure system on Scotland.

> There was no possibility of establishing a centralised, bureaucratic administration; no ruler had enough money to pay and supervise local officials. Therefore, local administration and justice, which is the essential work of any government, had to be left to the leading men in each district, that is, the lords.[1]

Where did feudalism come from? To begin with, the term is not particularly useful since, as historians have argued, the classic feudal pyramid did not truly exist anywhere.[2] In Scotland the process was even messier since the essence of feudalism (the authority of the Crown over territory) sat alongside pre-feudal institutions. This was inevitable since feudalism was imported by foreigners from Flanders, Normandy and England. David I's reforms of administration are credited with revolutionising the governance of Scotland. He erected Scotland's first burghs at Roxburgh and Berwick, founded monasteries, established sheriffdoms and, of course, granted feudal charters to the French knights who supported him and any native earls and lords prepared to accept the homage and fealty due to the monarch. Royal forests – hunting reserves where no one could hunt without the monarch's permission – were established together with baronial forests allocated to barons.[3]

As Mackintosh observes:

One marked characteristic of feudalism was the multiplication of hereditary offices. In Scotland this rose to excess. Hereditary officers of state, constables, marshals and so forth; hereditary sheriffs, baillies and stewards; hereditary keepers of castles, forests, parks and the like; hereditary functionaries on every hand.

The feudal nobles aped the royal state, and encircled themselves with a host of officers and vassals. They had their own sheriffs, chamberlains, constables and so on. In fact, they were a sort of little despots [*sic*] within their own territories.[4]

These developments were not only based on Anglo-Norman structures, they were populated by immigrants from the Anglo-Norman world. The burghs were run by an immigrant merchant class and the new class of landowner was almost entirely foreign. Feudalisation was thus, in essence, a form of colonisation. Land which had been owned by native aristocracy under pre-feudal arrangements was now held by a charter written in Latin which granted extensive privileges over the territory in return for money and military dues to the Crown. The beneficiaries were the new foreign nobility including Robert de Brus, Roger de Quincy, Robert de Balliol, Robert de Comines (or Comyn), Roger de Berkeley, Henry de Brechin, de Umphravill, de Morvills and de Sulis. They also included some of the native chiefs who calculated that it was in their best interests to secure a charter but who, at the same time, often continued with pre-feudal institutions of administration over their land.[5]

The whole process was, therefore, not unlike the British colonisation of Australia with its concepts of *terra nullius* – 'land belonging to no one' – a concept now discredited as a result of the Mabo decision (for which, see Chapter 9). The first land grab in Scotland was thus a process of colonisation by foreign forces aided and abetted by a process of internal colonisation whereby the native nobility was co-opted into the feudal system. It was the process of feudalisation that marked the beginning of the evolution of landownership as we know it today. The granting of feudal charters was a process of enforcing central authority and, just as the British colonialists co-opted indigenous tribal chiefs, so too did the early Scottish monarchs co-opt Scotland's indigenous aristocracy.

It is important to remember in this context that feudalism was imposed on Scotland. In contrast to England where William the Conqueror was careful to confiscate property legally before he began to grant it all away, no act was ever passed in Scotland that confiscated property to the Crown. As a result, one historian has argued that all Crown grants were therefore really ultra vires.[6] This can be illustrated by reference to what, in early feudal charters, is called the Quaequidem clause, the clause setting out the history of the property and how the rights came to be in the hands of the granter. Cosmo Innes argues that '[t]his clause is, however, too often wanting in our old charters', and where it existed, it often simply referred to the lands having been formerly held by 'our enemy'.

> I have observed some charters in Bruce's time, where the lands given by the King had formerly been in the possession of a Balliol or a Comyn, and that was sufficient account of their coming into the King's hands. You will find, I think, that the greatest number of the charters of King Robert I proceed on forfeiture.[7]

Feudal grants did not of course grant rights to the land as such but were contractual bargains between the superior who granted the feu with its attendant judicial and fiscal powers and the vassal who took possession and was under feudal obligations to the superior. The nature of the feudal obligation determined the character of the feu. Military tenure (wardholding) was granted in return for supplying knights or galleys. Blench tenure was more symbolic and obliged the feuar to supply certain services. For example, the Baron of Penicuik was obliged to provide three blasts on the horn in the forest of Drumsheugh on the Burgh Muir when the king hunted there. Of all the types of tenure, however, the predominant was feu farm – a feu in return for payment of an annual sum of money called the feu duty.

By the end of David I's reign, Scotland's native pre-feudal landowners still dominated the pattern of landownership but, across much of eastern Scotland, feudalisation had taken root though knights' fees, thanages, baronies and lordships.[8] In contrast to England, there was no wholesale displacement of the native aristocracy and, in 1200, all of the earls north of the Forth and Clyde were still of Celtic descent.[9]

David himself was educated in the English Norman court and had direct experience of how successfully feudalisation had subjugated England. From David I's reign to Robert I's accession to the throne, the feudalisation of Scotland not only accelerated but, more importantly, was consolidated in the hands of foreign Norman nobility, many of whom held extensive estates both in Scotland and in England. These individuals were almost always granted baronies. As Grant writes:

> In later medieval Scotland, the barony was an extremely common franchise. From Robert I's reign (1306–29), it was increasingly precisely defined as an estate to which specific 'baronial' powers were formally attached, while the main definition of 'baron' came to be a lord who possessed a barony and held it in liberam baroniam – that is, with the right to exercise those powers (it was possible to possess merely the lands of a barony, or part of one, without actually holding in liberam baroniam; technically, such a landowner would not be a baron). The baronial powers were those of 'pit and gallows, sake and soke, toll, team and infangthief'.[10]

That Robert I was responsible for developing this legal finesse is not surprising since, of all the medieval monarchs, he is the one who stood to gain most from feudalism. Of all the figures in Scottish history, no one, aside from William Wallace, is accorded more reverence than Robert Bruce. Already the next Homecoming celebrations have been proposed for 2014, the 700th anniversary of the Battle of Bannockburn at which Bruce is popularly regarded as having secured Scotland's independence at a crucial point in its history. But just why was Bruce on the field of Bannockburn on that June day in 1314?

To argue that Bruce secured Scotland's independence is to suggest that there was a polity called Scotland in 1314. There was not. Whilst the Treaty of Perth handed sovereignty of the Hebrides to Alexander III in 1266 and the Treaty of York defined the border between England and Scotland in 1237, the Highlands and Islands remained a law unto themselves as did much of the Borders. Scotland was not a nation state in any sense of the term as we understand it today but a kingdom. A kingdom is a very different place. It is a seat of power and it is that power that motivated Bruce to do battle with Edward. The prize was the Scottish Crown and the principal exercise of that power was in granting rights and privileges to Bruce's colonial friends who, after Bannockburn, became the beneficiaries of an exercise much like that carried out by the European powers during the Berlin Conference.

In reality, Robert Bruce was a medieval warlord – murderous, duplicitous, conniving and wholly devoid of any higher principles than his own advancement. His murder of Comyn is now considered to have been premeditated and, after capturing the Scottish Crown, he attempted to subjugate Ireland.[11] His elevation to national hero has more to do with the peculiar fixation with national myths in Scotland and the need to provide an ancient narrative of Scotland. But there is no conflict between being proud of Scotland and recognising Bruce for what he was.

The mistake is to think of terms such as 'freedom from English rule' as meaning the same to the medieval mind as it does to the modern mind. The modern nation state has no equivalent to the nobles and the church in the fourteenth century. The ordinary person then was a feudal serf and had no power, no land, no vote and no influence. Whilst there may be tempting parallels to be drawn, Bruce's actions should be considered in the context of the time in which he lived. It is true that no monarch after Bruce had to fight so hard to secure the throne and the kingdom but it is also true that he did so because that is what warlords do. Bruce was a member of a fractious elite class descended from Norman immigrants and his fight was a fight for feudal power, land and money. To place it any higher in the moral order of things is naive. Indeed there is something almost existential about the national hero myth and Bruce's role in securing the independence of Scotland. Had Bruce not won at Bannockburn, we would today most likely be contentedly English. We would no more mourn that fact than we mourn the fact that we are no longer Picts or Angles or

Britons or Vikings. Moreover, Bruce was hardly committed to Scottish independence. As Johnston so eloquently writes:

> On August 28th, 1296, as Earl of Carrick, he does fealty to the English King; in 1297 he renews his oath of fealty and raids Lanarkshire with the English. Then he joins Wallace, then surrenders to the English King at Irvine, and receives pardon for his temporary treachery to his feudal overlord. In 1298 he is in Edward's service in Galloway. In 1299 he sees an opportunity of striking a blow for his own advancement, so he attacks Edward's castle of Lochmaben. In 1302 he is surreptitiously appealing for aid to the King of France, whilst still assuring Edward of his loyalty; and in October of that year attends the English parliament. In 1303 he gets an advance of salary from Edward, and is appointed Sheriff of Lanark. In 1304 he attends King Edward's Parliament at St Andrews, and sends, at his own expense, engines of war to assist the English forces in the capture of Stirling Castle. In 1305 he gets the Umfraville lands in Carrick [and] attends the English Parliament.[12]

Robert Bruce's constant flipping of allegiance between the Scottish cause and fealty to Edward marks him as just another member of the nobility on the make. As the military historian Nusbacher put it:

> The ways to wealth for a Scottish nobleman were either to take it from someone else or to garner estates in England. Most of them tried to do both. The object of the game for a Scots nobleman was to have as much power as possible in Scotland, in order to safeguard his Scottish possessions, without having so much that the English king felt threatened. If the English king needed to beat a Scottish nobleman into line, he need only threaten to take away his English estates.[13]

His ambition was to secure power and he cared little from whence that power originated. He was the archetypal feudal tyrant.

Despite the intensive feudalisation of Bruce and later monarchs, indigenous forms of tenure did persist before the eventual triumph of feudalism. Parts of Scotland, such as Moray, remained in a state of open rebellion for centuries as the native aristocracy refused to acknowledge the legitimacy of the feudal charter granted by Robert Bruce to his nephew, Thomas Randolph.

An idea of the progress of feudalisation can be gleaned from the wonderful map prepared by Alexander Grant from Lancaster University (see Figure 1).

The map shows the 925 or so parishes that are likely to have existed in medieval Scotland during the first decade of the 1400s. Grant then surveyed each parish to determine under what type of charter the whole, most or some of each parish was held. The conclusions of his research are striking. They show that 869 of the 925 parishes were held wholly or mostly with at least a baronial charter and that two-thirds of Scotland was still held by charter within the pre-feudal earldoms and lordship structure. Another notable feature of this research is that over 64 per cent of ordinary baronies had the same name as the parishes they were located within, suggesting that many baronies were synonymous with parishes. Scotland, perhaps more than anywhere else in Western Europe, was overwhelmingly a land of franchises.

And that was that. Feudalism survived for another 500 years until its eventual demise on 28 November 2004. But, as the centuries passed, it evolved from a system that was essentially concerned with governance through the exercise of feudal authority to a system of land tenure and ownership. It is that story that this book focuses on because it is that transformation that resulted in the pattern of landownership we have today.

The reason feudalism is today consigned to the museums of rural life in every other country in the world but survived until very recently in Scotland is down to its successful adaptation to changing circumstances and the powerful role afforded to landowners in government. That it was never abolished until 2004 has everything to do with the political developments in Britain in the late seventeenth century whereby the Crown ceded control to the parliaments and, for over 200 years following the Union in 1707, the country was run by capitalists, landowners and the aristocracy. The rest of Europe delayed a while, long enough for the masses to rise up against the absolute power of monarchs and abolish feudal structures.

Feudalism, however, had lost much of its rationale by the late 18th century. Heritable jurisdictions had been abolished, vassals were free to sell their estate and feudal obligations were reduced to the simple obligation to pay an annual feu duty. It is worth concluding this chapter with an account of how feudalism was rejuvenated not in the rural estates of the nobility but in the heart of Scotland's capital city.

In 1766, the Town Council of Edinburgh used the Common Good Fund to acquire 37 acres of land to the north of the Nor Loch for the purposes of building the New Town based on a celebrated design by the young architect, James Craig. Almost immediately the Council began the process of feuing plots of land to developers. The problem it ran into straightaway was how to ensure that these developers followed an agreed design. Richard Rodger describes the problem in his magnificent book *The Transformation of Edinburgh* thus:

> In the absence of a planning code, no effective guarantees to investors existed that their house, its value and outlook would not be compromised by the actions of other builders, or by their neighbours' actions. Indeed, it was precisely to protect property interests that a system of burdens or obligations was introduced.[14]

Kenneth Reid, the architect of the abolition of feudal tenure in the 1990s claims that the importance of this system to the development of land tenure in Scotland 'is difficult to exaggerate'.[15]

Initially, in the feu charters granted to developers, very little was said, in the five pages or so, about how buildings should be constructed other than references to maintaining cellar supports and sewer connections. Instead, the essential design details necessary for conformity to Craig's plan were contained in a signed contract between the Council and the developer in which the feuar agreed to adhere to the feuing plan on display in the City Chambers. Thus it was the law of contract and not property that was used to ensure the uniformity of the Craig plan. However, the problem with this approach was that the terms of such an agreement were only binding between the initial parties – the Council

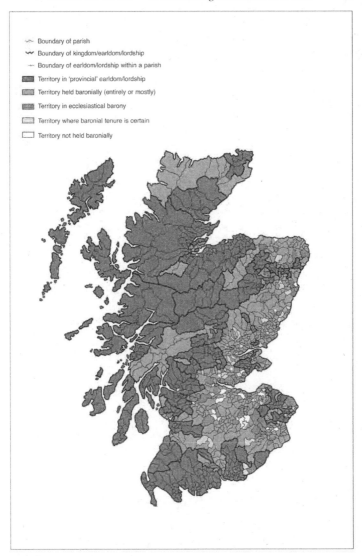

Boundary of parish
Boundary of kingdom/earldom/lordship
Boundary of earldom/lordship within a parish
Territory in 'provincial' earldom/lordship
Territory held baronially (entirely or mostly)
Territory in ecclesiastical barony
Territory where baronial tenure is certain
Territory not held baronially

Figure 1: Parishes, baronies, earldoms and lordships in early
fifteenth-century Scotland

Source: This map was produced by Dr Alexander Grant, University of
Lancaster, for his late-medieval history course

and the developer. Subsequent owners were free to disregard these conditions and this freedom led to the later incoherent changes to the frontages on Princes Street.

Initially, following a legal case, the Craig plan was regarded as having legal force[16] but a later House of Lords decision in 1818 overturned this and Lord Eldon insisted that 'to infer such a contract from the exhibition of such a plan, would be as violent a stretch in judicature as ever I met with in the course of a long professional life.'[17]

Much of the New Town was thus developed under the law of contract but landowners such as the Heriot's Trust and the Earl of Moray quickly realised that the means of enforcing control over development and thus maintaining the value and amenity of the estate was to include such conditions as burdens in the feudal title itself. The properties developed in the west end thus became known as the Moray feus. Edinburgh landowners then enthusiastically embraced the feudal title with its pages of conditions and rules and the lucrative future revenue in the form of feu duties and casualty payments or even repossession should any vassal fail to adhere to them.

At precisely the time that feudalism was being dismantled across the rest of Europe, it gained a new lease of life in urban Scotland. Lawyers and landowners across Scotland quickly took note and, following another important legal case in 1840, the feudal system thrived for the next 200 years as an indispensable tool in urban planning.[18]

But this is jumping ahead a bit. For feudalism to evolve as the structural architecture of landownership, others had to get in on the act and it was the Scottish nobility who launched the second land grab in the sixteenth century as they cast their covetous eyes on the extensive grants of land that the kings had made to the Church.

To Spoil the Kirk of Christ of Her Patrimony

The second land grab – the lands of the Church

The year 2010 was the 450th anniversary of the Reformation in Scotland, an event which, over the course of a seven-day sitting of the Scots Parliament, changed the culture, religion and power dynamics of Scotland forever. Across Europe as a whole, the Reformation had profound consequences and its founder, Martin Luther, remains one of the world's leading thinkers and revolutionaries. But just as little was done to mark the anniversary, so little attention has ever been given to the one very profound way in which the Reformation changed Scotland in terms that had nothing to do with religion and everything to do with the quiet appropriation of the extensive lands of the Church over the course of 100 years between 1520 and 1620.

This land grab is scarcely mentioned in history books other than by allusion and has attracted very little scholarly attention. By 1500, the landed class of nobles and gentry was well established. Most native chiefs had secured feudal charters and James IV had forfeited the Lordship of the Isles in an attempt to bring the Hebrides to heel. But the nobility was restless and unhappy with the growing power of the Stewart kings. Rebel nobles had defeated and killed James III at the Battle of Sauchieburn and as the sixteenth century progressed, his son James IV (who had led the rebels at Sauchieburn) proceeded to increase royal income through the more systematic exploitation of Crown lands and more diligent exercise of his power as feudal superior of the nobility's estates.[1]

He also began exploiting the Church by manipulating Church appointments, increasing taxes and by appointing members of his own immediate family to Church office. These were continued after 1512 by James V through increased feuing but, in particular, by what one historian has described as 'his increasingly ruthless exploitation of the resources of the church through taxation, the retention of revenues during episcopal vacancies and the shameless appointment of royal bastards to senior ecclesiastical offices'.[2]

During the 1500s, the nobility became increasingly restless and railed against the confluence of power that was the Church and the Crown. In 1500, the Church was the wealthiest landowner in Scotland, owning a quarter of the whole country, and responsible for half of the entire national land revenue.[3] It was venal and corrupt to boot and thus an obvious target for the second great land grab. What is often overlooked in histories of the Reformation is the economic and political context. In many ways, the theological arguments are secondary. John Knox and his fellow reformers were undoubtedly the architects of the Reformation in Scotland and many people did not need much convincing of the desirability of dealing with the corruption of the old Church. But they needed political support and this came from the Scots nobility. As Johnston argued:

> Not all the eloquence of Knox, though he did on occasion move three thousand persons to shed tears, nor all the manifest sorrows of the working class, could have caused the collapse of Roman ecclesiasticism in the sixteenth century, had not our old nobility allied itself to the Reformers, and allied itself with the fervour and enthusiasm generated by vision of immediate gain. The Church absorbed half the annual land revenue of Scotland: the nobles coveted that revenue. There is the secret of the Reformation![4]

Knox's plans, as laid out in *The First Book of Discipline*, were that the teinds[5] of all Church land should be used by the Reformed Church for three purposes, namely:

a) for the upkeep of the kirk
b) for the support of the disabled and the aged poor and the provision of work for the unemployed

and

c) for a public elementary school education for every child.

This was a radical manifesto for 1560 but it was dependent on the wholesale transfer of the substantial revenues from the old Church to the new. This never happened. By the time the Reformation had taken hold, the estates of the old Church had already been hugely depleted and the nobility was not about to let Knox and his reforming friends get their hands on any more.

In his *Book of Discipline*, Knox acknowledges that the game is up:

> With the grief of our hearts we hear that some gentlemen are now as cruel over their tenants as ever were the Papists, requiring of them whatsoever before they paid to the church; so that the Papistical tyranny shall only be changed into the tyranny of the lord or of the laird. We dare not flatter your honours, neither yet is it profitable for you that so we do. If you permit such cruelty to be used, neither shall ye, who by your authority ought to gainstand such oppression, neither [shall] they that use the same, escape God's heavy and fearful judgments. The gentlemen, barons, earls, lords, and others, must be content to live upon their just rents, and suffer the church to be restored to her liberty, that, in her restitution, the poor, who heretofore by the cruel Papists have been spoiled and oppressed, may now receive some comfort and relaxation.[6]

As Mackintosh makes clear:

> Many of the nobles, from motives of self interest, professed a willingness to embrace the reformed opinions, and gradually ranked themselves on the side of the Reformers; as time passed, and the prospects of the division of the spoil approached, they became more and more ardent in their adherence to the principles of the Reformation.[7]

England's Reformation took place thirty years before Scotland's and led directly to a process of disposing of Church lands. Scotland's Reformation, by contrast, came later and, when it came to dividing up the spoils, there was little left to distribute as the lairds and nobility had grasped monastic lands before the events of 1560.[8] Since around 1530, the nobility had embarked on a wholesale appropriation of Church lands although there had been much thieving taking place for centuries before that with Parliament constantly censuring the nobility for appropriation of Church property.

But it was the insidious entryism of the nobility into Church affairs in the sixteenth century that served to cause it to collapse as much from within as from attack from outside. The nobility managed to secure heritable bailieships by offering protection to bishops. Thus did the Lennox family secure control of the Bishopric of Glasgow and the Huntly family take over control of the Bishopric of Aberdeen, both of which were extensive and wealthy territories. Once in control, the third Earl of Huntly installed his son as Bishop in 1546. As Callander observed in his study of landownership in Aberdeenshire:

> In 1549, three years after becoming Bishop, he granted his first feu charter for lands in Birse. This charter was to his own elder brother, Sir Alexander Gordon of Strathaven . . . The Bishop disposed of all the lands in Birse during the next ten years, 18 out of the 24 towns and the extensive Forest of Birse all ending up with the Gordons. The position was much the same over the rest of the Bishop's Aberdeenshire lands, which had also included valuable salmon fishings, though not all the lands were lost willingly. In 1544, James Forbes of Corsindae had forcibly acquired a title to the church lands of Mountgarry. He robbed Bishop Gordon's predecessor of the bulk of the church's treasures when they were being removed for fear of another English invasion. James Forbes then held the treasures for ransom until he received a charter for the lands.[9]

Control of the Church permitted the control of the feuing of Church lands and thus a key form of entryism was the appointment of commendators – laypersons appointed to be entrusted with the custody of an abbey and in charge of the revenues for the duration of their life. Commendator abbots were not the working heads of abbeys and typically did not reside in the abbey but in a Commendator's House. It was this position that allowed the rot to set in. The final commendator of Kelso Abbey was Robert Ker of

Cesford, later Earl of Roxburgh. By the 1587 Act of Annexation, the valuable lands became his. Likewise the Earl of Haddington obtained Melrose.[10]

As one account of the period makes clear, the appropriation of the Church lands enriched the nobility significantly.

> Noble power was based primarily on their very considerable dominance of land, a dominance that increased in the later sixteenth century at the expense of the church and the crown. Huge tracts of former ecclesiastical land were acquired by secular landlords. Thus the estates of Newbattle abbey came into the hands of a branch of the Ker kindred, establishing the house of Lothian among the top ranks of the nobility. Other ecclesiastical land was feued to secular tenants, ranging from small 'bonnet lairds' at the bottom of the propertied community to the higher nobility. Even the 'teinds' or tithes of the income of certain land, formerly payable to the church, became the preserve of secular landlords. One effect of this was to disperse landholdings so that whilst most noble houses retained a territorial core of estates around their principal residence, landed possessions were scattered. By the early seventeenth century, the dukes of Lennox held property in fourteen shires, and the marquises of Hamilton owned land in thirteen shires. Some forty-eight noble houses had a landed portfolio extending to more than four shires, while 106 noble houses owned property in two or more shires.[11]

As the Reformation drew nearer, the nobles got organised. On 3 December 1557, a group of them came together, entering a bond of manrent (the signing of an agreement of mutual protection and association) and styling themselves the Lords of the Congregation. They were led by Archibald Campbell, fourth earl of Argyll, Alexander Cunningham, fourth earl of Glencairn, James Douglas, fourth earl of Morton, Archibald Campbell, Lord Lorne (fifth earl of Argyll from 1558), and Lord John Erskine. This was the first of the new religious covenants. Three years later,

> [t]he Reformation Parliament, despite the 100 lairds from various parts of Scotland who attended it, was orchestrated by

leading nobles. It was their kinsmen or dependants who filled it
to overflowing. There was no sudden power grab by a new elite
of smaller men. Control of politics rested, as before, with the
nobles.[12]

It was the Lords of the Congregation who commissioned Knox
to draw up the First Book of Discipline and to redraft it when it
failed to accord with their wishes. Whilst the radical reformers had
their own ideas about the reformed Church, their success was
conditional on the support of the nobles.[13] And so, with lightning
speed, the Reformation Parliament abolished the Mass and rejected papal authority. The Reformation was done and dusted in
seven days of Parliament in August 1560.

Meanwhile, the land grabbing continued and events in Ayrshire
in 1570 provide a dramatic example of the lengths to which some of
the nobility were prepared to go to secure titles to Church lands.

Crossraguel Abbey was a modest monastic institution in the
countryside south of Maybole. The Earls of Cassillis had, since the
Battle of Largs in 1263, built up extensive landholdings in Ayrshire
and Gilbert Kennedy, the fourth Earl of Cassillis, had cast
covetous eyes on the abbey's rich farmland. His uncle, Quentin
Kennedy, had been Abbot and famously argued with John Knox in
Maybole about the Mass. When he retired, Gilbert had hoped he
would be appointed Commendator, the trustee for life, of the
benefice of the abbey but was thwarted in this ambition and the
post went, instead, to Allan Stewart. In autumn 1570, Stewart
travelled to Crossraguel to visit what, in effect, was his own
property. He stayed with his brother-in-law, the Laird of Bargany,
also a Kennedy and a rival of Cassillis.

Late in August, Cassillis, with a party that included his brother
and son, kidnapped Allan Stewart in the Woods of Crossraguel,
took him prisoner and set off to Dunure Castle. There, Cassillis
demanded that Stewart sign over the lands of Crossraguel. Stewart
refused and so Cassillis had his baker, cook and pantryman take
him to the Black Vault of Dunure, strip him and bind him to a spit.
The servants poured oil over him so that he would roast slowly over
the fire. After several sessions of such torture, Allan Stewart was
persuaded to sign the charter and tack (lease). When the Earl of

Bargany heard what had taken place he secured support to attack Dunure and Stewart was taken to the Market Cross in Ayr where he denounced his persecutor, later submitting a detailed complaint to the Privy Council over his treatment. Cassillis was fined £2000 and ordered to restore the charters of Crossraguel to the Commendator.[14] One can only speculate as to the many and varied ways in which the nobility secured commendatorships and other offices in the Church since only the most brutal and violent would lead to such actions by the Privy Council.

Prelates and other churchmen had been allowed to feu lands since an act of 1457. One concern of the nobility was to ensure that these feus were now secure and that the liferent (the right to occupy but not own a property for a person's life) of commendators be changed to a feu. In 1587, James VI passed the General Annexation Act which transferred ecclesiastical properties into hereditary lordships and confirmed the nobility in their legal right to hold in perpetuity all land they had previously held in liferent as commendators. The lands of the Church fell thick and fast and, from 1587 until 1625, twenty-one abbeys, seven priories, six nunneries, two preceptories and two monasteries were erected into temporal lordships.[15]

Robert Pont was the father of the famous mapmaker Timothy Pont and one of the leading ministers in the reformed Kirk. In 1594, at the request of the General Assembly, he wrote three sermons against sacrilege.

> From the year of our Lord 1560 to this present time, the greatest study of all men of power of this land has been, by all kinds of inventions, to spoil the Kirk of Christ of her patrimony, by chopping and changing, diminishing of rentals, converting of victual in small sums of money, setting of feus under the value, long tackes upon tackes, with two or three life-rents, with many twenty years of a tack, annexations, erections of Kirk-rents into temporal livings and heritage, pensions, simple donations, erecting of new patronages, union of teinds, making new abbots, commendators, priors, and other papistical titles, which ought to have no place in a reformed Kirk and country, with many other corrupt and fraudful ways, to the detriment and hurt of the Kirk, the schools, and the poor, without any stay or gainsaying.[16]

This second great land grab hugely enriched the nobility and greatly impoverished the Church. The dreams of John Knox and the reformers were dashed. The newly propertied class was now a potent force commanding control of a vast extent of Scotland. But it remained vulnerable to the fickle whims of future monarchs and there was a pressing need to provide some greater level of legitimacy and security over the lands it now occupied.

It was at this point that the historic pact between property and the law was initiated. From now on, lawyers were increasingly entrusted with the important task of securing titles, defending property rights and legitimising the ownership of vast swathes of stolen property.

The Palladium of Our Land Proprietors

The third land grab – involving the lawyers

The period up to the establishment of the Court of Session in 1532 is often referred to as the Dark Age of Scottish legal history (though some date it to 1600). It was a time of political strife and weak government. Some remarkable statutes do, however, survive from this period. One example is the 1449 Leases Act which is still in force and which protected tenants against eviction before the end of their term.

> Item, it is ordained and decreed that for the security and favour of the poor people that labour the ground, that they and all others that have taken or shall take lands in time to come from lords, and have terms thereof, that, suppose the lords sell or alienate those lands, the takers shall remain within their tacks until the issue of their terms, regardless of whose hands those lands come to, for the same mail as they took them previously.[1]

The seventeenth century was a time of struggle between the Crown, which was interested in reasserting its power, and the nobility, who wished to preserve and strengthen theirs. As the power of the Crown grew and feudalisation progressed, legal process became more and more important in arbitrating and regulating power relations over land. And it was the craft of the lawyer that, next to the power of the Crown and the criminality of the nobility, cemented the institution of landownership and landed power in Scotland.

Having substantially secured the lands of the Church by the end of the sixteenth century, the nobility began a ruthless process of lawmaking to institutionalise and make lawful their rights. A significant motivation for this was James VI's belief in the divine right of kings and his and his son Charles I's enthusiasm for episcopacy. This would mean the king having the power to appoint bishops and thus bring the Church under his control. The nobility feared a return to Catholicism, and that would mean the prospect of losing the valuable Church lands they had spent the best part of a hundred years appropriating.

The strategy they adopted was to entrench their rights in law and perhaps the most important acts ever passed on land law were the Registration Act of 1617 and the Prescription Act of 1617. The Registration Act provided for the establishment of the Register of Sasines which remains in force today as a system of recording and thereby protecting rights in heritable property (of which more later). Given the vast transfers of land from the Church to the nobility, it is not hard to imagine the anxieties concerning the validity of their titles to their doubtful acquisitions which must have arisen to trouble the minds of the fortunate newly rich.[2]

The landed proprietors who met in Parliament on 28 June 1617 had a plan and the Register of Sasines and the introduction of prescription have to be seen as one coherent whole since the real intent of this act was to legitimise the extensive theft of Church lands. Were it not for the Reformation, there would never have been an act of 1617. The dismantling of the property of the Auld Kirk was a process of redistribution on a gigantic scale and so dubious was the basis upon which so many nobles had enriched themselves that it was felt necessary to institute both a register and a law to legitimise the ownership of stolen property.

The Parliament that met had little difficulty in pursuing such legislation. There was no right of debate and the Parliament was, in effect, beholden to the Committee of the Articles that developed and framed legislation. The Committee was elected on 17 June 1617 and included the Earl of Argyll, the Earl of Montrose, the Marquis of Hamilton and the Duke of Lennox. It was they who framed the legislation that, on 28 June, was presented to Parliament which passed twenty-three acts – dealing with everything from penalties for absence from Parliament to the regulation of dovecots and the punishment of drunkards (a £10 fine and twenty-four hours in the stocks for a third offence) – en bloc with no debate.

Prescription

Perhaps the most far-reaching of this mammoth session of law-making was the act 'regarding prescription of heritable rights' which conferred title to land to those who had possessed it for a period of forty years.

> Our sovereign lord, considering the great prejudice which his majesty's lieges sustain in their lands and heritages, not only by the abstracting, corrupting and concealing of their true evidents in their minority and less age and by the omission thereof, by the injury of time, through war, plague, fire or such occasions, but also by the counterfeiting and forging of false evidents and writs and concealing of the same . . . by the tenor of this present act, statutes, finds and declares that whatsoever his majesty's lieges, their predecessors and authors have possessed heretofore, or shall happen to possess in time coming by themselves, their tenants and others having their rights, their lands, baronies, annual rents and other heritage by virtue of their heritable infeftments made to them by his majesty, or others their superiors and authors for the space of 40 years, continuously and together following and ensuing the date of their said infeftments, and that peaceably without any lawful interruption made to them therein during the said space of 40 years, that such persons, their heirs and successors shall never be troubled, pursued nor deprived in the heritable right and property of their said lands and heritages foresaid by his majesty or others their superiors and authors, their heirs and successors, nor by any other person pretending right to the same by virtue of prior infeftments, public or private, nor upon no other ground, reason or argument competent of law, except for falsehood, providing they be able to show and produce a charter of the said lands and others foresaid granted to them or their predecessors by their said superiors and

authors preceding the entry of the said 40 years' possession, with
the instrument of sasine following thereupon.[3]

As John Rankine, the noted Professor of Scots Law at the
University of Edinburgh from 1888 to 1922 and author of *The Law
of Landownership in Scotland*, states:

> It was held that uninterrupted exclusive possession of lands for
> forty years under a charter and sasine, containing a description
> which can be so construed as to embrace the whole lands, though
> it may also be so construed as to embrace part of them only, is
> sufficient to exclude all enquiry, and to protect the person in
> possession against anyone holding even an express title, prior in
> date, to the whole or any of the parts of the lands . . . The subject
> of prescriptive consolidation is naturally connected with that of
> double titles.[4]

By double titles, he means situations where feu charters have been
granted over the same land to different people. Reading the act,
one might be forgiven for concluding that prescription is being
introduced to overcome the great prejudice sustained by landowners as a result of land rights being corrupted during their
minority or being rendered indefensible by war, injury, plague and
fire. In a Parliament attended by the Earl of Argyll, the Earl of
Montrose, the Earl of Lothian and the Earl of Roxburghe,
numerous lords and commissioners for the barons, the real intent
of this act, however, was not to correct the slights felt by the landed
class.

On the face of it, the act was indeed conceived of as a means to
resolve the conflicts that had emerged between, for example, land
held on feus granted by the Church prior to the Reformation and
the claims made on that same land by the nobility who had
managed to secure titles converting their previous liferent interests
into a feu. Quite whether a test of possession was very fair when so
often there was a huge disparity in political and economic power
between the parties in conflict is a moot point. But two things are
clear. Firstly, the 1617 act was not simply a means of resolving an
honest conflict of evidence. On the contrary, it was the means

whereby the powerful were able to call on the law to secure the advantage they sought to gain by having stolen the Church lands. Secondly, even if it was conceived of as a means of settling genuine conflicts in titles, it soon ceased to be used for such cases and became instead a means to legitimise the appropriation of land which had never been granted to the owner in the first place. As Rankine observed, '[T]he words of the protection given in the Act of 1617 to this favoured conjunction of title and possession are very full and sweeping, and have been applied . . . to many cases which were not properly within the purview of the Act.'[5]

As a means of settling disputes and uncertainties, it was a masterstroke, removing the ambiguities and doubts that would arise were titles to be strictly construed. The famous jurist Lord Stair eulogised the act as 'that excellent statute of prescription'[6] and the philosopher Lord Kames described it as 'the palladium of our land proprietors'.[7] Indeed the act 'as construed and extended by many generations of interpreters . . . was found to work so satisfactorily as not to require formal amendment till the year 1874'.[8] In 1874, the prescriptive period was reduced from forty years to twenty years.

The final triumph for landed proprietors came in 1880 when, in the case of Auld v Hay, it was re-affirmed that the original purpose of the 1617 act to provide a simple and expedient validation of rights to stolen property was, after all, the legitimate application of the doctrine of prescription. In that case, it was held that:

> uninterrupted and exclusive possession of lands for 40 years under a charter and sasine containing a description which can be so construed as to embrace the whole lands, though it may also be so construed as to embrace part of them only, is sufficient to exclude all inquiry, and to protect the person in possession against anyone holding even an express title, prior in date, to the whole or any part of the lands.[9]

In other words, it did not matter what had gone before, what the rights and wrongs were, whether the owner had ever been granted the land or what the circumstances were surrounding its acquisition. So long as a title 'can so be construed as to embrace the whole lands'[10] and so long as the claimant has possessed them, the title is settled.

Prescription continues to play an important part in the often controversial appropriation of private land and was central to the case of the Cuillin of Skye in 2000 where the doctrine of possession was claimed to be sufficient to assert ownership even in the face of a range of credible evidence that McLeod had never been granted the Cuillin (see Chapter 13). Prescription allows for making lawful property out of that which was not lawful (remember the story of the roasting of Allan Stewart). It achieves the opposite of the criminal offence of reset which, according to Section 51 of the Criminal Law (Consolidation) (Scotland) Act 1995, defines the current law thus:

> Criminal resetting of property shall not be limited to the receiving of property taken by theft or robbery, but shall extend to the receiving of property appropriated by breach of trust and embezzlement and by falsehood, fraud and wilful imposition.

It is interesting that the common law offences of theft and reset apply only to moveable property and not to heritable property. Anyone found in possession of stolen property can be found guilty of a criminal offence without limit of time. By contrast, if land had originally been obtained by fraudulent means, a recorded title and the law of prescription will now provide indemnity from prosecution.

An indication of the extent to which prescription was used to legitimise the dubious acquisitions of land by the nobility was provided as late as 1868 by the Duke of Argyll in the midst of a debate over who owned the foreshore. In a debate in the House of Lords, he claimed that 'there were rights acquired by individuals or public bodies in consequence of use and prescription, which was the foundation of a very great deal of the property held by Members of that House'.[11]

Prescription, however, was of no use without a title and, in order to claim ownership of land, the nobility decided to set up a public register and make their claims public for all to see.

Register of Sasines

The establishment of the Register of Sasines in 1617 allowed for the establishment of a public register in which deeds could be recorded which were then legally defendable. The Registration Act and the Prescription Act were, from a political standpoint, intimately related. The former provided a registrable title and the latter enabled any dubiety to be cured by the passage of time.

It is tempting to read more into the word 'sasines' than is proper. Derived from the French word *saisir* meaning 'to hold' or 'to seize', it is tempting to think that this is a reflection on how those registering their estates got their hands on the titles. However, the ceremony of taking sasine and the delivery of a handful of earth from the superior to the vassal had been taking place for centuries and, when writing became common, the term also came to embrace the written record of the ceremony. It was quite natural, therefore, to use this familiar term for the new register. Previous registers such as the Secretary's Register had existed but had proved to be ad hoc, open to conflict and fraud and inadequate in providing real legal meaning to property rights.

The reasons for the introduction of the register mirror those of the law on prescription passed in the same year. By 1617, there was widespread confusion and uncertainty over titles to land principally as a result of the conflicts mentioned previously. This confusion led, undoubtedly, to fraudulent dealings in titles as evidenced by the apparent rationale for the act contained in its opening sentence.

> Our sovereign lord, considering the great hurt sustained by his majesty's lieges by the fraudulent dealing of parties who, having alienated their lands and received great sums of money for that, yet, by their unjust concealing of some private right formerly made by them, renders subsequent alienation done for great sums of money altogether unprofitable, which cannot be avoided unless the said private rights be made public and patent to his highness's lieges; for remedy whereof, and of the many inconveniences which may ensue thereupon, his majesty, with advice and consent of the estates of parliament, statutes and ordains that

there shall be a public register in the which all reversions, regresses, bonds and writs for making of reversions or regresses, assignations thereto, discharges of the same, renunciations of wadsets [mortgages] and grants of redemption, and likewise all instruments of sasine, shall be registered within 60 days after the date of the same.[12]

But the greater impulse for this legislation was the anxiety and fear concerning the validity of many titles to the extensive lands of the Auld Kirk which had found their way into the hands of the nobility in the preceding century. In addition, there was widespread concern among the former tenants of the Church who, on obtaining new feus, were keen to see them afforded as much protection as possible. Finally, those who had been granted feus of common land in the royal burghs were well aware that, prior to the sixteenth century, these feus were illegal and so they too had good reason to welcome a more orderly and formal record of what, in many cases, had been obtained through nepotism, corruption and criminality.

All told, the effect of the Reformation and of the development of feuing manifested itself in the existence of a very large number of proprietors of land in the latter half of the sixteenth century who were by no means assured as to the security of their possessions. For those owners who took advantage of the opportunity to record deeds, the benefits were significant and, where there were doubts as to the validity of titles, forty years' passage of time permitted prescriptive rights to be claimed. The Register did not, however, make registration compulsory and, for 230 years, doubts and conflicts continued to arise over whether, when establishing the validity of titles, an unrecorded deed could have any force. This was an important question since the effect of the Sasine Register was supposed to be that it elevated a personal right contracted between a buyer and a seller into a real right defendable against all for all time. The question was put to rest in a court case in 1847 when at issue was the question as to whether an unregistered sasine could have any meaning in establishing whether someone owned land or not.

The proper object and effect of every valid seisin is to divest the granter of the heritable right, and to invest the grantee. When that legal act is once completed, it absolutely excludes the acquisition of any subsequent real right from the granter, preferable to that of the party seised, or, indeed, the acquisition of any real right, through any other medium than the right of the party so seised. An instrument of seisin, which has not in law that effect, is practically null as a seisin, i.e., an act completing a real right; for it does not produce the effect which it is the sole and peculiar object of a valid seisin to secure.[13]

By this judgement it was clear that registration was, in effect, compulsory if ownership of land was to mean anything at all and thus the Register of Sasines became the bulwark and the authority for the written title and ownership of land in Scotland. It remains in use to this day though, where land changes ownership and money changes hands, title is transferred to the Land Register, a computerised, map-based system providing a state-guaranteed title (see Chapter 11).

With a register to record deeds in and a legal basis upon which to legitimise possession, the institution of landownership was now well on the way to being liberated from the overbearing power of the Crown. If the first half of the seventeenth century was mainly concerned with strengthening the legal framework of landed property, the second half was very much concerned with securing the future of the landed families who had taken advantage of it by means of the law of succession and entail.

Succession

A key issue for the nobility had long been the question of succession or inheritance. The question was complicated by the fact that the nobility in medieval Scotland often held land in more than one jurisdiction – often in France and/or England as well as Scotland – and thus were subject to different laws in each place. In Scotland, the common law of inheritance to feudal estates was confirmed in 1292 by a court set up by Edward I to determine the succession following the death of Margaret, the Maid of Norway in

1290. In November 1292, this court reported to Edward that the right of succession to the Kingdom of Scotland was to be decided in the same way as the right of succession to earldoms, baronies and other impartible (indivisible) tenures were. This was based upon the principle of primogeniture whereby the eldest male son inherited. Females could inherit but only after all possible male lines had been exhausted. Primogeniture was a means of ensuring the perpetuation of the feudal system as it avoided any possibility of the division of landed wealth. The consequence of this was to sustain the large-scale pattern of landownership by denying children, other than the eldest son, any rights of inheritance.

Adam Smith was one of the many astute observers who was critical of primogeniture.

When land, like moveables, is considered as the means only of subsistence and enjoyment, the natural law of succession divides it, like them, among all the children of the family; of all of whom the subsistence and enjoyment may be supposed equally dear to the father. This natural law of succession accordingly took place among the Romans, who made no more distinction between elder and younger, between male and female, in the inheritance of lands, than we do in the distribution of moveables. But when land was considered as the means, not of subsistence merely, but of power and protection, it was thought better that it should descend undivided to one.

The security of a landed estate, therefore, the protection which its owner could afford to those who dwelt on it, depended upon its greatness. To divide it was to ruin it, and to expose every part of it to be oppressed and swallowed up by the incursions of its neighbours. The law of primogeniture, therefore, came to take place, not immediately, indeed, but in process of time, in the succession of landed estates, for the same reason that it has generally taken place in that of monarchies, though not always at their first institution. That the power, and consequently the security of the monarchy, may not be weakened by division, it must descend entire to one of the children. To which of them so important a preference shall be given, must be determined by some general rule, founded not upon the doubtful distinctions of personal merit, but upon some plain and evident difference which can admit of no dispute. Among the children of the same family, there can be no indisputable difference but that of sex, and that of age. The male sex is universally preferred to the female; and when all other things are equal, the elder everywhere takes place of the younger. Hence the origin of the right of primogeniture, and of what is called lineal succession.[14]

Primogeniture was at the heart of aristocratic privilege and, in concentrating power in so few hands, led to the revolutions that swept Europe in the late eighteenth century. The Napoleonic Code of 1804, which abolished privileges based on birth, ended primogeniture in France and was influential in ending it too in many other countries across Europe. The code, which still to this day forms the basis of French inheritance law, legally obliges landowners to divide their estate among their children equally.

In Scotland, by contrast, it was not until 1964 that primogeniture was finally abolished. The Succession (Scotland) Act 1964 governs succession to this day. Whilst it abolished primogeniture and thus opened up the *possibility* of heritable property being inherited by others beyond the eldest son, it was merely the possibility. The new law provided no legal *rights* to children to inherit landed property and it remained open to landowners to specify who should inherit landed estates. In practice, therefore, the old established habit persisted and continues to persist much to the irritation of many family members, to women in particular and, arguably, to society as a whole.

Of all the legal framework surrounding landownership, the law of succession in Scotland is the single greatest reason the pattern of private landownership remains so concentrated compared with the rest of Europe. Recent moves to reform the law are discussed in Chapter 28. With the abolition of feudal tenure having been secured on 28 November 2004, a full 200 years after the introduction of the Napoleonic Code, the laws governing inheritance represent one of the last bastions of landed privilege embodied in law.

Lord Stair, in his 1681 *Institutions of the Law of Scotland*, justified primogeniture as the means for 'the preservation of the memory and dignity of families, which by frequent divisions of the inheritance would become despicable or forgotten'.[15] Such were the times in which he wrote. Even today, over 300 years after these penetrating observations, the landed interest, as we shall see later, continues to oppose any reform of succession law to heritable property. Yet, this would be the one reform that would help to break down the pattern of private landownership more than any other.

But it was not just the laws of succession that were deployed to sustain landed hegemony.

Entail

Primogeniture was not sufficient in itself to secure the ownership of land in a family. What if the owner encountered financial difficulties or got into debt? What if the eldest son was more enthusiastic about partying than managing the family estate? These were real fears since land could be lost not simply by normal debts and bankruptcies but through the system of apprisal whereby the debts of landowners were marketable and could be sold by the creditor to third parties. This system was popular not only with those who managed to acquire land through it (often powerful landowners taking advantage of weaker ones) but also with creditors who received payment of debts sooner than they would otherwise have done. Indeed, a survey of land transactions in the seventeenth century found that a third of them involved apprisals.[16]

With many major families, including most nobles, suffering financial difficulties, a series of acts was passed in 1621, 1658, 1661 and 1672 to limit the use of apprisals. Their lack of effectiveness, however, led landowners to seek alternative legal remedies to prevent their estates from falling into the hands of creditors and the process known as entail or tailzies emerged whereby a line of succession could be secured and the estate protected against claims by creditors. The earliest recorded entail is that of the estate of Roxburgh in 1648 and others followed. But, as these did not enjoy any statutory basis, doubts arose as to their effectiveness and a test case was raised in the Court of Session in 1662. Although the

Court upheld the legality of entails by a narrow margin, most leading lawyers regarded the decision as flawed and, to dispel any remaining doubts, the 'Act concerning tailzies' (more commonly referred to as entail) was enacted in 1685.

Act concerning tailzies

Our sovereign lord, with advice and consent of his estates of parliament, statutes and declares that it shall be lawful to his majesty's subjects to tailzie their lands and estates and to substitute heirs in their tailzies with such provisions and conditions as they shall think fit, and to affect the said tailzies with irritant and resolutive clauses, whereby it shall not be lawful to the heirs of tailzie to sell, transfer or convey the said lands or any part thereof or contract debt or do any other deed whereby the same may be apprised, adjudged or evicted from the others substituted in the tailzie or the succession frustrated or interrupted, declaring all such deeds to be in themselves null and void, and that the next heir of tailzie may immediately, upon the contravention, pursue actions of declarator and serve himself heir to he who died last infeft in the seat and was not in contravention, without necessity in any way to represent the contravener.[17]

This act sheltered estates from creditors, prohibited any sale or lease and secured the line of succession by specifying precisely who should inherit. All entails were recorded in a new Register of Entails. In effect, it removed the entire landed interest from any interference by the market and mothballed it in perpetuity. An important motive for this act was the still volatile politics of the time only fifteen years after the Restoration when the Crown might still forfeit land at will, pass retrospective acts of annexation and declare treasonable acts which had been done in all innocence. Lord Stair, for example, was forced to flee to the Netherlands in 1682 one year after publishing his great work, *The Institutions of the Law of Scotland.* And it was not uncommon for estates of parties about to be tried to be made over to the Crown prior to their trials taking place in anticipation of the result![18]

The act was therefore as much about providing some measure of security against forfeiture as it was designed to protect estates from creditors. The hope was that any action taken might only be against the life interest of the possessor of the entailed estate and leave the heir secure to inherit. This hope was to prove short lived when, following the Union and the aftermath of the Jacobite uprising, estates of those convicted of treason were forfeited (though they were all restored in 1784).

Following the 1695 act, estate after estate was entailed. Samuel Shaw published a list in 1784 of the 772 entails recorded in the previous hundred years and, by 1846, the number had grown to 2046 recorded deeds of entail.[19] The proportion of Scotland covered by entailed land was around one fifth in 1785. It is estimated that, in 1825, fully half of Scotland was held as strictly entailed estates and the percentage continued to rise over the next fifty years.[20]

But entail had long been controversial. Reporting on the state of Scottish agriculture in 1814, Sir John Sinclair commented that:

> [m]any of our ablest writers are likewise of the opinion, that entails, carried to the extent of those in Scotland, are *absurd*, *unjust*, and *impolitic*. They consider it absurd, that any private individual should have the power of placing landed property *extra commercium*, and of regulating its descent, its disposal, and its use, to the end of time. They deem it unjust, that any proprietor should be deprived, by the act of a remote ancestor, of the power of making rational provisions for his wife and children. And on such strong grounds, they hold it to be *impolitic*, that any impediments should be thrown in the way of agricultural improvement. The irritant and restrictive clauses, which tie up the proprietor of an entailed estate, from the full management of his property, are so hostile to improvement, that they must be considered as objects of essential national concern; and in that respect entails ought to be, either still farther modified, or entirely abolished; for it is of paramount importance, that the land should yield the greatest possible quantity of produce, for the maintenance of an increasing population, which, in a free country, is constantly pressing hard upon the stock of subsistence.[21]

Sinclair continues:

> By this pernicious statute, every proprietor of land is empow-
> ered, out of his mere caprice, and without authority of any judge,
> to lock up his lands from commerce, (not only in favour of
> persons actually existing, whom he can see, and for twenty-one
> years farther, but), to all succeeding generations, as far as he can
> conceive and imagine . . . It is not easy to conceive any con-
> stitution of the holding of landed property, more completely
> calculated to damp, or totally to extinguish the spirit of im-
> provement in the proprietor, unless that which is said to take
> place in Turkey, where the Sultan is the sole heir to the property
> of his subjects.[22]

And the economist, Adam Smith, railed against the laws of entail
just as he had railed against primogeniture:

> Entails are the natural consequences of the law of primogeniture.
> They were introduced to preserve a certain lineal succession, of
> which the law of primogeniture first gave the idea, and to hinder
> any part of the original estate from being carried out of the
> proposed line either by gift, or devise, or alienation; either by the
> folly, or by the misfortune of any of its successive owners.

> They are founded upon the most absurd of all suppositions, the
> supposition that every successive generation of men have not an
> equal right to the earth, and to all that it possesses; but that the
> property of the present generation should be restrained and
> regulated according to the fancy of those who died perhaps five
> hundred years ago. Entails, however, are still respected through
> the greater part of Europe, in those countries particularly in
> which noble birth is a necessary qualification for the enjoyment
> either of civil or military honours. Entails are thought necessary
> for maintaining this exclusive privilege of the nobility to the
> great offices and honours of their country; and that order having
> usurped one unjust advantage over the rest of their fellow–
> citizens, lest their poverty should render it ridiculous, it is
> thought reasonable that they should have another.

Great tracts of uncultivated land were, in this manner, not only engrossed by particular families, but the possibility of their being divided again was as much as possible precluded for ever. It seldom happens, however, that a great proprietor is a great improver. In the disorderly times which gave birth to those barbarous institutions, the great proprietor was sufficiently employed in defending his own territories, or in extending his jurisdiction and authority over those of his neighbours. He had no leisure to attend to the cultivation and improvement of land. When the establishment of law and order afforded him this leisure, he often wanted the inclination, and almost always the requisite abilities. If the expense of his house and person either equalled or exceeded his revenue, as it did very frequently, he had no stock to employ in this manner. If he was an economist, he generally found it more profitable to employ his annual savings in new purchases than in the improvement of his old estate. To improve land with profit, like all other commercial projects, requires an exact attention to small savings and small gains, of which a man born to a great fortune, even though naturally frugal, is very seldom capable. The situation of such a person naturally disposes him to attend rather to ornament which pleases his fancy than to profit for which he has so little occasion. The elegance of his dress, of his equipage, of his house, and household furniture, are objects which from his infancy he has been accustomed to have some anxiety about. The turn of mind which this habit naturally forms follows him when he comes to think of the improvement of land. He embellishes perhaps four or five hundred acres in the neighbourhood of his house, at ten times the expense which the land is worth after all his improvements; and finds that if he was to improve his whole estate in the same manner, and he has little taste for any other, he would be a bankrupt before he had finished the tenth part of it. There still remain in both parts of the United Kingdom some great estates which have continued without interruption in the hands of the same family since the times of feudal anarchy. Compare the present condition of those estates with the possessions of the small proprietors in their neighbourhood, and you will require no other argument to convince you how unfavourable such extensive property is to improvement.[23]

By the beginning of the nineteenth century, figures such as Lord Rosebery were quite critical of entails and, in a debate in 1834 on reform, he argued that:

> The evils of these perpetuities had always been thought numerous and great. They were a constant impediment to the full improvement of the soil; they impoverished and depressed families whom it was their professed object to support and preserve; and they interfered with that interchange of land, which was not only injurious to the community, but hostile to one of the objects of a power to entail, that of gratifying the ambition to form families, besides depriving persons of the means, for centuries together, of making changes conformable to the varying circumstances of events.[24]

But the Duke of Hamilton was opposed to reform:

> He was decidedly opposed to the present Bill, as it would disturb the fundamental principles on which the law of property in Scotland was founded, as settled by the Act of 1685. That was an Act which had long been considered the fixed and settled law of the country; and if it were now unsettled, no law, or no principle in our Constitution, could in future be considered fixed or sacred. If there was any law in which there should be no positive change, it was this, which had so long been considered the fixed law on which the property of Scotland was held. This law had not only been carried down from their ancestors, and had been the means of preserving their estates through all the troubles which shook the country, but, by the Act of Union, it had been sanctioned and confirmed.[25]

Entails were weakened as a consequence of a number of acts in the nineteenth century and no new entails were allowed following the Entail (Scotland) Act 1914. Entails were finally abolished completely along with feudal tenure on 28 November 2004 and the Register of Entails was consigned to the safekeeping of the National Archives of Scotland.

Of all the institutions of landownership that have developed in

Scotland, primogeniture and entail are the two most responsible for the remarkable concentrated pattern of private landownership. I cannot put the argument better than Adam Smith himself:

> This original engrossing of uncultivated lands, though a great, might have been but a transitory evil. They might soon have been divided again, and broke into small parcels either by succession or by alienation. The law of primogeniture hindered them from being divided by succession: the introduction of entails prevented their being broke into small parcels by alienation.[26]

Feudalism in Transition

These legal reforms should be seen against the more long-term trends in the evolution of feudalism at this time and the historic shift in power from the Crown itself to the Crown and the Church and then, as the power of both of these institutions waned, to private landowners as we know them today.

At the earliest stages of feudalism, Crown feudal charters granted to native lords and immigrant Anglo-Normans were revocable by the king via acts of revocation at any time and this was the principal weapon used to maintain the loyalty and support of the nobles. During the Council, held in Scone on 6 November 1357 'for the king's maintenance, it was ordered that all lands, rents, possessions, and customs granted by him should be recalled to the Crown.'[27]

It was, in effect a one-way temporary transfer of power which could go no further and which, in any case would expire upon the accession of a new Monarch who, through an Act of revocation, would cancel all regalities – the highest feudal grant. The next reform was to enable the Crown to grant heritable feus, a process which gained momentum after an Act of 1503.

> Item, it is decreed and ordained by our sovereign lord and his three estates in this present parliament that it shall be lawful for his highness to set all his own lands, both annexed and unannexed, in feu ferme to any person or persons as he pleases, so that

it will not diminish his rental, grassums or other duties, and to set them with such clauses as he thinks expedient according to the aforesaid condition. And that the lands that he sets in his time, as is said, [are] to stand perpetually to the heirs according to the form of their condition. And that his statute is to last for the lifetime of the current king, our sovereign lord, only, so that the lands that he sets in his time with the aforesaid condition shall stand perpetually, and after his death the annexations which were made previously shall return again to the proper nature, so that his successors shall not have power to alienate or set in fee more than they had before this statute was made.[28]

And this power extended to the estates of the king's subjects:

Item, it is decreed and ordained that because the king's highness is of will and intention for the policy of his realm to set his own lands, both annexed and unannexed, in feu ferme, therefore he has granted to all his estates, with their advice, that every lord, baron and freeholder whatsoever, spiritual or temporal, shall have power throughout the days of his life to set all their lands in feu ferme or annual rent to any person or persons so that it does not diminish their rental, so that the alienation thus made of the most part of all their lands shall not be a cause of forfeiture either to the setter or to the taker, despite any statute or laws made to the contrary.[29]

Feuing developed rapidly in the sixteenth century and represented the first stage in what we would now recognise as modern landownership. The Church in particular was obliged to feu extensively to pay high taxes. However, although the feu was heritable, the superior's consent was required for it to be inherited and a further cash payment was due for renewing the feu. In effect, it was a lifelong tenancy. This power was later to be used effectively in the seventeenth century by larger landowners to reassemble estates that had become fragmented by re-acquiring feus when they came up for renewal.

A further important series of legal reforms followed the defeat of the Jacobite Rising of 1745. Wardholding was abolished as were heritable jurisdictions. Feuars (vassals in possession of a feudal charter from a superior) were also liberated from the obligation to obtain their superiors' consent for selling land and, by this reform, the beginnings of what is now recognised as Scottish landowner-ship can be identified. Landowners were free to develop their land with minimal interference from superiors or the Crown. Of course, they still had to abide by the terms of their feudal charter and the limitations that it laid down.

But not all legal authorities conspired to sanction the ease with which lawyers were able to annex land in the course of conveyances – annexations which, by subsequent occupation and further clever drafting, became part of their estates by stealth. Professor Cosmo Innes (1798–1874), the famous advocate and Professor of Uni-versal History and Greek and Roman Antiquities at the University of Edinburgh, wrote in his *Lectures on Scotch Legal Antiquities*:

> I do not suppose that any cruelty or injustice was ever pre-meditated by the legislature or the Government that there was any intention to favour the rich at the expense of the poor, but there are things in the history of our law that I cannot help censuring the more because I believe the evil was for the most part attributable to the straining of the law by lawyers. The books tell us what impediments the humane law in favour of the 'puir pepil that labours the grunde' had to encounter from the practising lawyers of the day. I think as little humanity has been shown in the divisions of commons. Looking over our country, the land held in common was of vast extent. In truth, the arable – the cultivated land of Scotland, the land early appropriated and held by charter – is a narrow strip on the river bank or beside the sea. The inland, the upland, the moor, the mountain were really not occupied at all for agricultural purposes, or served only to keep the poor and their cattle from starving. They were not thought of when charters were made and lands feudalised. Now as cultivation increased, the tendency in the agricultural mind was to occupy these wide commons, and our lawyers lent themselves to appropriate the poor man's grazing to the neigh-bouring baron. They pointed to his charter with its clause of parts and pertinents, with its general clause of mosses and moors

– clauses taken from the style book, not with any reference to the territory conveyed in that charter; and although the charter was hundreds of years old, and the lord had never possessed any of the common, when it came to be divided, the lord got the whole that was allocated to the estate, and the poor cottar none. The poor had no lawyers.[30]

Not only did the poor have no lawyers. They spoke no Latin either and were not in the habit of travelling to Edinburgh on a regular basis to examine the title deeds of the nobility.

Cosmo Innes

At this point it is worth saying something about the man whose quote above provides the title of this book. Cosmo Innes was something of a polymath. He was a prominent photographer and one of eight members of the Edinburgh Calotype Club – the first photographic club in the world. But it is for his twin interests in the law and antiquities that he is best known. He was born in the manor house of Durris in Kincardineshire on 9 September 1798 where his father, John Innes, of the family Innes of Innes, had purchased a ninety-nine-year lease, having sold lands in Morayshire. Interestingly, the 1695 Entail Act, which led to all sorts of legal disputes, was to lead to John's eviction from Durris. When the Duke of Gordon succeeded as heir of entail in 1819, he won an order evicting Innes on the basis that the original lease was contrary to the strict entail. John Innes was virtually ruined by the expensive litigation and then by the sums he had invested in the estate. The Duke of Gordon then secured an Act of Parliament allowing him to sell the estate in 1828.

Cosmo Innes became an advocate in 1822 and was appointed advocate-depute in 1833. From 1840 to 1852, he was Sheriff of Elgin and, from 1852 to his death in 1874, was Principal Clerk of Session. During this time he also began a lifelong interest in the records of Scotland, assisting Thomas Thomson, the Deputy Clerk Register for Scotland, in organising the ancient records of Scotland. As a result of this work, he published a number of scholarly works and was an editor of the Bannatyne, Spalding and Maitland Clubs, all leading antiquarian societies. He was also one of the Commissioners of the Municipal Corporations Inquiry (see Chapter 8)

In 1846, Innes was appointed Professor of Universal History and Greek and Roman Antiquities at the University of Edinburgh, a post he held until his death. According to one University of Edinburgh historian, Innes was 'the foremost record scholar of his generation and his editions of sources are still the everyday tools of the historians of Scotland'.[31]

Innes's appointment at the university allowed him to bring together his unrivalled understanding of Scotland's history obtained through his archival research with his legal training as an advocate and ongoing experience in charge of the Court of Session. One enduring result of this was a series of lectures to the Juridical Society which was published in 1872 as *Lectures on Scotch Legal Antiquities* and it is from one of these lectures that the quote above and the title for this book are derived. Innes's great contribution was to examine the historical basis of Scots law and to relate this to legal practice. Controversially, in the course of these lectures, he gently reminded his audience of the failings of the great institutional writers of Scots law such as Skene, MacKenzie, Stair and Erskine for not having rooted their work in the history of Scots law. Of Sir John Skene, he observed:

> I have tracked him and his manner of working, and I have not observed that he ever quotes an old charter, a brieve, or a step of old court procedure. He was satisfied with transferring to his work whole pages of the rambling note-books of nameless lawyers, and to attribute them to the legislation of fabulous kings from Malcolm Mackenneth downwards, while he put on his margins references to English books, wishing his reader to believe that these were borrowed from ours.[32]

Of George Mackenzie, the author of the *Institutions of the Laws of Scotland*, he notes:

> I have never found much satisfaction in consulting George Mackenzie's 'Observations on the Statutes'. That accomplished scholar to whom we owe, I suppose, the first foundation of our

noble library, directed his studies for the most part to more congenial pursuits. Neither his studies nor the bend of his mind were very historical, and not at all constitutional. His 'Observations on the Statutes' published in the worst time of our history (1686) are unfortunately suited to that bad time.[33]

And, of Lord Stair, he points out that, with all due respect to this giant of Scots legal writing:

His vigorous and well-trained intellect was directed to the philosophy of his youth, to the Divine law and the law of Nature, as the foundations of his system, and he wished to prove that the decisions of the Scotch Courts were not inconsistent with these. But a very slight attention to his great work will show that he had not bestowed much thought upon the historical foundations – the origin and progress of our peculiar law.[34]

And, finally, of Erskine, another of the towering figures in Scots legal scholarship, he says:

Unfortunately the taste for historical antiquities had not yet arisen when our *second* great institutionalist produced his well-known work. Erskine found the law of Scotland much elaborated since the days of Stair and settled by printed decisions. These he quotes, and supports his positions with citations from Craig's 'Jus Feodale,' Balfour's 'Practicks,' Bankton's 'Institutes,' Kames's works and Mackenzie's. But I suspect he was ignorant of our Scotch history; and for our peculiar and national law he is content to take it as given by Skene, and admits all Skene's materials as of excellent use towards understanding the history and gradual progress of our law. I do not find that Erskine himself anywhere seeks back to the antique origins of any branch of Scotch law; and now that we have so much printed of old styles and forms and examples of early litigation, Erskine's few contributions to legal antiquities seem to us very trifling.[35]

Innes's point is that all the institutional writers (some through no fault of their own as there were no systematic archives of the records of Scotland available at the time they wrote), failed to place Scots law (and, in particular, the law of property with which this book is concerned) in its proper historical context. Cosmo Innes was in an unrivalled position to do just that. He was the co-editor with Thomas Thomson of *The Acts of the Parliaments of Scotland 1124–1707*, published at the behest of the House of Commons in twelve volumes. This work remained the most complete record of the acts of parliament until the University of St Andrews Scottish Parliament Project launched their new record in 2008.[36]

His contribution was to subject the historical reality of much of what was and has been accepted as given law to forensic analysis. He remains one of the few (if not only) authority to undertake this kind of work and, given the subject matter of this book, a key source and the reason I have laid out, at some length, the facts about his life and work. Finally, on a personal note, many years ago when I first read his *Lectures* I noted, in passing, that, on the dedication page, Innes writes:

> To the Right Honourable John Inglis. Lord Justice-General of Scotland. My Dear Lord Justice-General, Allow me to dedicate to you this little book, which owes its existence very much to your Lordship's precept and example. I have the honour to be, Your most obedient Servant, C Innes. Inverleith Oct 14 1872.

I now live in the Inverleith part of Edinburgh and was intrigued to learn, from researching his background, that Cosmo Innes lived in Inverleith House, now part of the Royal Botanic Garden, from 1862 until his death. Cosmo Innes died on 31 July 1874 in Killin and was buried in Warriston Cemetery, not a stone's throw from where I am writing this book.

The Last Century of the Scots Parliament

In 1814, Sir John Sinclair, the Caithness improver and author of the first *Statistical Account of Scotland*, was moved to observe that in 'no country in Europe are the rights of proprietors so well defined and so carefully protected'.[37] The means by which that protection was afforded were largely put in place during the seventeenth century when, at times, the Scots Parliament appeared to do little but pass new laws affirming the institution of property. But securing favourable legal reforms was of itself not enough in what were turbulent times when the nobility was threatened with a return to episcopacy and having to restore the stolen church lands.

As if they needed any reminding of this, it came in the form of the Act of Revocation of Charles I. Introduced in 1625, it was passed by the Scots Parliament as one of no fewer than 168 acts passed throughout the ten-day Parliament during the king's only visit to Scotland in 1633. The act revoked all Crown land grants of Crown and Church property since 1542 and required the nobility to re-acquire them for a price, the income from which was to be used to refinance the Church and the Crown at the expense of the nobility.[38] This was an incendiary move which challenged the legitimacy of title to vast tracts of land (the bulk of the lands of the pre-Reformation Church) that had been acquired before and after the Reformation. There were few noble families left untouched by this threat and it compelled the landowners to rally to the support of the Presbyterian clergy. The nobility was compelled to act and, in 1638, not only joined the ministers but led them in signing the National League and Covenant in Greyfriars Church (the Earl of Sutherland was the first signatory). This document was motivated by a desire to safeguard landed property and is why it was widely known at the time as the Nobleman's Covenant.

Johnston argues that, had Charles I simply stuck to the act, the Church would have supported him and the nobility would have lost their lands. However, Charles's insistence on the divine right of kings, his scornful dismissal of Presbyterianism and his attempts to force his liturgy upon the Scottish Church drove the ministers into the arms of the aristocrats.[39] The nobility favoured a covenanted king – a king who would support the reformed church arrangements (and thus keep popery at bay) but who would also support the feudal status quo upon which the authority of their charters rested. The civil war which followed later that century led to the execution of Charles I but his son, Charles II, carried on in much the same vein, re-introducing episcopacy and restoring patronage. This, in turn, led to the Covenanting Wars – a movement again backed by the nobility in order to defend their landed property.

The legal and political reforms of the seventeenth century and the challenge presented by Charles I did not prevent the nobility from extending its ambitions to garner landed property and, throughout the seventeenth century, the third land grab was gathering pace and culminated in a decisive act of 1695 to divide the last great remaining commons. But, before exploring this, it is worth taking the time to note what was going on in the Highlands at this time – a region of Scotland where feudalisation had been slower to develop and where other, rather more drastic measures were taken to draw the Celtic aristocracy into the feudal grip of the Crown.

In Edinburgh They Hate Us

A short excursion into the Highlands

The historian James Hunter tells a story which sums up much of the relationship between the Highlands and the rest of Scotland.

> In the run-up to the 1979 devolution referendum, an old man in Sutherland, a man who couldn't have been more pro-Highland, told me he'd be voting to keep the status quo.
>
> 'Why?' I asked.
>
> 'Well,' he said, 'in London they don't give a damn about Highlanders, but in Edinburgh they hate us.'

In any discussions about land in Scotland, the Highlands loom large. There are a number of reasons for this – folk memory of the Clearances, romantic attachment to clans, crofting struggles, the aftermath of Culloden, the sporting estate, access and absentee landlordism.[1]

For a long time the Highlands and Islands were part of a Norse kingdom and then they enjoyed substantial autonomy under the Lord of the Isles. Seemingly forever, though, they have caused problems for those in power in Scotland. Older systems of land tenure and kinship-based society lasted longer there than in Lowland Scotland and, as a consequence, feudalism and the central authority that it embodied were slower to take root. As a consequence, a hybrid system of land tenure evolved, whereby native title, under the *dùthaich* system,[2] continued until well into the seventeenth century with feudal charters granted on an ad hoc basis as a means of imposing the Crown's authority and bending the native aristocracy to its will.

A key turning point occurred in 1462 when John, Lord of the

Isles, signed the treaty of Westminster-Ardtornish which, in return for becoming a liege of Edward IV, granted John half of Scotland north of the Forth if and when Scotland was conquered by England. Such a brazen treason led to the forfeiture of the Lord of the Isles in 1493 by James IV and, from then up until the Union of the Crowns in 1603, the Highlands were subjected to a systematic process of assimilation through feudal grants and central edicts. A deliberate strategy was adopted whereby feudal charters (*oighreachd*) were granted to clan chiefs which did not correspond to the territory actually settled by their clan society (their *dùthaich*) over which they exercised heritable trusteeship. Estates would be granted by feudal charter to the chief of another clan and the king would sit back and watch as strife was stirred up.[3]

This was the beginning of a long process whereby clan society began to break down as clan loyalties and native systems of governance yielded to the charter and the authority of the Crown. It was a time during which the most ruthless means were deployed against Highland society to promote assimilation into the Scottish state, to curtail the power of the chiefs, to suppress Gaelic culture and to exert feudal control over clan lands.

The elegant devices of Edinburgh lawyers were useless in this endeavour and, instead, the state adopted altogether more sinister methods. W. H. Murray, in his biography of Rob Roy MacGregor, describes how the Clan Campbell 'dragon' asserted its authority over Clan Gregor:

> The dragon refined its technique, turning from murder and rape to less open, more patient ways. The devices used to cheat men out of their homelands were the charter, the mortgage, the false promise, instigation to violence, false witness, the control of courts of justice, and Letters of Fire and Sword. The latter was the Privy Council's written authority to kill and burn, granted to men strong enough to harry an offending clan.
>
> By Act of the Privy Council at Stirling on 2 September 1563, Letters of Fire and Sword against the clan were granted to Sir John Campbell of Glenorchy and all nobles. The grants were repeated in 1588, 1590 and 1597 and were renewed at intervals over a hundred and thirty years. Their policy was genocide.[4]

In 1583, King James V issued a mandate against Clan Chattan, in which he charges his lieges to invade the clan 'to their utter destruction by slaughter, burning, drowning, and otherways; and leave no creature living of that clan, except priests, women and bairns'.[5]

In 1587, the General Band Act was passed 'for the quieting and keeping in obedience of the disordered subjects, inhabitants of the borders, highlands and isles' in which:

> considering the wicked inclination of the disordered subjects, inhabitants in some parts of the borders adjacent to England and in the highlands and isles, delighting in all mischiefs and most unnaturally and cruelly wasting, slaying, harrying and destroying their own neighbours and native country people, taking occasion of the least trouble that may occur in the inner parts of the realm when they think that care and thought of the repressing of their insolence is in any way forgotten, to renew their most barbarous cruelties and godless oppressions.[6]

Ultimately, the goal was to establish feudal authority and, in 1597, James VI passed an act aimed at consolidating feudal tenure in the Highlands by requiring all who claimed to own land to prove it by the exhibiting of a feudal charter. For the full flavour of royal hostility to the Highland clans, it is worth citing the act in its entirety:

The inhabitants of the isles and highlands should show their holdings

> Our sovereign lord, with advice of the estates of this present parliament, considering that the inhabitants of the highlands and isles of this realm, which are for the most part of his highness's annexed property, have not only frustrated his majesty of the yearly payment of his proper rents and due service properly indebted by them to his majesty out of the said lands, but that they have likewise through their barbarous inhumanity made and presently makes the said highlands and isles, which are most commodious in themselves, as well as by the fertility of the ground as by rich fishings by sea, altogether unprofitable both to

themselves and to all others of his highness's lieges within this realm, they neither maintaining any civil or honest society amongst themselves, neither yet admit others of his highness's lieges to traffick within their bounds with safety of their lives and goods. For remedy whereof, and that the said inhabitants of the said highlands and isles may the better be reduced to a godly, honest and civil manner of living, it is statute and ordained that all landlords, chieftains and leaders and clans, principal houses and householders, heritors and other possessors or pretending right to any lands within the said highlands and isles shall between this and 15 May next to come compear before the lords of his highness's exchequer at Edinburgh, or where it shall happen them to sit for the time, and there bring and produce with them all their infeftments, rights and titles whatsoever whereby they claim right and title to any part of the lands or fishings within the bounds foresaid . . . with certification to them and each one of them if they fail in the premises or to compear and find caution in manner and within the space foresaid, that they and every one of them who fails shall be discerned, likewise by this present act they are discerned to forfeit and lose all pretended infeftments and other right and title they have or may pretend to have to any lands whatsoever they have held or pretends to hold of his majesty either in property or superiority, which their pretended infeftments and titles thereof in case of failure foresaid are now as then and then as now declared by this present parliament to be null and of no value, force nor effect in themselves, and that the nullity thereof shall be received and admitted in all judgements by way of exception or reply, except any process, action or declaration of reduction to be given thereupon.[7]

This draconian act threatened forfeiture for any clan chief unable to exhibit a valid title to their land and no doubt induced much rummaging around in the family charter chests. Though the act was never fully implemented and, since the records of the Privy Council for the period up to 15 May 1598 have been lost, it is not certain how many chiefs complied. Many clearly didn't, including Rory Mor MacLeod on Skye whose lands were forfeited and handed to the Gentlemen Adventurers of Fife.[8] Most Highland chiefs did not have a current title (they may have had one previously but they tended to be revoked and forfeited with regularity), others had lost them and yet others had had them stolen by rival clans. Many charters had become ineffectual after the fall of the Lordship of the Isles since they derived from this forfeited estate.

According to William Skene, in some cases:

> where the right to the clan demesne was the subject of dispute between different septs, both parties had received at different times a quasi-title to them. In many cases the nominal superiority was feudally invested in an alien family, while the land was actually possessed by one of the clans; and in many others they had no title but immemorial possession, which they maintained by the sword; while on the other hand, those who already possessed a nominal right to the lands under feudal title which they had been unable to enforce, or who saw a great prospect, through the threatened forfeitures, of acquiring possessions in the Highlands and Isles, would eagerly avail themselves of the opportunity afforded them by this Statute. The chiefs of the clans thus found themselves compelled to defend their rights upon grounds which could compete with the claims of their eager opponents, and to maintain an equality of rank and prestige with them in the Herald's Office which must drive them to every device necessary to effect their purpose; and they would not hesitate to manufacture titles to the land when they did not exist, and to put forward spurious pedigrees better calculated to maintain their position when a native descent had lost its value and was too weak to serve their purpose.[9]

Cosmo Innes comments:

> But a time came when lawyers discovered that the lands of the tribe could not be held or vindicated, or perhaps could not have money raised upon them without writ, and then came the feudal investiture. The Crown-charter was taken, of course, to the chief who got the whole land of the tribe in barony. And in the

charters of the lands of a great clan the Crown-charter bestowed upon the chief all the rights of jurisdiction, civil and criminal, with pit and gallows, instead of his old patriarchal authority.[10]

The result was, of course, to sustain the chaos that arbitrary feudalisation had caused when superimposed on complex patterns of native kinship tenure.

As Johnston comments:

> As far back as the twelfth century, the King, in Council, had decreed that actual possession for four generations was no valid title; holders must secure feudal charters and the struggle and the turmoil between the twelfth and the eighteenth centuries was at bottom a struggle between the patriarchal tribe and the feudal baron, between the non-chartered, semi-communist Gaels and the ruthless, remorseless, grasping descendants of the pirates who had followed William the Conqueror to the plunder of England.[11]

In 1608, James VI embarked upon perhaps the most decisive attempt to pacify the Highlands. His previous attempt at colonising Lewis having failed, he decided on an alternative approach. He dispatched a naval force to Mull where a dozen of the leading Highland chiefs had convened a meeting. Andrew Knox, Bishop of the Isles, persuaded the chiefs to come on board for a religious service, whereupon the ship slipped its anchor and headed south where the kidnapped chiefs were incarcerated in Dumbarton, Blackness and Stirling Castles. Ten months later, they were released on condition that they sign the nine articles of the Statutes of Iona. At a court held on Iona on 24 August 1609, nine of the chiefs signed the document. By doing so they agreed, inter alia, that the ruinous kirks be repaired, that inns were to be established, that vagabonds be expelled, liquor be controlled, the eldest sons would be sent to the Lowlands for education and bards, the bearers of the culture, would 'be apprehended, put in the stocks and expelled the Islands'.

This was followed by an act of the Privy Council which sought to establish schools in every parish in the Highlands so that:

the youth be exercised and trayned up in civilitie, godlines, knawledge, and learning, that the vulgar Inglische toung be universallie plantit, and the Irische language, whilch is one of the chief and principall causes of the continewance of barbaritie and incivilitie amangis the inhabitantis of the Ilis and Heylandis, may be abolisheit and removeit.[12]

The chiefs who had signed these statutes were made to promise that all their sons would be sent to school in the Lowlands to be educated in English and it was ordained that none would be recognised as heirs to their fathers estates or be accepted as a tenant on Crown land who had not received this education.[13]

This was some assault and it is notable that such efforts were still being made 120 years after an earlier statute by James IV in 1496 that all barons and substantial freeholders must send their eldest sons to grammar schools and universities, 'so that they may have knowledge and understanding of the laws, through which Justice may reign universally through all the realm'.[14]

In the seventeenth century, landownership in the Highlands was far from clear-cut with the various statutes of the time creating a degree of confusion to add to the routine quarrelling and often murky financial transactions and family obligations that had been entered into. It is worth remembering that the 1617 Registration Act, which established the Register of Sasines, and the Prescription Act of the same year were passed not only to legitimise titles to the stolen lands of the Church but also to fortify feudal titles granted to Highland chiefs and others in the face of competing claims.

In the aftermath of Culloden, Jacobite leaders had their estates forfeited and heritable feudal jurisdictions and military wardhold-ing were both abolished. The feudalisation of the Highlands was complete. As Highland lairds sought to improve their social and economic position in wider British society in the seventeenth and eighteenth centuries, they sought to maximise rents to support such aspirations. This decisive change in the motivation of the Highland landowners, allied with wider economic factors, led to the introduction of large-scale sheep farming in the early nine-teenth century and to the period of voluntary and forcible eviction known as the Highland Clearances. Highland society's faith in the endurance of older understandings of land tenure was shattered as clan chiefs exercised their feudal authority and sold land to people with very different ideas about community relations, some of whom authorised acts which, to this day, endure as a manifestation of the despotism of much Highland landlordism at this time.

Landowning power in the Highlands and Islands was consolidated in the nineteenth century following the extensive forced sale of vast territories of clan land due to financial mismanagement. The historian Tom Devine points out that, from the 1820s, large areas of land in the western Highlands became available for sale on an unprecedented scale and that most sales were forced by the threat or reality of financial disaster. Lord Reay sold off his ancestral estates in the west of Sutherland and retired to a villa in Ealing; Walter Campbell's bankruptcy forced the sale of his Islay estate; a similar fate overtook MacNeil of Barra; and MacDonald of Clanranald had had to sell a number of his hereditary properties in Moidart, Arisaig and the Small Isles between 1813 and 1827 with his remaining Hebridean estate sold by his trustees in 1829. The Earls of Seaforth and the MacDonnels of Glengarry both lost their hereditary lands.[15]

Incoming landowners were in a position of unrivalled power enjoying unencumbered property rights and being afloat with cash. The law of prescription facilitated the appropriation of debatable lands and factors or local managers were introduced from outside whose influence on local affairs was, in many cases, greater than that of the owner. The scene was set for the dramas of the nineteenth century with a powerless peasantry, exiled and penniless clan chiefs and omnipotent landowners in possession of vast estates, some stretching from coast to coast.

The pattern of landownership in the nineteenth century became more concentrated as the new Highland elite extended their holdings. By 1870, for example, Sir James Matheson, who had amassed a vast fortune from trade in China, owned 424,560 acres of land. The Marquis of Breadalbane owned 458,421 acres across Perthshire and Argyll. The Duke of Sutherland held all but a few glebes and lighthouses across the 1.2 million acres of Sutherland. And, by 1900, over half the land area of the Highlands was owned by just fifteen landowners.

This powerful landowning hegemony remained unchallenged through most of the nineteenth century until, in 1886, the Crofters' Holdings (Scotland) Act provided security of tenure, fair rents, heritable rights and compensation for improvements to the crofters and cottars of the region. This act marked a watershed in property rights with a large class of tenants now beginning to enjoy legal rights for the first time. It was not, however, as radical as some had wished. It excluded the large Highland parts of Morayshire, Banffshire, Aberdeenshire and Perthshire. It gave very little to the thousands of landless cottars and did nothing to recover the customary rights held by the peasant class on the land from which they had been cleared. These shortcomings have never been addressed (though an extension of crofting tenure to the counties of Bute, Nairn, Moray and most of Banffshire was passed by the Scottish Parliament in 2010).

The history of land in the Highlands and Islands is distinctive but the essential legal framework was and remains the same as the rest of Scotland. One consequence of the very large-scale pattern of ownership was that Highland landowners did not participate to nearly the same extent in the fourth great land grab – the appropriation of the commonties to which we now turn our attention.

A State of Possession Already Subsisting Beyond the Memory of Man

The fourth land grab – the commonties

Despite the spread of feudalism and the depredations of ecclesiastical property, millions of acres avoided being feued during the first five centuries of feudal landownership in Scotland.[1] These lands formed Scotland's commons and the greatest part of them, the commonties, were next on the list of targets for appropriation by the landed class.

By far the most extensive type of commons in Scotland was the commonty. Strictly speaking, these were not genuine commons but uninhabited areas of land ranging from less than a hectare to a thousand hectares or more. The Commonty of Mey in Caithness was 14,126 acres in extent, the Commonty of Millbuie on the Black Isle was 7,117 acres, the Commonty of the Hill of Fare in Kincardineshire was 7,700 acres and the Commonty of Birsay in Orkney was 12,659 acres.[2]

Commonties were legally the undivided common property of neighbouring landowners over which extensive rights of common use persisted. Figure 2 shows the area of Scotland over which they existed. The closest parallel to commonties is the legal character of freshwater lochs. Loch Ness, for example, is not owned by any single landowner but is the undivided common property of the surrounding landowners. Where historically a loch fell wholly within the boundaries of a single property, however, the landowner has sole possession. Such is the case, strangely enough, with Loch

Parishes containing known commonties 2010
Undivided commonties 1840
Known former commonties that have been divided

Figure 2: Distribution of commonties showing the parishes
within which there are records of commonties

Source: Map derived from Adams, *Directory of Former Scottish Commonties*, 1971

Tay. At one time, the Earl of Breadalbane held all the land surrounding the loch – his holdings extended to around half a million acres stretching unbroken from Aberfeldy to the west coast of Scotland. With the bulk of the estate having been sold off in the early twentieth century, the solum of Loch Tay was sold in 1963. The solum is the ground underneath a building or other feature on or above the surface of the earth – in this case, the solum forms the bed of Loch Tay. Where a landowner owned the whole of a parish, commonties vanished, since, by definition, there were no land-owners to hold anything in common. This is one reason why so few survived in the Highlands and Islands with its large-scale pattern of landownership by Highland chiefs.

In the medieval period, the charters held by the nobility and the Church covered very extensive areas of land. Within these terri-tories, there were large tracts that had been subject to communal use since ancient times. Whilst commonties were well delineated on the ground (when it came to division, hundreds of beautiful maps were prepared), they were not delineated in the feu charters that landowners held but described only in general terms.

The institutional writers failed to define commonties with any degree of clarity (which reflects their ancient origins) and it was only when they came to be divided that their boundaries were ascertained. According to Rankine:

> [i]n most, if not all, of the conveyances of commonty to be found in ancient charters or spelt out of them by immemorial posses-sion, there is to be found not a new grant, but the recognition of a state of possession already subsisting beyond the memory of man, and too firmly rooted to be easily dislodged.[3]

And as Callander observed:

> Commonties were therefore not simply a remote relic that had survived outside the earlier feudal grants. The firmly rooted communal use of these areas continued unimpeded within the initial wide grants of land and then, as the number of landowners increased before the 17th century, they survived as areas of shared property. It was the increase in the number of landowners

that led to these areas becoming conspicuous as areas of common property, not just common use.[4]

Commonties were originally Scotland's genuine commons and satisfied the need for a huge variety of household goods and services. A commonty:

> usually offered the complete set of building materials: stone and the clay for mortar, timber for roofing and fixtures, the fail and divot for walls and roofs, a range of thatches, whether heather, broom, rushes or bracken, and in some areas, slate. The commonty met all fuel needs: usually peat and turf, with gorse and broom, sometimes wood and, in central Scotland, occasionally coal. The commonty . . . was the site for sheilings and grazings; it offered a reserve of arable land where an extra crop could be taken and it supplied a range of fertilisers, of which turf was the most typical but which might include limestone, marl or kelp. The commonty also offered the range of blossoms, berries and sap crops available from the native vegetation and which had many traditional uses as foods, drinks and medications. Commonties offered areas of free access whether for comings and goings, markets and fairs, or other events, particularly those needing to be more out of sight from the authorities, such as sectarian preaching.[5]

This extensive use contradicted the landowners' assertion that these areas were barren wastes.

Looking at any map of feuing in the fifteenth or sixteenth centuries masks the true extent of commonties. As Figure 1 on page 21 shows, most of Scotland's parishes in medieval times were covered by feudal grants of one sort or another and the majority were synonymous with parishes. Since parishes and feudalism originated about the same time, a deal of confusion grew as to the precise legal status of commonties with many people who used them believing them to be the common property of those living in the parish. But, as the feudal system consolidated, these parish commons came to be regarded as appendages to the estates of the property owners in the parish – the heritors. Callander remarks that the ambiguity of this transfer – a stealthy precursor to what was to come – was evident in many of the comments in the Statistical Accounts of the 1790s and 1840s where surviving commonties were described as parish land.[6]

The other stealthy precursor to formal division occurred where a whole parish fell into the ownership of one landowner or one feudal superior. In the first case, the commonty simply vanished as there were no owners to share in the rights of property. In the second case, vassals only had rights of servitude or use and not property so the commonty vanished. Thus, without the need to wait for the formal process of division that was to come, they too vanished. Since the number of landowners in Scotland contracted from the seventeenth century onwards, many commonties disappeared by default.

By 1600, many commonties had already been appropriated. The first act of the Scots Parliament to provide a legal framework for division was in 1608 but this required the consent of all heritors in the parish. This was followed in 1647 by an act that dealt specifically with commonties in the Lothians, Lanarkshire and Ayrshire. This act allowed for division where a majority of the parties were agreed.

Finally, in 1695, the act which led to the division and disappearance from the map of Scotland of over half a million acres of common land came into force.[7] Its success was based upon the fact that a commonty could be divided following a petition to the court issued by a single proprietor who had an interest in it. Not only did this make division easier, it also fell victim to a process of mutual suspicion and fear which led to division where otherwise there might be none.

As Rankine points out, the reason for this was that '[a]ll history shows that the tendency is . . . for the powerful to encroach on the ancient rights of the weak'.[8] This is backed up by the records of division which show that the pursuers were inevitably the smaller landowners whose rights to the commonty were being eroded by illegal encroachments from the bigger and more powerful proprietors. The smaller owners thus sought a division to ensure that they got their rightful share before it was stolen by others.

The 1695 Act was short and to the point:

Our sovereign lord, with advice and consent of the estates of parliament, for preventing the discords that arise about commonties, and for the more easy and expedited deciding thereof in time coming, statutes and ordains that all commonties, excepting the commonties belonging to the king and royal burghs, that is all that belong to his majesty in property, or royal burghs in burgage, may be divided at the instance of any having interest, by summons raised against all persons concerned before the lords of session, who are hereby empowered to discuss the relevancy and to determine upon the rights and interests of all parties concerned, and to value and divide the same, according to the value of the rights and interests of the several parties concerned, and to grant commissions to sheriffs, stewarts, bailies of regality and their deputes, justices of peace or others, for perambulating and taking all other necessary probation; which commissions shall be reported to the said lords, and the said processes ultimately determined by them. And where mosses shall happen to be in the said commonties, with power to the said lords to divide the said mosses amongst the several parties having interest therein, in manner foresaid. Or in case it be instructed to the said lords that the said mosses cannot be conveniently divided, his majesty, with consent foresaid, statutes and declares that the said mosses shall remain common, with free ish and entry thereto, whether divided or not. Declaring also, that the interest of the heritors having right in the said commonties shall be estimated according to the valuation of their respective lands or properties, and which divisions are appointed to be made of that part of the commonty that is next adjacent to each heritor's property.[9]

The act exempted Crown commons and those belonging to royal burghs. It also exempted mosses where they could not conveniently be divided. From 1695, commonty division proceeded apace and a whole new set of skills in surveying was developed as witnessed by the beautiful maps held for posterity by the National Archives of Scotland.[10] As the process of division advanced through the first half of the eighteenth century, the motives of landowners to pursue division evolved. Two forces were at work. The first was the desire to create and secure sole rights to property and the second was to initiate agricultural improvement.[11] From the 1760s onwards, however, agricultural improvement and the prospect of profit became the predominant motives of landowners and they and their agents engaged in a propaganda campaign to condemn commonties as archaic relics of the past. Sir John Sinclair, the agricultural improver, wrote of the Commonty of Millbuie on the Black Isle in 1795:

> It is asserted by the best judges, that the soils of the whole of this immense common are as good and as capable of every improvement as those of the rest of the peninsula, and that the plough may in fact reach any part of it. Several attempts have been made to have a division of this commonty lately . . . It will manifestly be rendering essential service to the tenantry and lower class of cottagers in this district to deprive them of the privilege of misspending and missapplying (*sic*) so much of their time and labour as are annually bestowed in collecting their miserable turf for firing, which is the chief and in fact the only benefit (if it can be so deemed) that they reap from this common; for if the face of it is examined, no person will pretend to advance that those who depend upon it for the pasture of a few hungry sheep and young cattle can possibly derive advantage from so wretched and cruel a system; nay, it is impossible that animals can exist upon such sustenance, and recourse must be had in consequence to depredation and encroachment upon property from which they are debarred, so that their very morals are affected by this same evil usage and privilege of common.'[12]

The act of 1695 was a simple and effective piece of legislation which allowed one owner – the pursuer – to raise a summons for division. Provided they could show documentary evidence of their claim to a share, the petition was admissible regardless of the wishes of other owners. The Court of Session would then issue an interlocutor and a commissioner was appointed to oversee the division. He, in turn, appointed a clerk, valuers and surveyors. All of those with a legitimate claim to a share had to produce documentary evidence attesting to the fact. Hearings were organised. Evidence was given and disputes resolved as to the share each proprietor was due. Lastly, the marches were perambulated, confirmed and a plan was prepared indicating each party's share. These plans survive today in the National Archives of Scotland.

Despite the extensive record of division, it is clear that not all commonties were divided. Some examples are analysed in Chapter 22. But the vast majority clearly were lost in what was the third and, certainly for the rural areas, the final major land grab by the landed class. But the 1695 act made an exception for the commons of the royal burghs on the basis that so many inhabitants depended on them. And it was these that were to be the subject of the next land grab.

Mere Miserable Starved Caricatures
of Their Former Greatness

The fifth land grab – the burgh commons

Another of the legacies of David I, alongside feudal tenure, is the Scottish burgh. As one historian observed, 'the vital connection between the surplus-producing landlords and tenants on the one hand and European markets on the other was provided by towns'.[1]

Burghs were established by way of a Crown Charter (for royal burghs) or Barony Charter (for burghs of barony) which define their powers and their obligations to pay the feudal superior the rents and customs collected. All surplus revenue was paid into the Common Good Fund. There were also ecclesiastical burghs and, later, police burghs. The burgh was differentiated from other settlements and the countryside in general by having a legal document granting it exclusive privileges in the form of monopolies on trade, levying customs taxes, holding markets and establishing guilds of merchants. All foreign trade was restricted to royal burghs and no one was to buy or sell any merchandise except from or to the merchants of the burgh. Burghs had their own form of tenure, known as 'burgage tenure'.

Importantly, royal burghs were granted parliamentary representation as one of the estates in Parliament following Bruce's Parliament in 1326 and, through the Convention of Royal Burghs, subsequently became a powerful political voice in medieval Scotland. The charter of the burgh included a grant of land, the rent from which was designed to sustain the burgh as well as provide essential resources for everyday sustenance. And, like the commonties, these lands were of significant extent and, as a consequence, were the subject of the last great land grab of Scotland's common lands. To appreciate how burgh commons disappeared quite so spectacularly, however, it is vital to understand the state of burgh democracy – or lack of it – in Scotland's burghs.

During the reign of James I, the artisan class within burghs was on the ascendancy and threatened the power of the merchant class of burgesses. Burgesses were the original freemen of the town and they were entitled to hold property under burgage tenure. They were the burgh elite, a wealthy class of merchants who controlled the burgh council and courts. They formed the electorate of the burgh and elected the Council on a yearly basis. Unsurprisingly, the unfree and the craftsmen resented the power of the burgesses and, when they saw that magistrates were continuing in office beyond the proper term of one year, they made their complaint known. The result was not the restoration of proper governance in the burgh but a direct assault on what little democracy existed. The remarkable piece of legislation that gave effect to this was the 1469 Officers of Burghs Act.

As touching the election of aldermen, bailies and other officers of burghs, because of the great disturbance and contention each year for the choosing of the same through the multitude and clamour of common simple persons, it is thought expedient that neither officers nor council be continued according to the king's laws of burghs for more than a year, and that the choosing of the new officers occur in this manner: that is to say, that the old town council shall choose the new council in such number as is suits the town, and the new council and the old one of the previous year shall choose all officers pertaining to the town, such as aldermen, bailies, dean of guild and other officers, and that each craft shall choose a person of the same craft who shall have a voice in the said election of officers for that time and similarly year to year. And further, it is thought expedient that neither captain nor constable of the king's castles, whatever town they are in, shall bear office within the said town as to be alderman, bailie, dean of guild, treasurer or any other officer that may be chosen by the town from the time of the next choosing onwards etc.[2]

This was a direct violation of the existing constitution of the burghs. In order to obviate the yearly trouble and contention at election times, the remedy was to abolish elections! Henceforth, the old council would choose the new one and together they would elect the magistrates to run the new council. The elite of the burghs, therefore, managed to subvert the early democracy that was emerging. Remarkably, this state of affairs persisted right up until the Burgh Reform Act of 1833 and the consequent lack of democratic scrutiny contributed directly to the crisis that was to befall the common good. As Johnston clearly argues:

> Until the Burgh Reform Act of 1833 the landowners and the commercial bourgeois class controlled all burghal administration of the common lands, and controlled it in such a way that vast areas of common lands were quietly appropriated, trust funds wholly disappeared, and to such a length did the plunder and the corruption develop, that some ancient burghs with valuable patrimonies went bankrupt, some disappeared altogether from the map of Scotland, some had their charters confiscated, and those which survived to the middle of the nineteenth century were left mere miserable starved caricatures of their former greatness, their Common Good funds gone, their lands fenced in private ownership, and their treasurers faced often with crushing debts.[3]

The story of how the patrimony of the burghs disappeared is a fascinating tale of corruption and bad governance. As early as 1491, a Common Good Act (which remains on the statute book) was enacted. It set down that the common good was for the use of the burgh and that the Great Chamberlain would be responsible for inspecting the books.

> It is decreed and ordained that the common good of all our sovereign lord's burghs within the realm be observed and kept for the common good of the town and to be spent in common and necessary things for the burgh by the advice of the town council at the time and deacons of crafts where they are, and an annual inspection is to be taken in the chamberlain ayres of the expenses

and disposition of the same. And further, that the burgh rents, such as land, fishing, farms, mills and other annual revenues, are only to be set for three years, and if any happen to be set [in] other ways, that they are not to be of any value, force or effect at any time in the future.[4]

Soon after, however, James IV's parliament of 1503 permitted the feuing of Crown land and that held by vassals of the Crown. Such rights were never granted to royal burghs but it was not long before they too managed to secure the rights. In 1508, James IV granted Edinburgh a charter, permitting it to feu the burgh commons. Similar charters were granted to Aberdeen and other burghs. Until then, the common good land could only be leased on short-term leases for a maximum of three years (see 1491 act above). The new charter allowed the magistrates to grant feus in perpetuity which generated far higher returns in annual feu duties than leases ever did. However, what the magistrates either did not appreciate or ignored was the fact that, whilst the terms of a lease could be renewed every three years and an appropriate rent set, the feu duty was fixed for all time and would quite quickly become a nominal sum.

As a parliamentary enquiry later noted, 'From this period, therefore may be dated the commencement of that system of maladministration which, with greater or less rapidity, has ultimately tended to the destruction of the far greater portion of the common good of the burghs royal.'[5] The story of Edinburgh provides a good example of the general trend. By the beginning of the sixteenth century, the burgh began the process of feuing land but, as the same parliamentary enquiry observed,

[a]s all such alienations were legally invalid, being in violation of the original intendment of the grants to burghs royal, as well as of the just rights of the community, the practice of feuing seems to have been at first adopted with hesitation and timidity.[6]

By the improvident exercise of the powers conferred on the corporation by the charter of King James IV, avowedly for the purpose of improving the condition of the burgh, and increasing its immediate revenue, the far greater part of the territorial property or common lands was speedily alienated, in return for annual payments in the current money of the kingdom, which have gradually dwindled down into what is no little more than a nominal and illusory quit-rent. The progress of these proceedings, and their operation in the impoverishment of the community, might be traced in the records of the council; but the result of the whole is so notorious and unquestionable, as to render any such deduction unnecessary.[7]

An act was passed in 1535 in an effort to stop the abuses but to little avail. Attempts by the merchants to investigate the affairs of the magistrates were frequently blocked. Johnston provides an example from Edinburgh:

When, in 1638, Captain Thomas Hamilton, an Edinburgh merchant, instituted a process before the Privy Council to force Sir James Fleming and Sir James Dick, two late Provosts, to produce the town's books, he was acting within both the letter and the spirit of an Act of 1535, which allowed inspection of documents relating to Common Good Funds. But the Council refused his request – 'it looking too popular and democratick'. Between 1807 and 1818, £28,000 worth of land was alienated, and between 1818 and 1833 land to the value of £7609 was sold; in 1832 the Council betrayed its legacy trusts by investing them for other purpose; and in 1833 Edinburgh once so wealthy a burghal community, became insolvent, and handed over its assets to trustees.[8]

The royal burghs, their charters having been granted by the Crown, were vassals of the Crown. All burgesses who held land under burgage tenure (the holding of land within a royal burgh) were thus also vassals of the Crown. By contrast, any sale of common good land was held under the feudal system with the magistrates, bailies and councillors as feudal superior. As common good land began to be alienated, a lucrative new market in superiorities was generated since a superiority worth 40 shillings was the qualification required to vote in parliamentary elections (this rose to £400 after 1743). Thus, the burgh could use feuing of the commons as a means of securing sympathetic parliamentary votes, significant revenues and valuable favours to friends and colleagues. The corruption and nepotism that took hold was, therefore, about a lot more than the accumulation of property – it was also concerned with who had a say in how the country was governed and who didn't as the following brief exchange over the 1832 Reform Bill in the House of Commons on 27 September 1831, demonstrates:

Mr. Robert A. Dundas presented a Petition from the Lord Provost and Magistrates of Edinburgh, being trustees of landed property, purchased by a legacy which had been devised for charitable purposes, complaining that the Reform Bill, by destroying superiorities, which they had hitherto sold, would take away their property. He contended, that superiorities were private property, and ought not to be taken away without compensation. The petitioners also prayed that they might be heard by counsel at the bar, and receive compensation.

Mr. Pringle supported the prayer of the petition, and deprecated the language which had formerly been used by the Lord Advocate.

Mr. John Campbell blushed for his na (*sic*) – country. To the honour of England, it ought to be stated, that not one demand for compensation had been made by any one of the proprietors of rotten boroughs which had been annihilated by this Bill. He was therefore sorry to find, that it was left for Scotland to ask compensation for the loss of that which she ought never to have had. No property would be taken away by this Bill from these Trustees, for the superiority would still remain unimpaired. The property would remain; but the right of voting attached to it would be taken away.

Mr. Dixon said, that the hon. and learned member for Stafford was misleading English Members, when he instituted a comparison between the rotten boroughs of England and the superiorities of Scotland. Did he mean to say, that the right of voting attached to a superiority was illegal? Superiorities might be legally sold—would the hon. and learned Gentleman say the same of a rotten borough?

Mr. Gillon was surprised at the extraordinary language held by the hon. member for Glasgow. In his opinion, the holders of superiorities had no more claim to compensation than the holders of rotten boroughs. He had heard with pleasure the declaration of the Lord Advocate, that he intended by his bill to destroy every rag and tatter of the abominable system of Scotch elections.

Sir Edward Sugden said, that the burgage tenures of England were quite as much legal property as the superiorities of Scotland, and yet the holders of burgage tenures had never put forth any claim to compensation, because much as they disapproved of the English Reform Bill, they felt that private advantage ought to give way to the public good. He was much surprised to hear so stanch a Reformer as the hon. member for Glasgow plead for compensation for the holders of Scotch superiorities. He (Sir E. Sugden) would never consent to give to the holders of Scotch superiorities that which had not even been asked for by the English holders of burgage tenures.

Mr. Kennedy contended, that the petitioners would lose no property by this Bill. They could not vote themselves on this superiority, but they could sell the right of voting on it to others; and it was only right that they should be deprived of that pecuniary advantage which others obtained from political jobbing.

Mr. Robert A. Dundas, in moving that this petition be referred to the Committee on the Scotch Reform Bill, took occasion to observe, that the petitioners, in bringing forward this petition, were influenced by public and not by private and selfish considerations.[9]

Robert Dundas, 2nd Viscount Melville was, of course, the latest in a long line of four Dundas heirs to have been MP for Edinburgh and would have been well acquainted with the corrupt practices of the burgh magistrates. The Reform Act (Scotland) of 1832 and the Burgh Police (Scotland) Act of 1833 were intended to bring an end to much of this corruption by extending the franchise to all males with £10 of land. The same held for the election of burgh councils under the 1833 act. Arguably, this had much the greater impact since it introduced a form of democracy for the very first time and brought an end to the system that had been in place since 1469 whereby each council had selected its own successors with all the nepotism, cronyism and downright despotism that this led to.

But the mode of election was not the only bone of contention. There was widespread concern at the depredations of the common good and the wider financial mismanagement of burghs. A House of Commons Select Committee to whom petitions from the royal burghs of Scotland was referred produced a voluminous report in 1819. It narrates in exquisite detail the shady goings-on in the burghs. On 8 July, the Committee interviewed William Arbuthnott who was Provost of Edinburgh from 1815 to 1817 and who had just acquired a superiority from the Town Council:

Are you acquainted with the sale of any superiorities during the year 1816?

I am.

Can you state by whose direction those were proposed in council to be sold?

It was myself, as lord provost, that brought forward the motion for the sale of those superiorities after consulting with some of my friends in the council as to the propriety of the measure.

What was the motive of your proposing to sell those superiorities?

I considered that there was a certain property belonging to the town council which was of no use to them and that it would be of material consequence to the funds of the town to sell that property.

In what way did you ascertain the value of those superiorities?

I know perfectly well it has elsewhere been insinuated, that I obtained the vote which I purchased myself, for a less price than was the real value of it; now I should be very loath, and I cannot persuade myself, that any agent, even to serve a political purpose, would calumniate a person's character, or say ought to their prejudice; but knowing how utterly unfounded that insinuation is, it cannot be surprising that I should feel much hurt at it, and should be very anxious that the matter should be sifted to the bottom. As soon as it was decided to sell the votes, I out of doors made the necessary inquiry respecting the price, for a considerable period previous to June 1816, with one exception, which was for three years before, in 1813; the highest price which had been given for votes, I was informed was 800 guineas; accordingly that was the price we meant to demand for our votes, but in a few days previous to the transaction taking place, I met Sir John Marjoribanks, who inquired what price we intended to put upon the votes of the town which were then on sale. I told him, I believed 800 guineas was the highest price which had been given, and that was the price therefore we meant to demand. Sir John then said to me, Mr James Gibson has just been with me, and informed me, one of their friends had purchased a county vote for £900; upon which I said to Sir John, I was extremely obliged to him for this information, for that I should have regretted exceedingly if one of the town's votes had been sold for less than could have been obtained for them elsewhere; that as far as depended upon me, none should; that I would begin by offering £900, and that I was persuaded no gentleman who had offered for the others, would wish to have them on more favourable terms.

Was any public information given that they were to be sold? No.

What was the price you ultimately gave for the vote you purchased?

£900 for the bare superiority and £60 for the feus.

Was any other of the votes then sold, disposed of to a member of council?

One other vote to Mr Mackinlay.

How many votes altogether were sold?

Four complete votes.

And none were exposed to public sale?

No.

Nor any public advertisement issued to intimate their being about to be sold?

None whatever.[10]

The inquiry was critical of the management of the burghs but failed to reach any radical conclusions. A follow-up report in 1820 fared scarcely better perhaps because, as observed in their pre-amble, 'First, that the documentary evidence obtained is necessa-rily made up by the very Official Persons, whose conduct the Petitioners arraign; and secondly, that such evidence is made up from records under the exclusive inspection and control of the same Official Persons.'[11]

As a consequence of the complaints raised and the reforms made to the electoral franchise, the government decided that it was time to set up a proper Commission of Inquiry and, in 1833, appointed Commissioners to inquire into the state of Municipal Corporations in Scotland. The membership included our friend Cosmo Innes. In total, the Commissioners visited eighty-four royal burghs and obtained evidence from forty-three burghs of regality and barony. The 'Local Reports' containing this evidence make for entertaining reading.

In Fortrose, they met Provost McFarquhar who, for twenty-three years, had exclusively managed the affairs of the burgh.

> He suffered no one to participate with him in power, and literally reduced the other councillors and burgesses to absolute nonen-tities. It was he, and he alone, who had prepared the documents exhibited to the Commissioners. He declared that 'he acted entirely on his own authority and on his own responsibility; that he previously consulted with nobody; that he afterwards shewed it to nobody; that he neither asked nor received any delegated power from the council; that he believed the council put entire confidence in him; and that there was nobody else in Fortrose, either in the council, or out of it, who knew anything on the subject.'

Upon questioning, it became apparent, however, that there was one person in whom he placed some confidence – a Mr Dempster, the innkeeper, whom he occasionally employed as an assistant. Mr McFarquhar kept sole possession of all the burgh records and accounts and all sums of money were paid to him and expended by him. The ledger book was all in the handwriting of Provost McFarquhar's friend, the innkeeper. The Commissioners, keen to speak to Mr Dempster, were told that he had run away some ten or twelve days before the inquiry commenced. Mr McFarquhar failed to provide an adequate explanation for his friend's absence, merely stating that he though he had gone to Glasgow but would be back any day soon. Further interrogation revealed that the accounts exhibited to the Commissioners had all been made up on one day – the 15th September 1833. Not only that but they had been made up especially for the Commissioners visit and were, in fact, a total concoction.[12]

Meanwhile, other burghs lost land though the greed of neighbouring landowners. As Johnston reports:

> Hawick (in 1833 drawing annual rents of £6,317) seems to have put up a spirited fight against the Duke of Buccleuch's attempt, in 1770, to appropriate its common muir. The case came before the Court of Session, and 'after having defended in court for some time, was by reason of the deficiency of the burgh funds, referred to arbitration of the Lord Chief Baron of Exchequer.' The result was a foregone conclusion; the Lord Chief Baron divided the common, donating a 'large part' to the Duke of Buccleuch and other conterminous heritors. In 1833 the people are, say the Municipal Commissioners, 'aggrieved, but the decreet arbitral, followed by possession for upwards of 50 years, bars all discussion as to the title of the proprietors. No blame can attach to the magistrates and council.[13]

He sums up the lamentable reports of the Commissioners:

> At one time Tain owned 3,000 acres of moorland, but on 'the conterminous proprietors making considerable encroachments,' the magistrates concluded that in whatever encroachments there must be, they, the magistrates, should be the encroachers, and so they feued out the moor among themselves at 6d per acre.
>
> Whithorn, whose Council was manned carefully by dependants of the Earl of Galloway, owned nothing in 1833 but a croft and a windmill; and the same noble family, by the same ignoble process, had secured for 'trifling feu-duties' almost the entire 1,200 acres which had constituted the ancient royalty of Wigtown. For a feu-duty of £16 the Earl, who was 'patron of the

place,' took over Wigton lands yielding an annual rent of £400; and it is a matter of some wonderment that the docile sycophants who constituted the magistracy did not also part with the lands of Gallowhill and Philiphall, the town hall, the ball rooms, and the schoolhouse.

Wick had lost in the law courts its limited right to commonty over the Hill of Wick, and owned no property; Abernethy owned nothing, nor did Alloa. Bathgate was the proud possessor of the site of a fountain and a right servitude over 4½ acres of moorland. Beith had no local government of any kind. Bo'ness owned nothing; Castle-Douglas owned a shop; Coldstream was stripped bare, not even possessing 'rights in its street dung'; Crieff had two fields; Dalkeith, nothing; Dunkeld, nothing; and Dunoon, nothing.

In 1785 the only remnant property of the Burgh of Dunse was an 'extensive common'; but in that year the common was divided between the neighbouring Superior and his feuars; in 1833 all was gone except 10 acres of moor and a whinstone quarry. The property of Fraserburgh – parks, links, etc. – was vested in the feuars. Eyemouth owned nothing, nor did Gatehouse-of-Fleet. Galashiels had not even a constitution. Galston owned nothing, and Girvan but a few houses.[14]

By 1835, the burgh commons were clearly much depleted but it would be wrong to suppose that they disappeared. As we will see later (in Chapter 23), common good did survive. Indeed, in the latter part of the nineteenth century, it expanded considerably as a result of two developments. The first was the coincidence of rapidly growing urban centres encroaching on to the lands of long-established rural estates. This provided a bonanza for the landowners in the form of capital receipts from land sales but it also led them to gift significant property to the burghs as parks, museums and town and village halls. These properties also became part of the common good and, in addition to the remnant lands of the original burgh charters, they constitute the major part of the common good in urban Scotland today.

The second development was the increase in litigation by burghs themselves in defence of the community's legal rights in common land.[15] These were important to a growing urban population who needed land for both recreational pastimes such as golf and industrial activity such as bleaching. A number of important cases came before the courts in the nineteenth century such as in Eyemouth where the Home family took out an action against women in the village to prevent them using a small area of land for drawing water and bleaching. The case, noted one of the judges, presented 'a question of great interest to the towns and villages throughout the country, a numerous class generally ill able to defend their own rights'. The case found for the women and the judges noted that what the feudal superior of Eyemouth was attempting to claim was an absolute and arbitrary power to deprive eleven hundred burgh inhabitants of rights necessary for their survival and intrinsic to the purposes for which the burgh of barony was erected. This case confirmed the existence of community land rights in public law.[16]

Another celebrated case concerned what was then known as the Pilmour Links and Commonty in St Andrews and is now better known as the Old Course, the most famous golf course in the world. In 1797, the Town Council was bankrupt and sold the town common to Charles Dempster, a rabbit farmer. The local inhabitants were furious at the fact that their historic commonty was to be turned into a rabbit warren. They obtained a legal ruling that they had a customary right to play golf and to destroy the rabbits. This led to a series of 'commonty riots' and twenty years of legal and physical war between the rabbit farmers and the golfers before the golfers prevailed and secured their rights. Without this action and the legal decision that upheld the townspeople's common rights, there would probably be no golf links in St Andrews today.[17]

Notwithstanding such victories, the loss of the vast patrimony of the burghs of Scotland was the last of the five great land grabs in Scotland. As a consequence, by the end of the eighteenth century, Scotland's landowners were a unified and powerful class. As Callander observed:

By the late 18th century, landownership had entered a highly profitable era. The powers that these major landowners had lost, for example through the Union of 1707 and the subsequent authority of a London based government, were countered by the extent of Scotland's land they had secured. The control of this land with all the political, social and economic values it still represented, allowed these landowners to retain their all-pervasive dominance of society in Scotland through into the 19th century.[18]

With no more land to appropriate in Scotland, that might have been the end of matters but, as luck would have it, there was land left to plunder beyond Scotland's shores and Scotland's landowners were enthusiastic participants in the imperial century following the defeat of Napoleon at Waterloo. And it was their adventures abroad together with the profits from the industrial revolution that made it increasingly possible to invest vast amounts of capital in their land back home and to turn much of Scotland into a huge playground for the nouveaux riches. It was the demand for wool during the Napoleonic wars that began the process of clearance across the Highlands. And it was the Berlin Conference of 1884–85 that carved up Africa among the European powers.

Colonialism was, in effect, the sixth land grab and it was conducted not by individuals on their own account but by individuals deploying state power. In a sense, this turns us full circle back to the early medieval period when the Scottish Crown was effectively colonising Scotland by imposing feudalism across the country. The next chapter explores this process of colonisation and the legal issues raised by it, many of which are returning today to challenge long-established ideas of property ownership.

I Hereby Take Possession of This Island of Rockall

The sixth land grab – colonial adventures

The annexation of one quarter of the world's land area by the United Kingdom represents the largest land grab ever undertaken. The land over which the sun never set was home to a quarter of the world's population and was secured through the same process of brute force and arrogance that Robert Bruce had engineered some 500 years earlier. Military might and the legal paraphernalia of declarations, renunciations and royal warrants and charters were deployed in the service of the monarch to subjugate lands and declare them *terra nullius*.

Old habits die hard. Just as the Crown had enforced its will over customary tenures in Scotland in the Middle Ages and now over the lands of the British Empire, so it continued to do until very recently. Britain's most recent colonial adventure took place in 1955 off the west coast of Scotland.[1]

Rockall is an isolated, uninhabited rock situated in the North Atlantic Ocean. It is only 19m high, 25m across and 30m wide. It is located 57°13′ north, 13°41′ west, some 187 miles west of St Kilda. The sea area around it, also known as Rockall, is well known to listeners of the BBC North Atlantic Shipping Forecasts.

The United Kingdom, Ireland, Iceland and Denmark all claim the rock as part of their respective territories. It is strategically significant as it sits on the Rockall Bank which is believed to contain significant deposits of oil and natural gas. But, back in the 1950s, its importance was strategic and, with the Cold War underway, there were fears that the rock could be used by a foreign power to track missiles which were shortly to be tested from the rocket range on the island of South Uist.

The problem of how to go about securing possession of the rock exercised the government in 1955 and it sought the advice of, appropriately enough, the Colonial Office on how the empire should be expanded. Precedents from the past were considered such as Christmas Island and Tristan da Cunha and the mandarins responded thus:

> In the case of uninhabited and virtually uninhabitable territories all that seems to be required in municipal law is formal annexation, though, of course, international law probably requires some actual exercise of sovereignty to make the title good. It seems . . . that the formal annexation could be achieved either by an issue of an Order in Council or other appropriate instrument under the Royal prerogative or . . . by the reading of a proclamation on it by some duly authorised officer.[2]

Underlying this opinion was the charge given to Captain Cook in 1768 to take possession of 'such islands as you may discover in the course of your voyage that have not hitherto been discovered by Europeans'.[3]

On 18 September 1955, Captain Connell of HMS *Vidal*, acting in pursuance of a royal warrant, led a naval expedition which landed on the rock, planted a Union flag, affixed a bronze plaque and formally annexed Rockall to the British Crown. Lieutenant-Commander Scott announced to his two companions on the rock and to the bemused puffins, guillemots and other seabirds in the area, 'In the name of Her Majesty Queen Elizabeth II, I hereby take possession of this island of Rockall.' (See Plates 8 and 9.)

The three men stood to attention as the flag was raised and HMS *Vidal* sailed past and unleashed a twenty-one-gun salute as the final act of territorial annexation in the history of the British Empire drew to a close. Both the plaque and the flag were washed away long ago. The following is what was inscribed on the plaque:

BY AUTHORITY OF
HER MAJESTY QUEEN ELIZABETH THE SECOND,
BY THE GRACE OF GOD OF THE
UNITED KINGDOM OF GREAT BRITAIN
AND NORTHERN IRELAND AND OF
HER OTHER REALMS AND TERRITORIES, QUEEN,
HEAD OF THE COMMONWEALTH,
DEFENDER OF THE FAITH ETC, ETC, ETC,
AND IN ACCORDANCE WITH HER MAJESTY'S
INSTRUCTIONS DATED THE 14.9.55.
A LANDING WAS EFFECTED THIS DAY UPON
THIS ISLAND OF ROCKALL FROM H.M.S. VIDAL.
THE UNION FLAG WAS HOISTED AND
POSSESSION OF THE ISLAND WAS TAKEN IN THE
NAME OF HER MAJESTY.

[SIGNED] R H CONNELL
CAPTAIN H.M.S. VIDAL,
18 SEPTEMBER 1955.

But stranger things were yet to happen. In 1971, the UK became increasingly concerned about rival claims to Rockall from Denmark, Ireland and Iceland, who were all interested in the fisheries and potential oil and gas deposits. Rockall was also not legally part of the UK (and thus had a similar status to other Crown possessions such as Pitcairn and the Christmas Islands) and thus important fisheries legislation did not apply. Moreover, the UK was about to join the European Common Market and Rockall provided an important extension of the UK's sovereignty. To attempt to fortify its claim, the UK enacted the Island of Rockall Act 1972. One of the shortest acts on the statute book, it states boldly:

An Act to make provision for the incorporation of that part of Her Majesty's Dominions known as the Island of Rockall into that part of the United Kingdom known as Scotland, and for purposes connected therewith.

Be it enacted by the Queen's most Excellent Majesty, by and with the advice and consent of the Lords Spiritual and

Temporal, and Commons, in this present Parliament assembled, and by the authority of the same, as follows:-

1. As from the date of the passing of this Act, the Island of Rockall (of which possession was formally taken in the name of Her Majesty on 18th September 1955 in pursuance of a Royal Warrant dated 14th September 1955 addressed to the Captain of Her Majesty's Ship Vidal) shall be incorporated into that part of the United Kingdom known as Scotland and shall form part of the District of Harris in the County of Inverness, and the law of Scotland shall apply accordingly.

2. This Act may be cited as the Island of Rockall Act 1972.

Then the really silly business started. A Glasgow solicitor, noting that Rockall was part of Scotland and subject to Scots law, decided to claim ownership. Since the Crown's claim was, in law, merely one of sovereignty (attempting to make Rockall part of the UK), the rock was owned by no one. In such circumstances, it is possible to prepare and record an *a non domino* disposition (for a full discussion on the term *a non domino*, see pp. 278–80). Thus, on 8 June 1975, Alexander Harper, an engineer of 1103 Argyle Street in Glasgow, granted ownership of Rockall *a non domino* to Daniel Gardner, a solicitor of 105 West George Street, Glasgow.

What followed was something of a farce as the Keeper of the Registers of Scotland realised the potential significance of the deed. He returned it to them on the spurious grounds that they did not appear to have paid stamp duty – tax paid on property transactions. As a transaction of no value, however, stamp duty was not liable. However, this delay allowed the Crown Office to be alerted and gave them time to prepare a deed, in the name of Her Majesty, which was promptly recorded (with no stamp duty payable) on 7 August 1975. By the time Gardner had verified the non-liability to stamp duty, therefore, and resubmitted the deed, the Queen had got there before him.[4]

Rockall remains the subject of international disagreement and whether the UK's claim is valid or not will probably only eventually be determined if and when oil, gas or other minerals are found. Then, Ireland, the UK, Denmark and Iceland will resume negotiations.[5]

The annexation of Rockall involved exactly the same sort of procedures as were involved in the colonisation of much of the British Empire with the single exception that there were no native people to deal with in the North Atlantic. Following the Union in 1707, Scots embraced the opportunities provided by imperial expansion. Families such as the Jardines, Mathesons, Flemings and Dundases became key players in the commercial exploitation of the British Empire and the newly acquired profits from tea, rubber, narcotics, tobacco and finance provided the capital necessary to develop both Highland and Lowland estates.

British imperial authority in North America, Australia, India and East Africa was underpinned by the sovereignty of the Crown. Just as on Rockall, it was considered that proclamations, ceremonial flag raising, the popping of a few cannons and assertions of Crown dominion were all that was required to establish British rule in the empire. But the legitimacy of these imperial land grabs has remained a problematic issue for Britain's colonies even long after decolonisation – as witnessed in present-day Zimbabwe.

In the USA, the colonists were astute enough to negotiate (though that is a rather generous term to apply to what were actually threats backed up by force) treaties and agreements with the native population across the country. Latterly, they simply wiped them out. In Canada the same process took place but few treaties were agreed west of the Rockies – the so-called British Columbia anomaly – which was a consequence of the 1763 Royal Proclamation by George III that no title to Indian territory was to be extinguished merely by conquest or occupation. This remains the case today and leaves the province in something of a quandary.[6] Despite a process of treaty negotiations initiated in 1991, none has yet been signed. The Auditor General of British Columbia recently concluded that the lack of treaties between the British Columbia Government and First Nations 'is detrimental not only to First Nations, but also to the province's economic development and social well-being'.[7]

In other British colonies, the same attention was not observed to such legal niceties and the territory was simply annexed in the name of the Crown much as Rockall was to be many years later. This was to lead to significant problems for the indigenous population, not only in the immediate aftermath of de-colonisation but also many years after when such apparently simple claims were tested in the courts. Perhaps the best example of this is the recent decision in Australia in the so-called Mabo case.[8]

This was a test case brought by Eddie Mabo, David Passi and James Rice to determine the legal rights of the Meriam people on the islands of Mer (Murray Island), Dauar and Waier in the Torres Strait which was annexed to the State of Queensland in 1879. Mabo claimed that he and his colleagues held native title and that the Crown had an obligation to uphold their rights. This posed a direct challenge to the notion that colonisation had extinguished native title in an Australia that had long asserted the supremacy of the Crown. Crucially, in this case, the High Court begged to differ:

> The proposition that, when the Crown assumed sovereignty over an Australian colony, it became the universal and absolute beneficial owner of all the land therein invites critical examination. If the conclusion at which Stephen C.J. [Chief Justice] arrived in Attorney-General v. Brown be right, the interests of indigenous inhabitants in colonial land were extinguished so soon as British subjects settled in a colony, though the indigenous inhabitants had neither ceded their lands to the Crown nor suffered them to be taken as the spoils of conquest. According to the cases, the common law itself took from indigenous inhabitants any right to occupy their traditional land, exposed them to deprivation of the religious, cultural and economic sustenance which the land provides, vested the land effectively in the control of the Imperial authorities without any right to compensation and made the indigenous inhabitants intruders in their own homes and mendicants for a place to live. Judged by any civilised standard, such a law is unjust and its claim to be part of the common law to be applied in contemporary Australia must be questioned. This Court must now determine whether, by the common law of this country, the rights and interests of the Meriam people of today are to be determined on the footing that their ancestors lost their traditional rights and interests in the land of the Murray Islands on 1 August 1879.[9]

The judges in this case made the important observation that, although Australian law is 'the prisoner of its history, it is not bound by decisions of courts in the hierarchy of an Empire then concerned with the development of its colonies'. Since the Australia Act of 1986, 'the law of this country is entirely free of Imperial control. The law which governs Australia is Australian law.'[10]

Eddie Mabo and his fellow plaintiffs had been pursuing legal actions for some time but with only limited success. This action, in the High Court of Australia, sought a declaration that the Meriam people are entitled to the Murray Islands as owners, possessors and occupiers, that the Murray Islands were not and had never been Crown lands and that the State of Queensland was not entitled to extinguish the title of the Meriam people. Their petition was upheld:

> [S]ix members of the Court (Dawson J. dissenting) are in agreement that the common law of this country recognises a form of native title which, in the cases where it has not been extinguished, reflects the entitlement of the indigenous inhabitants, in accordance with their laws or customs, to their traditional lands and that, subject to the effect of some particular Crown leases, the land entitlement of the Murray Islanders in accordance with their laws or customs is preserved, as native title, under the law of Queensland.[11]

The Court concluded by declaring that 'the land in the Murray Islands is not Crown land within the meaning of that term in s.5 of the Land Act 1962'.[12]

This was a revolutionary ruling. It ended the colonial fiction that Australia was *terra nullius* when the British arrived and established the fact of there being in existence such a thing as native title at common law and thus native land tenure. But it also highlighted an important distinction between, on the one hand, the Crown as a sovereign authority and, on the other, the Crown as the holder of title. Eddie Mabo won this case because the land of the Meriam people, with some minor exceptions, had never been disposed of, granted or alienated by the Crown. Thus, whilst the Crown (now the state of Australia following the Australia Act 1986) remained sovereign and Mabo recognised this in the authority of the Court itself, it was argued and decided that the land remained under native title because the Crown had never exercised its power to alienate it. Had it done so, any claims by the Meriam people would have been extinguished.

Dùthaich

The very real legal issues raised by Eddie Mabo and the rather more superficial activities of HMS *Vidal* and Mr Gardner highlight important questions of the legitimacy of titles to land.

In 1999, I acquired the title to an acre of land and have the deeds to prove it (see Plate 1). The land is not in Scotland or the UK nor, indeed, is it on Planet Earth. It is in the Oceanus Procellarum on the lighted side of the Earth's moon, specifically Lot 032/0827 in Area F–4 of Quadrant Charlie and was purchased from Dennis M. Hope, Head Cheese and Lunar Ambassador to the United Kingdom. My Lunar Deed is accompanied by a Plan showing the location of my land.

The validity of this title relies on the authority of the legal code that underpins it. Unfortunately for me (and other lunar title holders), Mr Hope, the Head Cheese, lodged claims with the UN to own the moon and other stellar objects and, since then, he has sold in excess of 2.5 million titles. Of course this is all a gimmick. The 1967 Outer Space Treaty debars any state claiming ownership of the moon. Mr Hope argues that this convention only applies to states and not to individual citizens of those states and thus his claim is valid. However, any claim I have as a result would have no legal validity because there is no legal power underpinning my title and, therefore, no authority prepared to defend my claim. This serves to remind us that, at a certain level, all land tenure systems are made up – fictions that are true only for as long as people believe in them or believe there is no alternative. When the possibility of a different future emerges, old rules can be swept aside overnight as happened during the French Revolution or, in the twentieth century, in the Soviet bloc and in post-independence India.

In Scotland, the main architecture of our system was devised and given legal effect by the actions of a few hundred self-serving aristocrats in the sixteenth and seventeenth century. It was a wholly manufactured system designed to serve the interests of a tiny number of the landed elite who happened to make the laws. The same fictions were being perpetrated by Her Majesty and her royal warrants in 1955 as were being perpetrated decades later by Mr Hope. The difference of course is that Mr Hope is a self-appointed lunar entrepreneur whilst the UK is a sovereign state governed by the rule of law with legal codes to arbitrate land rights and a court system to give effect to them.

We can, therefore, if we wish, change these land laws as easily as they were made in the first place and with more authority, given the greater level of democratic governance we now enjoy. The Abolition of Feudal Tenure etc. (Scotland) Act 2000 is one example of this authority in action. Feudal superiorities were abolished overnight. There was no compensation and no feudal estate was allowed to be created from that day on.

Questions of the sort raised by colonialism, the Mabo decision, my moon deed and the abolition of feudal tenure also apply to Scotland. Does Scotland have any system of native title whereby claims might be made to land alienated by historic colonisation? Interestingly, a petition to the Scottish Parliament raising exactly this question was presented in 2009 by Ranald Alasdair Mac-Donald of Keppoch in which he called on the Parliament to urge the Scottish Government to investigate the *dùthaich* system of land tenure.[13]

Prior to the imposition of feudalism in Scotland, a range of native tenure systems existed though we know little about how they operated. Feudalism was superimposed on these systems of native title and, in many instances, ran concurrently alongside them. The most common of these native tenure regimes, certainly in the Highlands, was *dùthaich*, a Gaelic term meaning 'land, native country or territory over which hereditary rights are exercised'. Typically it represents the territory regarded as the homeland of a clan or other kinship group. The process of granting feudal titles to clan chiefs was to cause much grief as the areas of both seldom coincided (see Chapter 6). When the authority of *dùthaich* clashed with that of a feudal grant, the clan chiefs all chose to respect their feudal charters to enrich themselves as landowners. *Dùthaich*, it can be argued, died the day a feudal charter was granted over the ancestral lands of the clan.

By 1600, feudal tenure was firmly established and all land was held by the Crown and granted out by feudal charter. The Scottish state and its judicial system never recognised native title of any sort although remnants of it persisted in the various non-feudal tenures that still exist – for example, in the modes of organisation of crofting tenure.

Mr MacDonald argued that the Abolition of Feudal Tenure etc. (Scotland) Act of 2000, failed to acknowledge *dùthaich* in the same way as it acknowledged the survival of udal law in Orkney and Shetland. Udal law was not, however, a native system of land-holding but was introduced by the Vikings upon their conquest of the Northern Isles. The introduction of feudal tenure in the eleventh century did not affect udal law since the Northern Isles did not become part of Scotland until 1567. Thereafter, udal law continued to this day to govern landholding in Orkney and Shetland.

Ranald MacDonald's assertion of *dùthaich* is a tricky issue to sustain since, although feudal tenure was imposed on Scotland, it was imposed by Scotland's own rulers who through it asserted their ultimate ownership of all land in the kingdom. All land-ownership was subsequently derived of the Crown until 28 November 2004 when the system was abolished. Under these circumstances, could any land now be considered to be held under a pre-feudal system of land tenure?

The central problem for the petitioner was that there is no instance where *dùthaich* has been raised and upheld in any Scottish court of law as a prior and thus legitimate form of land tenure. If an attempt was made though, what would be the chances of success?

First of all, to succeed, any case would have to be brought over land that was not held under a recorded feudal title (or, since 2004, derived from one). Any other claim would be easily countered by the well-established law of landownership and it is unlikely that any court would overturn centuries of legal precedent. But is this not precisely what happened in Australia in the Mabo case? Can feudalism be equated with the Crown's rights in Australia and *dùthaich* with Australian native title? To an extent it can but the Mabo decision does not offer any comfort for anyone seeking to recover land formerly held under *dùthaich* since the High Court of Australia also found that:

> Native title to land survived the Crown's acquisition of sovereignty and radical title. The rights and privileges conferred by native title were unaffected by the Crown's acquisition of radical title but the acquisition of sovereignty exposed native title to extinguishment by a valid exercise of sovereign power inconsistent with the continued right to enjoy native title.
>
> Native title has been extinguished by grants of estates of freehold or of leases . . . Thus native title has been extinguished to parcels of the waste lands of the Crown that have been validly appropriated for use . . . and used for roads, railways, post offices and other permanent public works which preclude the continuing concurrent enjoyment of native title.
>
> Native title continues where the waste lands of the Crown have not been so appropriated.
>
> Native title to particular land and the persons entitled thereto are ascertained according to the laws and customs of the indigenous people who, by those laws and customs, have a connection with the land.[14]

In other words, native title survived where it had not been extinguished by Crown grants. That observation must have come as a relief to everyone who owns property in Australia as, otherwise, every title for every acre of Australia would be open to challenge! It also underpins MacDonald's assertion that *dùthaich* might well survive in Scotland but, for any land held under *dùthaich* to survive, it would be necessary to demonstrate that it had never been the subject of any feudal grant and that any feus which had been granted are invalid.

Even in those circumstances, however, any 'waste lands' not so alienated would, today, still be owned by the Crown. Despite feudal abolition and the abolition of the ultimate superiority of the Crown, any land that was never granted to others remains held allodially by the Crown.[15] Could this be challenged by asserting a pre-feudal system of tenure? It is unlikely for two reasons. First of all, to do so would be to challenge over 800 years of feudal legal history and the authority of kings, queens and parliaments and court decisions. Secondly, for any indigenous people to submit a valid claim, they would have to demonstrate a historic and continuous connection with the land. According to the Mabo decision:

> Native title to an area of land which a clan or group is entitled to enjoy under the laws and customs of an indigenous people is extinguished if the clan or group, by ceasing to acknowledge those laws, and (so far as practicable) observe those customs, loses its connection with the land or on the death of the last of the members of the group or clan.[16]

The MacDonalds of Keppoch, along with all the other clans of Scotland, ceased to acknowledge such laws and customs long ago – indeed, there was no chief between 1848 and 2006 – and, thus, could not assert such rights in any court of law. Furthermore, unlike Eddie Mabo and the Meriam people who belong together by their common ancestry, if you wish to become a member of Clan Ranald of Lochaber (Keppoch), the current chief, who submitted the petition, charges £200 for life membership![17]

But it has not only been clan chiefs in fancy dress enacting bizarre rituals from the pages of history to establish dubious claims of authenticity who have attempted to claim indigenous land rights in Scotland. Recently, the Scottish Crofting Foundation (formerly the Scottish Crofters Union) has spent some considerable effort promoting the claim that crofters are indigenous people of the Highlands and Islands. In a paper it published in 2008, it claims at one point that they are *the* indigenous people of the Highlands and Islands – although the author does stress that indigenousness is an inclusive concept and is primarily to be regarded culturally rather than racially or genetically. The motivation for this paper was to explore whether international policies and the human rights framework around indigenous peoples could assist the crofting community in defending their way of life against what they saw as the latest in a long history of attempts to marginalise their way of life, their system of land tenure and their culture. It concludes by calling on the government:

> to recognise crofters as indigenous people of the Highlands and Islands; respect the growing body of international law on indigenous peoples; and devolve power and decision-making on indigenous issues to the people who maintain the indigenous cultures of the Highlands and Islands.[18]

Whilst such a call is, in itself, perfectly reasonable, it does contain within it the seeds of much discontent and conflict. To recognise crofters as indigenous people implies the denial of that status to those – including Ranald Alasdair MacDonald of Keppoch, Chief of the Honourable Clan Ranald of Lochaber Mac Mhic Raonuill – who are not crofters or it at least implies that others need to make their own case.

What about those who, but for an accident of history do not enjoy the tenure of a croft but in every other respect are indigenous by virtue of their culture and language? There are many good reasons to provide greater self-governance of crofting by crofters and to secure and develop the system of crofting tenure – as is being done by extending it to parts of Banffshire and Arran. However, arguing that a certain class of people who enjoy rights under a relatively recently created form of land tenure are any more indigenous than any other group is problematic and does little to serve anyone's interests, least of all crofters'.

I should stress that my dismissal of the foregoing claims to restore forms of native title does not mean that I am unsympathetic to any move to assert alternative constructions of land rights in Scotland. I am most certainly actively pursuing the identification and assertion of various forms of common land rights (see Chapter 22). However, it is important – and, indeed, it is the only realistic way forward – to pursue any such claims within the framework of law as it currently stands. This is what Eddie Mabo and his colleagues did in Australia and what many groups of people around the world are currently doing. However, it does no one any good to invent notions that have no basis in contemporary reality. Such moves only serve to confuse the important issues at stake and, in some cases, to promote the vested interests of one group to the disadvantage of another.

As the above examples show, land rights remain in a state of flux, legal certainties continue to be challenged (in some cases successfully) and politics is an ever-present factor as the case of Rockall continues to demonstrate. Law is a human construction, a set of rules determined by people to govern the affairs of society. We have the land law we have in Scotland because, until very recently, it was the landowners who made that law.

Time, then, to turn to the politics of landownership.

Look Here, Boy, Steady On. Let's Get This Thing Straight

Politics and the Landed Elite

It is notable from even a cursory glance at history that the landed class had one huge advantage when it came to legislating over land matters. Put simply, they were the legislators. Until the Representation of the People (Scotland) Act 1832, the Scots and British Parliaments had remained dominated by the landed class both in terms of MPs and voters. In 1830, the whole electorate in Scotland was probably less than 4,500 out of a population of 2,300,000.[1] It comprised the county franchise based on a statute of 1681 (comprising landowners) and the representatives of the burghs (who themselves elected their own successors) whose authority was based upon a statute of 1469.

The old Scots Parliament, far from being a noble institution, was, in the words of Johnston, 'not a national Parliament: it was a feudal oligarchy – venal, corrupt, and despicable, servile to the Crown, and tyrannical to the people'.[2] This was the institution that passed Scotland's land laws.

In 1427, the numbers of the clergy, barons and Crown vassals entitled to attend Parliament had grown unwieldy and a system of representation was developed whereby each county could be represented by a minimum of two delegates.[3] Thus was born the landowning franchise or electorate who held sway until reform began hesitantly in 1832. Only those who held land directly from the Crown had the vote and this was one reason why feuing was popular as opposed to outright sale of land as this would create a new vassal of the Crown with a vote.

The county franchise consisted of two types. The first consisted of those who held a feudal superiority worth at least £2 at a valuation conducted in the fourteenth century! The other, established in 1743, granted the vote to superiors who held land worth £400 Scots (about £35 sterling). Vassals had no vote at all. Scottish landownership was concentrated in very few hands and superiors were an even more concentrated class of people. As a consequence, the total rural electorate in 1820 numbered 2,889 people whereas, in England, it stood at 190,000 and, in Wales (with about half the population of Scotland), it was 18,700.

What is more, since the right derived from the superiority rather than the actual land itself, it was feasible for a landowner to have his lawyers separate the properties and superiorities on his estate so that he could retain his land while parcelling out £400 superiorities to enfranchise his supporters.[4] These voters were known as paper, faggot or fictitious voters as few of them had any connection with the county. They were frequently Edinburgh lawyers, landowners from other parts of the country or sympathisers with the political party of the superior. By the end of the eighteenth century, it has been estimated that fully one half of the county voters were fictitious and, in eighteen seats out of a total of forty-five, fictitious voters formed the majority. In Bute, only one of the twenty-one electors was a 'real' voter![5]

Even after the Scottish Reform Act of 1832 with its £10 franchise, it remained possible to divide up estates into a joint ownership, generate 'new' voters and insert a clause in the deeds reserving the original owner's right to reclaim the created vote.[6] This caused a good deal of consternation and, in 1837, the Select Committee on Fictitious Votes in Scotland was established to inquire into the practice. It published its first report later that year and, as noted by the radical nineteenth-century philosopher MP, Joseph Hume, in one of his tracts, 'great efforts have, in many counties in Scotland, been made by men of wealth and influence, and especially by large landed proprietors, to neutralise and overpower the Local Constituencies which a £10 franchise has created, and to regain the political power which, under the old system, they had long and unsparingly exercised'.[7]

The Committee made a detailed study of the county of Selkirk where, in the 1832 election following the passing of the Reform Acts, there were 280 registered voters of whom 133 voted for the Whig, John Pringle of Clifton, and 124 voted for Alexander Pringle of Whytbank, the sitting Tory. Alexander Pringle was re-elected in 1835 and we will see why.

The political agents of the Tory Party arranged for the purchase of the County Inn in Selkirk by eleven joint owners, making each eligible for the vote, having a £10 interest in property. Seven of them were lawyers and advocates in Edinburgh and all of them lived outside the county of Selkirk. A further five outside interests were then enfranchised by the purchase of the farm of Batts. The Tories justified the creation of these joint proprietorships on the basis that 'property ought to be represented, and that therefore a landed proprietor is entitled to secure the representation of his property, by splitting his whole estate into £10 qualifications, and distributing them among parties whether resident or non-resident'.[8]

The Committee went on to note that a total of 277 voters were created across the county by these fictitious methods of whom 222 were non-resident – almost as many as there had been in total at the 1832 election.[9] In evidence, Mr Adam Paterson, an Edinburgh lawyer who had been closely involved in property transactions in the county, stated that a total of fifty-five new voters had been added in the town of Selkirk alone, of whom twenty-six were advocates, writers to the signet and writers resident in Edinburgh. And that's why Mr Pringle of Whytbank won the seat back in the 1835 general election.

Furthermore, it was not until 1889 that there was any form of elected county government. Local administration in the shires was handled exclusively by those holding land worth over £100 per year. They formed the Commissioners of Supply and their existence dated back to 1667 when they were first appointed to collect the land tax.[10] According to historians Graeme Morton and Bob Morris:

> It was the lateness, and the weakness, of this reform which provided the opportunity for the survival of aristocratic influence over the people of the county. In the Borders, the Dukes of Buccleuch and Roxburghe maintained their dominance as

county office-bearers (until the reorganisation of local government in 1974) and used their influence to suggest appropriate appointments for the legal office of sheriff-depute.[11]

The ordinary residents of the county, even those who had a vote in parliamentary elections, had no input to local government until more than sixty years after the first Reform Act. Arguably, the reforms of 1889 were as radical as those earlier Reform Acts though it took some time for changes to take effect. The Earl of Dalkeith, for example, stood unopposed in Selkirk and two thirds of the new county council convenors in 1892 were landowners. As late as 1940, half of them were still in the hands of the gentry with seven being peers and ten Lord Lieutenants.

It was only in 1928 that men and women eventually secured the vote on an equal footing. The implications of this are that the vast majority of the land laws in place have no legitimate democratic sanction beyond the fact that they have not as yet been repealed or reformed. It is little wonder there was pressure for reform. For virtually the first 700 years of feudal landownership, a tiny number of feudal superiors made the very laws they stood to benefit from and ran the day-to-day administration of counties. This was the landed elite whose hegemony was total and whose influence continued to exert a substantial influence over public life until very recently.

The power that derives from landownership in Scotland has, historically, been all encompassing. It was the basis for economic and political influence for the best part of 800 years and only began to wane at the end of the nineteenth century, long after its demise in most other European countries. Why was this?

Clearly the political power enjoyed by landowners was eroded by the reform acts of the nineteenth century when the franchise was extended beyond landowners and then again in 1928 when all adult men and women got the vote. It was further eroded by economic and political events such as the reforming zeal of the Lloyd George government, legislation such as the crofters' acts and smallholders' legislation and by post-war statist policies. Most recently, landowners have had to adjust to the new reality of the Scottish Parliament. The twentieth century was very much a century of mixed fortunes for the landed elite. On the one hand, hostile governments imposed punitive taxes, such as death duties, which resulted in the break-up of many of the estates of the nobility. Laws designed to provide more statutory protection to tenant crofters and farmers and the nationalisation of planning in 1948 all eroded the freedom of landowners to manage their affairs as they saw fit. On the other hand, the unregulated nature of the land market, the robust legal framework for landownership and the emergence of new generations of wealthy industrialists meant that there was a ready market for their land.

The thesis presented by David Cannadine in his book *The Decline and Fall of the British Aristocracy* is, as the title suggests, broadly accurate but it would be wrong to assume that, as a consequence, landed power was necessarily marginalised. Certainly the impact of the reform acts, the abolition of the House of Lords' powers to veto legislation, punitive taxes and the slaughter of the First World War succeeded in emasculating the former power of the old aristocracy and the great noble families. But, whilst these events hugely reduced the extraordinary power and influence of the dukes, marquesses and earls, they did not diminish the institution of landed property to the same extent since new wealth simply replaced them. In place of the Duke of Sutherland, the Duke of Hamilton, the Marquess of Breadalbane and the Earl of Fife, there appeared the industrial and commercial wealth of the Burton, Wills, Whitbread, Cayzer, Fleming, Jardine, Matheson, Pilkington and Inchcape families.

During all these disruptions, the formidable power built up over centuries through assiduous attention to the legal framework provided a bulwark against what reforming politicians could achieve. Although as a class, the landowners no longer governed, the institution of landownership remained remarkably resilient particularly in comparison to the rest of Europe. This survival is illustrated by the following facts:

- primogeniture lasted until 1964 and children still do not have the right to inherit landed property;
- some 30 per cent of Scotland is still occupied by tenant farmers, long after their counterparts in the rest of Europe became owner-occupiers;

- rural landowners have successfully secured the abolition of all 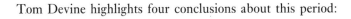 taxes on land and, despite professing to be rural businesses, still enjoy exemption from business rates.

Tom Devine highlights four conclusions about this period:

FIRST, from the later 1930s, the selling of land on a significant scale by the great estates declined, a pattern that continued after the Second World War and lasted through to the 1970s. The tide of owner-occupation which had threatened to engulf the traditional estate structure had ebbed considerably.

SECOND, there has been a remarkable continuity in Scottish landownership which the malaise of the decades from the 1880s to the 1930s has obscured. The nation still has the most concentrated pattern of landownership in Europe with 75 percent of all privately owned land in the 1970s held in estates of 1,000 acres or more and over one-third in estates of 20,000 acres or more. By the 1990s this remarkable level of concentration had, if anything increased further. The extent of land possessed by these mammoth estates has fallen since the 1870s, but the traditional structure of concentration has survived and has done so to a greater extent than in any other European country.

THIRD, the continuities are deeply significant, as a core of fewer than 1,500 private estates have owned most of the land in Scotland during the last nine centuries. Among the owners of great estates are several families who have been in hereditary occupation for more than 30 generations. Several landed families may have lost their estates in whole or part, but the great houses of Buccleuch, Seafield, Roxburghe, Stair, Airlie, Lothian, Home, Montrose and Hamilton and others still own extensive acreages.

FOURTH, the historic infiltration of newcomers into Scottish landownership has persisted in the 20th century. Merchant bankers, stockbrokers, captains of industry, pop stars, oil-rich Arabs and wealthy purchasers from Holland and Denmark are among the groups that have acquired Scottish estates in the past few decades. Nevertheless, this has not generally resulted in the break-up of the larger traditional properties, as most buying and

selling has been of land that has usually had a higher turnover of
ownership in the past.[12]

Somewhat surprisingly, then, the institution and the concentrated pattern of large-scale private landownership have survived
thanks to a generally favourable political climate, increasing land
values, public subsidies, tax breaks and a distinct absence of
much in the way of a land reform movement for much of the
twentieth century. Before exploring this survival further, it is
worth considering why Scotland, at the beginning of the twentieth century, remained in the grip of feudal power at a time
when, all over Europe, it had been swept away with revolutionary alacrity.

The political revolutions in Europe were concerned with the
dismantling of feudal regimes that were still in the hands of
absolute monarchs. Frustration and anger at the iniquity and
injustice of serfdom led to political uprisings, the consequences
of which were both the reform of political power structures and the
reform of landownership. As a result of this process (and in stark
contrast to Scotland), the extensive lands of the Church and the
nobility ended up in the hands of peasant proprietors and of the
communes and municipalities of France, Germany, Denmark and
the rest of Europe, liberated from the grip of the aristocracy.

Britain missed out on all of this and a key factor was the 1688
Glorious Revolution in England and the 1689 Claim of Right in
Scotland. These effectively wrested political power from the
Crown and, following the Union of 1707, the Scottish nobility
together with their English, Welsh and Irish counterparts ended
up with the political power, the landed power and the military
power. It was a force against which a peasant uprising was never
going to succeed, as a number of failed attempts in the eighteenth
and nineteenth centuries were to prove.

The political power of European peasants in the nineteenth
century was never to be enjoyed by those who lived on the land in
Scotland. They suffered the consequences in the Clearances and
the challenge of living in the slums of industrial Scotland whilst
their counterparts in Scandinavia and Western Europe, though
poor, at least had land. The heirs to that land today are the

prosperous small proprietors scattered throughout the countryside of Continental Europe.

The disempowered peasantry of Scotland were provided with alternative distractions to political agitation – serfdom in the coalmines and factories of industrial Scotland and living in the slums associated with them. In the country, a waged labouring class found employment on farms and the estates of the landed classes. Periodically, they were drawn or dragooned into serving the British Empire overseas, a situation that caused a number to be in the unfortunate position of laying their life on the line for a government which turned a blind eye to evictions and clearance of their families' holdings back home.

Britain's political system accommodated and responded to dissent and the need for reform by conceding incremental change. As a consequence, the revolutionary focus provided by an absolute unyielding monarchy was absent and the landed privileges associated with the ruling class survived such a long slow process in contrast to the revolutionary zeal of mainland Europe. There had been insurrection of course. Glasgow lawyer Thomas Muir established the Friends of the People Society in 1792, and the Radical War of 1820, involving John Baird and Andrew Hardie, was the most prominent among early revolutionary movements. But these were never a match for the might of the British state and thus land reform, if it were to be pursued, would have to be achieved within the context of a state very much under the control of landed power. That this state of affairs has persisted until the very recent past in the form of the legislative role of the House of Lords is nothing short of astonishing to any neutral observer from, for example, the Netherlands, France or Denmark.

It was the economic depression of the 1870s and 1880s that brought rural discontent to a head. A number of political organisations were formed to campaign for land reform, among them the Highland Land League, the Scottish Land Restoration League and the Scottish Land Reform Alliance (SLRA). Much has been written about the Highland Land League and crofter agitation in the North and West Highlands and how it led to the far-reaching Crofters' Holdings (Scotland) Act of 1886 but demands for reform came from across Scotland.

The Scottish Land Reform Alliance was the main organisation in Scotland pushing for land reform. It demanded abolition of hypothec, entails and primogeniture, the reform of game laws, tenants' right of compensation and the granting of secure and heritable agricultural tenancies. Inspired by the earlier efforts of the Chartist Land Plan and the National Land Company, movements such as the Commercial Land Company emerged, aimed at organising the break-up of large landholdings and the creation of peasant holdings.[13] But the collapse of Gladstone's government in 1894 and the convolutions of Irish Home Rule contributed to the lack of success of these movements and of the agitators and campaigners of the wider land reform movement such as the Crofters' Party.

But, if the Highlands appeared to be in the vanguard of land reform during this time, it was as much to do with the weaker political power of landowners in the region as it was to do with the strength of the Highland peasants' case for some redress. In Aberdeenshire, for example, crofters in the SLRA burnt an effigy of a particularly despised laird, Alexander Burnett of Kemnay in 1886. They were also at the forefront of attempts to include Aberdeenshire and the north-east within the scope of the Crofters Bill then going through Parliament despite the opposition of the Liberal government who were keen to restrict it to the seven counties of Shetland, Orkney, Ross and Cromarty, Caithness, Sutherland, Inverness and Argyll. This attempt was to have an echo over a hundred years later in the formulation of the community right to buy (see Chapter 27).

On every criterion that the government put forward – small size of average holding, existence of Gaelic, historical evidence of common grazing – the SLRA countered by showing that these applied equally to the rest of the Highlands outwith the seven counties. In the end, the Lord Advocate despaired of finding a rational basis for limiting the application of the bill and declared that only the counties visited by the Napier Commission – a commission established by Prime Minister William Gladstone to inquire into the condition of crofters in the Highlands and Islands in 1883 – would be included, despite the 1886 bill bearing very little relationship to the recommendations of the Commission which had, among other suggestions, proposed that crofters paying less than £6 per year rent should be assisted to emigrate![14]

But continued unrest and demands for more land did lead to Scotland-wide legislation in 1911 (The Small Landholders Act) which extended crofting tenure to the rest of Scotland. It was too little too late for the Lowland peasantry but one thing it did, in contrast to the Crofters' Act, was stimulate landed interests to become better organised politically.

Up until the beginning of the twentieth century, landowners were in little need of any structured organisation to represent their interests. Their status as part of the ruling elite negated the need for any more formalised arrangements. But, as land reform initiated at the end of the nineteenth century gained momentum, landowners began to feel the need to organise themselves. In November 1906, on the back of a furious outcry by landowners over the Small Landholders Bill, the Scottish Land and Property Federation was formed to protect landowners' interests. Its successor was the Scottish Landowners' Federation, (recently rebranded in 2011 as Scottish Land and Estates). The proposals, which eventually became law in 1911, were defeated by the House of Lords twice and only passed after the Lords' veto had been abolished by the Parliament Act of 1911.

These events, culminating in the Land Settlement (Scotland) Act of 1919, marked the last attempt at serious land reform in Scotland other than the Agricultural Holdings Act 1949 which gave tenant farmers security of tenure.[15]

The survival of a landed elite in Scotland is thus quite remarkable and research has yet to reveal any country (outside of absolute monarchies) with a pattern of private landownership so concentrated as Scotland. Effective political organisation has delivered to the modern Scottish landowner far more public financial assistance than their ancestors ever enjoyed and a tax regime far more benign than anything enjoyed by their predecessors.[16] Scottish landowners embraced the heritage industry as a means of justifying the existence of large estates, mansion houses and titles and monopolised control of The National Trust for Scotland until relatively recently. The titled among them enjoyed the position of legislators in the House of Lords as hereditary peers until most

The Education of the Edinburgh Bourgeoisie

Private Schools and Landownership in Edinburgh

Edinburgh is a strange and somewhat discomfiting place to bring up children due to the educational apartheid between those who send their children to the local public school and those who choose private fee-paying education. Friendships can end over the topic and I don't propose to pursue it any further here. But one aspect of this is interesting in the context of land-ownership and that is the extent to which the wealth of these schools was generated by their involvement in the land market.

Landownership played a significant role in the evolution of private education in Edinburgh and no one did it better than the trustees of George Heriot. As the leading chronicler of Edinburgh's land observed:

> An exclusion zone was imposed on Edinburgh by the activities of the Heriot Trust's property acquisitions in the years 1626 to 1706; it was simply impossible, thereafter, for an individual or institution to acquire sufficient property within the immediate vicinity of the city to challenge the dominance of the Heriot Trust.[17]

When George Heriot bequeathed his wealth in 1624 to found a 'Hospitall and Seminairie of orphans, for educatione, nursing and upbringing of youth, being puir orphans and fathirles childrene of decayit burgesses and freemen of said burgh, destitut and left without meanes', he had already acquired various estates, mortgages and superiorities in the City of Edinburgh. Heriot's trustees embarked upon an odyssey of land acquisition aided by an incestuous relation-ship with corrupt officials of the Town Council who were appointed as trustees. The site of the Heriot's School itself was broken in June 1628 by gangs of workers, some of whom were shackled prisoners including women. In the fifteen years from 1634, the Heriot's trustees initiated an unprecedented wave of land acquisition across the north of Edinburgh. By the end of the nineteenth century, the school owned over 1,700 acres of land and feus. The governors noted with satisfaction that 'scarcely an acre of land in the vicinity of Edinburgh had not been purchased for the benefit in perpetuity of the Heriot Trust'.

Meanwhile all the other private schools were busy acquiring property portfolios with the Edinburgh Merchant Company noting proudly in 1879 at the opening of the new Merchants' Hall, that 'our company holds nearly 8000 acres of lands, these estates being in five different counties'.[18]

In 1850, land owned by these institutions included the following:

School	Acreage	District
Heriot's	1,700	Edinburgh
George Watson's	1,584	Spylaw, Kelso
	95	Preston, East Lothian
	1,017	Cockburn, Midlothian
	349	Carstairs
	unknown	Breich
	464	Gilmerton, Fife
Merchant Maiden's	2,674	Peterhead
	842	Heiton, Kelso
Stewart's	900	Bathgate, Balbardie[19]
James Gillespie's	693	Spylaw, Bonaly

The extensive urban estates of Edinburgh's private schools have been a key element in providing for the education of the Edinburgh bourgeoisie. It is no coincidence either that these schools and their FP rugby clubs have provided the social glue that has forged generations of Edinburgh lawyers, financiers and land agents into the cohesive class that has both formulated and sustained landed hegemony in Scotland.

were evicted in 1999 and many often governed as ministers in sympathetic UK administrations. Apart from a few crises of confidence – such as the 1909 budget – little has happened to disturb the sleep of those who own Scotland.

Lairds were also prominent in government land use agencies for much of the twentieth century. Prominent landowners, such as Lord Arbuthnott, Lord Dulverton and Lord Montgomery, commanded considerable influence over debates and policies on land.

The web of influence by landowners within all sorts of bodies is well illustrated by 2nd Baron Dulverton. A member of the Wills tobacco family, Dulverton owned the Glenfeshie Estate in the Cairngorms as well as Fassfern in Lochaber. He was a keen forester and conservationist. He was also at various times a member of the Nature Conservancy Council's Scottish Committee, the president of Timber Growers (the woodland owners' association), a member of the Red Deer Commission and a trustee of the World Wildlife Fund (WWF), and a member of the House of Lords from 1956 until his death in 1992. In 1986, he provided a rare interview to the *Glasgow Herald* amid growing criticism over the way in which private forestry was being funded by generous tax breaks. Keen to stifle any reform of a system which funded him and his landowning colleagues very generously, he admitted to an overt campaign to silence the key conservation bodies in Britain, saying, 'I did have a word with the World Wildlife Fund chaps. I did have a word with the Royal Society for the Protection of Birds. And I did have a word with the Campaign for the Protection of Rural England.' He met with Tim Walker, the Chairman of the WWF trustees and told them, '[L]ook out, boys! We've given you quite a lot of help. So for God's sake don't go on like this.' His Dulverton Trust at that time was contributing around £70,000 a year to WWF. In his phone call to the Director General of the RSPB, he said, '[L]ook here, boy, steady on. Let's get this thing straight.'[20]

I was personally involved in the politics of nature conservation, forestry and the Cairngorms in the 1980s and was well aware of this kind of pressure. It was not usually so explicit but it was all-pervasive. Aside from the House of Lords, this influence has been mediated by the landowners' trade union, the Scottish Landowners' Federation (SLF). Prior to 2004, voting membership was restricted to those owning at least 10 acres of land. In 1975, the SLF had 3,712 members owning 7 million acres of land. By 1994 membership had declined to under 3,000 though the acreage is unknown. Whilst it includes many large-scale landowners, 40 per cent of its membership in 1994 was from the counties of Aberdeen, Ayr, Perth and Angus or from England. The majority of members own holdings of less than 1,233 acres and in 1994, the SLF claimed that 55 per cent of its members owned less than 500 acres. [21]

The one event apart from the 1909 budget that has caused most concern to landowners in the twentieth century was the establishment of the Scottish Parliament for the simple reason that they could no longer directly influence legislation in the way that their supporters in the House of Lords had been able to do. It caused real anxiety and discomfort to the SLF. Shortly after the devolution referendum held on 11 September 1997, the then convenor of the SLF wrote a letter to all members.

25 September 1997

Dear

There can be little doubt that issues relating to the private ownership of land in Scotland are under ever-increasing public scrutiny.

In recent years we have seen traditionally private estates purchased by conservation and community interests who believe that they can 'do better' than previous owners . . . at least in-so-far [*sic*], as their particular focus is concerned. We have also seen the growth of a significant land reform lobby challenging the pattern of private landownership in terms of rights and responsibilities. Even acting fully within their legal rights, landowners and their managers have found themselves severely criticised by press and politicians.

A great number of these issues were local in a UK context, but the overwhelming result of the Referendum for a Scottish Parliament raises their profile to an extent where legislative change is now easily conceivable. Our understanding is that almost all the matters which pertain to land and estate management in Scotland will fall within the jurisdiction of the Scottish Parliament. We have heard within the last week of intentions to introduce National Parks to Scotland and we know that the Parliament will be looking at the question of public access. Given the distribution of Scotland's population it is unlikely that the majority of members of the new Parliament will have much real understanding of, or sympathy for rural issues, but they will nevertheless have powers over us all.

I do not believe that there has ever been another occasion upon which the private landowners in Scotland have needed to come together to meet the challenges which they face. As Convenor of their representative body, the Scottish Land-owners' Federation, I am considering how best to ensure that landowner's [sic] rights are properly protected and that all perspectives of land management are understood.

My purpose in writing is to invite you and your Factor to a presentation of our plans to enhance the work and profile of the Federation. I am inviting all the major estate owners in Scotland, those we believe to have most at risk from unchecked land reform and environmental legislation, to the Jarvis Ellersly House Hotel, Edinburgh on Friday 17th October, commencing at 11.00am. I enclose a map showing the location of the hotel. We plan a series of short presentations, a discussion session and lunch.

I do hope you will be able to attend and look forward to meeting you. The Federation needs your support . . . so that it can support you and your interests.

Yours sincerely,
Andrew Dingwall-Fordyce
Convener

There is a PhD to be written exclusively on this letter and close textual analysis is fascinating but the tone and content confirms the onset of the Scottish Parliament as a historic threat to the interests of landowners. In a somewhat comical aside to this meeting, one member of the SLF asked Alastair McIntosh, an academic who campaigns on land reform, to be his representative at the meeting (his 'Factor'). Alastair tried to gain access but was gently but forcibly escorted out backwards through a narrow exit whereupon he almost collided with the Duke of Buccleuch who greeted him warmly and was informed of the circumstances of Alastair's eviction![22]

Some measure of the influence which the SLF up to that point had taken for granted is revealed in recently released Scottish Office files which provide an interesting insight into the relationship between the SLF and the then Conservative government of 1979–1997.

The SLF had been accustomed to having a meeting with the Financial Secretary to the Treasury in advance of the Budget to press their interests in matters of finance and tax. In 1984, however, the Treasury refused to meet with them. This upset Alexander Trotter, the convenor of the SLF, who wrote to Lord Gray of Contin, the Minister of State in the Scottish Office responsible for agriculture. Lord Gray had lost his seat in the election in 1983 to the youthful Charles Kennedy but was promptly made a lord and a minister in the Thatcher government.

7 Feb 1984

Dear Minister,

I am writing to let you know that the Federation has been refused a meeting with the Financial Secretary to the Treasury, which it has previously been the custom to hold prior to the Budget. We are most concerned that this has happened in a year when we attach great importance to fiscal change in order to achieve the aims and objectives of the Agricultural Holdings (Amendment) (Scotland) Act, 1983.

I would be most grateful if you could use your influence on the Financial Secretary to help obtain a meeting for us, even at this late stage.

Alexander Trotter

Lord Gray wrote to the Financial Secretary on 14 February:

I attach a copy of a letter I have had from Sandy Trotter, Convenor of the Scottish Landowners' Federation. It speaks for itself. I can well imagine that it is tedious for you and your colleagues to undertake series of meetings in the run-up to the budget with bodies whose views are already well known and I can understand if you have decided to apply a different approach this year. But as you can see the Federation have taken your decision badly and I wonder if there would be even now the prospect of your giving them their customary hearing. They are an important and influential body in Scotland with whom we enjoy good relations and to whom, along with the Scottish National Farmers Union, we are particularly indebted for the co-operation they gave us last year on our agricultural holdings legislation. They are also of course overwhelmingly our political supporters. If you could meet them I am sure it would be most appreciated.[23]

The SLF did not get their meeting but the exchange demonstrates the extent to which the SLF (and NFU Scotland) enjoyed regular access to those in the corridors of power.

Faced with the difficulties of a Scottish Parliament, however, the SLF's performance since 1999 did not impress those who own the very largest estates in Scotland. In 2002, they proceeded to set up their own organisation, the Scottish Estates Business Group (SEBG). It was formed to represent the interests of Scotland's 'progressive rural estates with significant business interests'. It has developed an approach all of its own, conscious perhaps that the SLF had failed to champion the interests of its members rigorously enough. The SEBG consists of twenty of the largest landed estates in Scotland, including Atholl, Buccleuch, Seafield, Argyll, Dunecht, Roxburgh and Lothian. It has taken a robust approach to asserting the interests of its members and is keen to change the terms on which the land reform debate takes place by portraying estates as vital rural businesses playing a central role in rural development.[24] An early attempt to provide some solid research to back this up, however, turned out to be little more than a public relations exercise.[25]

But it is not only the PR consultants who are having to work hard. Lawyers too (or a small but significant number of them) are busy also defending landed power. One particular firm, Turcan Connell, has crafted a specialisation out of providing advice to large estates and has not been shy of offering its opinions to politicians on behalf of its clients.[26] This is all perfectly legitimate and, indeed, it is to be welcomed. Part of the adjustment that landed interests have had to make in response to the advent of the Scottish Parliament has been to come into the open with their views and opinions. This has been most refreshing and it allows for an honest debate.

There remains a powerful landed elite in Scotland owning a disproportionate amount of land. Whether it survives or not is very much dependent on how it responds to public debate and interest. The Scottish Parliament has created a very different and potentially hostile political terrain for landowners but one that, in the long term, can only be good for the institution of landownership which, if it is to survive in whatever form, requires the informed political consent of the people of Scotland. The extent to which that has been given is explored later but now it is time to have a look at who actually owns Scotland in 2012.

Lord Derby, Lloyd George and John McEwen

A Tory, a Liberal and a Socialist try to find out who owns Scotland

Finding out who owns the country has exercised the minds of many people for well over a century. Why it should is something of a paradox when Scotland possesses perhaps the earliest land registers in the modern world. Registers were kept in Edinburgh Castle from about the thirteenth century and the Register of Sasines was established by an act of the Scottish Parliament in 1617. But this has not stopped the public and politicians from calling for more information to be made available on who Scotland's landowners are.

To determine the location and extent of even one landholding together with its current ownership can take the best part of a day of poring through interminable legalese and complex conveyancing descriptions often covering over a hundred years in one document with numerous references to other deeds and, more than likely, no plan to help in identifying what land is being described. Faced with such a taxing job, it is little wonder that people have become frustrated and no wonder at all that no overall picture or pattern can be obtained in any reasonable time frame of who owns a particular parish or a county. The only people who have had regular access to these records and the knowledge of how to interpret them have been legal specialists.

The reason for this apparent contradiction between long-established records and complexity is that the Register of Sasines is a register of deeds documenting legal transactions in land. It is thus a vast repository of text entries recording dispositions, securities, bonds, leases and other legal matters. The current Keeper of the Registers of Scotland is Sheenagh Adams and she has a statutory duty to record deeds presented to her and to ensure their orderly availability for public inspection in the Register of Sasines. The burden of interpreting such deeds and working out who owns what is, however, up to the public, solicitors and the purchasers of property. The Keeper can make no claims about the legal ownership of land in the Sasines Register. Solicitors have, by and large, regarded the Register as their domain and there is no allowance made for the needs of non-legally trained users. One of the most defective aspects of the Register of Sasines is that many deeds do not have any plans and thus it can be difficult to identify where exactly the boundaries of any property lie. Where plans do exist, they are often poor photocopies in black and white, purporting to show 'the boundaries as delineated in red on the attached plan'![1]

During the twentieth century, a number of legal reviews concluded that Scotland's system of land records should move from a register of deeds affecting land to a register of title – a definitive record of who owns what. In response to these calls, the Land Registration (Scotland) Act was introduced in 1979 in some haste during the dying days of the Labour government. This 1979 act was a radical departure from previous practice in three main ways. First of all, it introduced the principle that the Keeper would record titles to land and not simply the deeds from which titles were derived. In other words, by inspecting the Land Register, the identity of the owner is immediately apparent. Secondly, titles (or land certificates) included an Ordnance Survey map clearly showing the boundaries. Finally, the Keeper would, before issuing the Land Certificate, conduct a once-and-for-all search of the historic deeds affecting the property and determine the true ownership. This would provide a guarantee of the title and indemnity for any defects.

The Land Register was introduced on a rolling basis, county by county, starting with Renfrew in 1981. In 2003, the last six counties of Ross and Cromarty, Caithness, Moray, Orkney, Shetland and Sutherland went live and began admitting registrations. Today, any property that changes hands for value (inheritance and gifts do not, for example, trigger an entry in the Land Register) will transfer from the old Register of Sasines to the new Land Register. In February 2010, the Scottish Law Commission (SLC) published proposals for dealing with some of the defects of the 1979 act by extending the coverage of registered land and making the process of recording ownership more streamlined and straightforward.[2]

Currently, almost 60 per cent of titles have transferred to the Land Register although, because the bulk of these are domestic, urban properties, the percentage of titles does not reflect the extent of land now registered. Since most of the 1,500 estates that dominate rural Scotland are not yet on the Land Register, the extent of land registered is only around 18 per cent. This contrast is shown in the maps in Figures 3a and 3b.

The map in Figure 4 shows the actual areas of land registered in the Land Register. The extent of registered land across the built-up areas of the Central Belt, for example, highlights the fact that ownership of houses changes quite frequently and therefore triggers registration whereas, for the bulk of rural property, the turnover is slower. This map has never before been published and was kindly supplied by the Registers of Scotland.

One interesting aspect of the new Land Register is that, because the Keeper is required to conduct a once-and-for-all examination of titles in order to provide the Land Certificate and indemnify the owner against defects, she frequently encounters claims of ownership that cannot be substantiated by the existing evidence in the Register of Sasines. In such circumstances, she has the power, under Section 12 (2) of the 1979 Land Registration Act, to withhold indemnity over any or all of any area of land. Such land is delineated on the Title Plan as being excluded from indemnity. Given the rigorous scrutiny applied when land is first registered (the process can take up to five years in complex cases), areas of land excluded from indemnity are a good proxy for assessing the extent of land with no legitimate title. The Keeper was unable to provide exact information on the extent of such land but I have examined many titles and found that between 10 and 20 per cent of them include areas where indemnity is excluded.

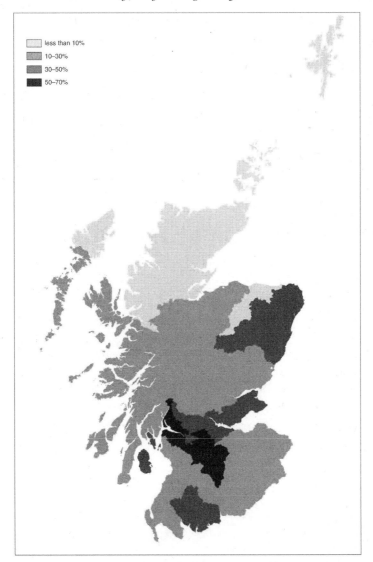

Figure 3a: Land Register coverage – titles

Source: Data derived from Scottish Law Commission, *Report on Land Registration*, p. 607

Figure 3b: Land Register coverage – area

Source: Data derived from Scottish Law Commission, *Report on Land Registration*, p. 609

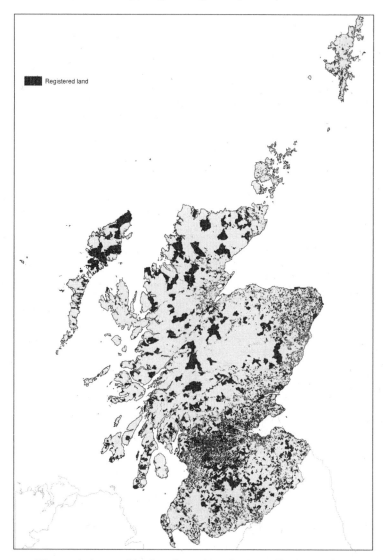

Figure 4: Areas of land registered on the Land Register (2012)

Whilst the Registers of Scotland are the place to find out who owns Scotland, they are difficult to penetrate for anyone other than trained specialists and they cannot provide an overview of specifics like who owns all the land in a certain glen or what the pattern of ownership is in a particular parish. They can be used to derive such information (see for example the www.whoownsscotland.org.uk project) but they remain primarily a resource for conveyancing lawyers to use. For the public, politicians, researchers and others interested in such questions they have not been the first port of call and there are a number of other initiatives that have taken place over the years that do meet these demands rather more easily. It is time to explore the history of land information.

1872–73 Return

Serious inquiry into who owns land dates from the late nineteenth century and was associated with land agitation in England and attempts to set up a land registration system. Then, the British landed classes held estates so vast that only the aristocracy of Austria, Hungary and Romania could rival their territorial dominance. They were probably collectively the wealthiest of the European territorial elite and, of course, they wielded enormous political control from the towns all the way to the Palace of Westminster.[3]

As early as the 1840s, politicians such as Richard Cobden and John Bright, leaders of the Anti-Corn Law League, had campaigned against what they saw as the excessive concentration of landownership in the hands of a small number of the aristocracy. Following the 1861 census, John Bright claimed that fewer than 30,000 people owned land in the UK and that fewer that 150 men owned half of England. It was an argument over whether this figure was accurate or not that eventually prompted the first statistical assessment of landownership in the UK. Bright's political opponent, Lord Derby, argued that there were, in fact, many more landowners than had been revealed by the census and that Bright and his friends were making the 'wildest and most reckless exaggerations' about the true numbers.[4] Lord Derby, himself an owner of 70,000 acres, argued that the true figure was around ten times as many.

On 19 February 1872, Lord Derby led a debate in the House of Lords in which he proposed a statistical return be made of all owners of lands and heritages in Great Britain and Ireland. The survey was approved by the government and was to include the names, acreages and value of all holdings of land in excess of an acre together with an aggregate figure for all those holding less than an acre. It was to be comprehensive, covering both urban and rural land.

In Scotland, the Comptroller-General of the Inland Revenue, Angus Fletcher, was charged with the job. The data was collated on the basis of counties with a separate return compiled for the municipal burghs of over 20,000 inhabitants, these being Aberdeen, Dundee, Edinburgh, Glasgow, Greenock, Kilmarnock, Leith, Paisley and Perth. It was thus intended to be a comprehensive account of the ownership of the whole of Scotland and indeed remains the only such statistical account ever published.

The practical task of compiling the return was given to the Surveyors of Stamps and Taxes who made enquiries locally. According to Fletcher, 'The duty imposed on these officers in ascertaining the estimated extent or acreage of properties was one of considerable difficulty, and, occasionally, of some delicacy.'[5] Early in 1873, Fletcher sent a circular to the known agents of landed proprietors asking them to provide information on owners and acreage. Where no satisfactory response was obtained, the Surveyors were instructed to 'select persons of local knowledge and skill to aid them in ascertaining the acreage of properties'.[6] Angus Fletcher and his team completed and published the *Return of Owners of Lands and Heritages Scotland 1872–1873* in Scotland on 25 February 1874 (see Plate 12).

Completed in less than two years, it was a remarkable piece of work. It showed that fully 18,031,066 acres of Scotland (92.3 per cent) was owned by just 1,809 landowners and 13,503,743 acres of Scotland (69.1 per cent) was owned by a mere 345 people.[7] Out of a total population of 3,559,847, only 132,230 (a mere 3.7 per cent of the population) owned any land at all, urban or rural. Fully 96.3 per cent of the population were tenants of one sort or another. This was a pattern of private landownership that was more concentrated and monopolistic than almost anywhere else in Europe.[8]

In the aftermath of the 3rd Reform Act, such revelations led radicals to question why so few people were drawing so much in the way of unearned income. The return provided a statistical gold mine and formed the basis for Tom Johnston's 1909 philippic, *Our Scots Noble Families*.

The People's Budget

In my book *Who Owns Scotland*, I observed that 'There has only ever been one official survey of landownership in Scotland – that conducted by the government in 1872–73.' I was wrong. During my research in 1995, two informants told me of the impressive records of landownership held by the Inland Revenue. One told me that these had recently been 'moved to Edinburgh'. With much to do and not much time to do it, I failed to make sufficient effort to locate them. In fact there *was* another official survey and it is by far the more impressive. Its origins lie with the *Return*.

In 1874, the public could go into their local library and consult the *Return of Owners of Lands and Heritages* and find out who owned all the land in Selkirkshire or in Edinburgh. As a statistical account, it has yet to be bettered. And it was those statistics that motivated David Lloyd George in his campaign to tax land. The Edwardian period was characterised by growing working-class mobilisation on the one hand but immense patrician wealth and power on the other. As Cannadine wrote:

> All his life, Lloyd George had believed in attacking landlords, and in breaking their monopoly of the soil as the necessary prelude to overthrowing their social privileges and political power. Quite simply, and quite sincerely, he hated the grandees and the gentry, and everything they represented . . . In his 1906 election campaign, he promised that 'the next great legislative ideal' was the emancipation of ordinary people from 'the oppression of the antiquated, sterilising and humiliating system of land tenure'.[9]

At the end of the nineteenth century, there was widespread land agitation in Ireland, in Scotland and in Wales. Meanwhile, the

American social reformer, Henry George, had made the link between desperate levels of poverty on the one hand and what he termed the unearned increments in land values on the other. His book *Progress and Poverty* articulated his ideas and it sold over three million copies worldwide. His argument was simple and compelling:

> Next take some hardheaded business owners who have no theories, but know how to make money. Say to them: 'Here is a little village. In ten years, it will be a great city. The railroad and the electric light are coming; it will soon abound with all the machinery and improvements that enormously multiply the effective power of labor.'
>
> 'Now ask: 'Will interest be any higher?'
>
> 'No!'
>
> 'Will the wages of common labor be any higher?'
>
> 'No,' they will tell you. 'On the contrary, chances are they will be lower. It will not be easier for a mere laborer to make an independent living; chances are it will be harder.'
>
> 'What, then, will be higher?' you ask.
>
> 'Rent, and the value of land!'
>
> 'Then what should I do?' you beg.
>
> 'Get yourself a piece of ground, and hold on to it.'
>
> If you take their advice under these circumstances, you need do nothing more. You may sit down and smoke your pipe; you may lie around like an idler; you may go up in a balloon, or down a hole in the ground. Yet without doing one stroke of work, without adding one iota to the wealth of the community–in ten years you will be rich!
>
> In the new city you may have a luxurious mansion. But among its public buildings, will be an almshouse.[10]

George's solution was equally elegant:

> I do not propose either to purchase or to confiscate private property in land. The first would be unjust; the second, needless. Let the individuals who now hold it still retain, if they want to, possession of what they are pleased to call *their* land. Let them

continue to call it *their* land. Let them buy and sell, and bequeath and devise it. We may safely leave them the shell, if we take the kernel. *It is not necessary to confiscate land; it is only necessary to confiscate rent.*[11]

Within Parliament, there were no fewer than fourteen bills and resolutions introduced between 1889 and 1906 on the subject of taxation of land values. Following the Liberal landslide in 1906, land taxation was firmly on the agenda and, following two defeats in the House of Lords, Lloyd George, now Chancellor, introduced a land tax in his famous People's Budget of 1909. This was to lead to a further rejection in the Lords, the constitutional crisis of 1909– 10 and the eventual passing of the Parliament Act 1911 which abolished the Lords' veto on money bills. Two thirds of the Lords who rejected the proposals in 1909 owned at least 5,000 acres of land and the *Daily News* of 28 December 1909 claimed that the 'lords who killed the Budget' owned some 10.4 million acres of land between them.[12] Eventually, following the election of 1910, the bill was reintroduced, passed by both houses of Parliament and entered the statute books as the Finance (1909–1910) Act. Section 26 (1) reads as follows:

The Commissioners shall, as soon as may be after the passing of this Act, cause a valuation to be made of all land in the United Kingdom, showing separately the total value and the site value respectively of the land, and in the case of agricultural land the value of the land for agricultural purposes where that value is different from the site value. Each piece of land which is under separate occupation, and, if the owner so requires, any part of any land which is under separate occupation, shall be separately valued, and the value shall be estimated as on the thirtieth day of April nineteen hundred and nine.[13]

The act was designed to provide a levy on the so-called incre- ment value of land (increment value duty) – to tax that part of the capital appreciation of land that was derived from the site and not from the improvements upon it. According to Cannadine, the importance of the land tax to Lloyd George was not so much in its revenue-raising potential but the fact that it would involve a survey and valuation of all land in the country.[14]

Before the provisions even passed into law, the Inland Revenue had begun planning for its implementation and, by September 1915, had achieved remarkable progress. It had identified and mapped 19,408,700 acres of Scotland and valued 1,333,200 hereditaments (individual property parcels) representing 99.7 per cent of the country. It was an astonishing exercise for the Edwardian period and meant that the whole of urban and rural Scotland was mapped and the owners and tenants identified and recorded. Nothing like it had ever been attempted before or since and it stands as a remarkable legacy to both the political diligence of Lloyd George and the work of the 152 staff of the Valuation Office in Scotland.

The land tax provisions of the 1910 Finance Act were eventually repealed by the Finance Act of 1920 but the Inland Revenue kept hold of the plans and they continued to be of use in administering various land-related taxes such as capital gains tax and death duties. The Inland Revenue kept hold of all of these records until 1985 when the maps were deposited in the National Archives of Scotland with the field books following in 1990 and the collection was only open for inspection some years later.

When I did eventually locate the records, what I found astonished me. There are a total of 14,050 plans covering the whole of Scotland at scales of 6 inches and 25 inches to the mile. They are extraordinarily detailed with comprehensive coverage of boundaries drawn neatly in red or purple ink (see Plate 3). Not only this but each parcel of land delineated was not simply a landownership unit but a hereditament – a taxable unit which could be a house, a shop or a farm as this was, after all, a survey that was to form the basis of a land tax. Thus, on any one sheet covering a rural area, there might be thirty or so such units in a small village together with six or eight farms. All might be owned by one landowner but they are delineated individually. This is invaluable since it was at a time when title deeds contained no such map-based bounding information.

As Brian Short observed in his masterful study of the 1910 survey:

The significance of these maps is clear. At no other time do we have reliable contemporary maps covering the entire country which delineate property boundaries in both town and country. And given the wealth of supplementary information . . . it will be clear that this is a resource of the utmost importance.[15]

The maps are annotated with index numbers, unique to each parish, to identify each parcel of land. These can be used to locate detailed information about the ownership and occupation of the land in the associated field books which are where the surveyors recorded a range of detailed information about the property, often covering up to four pages, including the name of the owner and tenant, improvements, valuations, and detailed plans and layouts of the property.

The data contained is highly authoritative as it was compiled by the Inland Revenue for taxation purposes. Existing sources such as Rates and Valuations Lists were used to identify properties and landowners were obviously keen to ensure that the information was accurate since they would not want to pay any more taxes than necessary.

The value of these records is that they provide a clear map-based register of landownership in 1910 – a record that had never until then existed and which has never been repeated since. Thus, with knowledge of who owned a parcel of land in 1910, it is that much easier to interrogate the official Register of Sasines to determine who owns it today.

But, as the twentieth century wore on, people forgot that there had ever been such records. The public had never had access to them in any case and, since they were held by the Inland Revenue and considered by many to contain sensitive information, their very existence was very effectively concealed from all but those working in the Inland Revenue and valuation profession. Sandy Mather, an Aberdeen geographer, wrote a research note in the *Scottish Geographical Magazine* in 1995. He never mentioned the Inland Revenue survey. Indeed, his introductory paragraph is now clearly misleading:

The ownership and occupancy of land in Scotland is an emotive subject on which it is difficult to carry out objective research.

The fact that no comprehensive national inventory has been published during the twentieth century is significant. It is eloquent, if silent, testimony to the technical problems involved in such an exercise, and to the political sensitivity of the subject.[16]

Mather was, in fact, strictly-speaking correct to comment that no inventory had been published because the Inland Revenue material remained private – indeed, it was probably confidential. But it is an interesting reflection on the abyss into which the 1910 survey fell that Scotland's leading geographer on landownership did not know about this material until I told him about it in 2002.

When, in the 1960s, the Countryside Commission for Scotland (CCS) decided to carry out some research into how to plan for the growth in outdoor recreation in Scotland, it quickly realised that some understanding of the pattern of landownership would be useful. It therefore appointed Dr Roger Millman, a geographer at the University of Aberdeen, to undertake a survey of the landed estates of Scotland. The Proprietary Survey of Rural Scotland was funded by CCS, the Highlands and Islands Development Board, the Scottish Landowners' Federation and two academic trusts. Millman's survey was recorded on one-inch-to-the-mile maps which are now deposited in the National Archives of Scotland together with a series of 10,000 index cards (though these were never published).[17]

This survey was, again, quite revolutionary in its own small way as nothing like this had been attempted since the Inland Revenue Survey (IRS) which Millman was unaware of. Having been deposited in the National Archives of Scotland in 1972, the survey became the standard reference for anyone wishing to find out who owned land over an extensive area – say a parish or county. The public at large, however, was largely unaware of the Millman survey since the results were published in an academic journal and no attempt was made to place them in any sort of context in terms of the pattern of landownership in Scotland. Indeed, Millman himself was at pains to make it clear that the survey was in no way an attempt to open up landownership to public scrutiny nor was it to be interpreted as being critical of the pattern of landownership.

No data on private ownership has been included in the inventory accompanying the map since this must remain confidential . . .

It should be stressed that the publication of the map and inventory is in no way intended to prejudice the concept or tradition of the private ownership of land in Scotland which, despite many defects in both the attitudes of owners and the management of estates, continues in the opinion of many rural management consultants to be the most expedient form of land occupancy.[18]

Others were not so shy though and, in the 1970s, land issues began to feature on the political scene with the Labour Party, the Scottish Labour Party, led by Jim Sillars, and the Scottish National Party all adopting policies on land. The Perth and Kinross Fabian Society undertook research in Perthshire on who owned the county and the results were published in 1971 in a pamphlet entitled 'The Acreocracy of Perthshire: Who Owns Our Land?'. One member of the Society who was involved was a forester from Blairgowrie called John McEwen. From his boyhood in Perthshire, living and working on estates, to his later career as a forester with the Forestry Commission and as a self-employed forestry consultant, he had cared passionately about land, its ownership and its use for over sixty years. In 1972, following the publication of 'Acreocracy', McEwen discovered that Millman's maps had been deposited in the then Scottish Records Office. In his words, 'this was a terrific breakthrough'[19] and he proceeded to order copies of the maps. Over the next five years, he marked up these maps, clarifying the boundaries, and used a planimeter to measure the acreage of each estate. In 1977, the work was published by Edinburgh University Press as *Who Owns Scotland*.

One of the main criticisms levelled at his work was that it contained major inaccuracies. This was undoubtedly true but what was remarkable was that despite them, the overall pattern of ownership he presented was, by and large, accurate. Why he made mistakes – and he understated as well as overstated the extent of land holdings – is of some limited interest.

The maps he used were photocopies of Millman's maps which

are lodged in the NAS. There are three main sets. The first is a set of 1-inch (1:63 360) maps giving rough coverage for the whole country. The second is a set of 2.5-inch (1:25 000) maps which give greater detail and finally there is a neat set of 1-inch maps transcribed from the first set by a student assistant. Roger Millman left extensive suggestions for tidying up his information with staff in the archives. Unfortunately these were never followed up. As a result, it seems that McEwen received copies of the first rough set which had two major deficiencies. They were roughly drawn and therefore not clear when photocopied and secondly they did not include some information which was instead contained on the 1:25000 set. Even taking his sources into account, it remains something of a mystery why McEwen made some of the errors he did. One clear reason is that the maps he obtained contained references to superiorities, farms having a feudal superior in common. These were marked as feued farms but often interpreted by McEwen as being under one ownership. In other cases, there is no explanation. Cawdor Estate is a case in point where the acreage is actually much greater than that recorded by McEwen. Of more importance are the alleged gaps in the Southern counties which resulted in some inaccuracies in McEwen's data. This is almost certainly the result of McEwen not having access to the most comprehensive of Millman's maps which are as comprehensive of the south as they are of the north.

Such errors as there were do not detract from the valuable work done by John McEwen which remains a remarkable achievement – he was ninety years old when he finished – and was motivated by the desire to see this information publicised. It was the simple act of publishing the details of all estates of over 1,000 acres in 1977 that was McEwen's great contribution to the debate although it was not appreciated by some. One John Christie of Lochdochart, a leading member of the Royal Scottish Forestry Society (of which John McEwen had been the only working forester ever to be president), wrote in the Society's magazine:

[I]t is sad when the family and friends of a very old man cannot dissuade him from exhibiting in print his envy of those more fortunate, hard working and thrifty than himself and his ignor-

ance of an industry in which he claims to have worked for a
lifetime . . . My main regret is that the early thinnings of
privately owned and managed woods may have been pulped
to produce the paper upon which this silly little booklet was
printed.[20]

Aside from a few academic studies of particular localities, no one
ever followed up Millman and McEwen's work. As a result, their
work became the standard reference until 1996.

As a student of forestry at the University of Aberdeen in the
early 1980s, I had become aware of McEwen's work. In a rather
conservative department of forestry, he was regarded with some
suspicion. My own interest in landownership was inspired by
regular trips into the Cairngorms and discussions in bothies about
characters such as the Panchaud brothers, Swiss businessmen who
owned the Mar Lodge Estate at the time, and, increasingly, about
the spread of commercial forestry across Deeside which was being
driven by very generous tax arrangements. As a consequence, I met
and got to know leading figures in the conservation world such as
Drennan Watson and Adam Watson (no relation) and became
involved in the North East Mountain Trust, an environmental
campaigning body consisting of mountaineering clubs in the north-
east. Very soon, I was drafting letters opposing new forestry
developments in Glen Dye, on Mar Lodge and in the hills above
Tarland.

But it was the controversy over the afforestation of the so-called
Flow Country in Caithness and Sutherland and, in particular, the
lavish exposé of the tax breaks given for forestry being enjoyed by
the likes of Terry Wogan and Dame Shirley Porter in the *Observer*
colour supplement of 14 February 1988 that convinced me that
forestry and similar land uses were not just scientific issues but
highly political. What became evident to me was that no analysis of
land use could ignore the question of power relations and, as the
controversy over both the tax and environmental impacts of this
afforestation grew and moved to the corridors of power in London,
I became more and more interested in landowning politics.

Fast-forward a decade and I had done a number of jobs all with
an environmental flavour but had never lost sight of or interest in

who owns Scotland. In 1995, I heard that the Edinburgh publishers, Canongate, were interested in a new version of McEwen's classic text. I approached them and we signed a contract. So, in the summer of that year, I began the task of trying to produce a new analysis of who owned Scotland. The methodology, a mixture of documentary research and direct approaches to landowners, is outlined in Chapter 5 of *Who Owns Scotland*.

The results of this work showed that landownership in Scotland was still dominated by a relatively small number of very large landholdings. It confirmed that the decline and fall of the aristocracy, that Cannadine argued, was real but that the old aristocratic order (Buccleuch, Roxburghe, Seafield, Argyll, Atholl and Lothian) still held huge estates and that new owners from business, finance and overseas had moved in to replace others. I concluded *Who Owns Scotland* by outlining a series of reforms I felt were important to redistribute control of land more equitably and concluded that only with a Scottish Parliament would some of the issues raised be properly dealt with. That land reform process is looked at in some detail in Chapter 25.

Over the five years following publication, it became evident that I had made some mistakes and that, aside from the politics of land, there was a demand from a purely practical perspective for information on who owned particular parcels of land. There is a wide range of instances where people need access to straightforward reliable information on the ownership of land. Utilities need to negotiate wayleaves. Local authorities need to survey new road alignments. Scientists need permission for wildlife survey work. Local people wish to contact landowners for a range of purposes. Emergency services need to contact landowners in the event of incidents such as flooding or forest fires. Researchers need basic information to study the ownership and occupation of land. Many other people ranging from film companies and outdoor activities organisers to mineral prospectors, renewable energy companies and developers have similar needs.

Historically, there was only one place where people could always go to find out who owned property and that was the Register of Sasines. From 1981, this has steadily been replaced by the Land Register which is where all sales of land are now recorded. The

Register of Sasines is a record of deeds lodged with the Keeper of the Registers of Scotland. They are descriptive and are cross-referenced with other older deeds that, more often than not, lack plans, are not spatially organised and are difficult and time-consuming to access. These records are the definitive source for information on who owns what but are not the place to go if you want a quick answer to a question of who owns a specific parcel of land. In time, as the Land Register covers more of Scotland, it may be modified to allow quick and easy access by the public but until the larger properties are included, which may be some decades away, its coverage remains patchy. I used the Register of Sasines in 1995 but, given the time-consuming nature of conducting research in it, was obliged to follow other lines of enquiry, such as direct approaches to landowners, in order to achieve anything like a significant coverage of Scotland.

It was evident, however, that there was a growing interest in the topic following the 1997 general election and the establishment of the Scottish Parliament in 1999. A more accurate, accessible and comprehensive source of landownership information was needed. However, there was no serious political support for any initiative of this sort from elected politicians in Holyrood but there was from councillors in Highland Council and, later, in Argyll and Bute Council.

In April 1997, I was commissioned to produce a database of landownership in the Highland Council area. It was decided that the information should meet the following criteria:

- the process had to be <u>efficient</u> in terms of time and resources
- it had to yield information of <u>known</u> quality in terms of accuracy and precision
- information had to be of a reasonably <u>consistent</u> standard
- it had to provide data in a way which enabled it to be <u>updated</u> systematically

The final database would aim to account for all holdings over 20ha (50 acres) in extent. Importantly, the results were to be made available to the public. This contrasted with other government initiatives which held useful information on landownership. For example, the Scottish Executive Rural Affairs Department held over 30,000 records of farm units in Scotland and Scottish Natural Heritage had recently commissioned a database of landholdings in the former Cairngorm Partnership Board area. Both remained and remain today confidential since landowners were assured of secrecy when they were initially approached to cooperate.

By August 1998, I had identified a total of 2,747 landholdings covering 5,132,848 acres of land or 97.3 per cent of the Highland Council area. Of these, 1,204 were included in the database covering 4,998,410 acres of land or 94.8 per cent of the area. This work was later extended to Argyll and Bute.[21]

Having completed this work, it was obvious that the task was manageable and, when tied in to the Registers of Scotland, could be updated and checked as and when required. Might it be possible to roll this out across Scotland?

By this time, the context in which this might be done had changed significantly from back in 1995 in six key respects. Firstly, another revised edition of *Who Owns Scotland* was out of the question since the financial returns were quite simply not adequate to justify spending another year researching and writing a book. Secondly, the Internet and the World Wide Web as means of communicating information were growing fast and appeared to be a more sensible way of distributing such information than the physical pages of a printed book. Thirdly, an Internet-based approach could convey far more information than could be contained in the pages of a book. People were interested in contacting landowners and so wanted names and addresses and other information – plus landowners themselves were beginning to set up websites. Fourthly, the Register of Sasines and the Land Register were now available online via a new service called Registers Direct. The registers themselves remained complex to interrogate but at least this could be done from home and did not require a visit in person to their offices in Meadowbank House. Fifthly, the Ordnance Survey had begun to make available digital versions of their 1:50,000 maps which could never be reproduced in a book but could, potentially, be displayed easily on a website. And, finally, Geographic Informations Systems (GIS) software was now available (though it was expensive) and it enabled the generation and manipulation of geographic data and map production in a far more flexible manner than was possible with paper maps.

Meanwhile, the Scottish Executive had, as part of its land reform proposals, decided to explore the rationale for a database of rural landholdings constructed along the lines of the Highland Council model. It announced a research study in Parliament on 11 May 2000. Later that year, on 11 November, the Scottish Liberal Democrat leader, Deputy First Minister of Scotland and Minister for Justice, Jim Wallace, announced that he would not be pursuing any new database but, instead, would publish a leaflet telling people where they could find such information.[22]

I disagreed with this conclusion and decided it was time to develop a website myself which would contain information on who owns Scotland, including names, addresses, maps and further contacts that had been updated as far as possible. A prototype was launched in November 2001 and, on 1 May 2002, the website was launched. The original target was to document 75 per cent of Scotland within three years. However, like the Highland Council study, I was using the original title deeds as the basis for determining ownership information and this proved time-consuming. With no funding to cover the time spent on the project, it soon became a spare-time activity but, nevertheless, managed to cover 50 per cent of Scotland by 2007 – well behind schedule but within sight of the finish.[23]

Two things then happened which changed the course of the project. The first was the finale of a dispute with the Ordnance Survey over costs of digital maps. It became clear that they were prepared to breach their original agreement and increase costs to well over £10,000 per year and, in February 2007, I removed all OS maps having concluded that I could no longer work with them.[24] The next event was in 2009 when, in April, I was informed that the arrangements I had enjoyed up until then whereby I had research access to the Registers of Scotland would no longer apply and that full fees would, from then on, be due. This increased the annual costs by around £5000 and, at this point, I took the decision that the project could no longer continue as a not-for-profit free-to-access website. On 1 October 2009, the Who Owns Scotland website was relaunched as a redesigned subscription-only service.

For individual records of ownership, users are invited to subscribe to the site.

The Land Register, meanwhile, continues to expand. The 18 per cent coverage combined with the data from the Who Owns Scotland website and the public sector estate now accounts for close to 75 per cent of the country. We are becoming better informed than at any time in the past about the pattern of landownership in Scotland.[25] So what does this tell us about who owns Scotland today?

Who Owns Scotland?

The facts

Who does own Scotland, then? As outlined in Chapter 11, this question is a little tricky. If you wish to find out who owns a certain field or a house or a forest or an office block, then the Registers of Scotland should be able to help. If there is an address then it should be quite straightforward. If there is no address – for example, a field – then, unless it is on the Land Register, it may be impossible since the Register of Sasines is not plan based. In any event, as the Land Register coverage expands, things will get easier. Meanwhile the Who Owns Scotland website contains details of over 2000 landholdings covering 10 million acres.

However, if you wish to find out the pattern of ownership over a parish or a county or want to know how it has changed over time or want to know the breakdown between different kinds of owners or the amount of land held in community ownership, then the official records are of no help. It was to answer these kinds of questions – questions of public interest – that I wrote *Who Owns Scotland* in 1996 and subsequently launched the Who Owns Scotland project and website. So what does all this data tell us?[1]

Landownership in Scotland, 2012

Scotland comprises	Acres
Inland water	36,868
Land	19,432,565
Total area	19,469,433

Table 1a
Source: Author's own data

Urban/rural landownership in Scotland breakdown, 2012

Of the land area	Acres	Percentage
urban	508,049	2.6%
rural	18,924,516	97.4%

Table 1b

Source: Author's own data

The rural land is owned by four broad categories of owner:

Four broad categories of rural landownership

Category	Acres	Percentage
Heritage sector	480,739	2.5%
Community sector	425,739	2.2%
Public sector	2,295,751	12.1%
Private sector	15,722,287	83.1%
Total	18,924,516	

Table 1c

Source: Author's own data

Concentration of private rural landownership in Scotland, 1872–2012

Percentage of private rural land	Numbers of owners				Acres
	1872	1970	1995	2012	
10%	3	18	17	16	1,624,836
20%	21	51	53	49	3,145,430
30%	34	110	116	110	4,721,261
40%	63	207	220	221	6,288,869
50%	118	370	412	432	7,861,437
60%	196	1180	854	963	9,433,791

Table 2a

Source: Author's own data

Breakdown of private rural landownership in Scotland for 1970, 1995 and 2012

Date	Number of owners	Percentage of private land owned	Average number of acres held per owner
1970	1180	60%	8,389
1995	854	60%	11,478
2012	963	60%	9,796

Table 2b

Source: Author's own data

Tables 1a, 1b and 1c show the broad breakdown of Scotland by land area and by type of ownership and Tables 2a and 2b show the concentration of private rural landownership and the breakdown of that ownership for the years 1970, 1995 and 2012.[2] What is revealing about these figures is the persistent pattern of very concentrated private ownership of land which has remained virtually static since 1970. The number of owners owning 50 per cent of the privately owned rural land has increased by only 17 per cent in forty years. The number of landowners of 60 per cent has in fact decreased since 1970 from 1180 to 854 in 1995 and to 963 in 2012. The reason for this decrease is probably the steady amalgamation of farms and the acquisition of multiple holdings across Scotland by some recently established landowners. Were the analysis to continue to 70 per cent, it is almost certain that the same increasing concentration would be observed though a close analysis of the data would be required to say for certain. Today there are over 9.4 million acres of land held by a mere 963 landowners and over 10 million acres of land are held by a mere 1,545 private landowners in estates of 1,000 acres and larger (see Table 3).

Whereas the pattern of private ownership has remained much the same (though in a reduced total acreage), the extent of land under community ownership and other forms of not-for-profit ownership, such as conservation bodies, has more than doubled from 440,000 acres in 1995 to over 900,000 acres in 2012. These developments are explored in later chapters. Meanwhile let's look in a little more detail at the various sorts of landowners in Scotland.

Breakdown of private rural landownership in Scotland, 1970–2012

Acreage of holding	1970		1995		2012	
	Number	Acres	Number	Acres	Number	Acres
⩾ 100,000	5	706,400	4	613,025	5	763,220
75,000–99,999	6	508,800	6	527,139	6	534,618
50,000–74,999	21	1,256,700	16	939,218	17	987,489
40,000–49,999	19	828,100	10	457,784	10	440,742
30,000–39,999	21	720,100	22	776,283	24	846,674
20,000–29,999	47	1,120,000	56	1,355,649	42	1,030,165
10,000–19,999	174	2,444,590	144	1,999,973	142	1,947,705
5,000–9,999	258	1,743,500	215	1,502,413	199	1,376,758
4,000–4,999	98	430,800	114	495,114	89	394,625
3,000–3,999	194	662,100	117	389,481	119	409,465
2,000–2,999	351	842,100	230	526,773	239	568,102
1,000–1,999	552	745,300	465	609,269	653	882,389
Total	1,746	12,008,490	1,399	10,192,121	1,545	10,181,952

Table 3

Source: Author's own data

The Public Owners

Scottish Ministers, the legal name for the Scottish Government and the successor entity to the Secretary of State for Scotland, is the largest landowner in Scotland, owning 1,901,607 acres of land – 9.8 per cent of the land area of Scotland. Other publicly owned land, such as Scottish Water land and Ministry of Defence land, totals a further 394,144 acres. The total extent of publicly owned land in Scotland is 2,295,751 acres – 11.8 per cent of Scotland (see Table 4 and Figure 5).

Land held by Scottish Ministers consists of two main holdings, namely the national forest estate managed by the Forestry Commission and the agricultural estates managed by the Scottish Government Rural Payments and Inspections Directorate (things were clearer when it was simply the Board of Agriculture). Contrary to popular opinion, the Forestry Commission owns no land in Scotland. The national forest estate covers 1.65 million acres of land and is merely managed by Forestry Commission Scotland. The agricultural estate is dominated by large estates principally in the Western Isles, Skye and Sutherland which were acquired early in the twentieth century to create smallholdings and crofts. An additional 8,895 acres of land on Barra was acquired in 2003 when MacNeil of Barra gifted it to the government. The Transfer of Crofting Estates (Scotland) Act 1997 provides a right for crofting townships to take over ownership of Scottish Ministers' land. The first and only transfer to date took place in January 2010 when 16,255 acres comprising the three townships of Borve, Luskentyre and Scaristavore in west Harris were acquired by the West Harris Trust. Other land held by Scottish Ministers includes land managed by the Crofters Commission, Science and Advice for Scottish Agriculture and the Royal Botanic Garden Edinburgh.

Landownership by public bodies, 2012

Organisation	Acres
Scottish Ministers (Forestry Commission)	1,648,193
Scottish Ministers (agricultural estates)	242,267
Local Authorities	82,771
Crown land	89,000
Scottish Natural Heritage	88,463
Scottish Water	70,000
Secretary of State for Defence	53,522
Scottish Ministers (other land)	11,147
Highlands and Islands Enterprise	10,388
Total	2,295,751

Table 4

Source[3]

The Crown Estate Commissioners (CEC) administer Crown land which includes 89,000 acres of rural land in Scotland principally at Glenlivet and in Dumfriesshire. It also includes Crown foreshore and the 100,000 square kilometres of seabed out to the 12-mile territorial limits of Scotland (the seabed is not included in the figures in Table 4). In addition, the Crown in Scotland has

Figure 5: Rural land owned by Scottish Ministers and public
bodies under their direction, 2012

The Poor Had No Lawyers

property rights over the continental shelf to the 200-nautical-mile limit. This represents one of the most valuable public estates in Scotland and has been the subject of much recent debate (see Chapter 14).

Scottish Natural Heritage was established in 1992. It is the Scottish Government's conservation agency and inherited its 88,463-acre landholding from its predecessor, the Nature Conservancy Council. It consists mainly of National Nature Reserves, the largest of which are the Island of Rum, Beinn Eighe and Creag Meagaidh (see Table 5).

Land owned by Scottish Natural Heritage

Property	County	Acres
Rum	Inverness	26,400
Beinn Eighe	Ross and Cromarty	10,297
Creag Meagaidh	Inverness	9,756
Invereshie	Inverness	7,618
Ben Wyvis	Ross and Cromarty	5,780
Rannoch Moor	Perth	3,704
Cairnsmore of Fleet	Kirkcudbright	3,247
Glen Roy	Inverness	2,886
Loch Druidibeg	Inverness	2,577
Ben Lui	Argyll	2,380
Sands of Forvie	Aberdeen	2,511
Glencripesdale	Argyll	1,505
Claish Moss	Argyll	1,391
Moine Mhor	Argyll	1,218
Dunnet Links	Caithness	894
Taynish	Argyll	872
Abernethy	Inverness	657
Mealdarroch	Argyll	506
Glen Tanar	Aberdeen	450
Glasdrum Wood	Argyll	418
Coire Fee	Angus	395
Tentsmuir	Fife	299
Various other properties		2,702
Total		88,463

Table 5

Source: Scottish Natural Heritage

The Secretary of State for Defence owns 53,522 acres of land principally around the Garelochhead with a range of smaller RAF bases and training grounds across the country (see Table 6).

MoD land owned by the Secretary of State for Defence

Property	Acres
Cape Wrath	5,973
Garelochhead	3,339
Dundrennan	1,989
Eastriggs	1,292
RAF Tain	1,196
Range West Freugh	1,185
Barry Buddon	1,174
Hebrides	929
Castlelaw	773
RAF Kinloss	666
Coulport	648
RAF Lossiemouth	580
RAF Leuchars	357
Glen Douglas	223
RM Condor	201
RAF Crimond	197
Kirknewton Airfield	95
Faslane	87
RAF Buchan	65
Rona Range	59
Black Dog	54
Aird Uig Timsgarry	41
Fort George	39
NATO Campbeltown	38
NATO Poolewe	38
NATO Loch Striven	33
Craigie Hall	31
Finnart	22
OFD Garelochhead	20
Old Man of Wick	19
Stirling Training Camp	13
Vulcan	9
RAF Saxa Vord	8
Balmacara	7
Lerwick Observatory	7
RAF Benbecula	6

Table 6

Source: MoD Defence Estates Development Plan (DEDP), 2009 (updated to 2012)

Highlands and Islands Enterprise owns the Cairngorm Estate which includes the Cairngorm ski resort. This was originally part of the Forestry Commission's Glenmore Estate but was transferred to the Highlands and Islands Development Board in 1971 for the purposes of developing downhill skiing facilities. In 2006, a consultation was launched on future ownership options but plans were abandoned in 2007. In 2009, the Scottish Parliament published a report critical of the millions of pounds spent on the controversial funicular railway.

Local authorities own a substantial amount of property and under this category is included common good land. Their rural holdings consist mainly of common land belonging to burghs in the Borders and a large estate in Shetland. Despite ongoing efforts to improve the asset registers of local authorities, there is no central register of land and property owned by them. Some property dates back to the original burgh charters and is, therefore, not even in the Register of Sasines as its ownership has never changed except by virtue of the various statutes reforming local government structures.

Scottish Water inherited the holdings of the old regional water boards in 1996 and manages them for the supply of water. Its largest holdings are at Lintrathen in Angus and the Loch Katrine estate north of Glasgow which has been leased on a long lease to the Forestry Commission.

As part of an ongoing process of pursuing efficiencies in government, the Scottish Government published a review of all land held by Scottish Ministers and agencies in 2009 which made various recommendations for managing the estate more efficiently.[4]

The Private Owners

Private landownership in Scotland is characterised by a mixture of large estates, owner-occupied farms and private forestry holdings and by a range of ownership vehicles from the personal to companies, offshore trusts, family trusts and farming partnerships. It is also characterised by a very open and unregulated market in land. Recent reforms have promoted the concept of community ownership and this has been the most prominent change in the pattern over the past fifteen years but, on the question of the rest, there remains considerable disinterest. This is unusual since it is perfectly possible to apply the same evidence-based analysis to the question of how land should be held as it is to any other aspect of public policy. As a consequence, apart from the growth in state ownership in the early twentieth century, the pattern of private ownership has been left to the market. Table 7 lists the top one hundred private landowners in Scotland in 2012.

Who Owns Balmoral Estate?

Balmoral is the archetypal Highland estate but all is not as it seems and the way in which the Queen has arranged her affairs provides an insight into how the upper classes have managed to protect their wealth and land and reveals deep-seated questions that lie at the heart of the debate on land reform in Scotland. Who owns Balmoral?

Contrary to popular belief, Queen Victoria did not fall in love with Balmoral and purchase it in the nineteenth century. Likewise, the Queen who is regarded as the owner of Balmoral Estate, in fact, is not. If you look at Balmoral's website you will see the following claim:

> Purchased by Queen Victoria in 1848, the Estate has been the Scottish Home of the British Royal Family ever since.

And

> The Estate is owned and funded by Her Majesty The Queen, personally rather than as Sovereign.[5]

Both claims are wrong.

Queen Victoria took a *lease* of Balmoral Estate in 1848 from the Trustees of the Duke of Fife. The estate was then purchased in 1852 not by Queen Victoria but by Prince

Albert. The 1760 Civil List Act meant that any property bought by the monarch would become part of the Crown Estate, the revenues of which are surrendered to Parliament in return for the Civil List, and, since Queen Victoria had no wish for that to happen, the title was acquired in Albert's name. In the same year, the Balmoral Estates Act was passed to avoid any questions arising over the legitimacy of this arrangement. The Crown Private Estates Act was then passed in 1862 to enable Victoria to inherit Balmoral in her private capacity following Albert's death.

This same act further stipulated, in Section 4, that all property owned by the monarch in their private capacity would be held not by them personally but be vested in trustees. Balmoral is therefore owned by Trustees under Deeds of Nomination and Appointment by HM Queen Elizabeth II and the Queen is the beneficiary of this trust. In 1997, the three trustees were Rt Hon. David George Coke Patrick Ogilvy, Earl of Airlie (Cortachy Castle, Cortachy, Kirriemuir, Angus), Sir Iain Tennant KT LLD (Lochnabo, Llanbryde, Moray) and Sir Michael Charles Gerrard Peat CVV, Keeper of the Privy Purse (St James Palace, London).

So what do the Queen's trustees actually own?

First of all they own the Balmoral Estate itself which was extended in 1947 by the purchase of lands in Angus – Bachnagairn and White Mounth in 1947 and Glen Doll in 1997. In addition the trustees have a long lease of Abergeldie Estate and bought two parts of Delnadamph Estate in 1977 and 1980. In total, they own around 61,500 acres and have a long lease on the 11,700 acres of Abergeldie. This makes them the sixteenth largest private landowner in Scotland – up from twentieth in 1995 and seventy-fifth in 1970.

Private landownership in Scotland remains a small, inter-related and privileged club which is proud to have the Queen as a member. But, with land reform such an important part of public policy, what message does it send out when the Queen continues to play the role of Highland laird? The Queen is supposed to set an example. In Scotland, public policy on land reform is to secure a 'rapid change in the pattern of land ownership'.[6] The Queen is running counter to that by being the owner of a large and expanding estate.

The Queen, who, like other large landowners, owns estates to provide her with a place to spend her holidays, can continue to enjoy her holidays as others do by renting a castle or country hotel. Under state or community ownership, the Queen could even continue to enjoy holidays at Balmoral if she wished. Any serious attempt at dismantling the concentrated pattern of private landownership in Scotland will get nowhere if it does not face up to the fact that the Queen's ownership of Balmoral is a central part of the selfsame problem. It remains an obstacle to radical land reform since its continued existence legitimises large-scale private landownership.

This situation will be exacerbated when Balmoral is inherited by Prince Charles as heir to the throne. He will pay no inheritance tax because, although the Queen's estate is subject to inheritance tax, bequests from sovereign to sovereign are exempt. The monarchy website provides a rather bizarre reason for this – 'This is because the Sovereign is unable to generate significant new wealth through earnings or business activities, and to recognise the requirement for the Monarchy to have a degree of financial independence.'[7]

Whilst increasing numbers of people face 40 per cent inheritance tax bills on their parents' houses, and quite rightly so, the Queen's heir will not. And, whereas many ordinary people will have to sell inherited assets to pay the bill, the argument is that the sovereign does not generate enough wealth to do this. But Prince Charles, who would have to foot the bill were he to be liable, earned over £15 million last year from the Duchy of Cornwall. Moreover, when any normal family inherits property, each child will usually receive an equal share. But the sovereign is still subject to the laws of male primogeniture so Princess Anne, Prince Andrew and Prince Edward will inherit nothing of Balmoral. If they did, it would at least do something to break down the pattern of ownership.

Any moves to change the pattern of ownership should not be regarded as an attack on the Queen personally – her attitudes about how to manage Balmoral are as progressive as those of many modern landowners – but as a challenge to the idea that Scotland can ever truly create a modern democracy when its land continues to be in the hands of so few people and when, on issues such as inheritance tax and succession, they are subject to different rules from the rest of society.

Balmoral Estate is a block on land reform and, for as long as its ownership remains unquestioned, so too will the wider pattern of large-scale unregulated private ownership. Balmoral is the personal property of the Queen rather than part of the Crown Estate but the time has come to end this peculiar situation which continues to stand in the way of meaningful land reform.

The 100 largest landholdings in Scotland, 2012

Position	Property	Owner	Acres
1	Buccleuch Estates	Buccleuch Estates Ltd	241,887
2	Glen Feshie & other estates	Anders Povlsen	159,274
3	Atholl Estates	Trustees of Atholl Estates, Blair Charitable Trust, Bruar Trust	124,125
4	Invercauld and Torloisk Estates	Trustees of Captain Farquharson's Invercauld No. 1 Trust and Trustees of Captain Farquharson's Invercauld No. 2 Trust	120,685
5	Alcan Estates	British Alcan Aluminium Ltd	117,249
6	Seafield Estates	Earl of Seafield	95,815
7	Westminster Estates	Trustees of Hugh R. A. Grosvenor, Trustees of Gerald H. Grosvenor, fourth Duke of Westminster, and Gerald C. Grosvenor, sixth Duke of Westminster	94,817

The 100 largest landholdings in Scotland, 2012—contd

Position	Property	Owner	Acres
8	Blackmount, Dalness and Etive Estates	Philip Fleming, Robert Fleming and Trustees	92,141
9	Sutherland Estates	Elizabeth Janson, Countess of Sutherland, Charles Janson and Trustees of Elizabeth Janson, Countess of Sutherland	87,898
10	Letterewe, Heights of Kinlochewe and Tournaig Estates	Clyde Properties NV and Utrechtse Beheer Maatschappij Catharijne BV	87,066
11	Locheil Estate	Donald Andrew Cameron, Cecil N. T. Cameron and Trustees of said Donald A. Cameron	76,881
12	Glenavon and Braulen Estates	Glenavon Ltd and Andras Ltd	71,383
13	Strathconon Estate	Kirkbi Estates Ltd	69,845
14	North Uist Estate	Trustees of Doon Aileen, Countess Granville	62,200
15	Killilan, Inverinate, West Benula and Glomach Estates	Smech Properties Ltd	61,961
16	Applecross Estate	Applecross Estate Trust	61,609
17	Balmoral and Delnadamph	Trustees under Deeds of Nomination and Appointment by HM Queen Elizabeth II	61,507
18	Drummond Estates	Nancy J. M. H. Drummond Willoughby, Baroness Willoughby de Eresby, Drummond Foundation and Grimsthorpe and Drummond Castle Trust Ltd	60,939
19	Bute Estates	Bute Estate Ltd	56,772
20	Loch Ericht Estates	Argo Invest Overseas Ltd, Hanbury Family and Compania Financiera Waterville SA	56,510

The 100 largest landholdings in Scotland, 2012—contd

Position	Property	Owner	Acres
21	Roxburghe Estates	Roxburghe Trusts, CIC (Guernsey) Ltd, First Roxburghe Bahamian Trust and Sunlaws Development Company Ltd	55,136
22	Dunecht Estates	Hon. Charles Pearson	55,051
23	Assynt Estates	Edmund Vestey and family and trusts	54,754
24	Gairloch (Flowerdale and Shieldaig) and Conon Estates	John A. Mackenzie of Gairloch and Trustees of John A. and Frances M. S. Mackenzie	53,625
25	Cawdor Estate	Cawdor Trusts, Colin R. V. Campbell, 7th Earl of Cawdor, Isabella Campbell, Countess of Cawdor, and Angelika Campbell, Dowager Countess of Cawdor	52,920
26	Argyll Estates	Trustees of the tenth Duke of Argyll	51,667
27	Islay Estate	Islay Estates Company Inc.	51,563
28	Burton Estates	Burton Property Trust and Alexander J. Baillie	50,047
29	Corrour Estate	The Corrour Trust	47,845
30	Stair Estates	Trustees of the Earl of Stair	46,613
31	Invermark and Brechin Castle Estates	Dalhousie 2006 Trust	46,362
32	Douglas and Angus Estates	Douglas and Angus Estates	46,337
33	Langwell and Braemore Estate	Wellbeck Estates Company Ltd	45,828
34	Uig and Hamnaway Estate	Peter J. Cresswell, Trustees of Charles P. Fairweather and Mark G. Cresswell	45,131

The 100 largest landholdings in Scotland, 2012—contd

Position	Property	Owner	Acres
35	Sinclair Estates	Sinclair Family Trust and John Sinclair (or Thurso), Viscount Thurso	40,977
36	Ardverikie Estate	Ardverikie Estate Ltd	40,815
37	Glenfiddich and Cabrach Estate	Golden Lane Securities Ltd	40,764
38	Dunvegan and Glenbrittle	Executors of John MacLeod of MacLeod	40,070
39	Coignafearn Estate	Coignafearn Estate (Tomatin) Ltd	39,560
40	Barachander and Conaglen	John Guthrie	39,405
41	Eishken Estate	Eishken Nominees Ltd	39,000
42	Soval Estate	Richard P. Kershaw and Marie D. Kershaw	39,000
43	Fasque and Glendye Estate	Charles A. Gladstone and Trustees under Settlement between Sir Erskine W. Gladstone and others	38,632
44	Wemyss Estates	Lord Wemyss Trust	38,113
45	Various properties	Edinmore Properties Ltd	37,464
46	Strathvaich and Strathrannoch	Dickinson Trust Ltd, Trustees of Dione Angela Countess of Verulam, Trustees under Creasey Trust, Pictet Bank and Trust Ltd and Spero Trustee Company and Nicholas Westwood Smith	37,228
47	Luss Estate	Luss Estates Company	37,191
48	Dunbeath and Glutt Estates	Stuart W. M. Threipland and Claire R. M. Threipland	36,978
49	Meggernie and Lochs Estate	Beverley Jane Malim	36,790

The 100 largest landholdings in Scotland, 2012—contd

Position	Property	Owner	Acres
50	Altnaharra Estate	Altnaharra Estate Ltd	36,266
51	Ardtornish Estate	Ardtornish Estate Co. Ltd	35,357
52	Skelpick and Rhifail Estates	Firm of Skelpick and Rhifail Estates	35,088
53	Barvas	Barvas Estate Ltd	34,600
54	Dundonnell Estate	Regina Anna Properties Ltd	33,201
55	Moray Estates	Moray Estates Development Co.	33,143
56	Balnagown and Invercassley Estates	Bocardo Société Anonyme and Ross Estates Co.	32,289
57	Corriemulzie, Loubcroy and Caplich Estates	Trustees of Patrick F. J. Colvin	32,206
58	Kinlochewe, Lochrosque and West Fannich Estates	Patrick C. G. Wilson and Family and Trust	32,184
59	Loch a Choire Estate	Andrew H. Joicey, James M. Joicey, David R. Knowles and David H. M. Leslie	31,185
60	Loch Naver, Syre and Rhifail Estates	Yattendon Estates Ltd and Firm of Mynthurst Estates	30,890
61	Wester Glenquoich Estate	Andrew D. Gordon and Trustees of Duncan Gordon 1999 Trust	30,787
62	Tulchan Estate, Lugate, Ferniehurst, and Bowland Estates	Tulchan Sporting Estates Ltd. (Leon G. Litchfield)	30,117
63	Glen Tanar Estate	Michael A. Bruce	29,217
64	Attadale Estate	Trustees of Carolyn Mary Macpherson	29,099
65	Lochluichart Estate	Lochluichart Estate Co. Ltd and Ian H. Leslie Melville	29,022
66	Scone Estates	Earl of Mansfield and Trusts	28,480

The 100 largest landholdings in Scotland, 2012—contd

Position	Property	Owner	Acres
67	Badanloch Estate	Executors of Philip William Bryce, Viscount Leverhulme	28,424
68	Corrielair Estate and others	Firm of Ian Brown and Sons and I. and H. Brown Ltd	28,398
69	Inver and Ormsary Estate	Sir William J. Lithgow and Inver Farmers	28,342
70	Various properties	Charles Connell & Co. (Colquhalzie Farms) Ltd	27,856
71	Dalmeny Estates	Harry R. N. Primrose, Lord Dalmeny and Trustees of Lord Dalmeny	27,465
72	Bighouse Estate	A H G Group Ltd	27,172
73	Pairc Estate	Pairc Crofters Ltd	26,800
74	Bays of Harris Estate	Rodney and Patricia Hitchcock	26,400
75	Castlemilk Estates	Sir Archibald B. C. Edmonstone and Andrew R. J. Buchanan-Jardine as Trustees, under deed of trust of Sir Andrew R. J. Buchanan-Jardine, and Trusts	25,896
76	Mar Estate	Mark M. Nicolson, Merlin S. V. G. Hay, Earl of Hay and Slains, and Michael A. Hayes	25,143
77	Ardleish and Glenfalloch Estates	Felicity Richardson, Philippa Hanbury, Anthony Lowes, Jeremy Lowes, Thomas Lowes and David Lowes	24,832
78	Various properties	Greentop Lands & Estates Ltd	24,729
79	Ardgour Estate	Robin Michael Maclean of Ardgour and Trustees of said Robin Maclean	24,719
80	Gruinard, Achnegie and Fain Estates	Trustees of Lady Huntly's 1987 Children's Settlement	24,571

The 100 largest landholdings in Scotland, 2012—contd

Position	Property	Owner	Acres
81	Sallachy and Creanich Estates	H. H. Roesner Property Management Ltd	24,557
82	Dougarie Estate	Stephen C. Gibbs and Trustees of Stephen & Lavinia Gibbs	24,539
83	Drumochter and Ralia Estate	Eira Drysdale, Alasdair J. Findlay and Trustees of Eira Drysdale	24,350
84	Foich and Inverlael Deer Forest	Beleggingsmaatschappij Festeyn BV, Inverlael BV, Hendrik J. E. van Beuningen Sen., Hendrik J. E. van Beuningen Jun., Christine E. Vaandrager-van-Beuningen, Elisabeth M. van der Hoever-van-Beuningen and Julia Hurst-van-Beuningen	24,338
85	Rothiemurchus Estate	Trustees of John P. Grant and Rothiemurchus Estate Trust	24,330
86	Dinnet Estate	Edward C. M. Humphrey and Wester Coull Trust	24,317
87	Fearann Eilean Iarmain	Lady Lucilla Noble	24,017
88	Broadland Estates	Broadland Properties Ltd	23,534
89	Coulin Estate	Trustees of Philip Reginald Smith	23,256
90	Alladale and Deanich Estates	Paul, Sylvia and David Lister and Graham Chambers as Trustees of Sylvia Lister, 2002 No. 1 Settlement	23,252
91	Achentoul Estate	Achentoul Estate Co.	23,113
92	Merkland and Ben Hee	Trustees of Sheelagh M. G. Garton	22,898

The 100 largest landholdings in Scotland, 2012—contd

Position	Property	Owner	Acres
93	Altnafeadh	Andre Valentin, Vicomte Adolphe de Spoelberch and Henrietta N. Marie, Vicomtesse Adolphe de Spoelberch and Rodolphe and Diane de Spoelberch	22,883
94	Glendoe and Ardachy Estates	Hillhouse Estates Ltd	22,597
95	Ardlussa Estate	Trustees of Andrew C. Fletcher	22,419
96	Borrobol Estate	Michael I. Wigan	22,393
97	Tressady Estate	Tressady Estates Ltd	21,580
98	Strathmore Estate	Dora H.G. Gow	21,125
99	Ballindalloch Estate	Trustees of Clare Nancy Russell	21,068
100	Meoble and Lettermorar	Mark Ziaini de Ferranti	21,031

Table 7

Source: Author's own data

The Aristocracy

Despite David Cannadine's thesis of the decline and fall of the British aristocracy, the traditional landed class have survived in Lowland Scotland although, like the rest of Britain, their grip loosened considerably in the first quarter of the twentieth century.

The Highland aristocracy, however, and the holders of all the land in the Highlands and Islands for centuries, more or less disappeared completely by the end of the nineteenth century. The victims of external forces and their own financial woes, the clan elites failed to weather the transformations that took place in the 1800s. Tom Devine points out that the Mackenzie of Seaforth lands in Lewis, Kintail and Glenshiel were virtually gone by 1844.

Walter Campbell of Islay, once the owner of the entire island was bankrupt by 1848 and sold up in 1853. The MacNeils of Barra, MacLeod of Harris, MacDonald of Bornish and MacDonald of Boisdale had all lost their hereditary estates in the three decades after the end of the Napoleonic Wars. He estimates that the acreage of the Highlands in new ownership by the last quarter of the nineteenth century was at least 70 per cent of the mainland and insular parishes of western Argyll, Inverness and Ross. They were replaced by wealthy commoners such as James Morrison who bought Islay from the bankrupt Walter Campbell and James Matheson who bought Lewis in 1844 from the bankrupt Earl of Seaforth.[8]

The Lowland aristocracy fared substantially better and indeed consolidated their position in the years leading up to the end of the nineteenth century. Most of the large landed estates of the north-east, south-west and south-east of Scotland entered the twentieth century virtually intact. The big changes came in the years following the First World War when, for example, landownership in Galloway was transformed out of all recognition from the position before 1900.

A significant amount of land is still held by those families who succeeded in acquiring it many centuries ago. It is estimated that at least 25 per cent of estates of over 1000 acres in extent have been held by the same family for over 400 years and the majority of the aristocratic families that owned land in 1872 still do so today.[9] These families are based predominantly in the Lowlands and still own 2.24 million acres (28.1 per cent) of the 7.79 million acres of land held in estates of 5000 acres and over.

Overseas Interests

Ownership of land by overseas interests remains controversial and, as discussed in Chapter 29, it can pose real challenges to Her Majesty's Revenue and Customs. Around eighty estates covering around 905,000 acres are held by overseas individuals and offshore trusts (see Table 8). Periodic calls for tighter regulation or even abolition of overseas ownership of land (particularly land owned in offshore tax havens) have failed to lead to any reform.

The 50 largest offshore landholdings in Scotland, 2012

Position	Property	Owner	Acres
1	Glen Feshie & others	Anders Holch Povlsen	159,274
2	Letterewe, Heights of Kinlochewe and Tournaig Estates	Clyde Properties NV and Utrechtse Beheer Maatschappij Catharijne BV	87,066
3	Glenavon and Braulen Estates	Glenavon Limited and Andras Ltd	71,383
4	Killilan, Inverinate, West Benula and Glomach Estates	Smech Properties Ltd	61,961
5	Loch Ericht Estates	Argo Invest Overseas Ltd, Hanbury Family and Compania Financiera Waterville SA	56,510
6	Coignafearn Estate	Coignafearn Estate (Tomatin) Ltd	39,560
7	Balnagown and Invercassley Estates	Bocardo Société Anonyme and Ross Estates Co.	32,289
8	Braeroy and Tulloch Estates	Braeroy Estate Ltd	30,215
9	Various properties	Greentop Lands & Estates Ltd	24,729
10	Sallachy and Creanich Estates	H. H. Roesner Land & Forestry Management (Scotland) Ltd	24,557
11	Foich and Inverlael Deer Forest	Beleggingsmaatschappij Festeyn BV, Inverlael BV, Hendrik J. E. van Beuningen Sen., Hendrik J. E. van Beuningen Jun., Christine E. Vaandrager-van-Beuningen, Elisabeth M. van der Hoever-van-Beuningen and Julia Hurst-van-Beuningen	24,338
12	Altnafeadh	Andre Valentin, Vicomte Adolphe de Spoelberch and Henrietta N. Marie, Vicomtesse Adolphe de Spoelberch and Rodolphe and Diane de Spoelberch	22,883

The 50 largest offshore landholdings in Scotland, 2012—contd

Position	Property	Owner	Acres
13	Balmacaan Deer Forest	Balmac Forest Ltd	19,082
14	Tarbert Estate	Ginge Manor Estates Ltd	18,736
15	Balnacoil Estate	A.M. Ejendomme ApS	18,344
16	Dalnacardoch Estate	Hunting Stalcair Ltd	18,000
17	Blackford Estate	Park Tower Holdings Establishment	14,600
18	Dorback Estate etc.	Salingore Holding Ltd	14,535
19	Lochindorb, Logie and Relugas Estates	Alexander W. G. Laing and Saltire Trustees (Overseas) Ltd	13,835
20	Kilchoan Estate	Kilchoan Estate Ltd and Eric Delwart	13,212
21	Inverailort Estate and Ranachan	Cairns Number Three Settlement between Niall Cairns and Trustees	12,886
22	Glenure or Glencreran Estate	Establissement Entraide et Solidarite	12,567
23	Kirklawhill etc.	Multioptique Ltd International SA	12,432
24	Pitmain Estate	Lucas Aardenburg	12,039
25	Glen Banchor and Strone Estates	Beaverton Property LLC	11,705
26	Glencassley	Glencassley Ltd	11,098
27	Gleann Leac-na-muidhe etc.	Domenico Felice Berardelli	10,933
28	Forrest Estate	Forrest Estate Ltd	10,858
29	Durness Estate	Vibel SA	10,488
30	Carsaig and Pennyghael	Participatiemaatschappij Epsilon BV	9,795
31	Wester Guisachan Estate	Reynout Kwint	9,342

The 50 largest offshore landholdings in Scotland, 2012—contd

Position	Property	Owner	Acres
32	Fannich Estate	Medieval Industries Inc.	9,293
33	North Affric Estate	Beaufort Enterprises SA	8,974
34	Arisaig Estate and Borrodale House	Amphill Investments Ltd	8,940
35	Camusrory Estate	Camusrory Estate Ltd	8,080
36	Carskiey	Carskiey Aktiengesellschaft	7,472
37	Inversanda Estate	Orion Holdings Ltd	6,708
38	Scalpay, Longay and Guillamon	Ibercasa Anstalt	6,231
39	Glenmassan	Arkady Ltd	5,680
40	Various forests	Vecata A/S	5,672
41	Kildrummy Estate	Kildrummy (Jersey) Ltd	5,661
42	Glenborrodale Estate	Luna Ltd	5,536
43	Gledfield Estate	Gledfield Estate Ltd	5,177
44	Achany	TAP UK Ltd	5,072
45	Dalmigarry	Supreme Leader Inc.	4,521
46	East Benula Estate	Chooky Corporation	4,375
47	Balmacaan Estate	Arran Ltd	4,190
48	Woodcock Beheer Estates	Woodcock Beheer BV	4,057
49	Scoor Estate	Ospinter Ltd	3,293
50	Various properties	Gong Hill Ltd	2954

Table 8

Source: Author's own data

Institutional Owners

Many of the institutional owners of land, such as Eagle Star and Prudential, have sold their land in Scotland and the extent of such ownership is much reduced from what it was in the 1970s. Pension funds still include land as part of their investment portfolio but now seem to prefer urban to rural. Forestry investment by pension funds is still prevalent and institutional or industrial ownership of forests by the timber industry has been growing steadily over the past decade or so.

Changes since 1995

In 1995 there were 258 privately-owned estates larger than 10,000 acres covering 6,669,071 acres. By 2012 this had reduced to 246 covering 6,550,613 acres, a reduction of 118,458 acres. In this period, six estates covering 281,484 acres were taken over by community landowners (see Table 9 on p. 200). The remaining 252 estates were consolidated into 246 landholdings and expanded in extent by 163,026 acres.

Of these 246 estates, fifteen (6 per cent) have changed hands since 1995, which represent 5.6 per cent of the acreage. Of these, two have been by inheritance and thirteen by sale. Remarkably, in the top one hundred landowners of 2012, the Danish businessman, Anders Povlsen, and Hugh MacLeod, who inherited Dunvegan Estates from his father, are the only newcomers.

The most significant change since 1995 is the marked increase in the extent of land owned by community organisations and, to a lesser extent, by conservation bodies (see Chapters 15 and 16). Community ownership has more than doubled in extent and conservation bodies such as the RSPB have increased their holdings by 44 per cent since 1995. The vast bulk of the expansion in the landholdings of these two types of owner has been in the north and west Highlands and Islands.

The next few chapters explore in detail some aspects of landownership, including crofting, forestry and housing. But, before we look at these, I want to take a brief diversion to tell the story which, in 2000, thrust the whole question of who owns what back into the public spotlight.

A Considerable Ridge of Very High and Lofty Hills

The Cuillin, MacLeod and a leaky castle

What follows is a rather lengthy exposition about the sale of the Cuillin. The reason for recounting it at length is that it provides a valuable insight into the manner in which land was appropriated and the role of the law in legitimising the theft of the commons. As I said at the outset, we need to have a better understanding of how land rights have evolved if we want to secure meaningful land reform. It is also instructive as a contemporary moral tale of how close the whole edifice of land rights came to collapsing but how it was saved by the lack of decisive action by those with the power to take it. It exposes the bluster and wilful ignorance of vast swathes of official Scotland which, deluded by centuries of acquiescence to legal fictions, missed the opportunity to get to grips with the substance of the issue – namely, how come so much land ended up in so few hands, was this lawful and why did the legal establishment contrive to make it so?

In what follows I must pay tribute to the tireless work of Alan Blackshaw who, on behalf of Ramblers Scotland, doggedly pursued the question of who owns the Cuillin. Much of the evidence cited here derives from his work.

On 17 March 2000, FPD Savills, who describe themselves as 'international property consultants', issued a notice of a press briefing to be held in their Edinburgh office in Charlotte Square at 11 a.m. on 22 March. There was to be an announcement about the sale of a Scottish estate of 'national importance'. Speculation began immediately as to where this could be and quickly became ridiculous. Maybe the Queen was selling Balmoral? The Cuillin came to mind but it was not until two hours before the press conference that I got a telephone call to tell me that it was indeed the Cuillin.

On 22 March, twenty or so of us squeezed into a small room in the basement of Savills' plush Edinburgh office. At 11 a.m., in came Guy Galbraith of Savills, a gentleman in a kilt, an older man in a suit and a younger man in a suit. None of them looked terribly comfortable and I recognised the kilted man immediately as John MacLeod of MacLeod, the 29th Chief of the Clan MacLeod. He was accompanied by his factor, John Lambert, and his son Hugh MacLeod.

The announcement was made and a press release handed out together with the sales particulars – which would be available to the rest of the public for £20! The Black Cuillin of Skye were being placed on the market at offers over £10 million (see Plate 5 and Figure 6). The reason given was economic. John MacLeod's home, Dunvegan Castle, needed substantial repairs to a leaky roof. In addition, the estate wanted capital to invest in a number of conservation and tourism projects. In total, they were seeking to raise £18 million with an additional £5 million from public grants and bank loans and cash flow providing the remaining £3 million.

What followed was characteristic of what so often happens when an iconic part of Scotland is put up for sale. There were the usual howls of outrage that Scotland can be bought and sold at a whim and calls for the mountains to be preserved for the nation. *The Herald* ran an editorial 'Sale of the Cuillins Idea of private ownership is offensive'. The *Scotsman* ran the story under 'Public held to ransom over sale of the Cuillin'. Calum MacDonald MP, who had until recently been a minister in the Scottish Office, commented that:

> [t]he idea of selling the Cuillin is ridiculous but at such a price it's obscene. MacLeod should hang his head in shame for trying to exploit what God has given the people of Skye. It goes to show that the one thing worse than a greedy foreign landlord is a greedy Scottish one.[1]

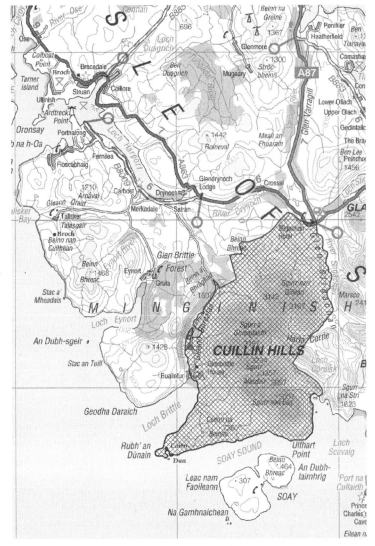

Figure 6: Map of the Cuillin showing extent of land offered
for sale in 2000

Source: Author's own data. Contains Ordnance Survey data Crown
copyright and database right 2013

In the Scottish Parliament, Alasdair Morrison said:

The episode raises a number of issues. John MacLeod of MacLeod did not buy the estate; he got it because he is the clan chief. I hope, for the sake of the people of Skye and Scotland, that MacLeod of MacLeod will come to a solution that will be sympathetic to his kinsmen in Skye. Incidentally, the matter raises the wider issue of how some clan chiefs became private landowners. I hope that this episode can shed light on that great mystery.[2]

Conservation organisations such as the John Muir Trust had an interest in the sale but publicly refused to countenance paying anything like the £10 million that was being asked – a figure that Savills confirmed was based on the price The National Trust had recently paid for Snowdon in Wales. Heightened publicity surrounded the sale following the announcement at the beginning of April that the John Muir Trust was taking ownership of the summit of Ben Nevis – a 4181-acre estate – for £450,000. This equated to £107 per acre compared with the £435 being sought for the Cuillin. It was rapidly becoming clear that there was probably little chance of anyone buying the estate for £10 million. Even if there was, they would have been troubled by a more fundamental question which quickly came to the fore as the *West Highland Free Press*, based on Skye, challenged Mr MacLeod to 'show us your title deeds'.[3] Did MacLeod actually own the Cuillin in the first place?

This echoed the call from land reformers down the centuries who, believing that land had been simply stolen, argued that the owners had no legal claim. If they did, then they should exhibit their deeds. The bitter truth was, however, that most landowners did have good title. It also neatly linked back to the origins of the Cuillin title. The Skye estates had been forfeited as part of the 1493 forfeiture of the Lord of the Isles and granted to MacLeod by a charter in 1498. In 1597, James VI required all who claimed land in the Highlands and Islands to produce their title deeds before the Scottish Privy Council (see Chapter 6). MacLeod had failed to do this and his lands were forfeited once again. Only after he had signed the Statutes of Iona and received a royal pardon was he given a fresh barony charter granting all the lands he had been granted under the 1498 charter. This charter of 1611 is the deed upon which MacLeod's claim to own the Cuillin ultimately rested. What made this case unique was that the Cuillin had never been offered for sale before and they remain one of the few parts of Scotland not to have ever been sold since its original feudal grant.

On 6 April 2000, the Scottish Executive announced it would be taking no action over the sale:

> Mr Duncan Hamilton (Highlands and Islands) (SNP): To ask the Scottish Executive whether it plans to take any action regarding the proposed sale of the Black Cuillins on Skye.
>
> Sarah Boyack: We do not propose to intervene in the private sale of the Cuillin Estate.[4]

If the Cuillin had never been granted to MacLeod's ancestors, then it would be Crown land but the Crown Estate Commissioners quickly announced that they would not be conducting any investigation of the title. However, by mid-May, their position had become untenable. Following interventions by Charles Kennedy MP and clear signals from Scottish Office Minister Brian Wilson and John Reid, the Scottish Secretary, that they would pursue this, the Commissioners made a U-turn and announced, on 18 May, that they would, after all, investigate. Michael Cunliffe, Head of Scottish Estates at the Crown Estate office, said, 'Although the evidence so far does not suggest a strong basis for Crown Estate ownership of the Cuillins, there are clearly questions which need to be answered regarding title to the area.'[5]

Meanwhile the politicians were prevaricating. Jim Wallace, the Minister of Justice, had given a talk to the Scottish Landowners' Federation a month previously in which he demonstrated all the characteristics of the pusillanimous legally-trained politician.

> Landowners are part of the solution, not part of the problem. This is the basis for my key message today – that the Executive is not hostile to private landownership provided that it is responsible private landownership. In other words, good landowners have nothing to fear.

It is for this reason that the Executive see no need for intervention simply because an area such as the Cuillin Estate on Skye comes on to the market. I fully understand the clear public interest and the present feeling of uncertainty on Skye regarding the future of this important heritage area. Indeed such is the importance of this robust landscape in natural heritage terms that the Cuillins are protected by a Site of Special Scientific Interest designation and that would continue after the sale. Moreover, the access currently enjoyed by walkers and climbers will be buttressed by our forthcoming access legislation. But private ownership has worked well for this estate so far and I see no reason why another private owner should not make a success of managing the estate. What matters most here, as elsewhere, is that ownership should be exercised responsibly. That is the critical issue – not whether land is in public or private ownership.[6]

By contrast, Brian Wilson, now a Minister in the Scottish Office and someone who had a history as a campaigning journalist with strong views about landlordism, told the *Guardian* following the Commissioners' volte-face:

I regard it as a landmark because for the first time the assertion of landownership has been challenged. I have always believed that if some of the so-called landowners in the Highlands were required to provide valid deeds, they would be in trouble.[7]

The investigation by the CEC proceeded in two stages. First of all, it sought advice from Alan Menzies, the Crown Estate Solicitor in Scotland. He prepared a sixteen-page advice memorandum containing evidence gathered from MacLeod's private papers and from public records. This was then handed over to James Drummond Young QC for Opinion of Counsel.[8] Critically, the CEC did not seek a view on the question of whether MacLeod had ever been granted title to the Cuillin. Instead, they sought an opinion as to MacLeod's claim of ownership. As we will see, the difference is significant and reflects one of the core themes of this book – namely, that the law has been constructed in such a way as to render irrelevant what an owner was granted and focuses instead on which claims can be defended.

Some of the joys of reading legal opinions and judgements are the disciplined logic of the argument, the elegance of the language and the synthesis of facts, evidence and the law. One expects to be able to see in plain terms the facts and evidence that have been drawn upon in reaching a legal opinion of the sort provided by James Drummond Young so that, even if one may disagree with it, there can be no doubt as to why the decision was reached.

Mr Menzies' advice memorandum pulls together all the evidence that he could obtain both from the public records and from MacLeod's own archives. His conclusion is that Macleod's title is 'not sufficiently clear to enable it to be applied on the ground without the introduction of external evidence to assist the interpretation'. He goes on to say that 'there is strong evidence to suggest that [the title] includes at least part of the Cuillins' and he names the relevant parts. But he then says, '[T]he question is do they extend to the whole or only part of the Cuillin?'

This is indeed the question that everyone was asking and Mr Menzies' conclusion was that, in his view, 'the only evidence that is capable of being produced to determine whether Mr MacLeod's title does extend to part only or the whole of the Cuillins is the extent of possession enjoyed'. He goes on to say:

> I therefore conclude that Mr MacLeod has a title which is insufficient of itself to identify the extent of his land but when taken with the evidence of possession leaves the Crown with no direct evidence to refute Mr MacLeod's claims.[9]

Having assembled the evidence, it was now up to Mr Drummond Young QC to provide an Opinion. He took the view that MacLeod had a good title on the basis of possession and the bulk of his argument is concerned with demonstrating this possession. At which point, we should pause for a minute and remind ourselves of what is being said by these two learned gentlemen. They are both saying that we cannot know what land was granted to MacLeod originally in 1611 but that, nevertheless, his claim to now own the Cuillin is valid because he has 'possessed' it for the required period of twenty years. In the rest of this chapter, I want to explore this claim in some greater depth.

As was made clear in Chapter 5, prescription is a legal device that allows land to be legally owned by the fact of having a recorded title and a person having possessed it for the requisite period. However, certain tests must be met before prescription can be claimed and, where it is claimed, certain further tests must be met. We will come back to the question of whether prescription can in fact be claimed but, for the moment, let us assume that it can. To demonstrate prescriptive possession, two things must be shown. The first is that there must be a recorded deed that is *habile* (meaning 'apparently sufficient' or 'in terms capable of being so construed') to include the land and the second is that possession can be demonstrated openly, peaceably and without any judicial interruption for twenty years following the recording of the title.[10]

So, does MacLeod have a *habile* title – a title that is capable of being interpreted as including the Cuillin? One might expect that Mr Drummond Young would have spent some time and effort in adducing the facts and evidence relating to whether MacLeod had a *habile* title since, unless he has, any discussion of possession is meaningless and irrelevant. Astonishingly, however, he deals with this important question in one sentence of a thirteen-page Opinion and in this quick dismissal is found the essence of the question not only to the validity of MacLeod's alleged title but to the validity of the titles covering most of Scotland. In an Opinion stretching to over 7000 words, less than 250 are devoted to the question of whether the title is *habile*:

It is reasonably clear that the Cuillins lie within the Parish of Bracadale and within the areas generally known as Bracadale and Minginish. It follows that the three deeds in question, those of 1611, 1931 and 1966, are all capable of including the Cuillins among the subjects conveyed.

Mr MacLeod's title, as contained in the deeds of 1611, 1931 and 1966, is in my opinion clearly capable of including the Cuillins.

There is no doubt that a substantial area of land was conferred on Roderick MacLeod and his successors by the Crown in 1611

. . . That area of land included subjects in Bracadale and Minginish.

So what does MacLeod's title tell us about what was granted? The subjects in the 1611 charter are obviously on Skye and they are described as being, inter alia, four *unciates* of land at Bracadale (the term '*unciate*' will be explained shortly), one *unciate* at Lyndale, four *unciates* at Minginish and five *unciates* of land at Waternish. Lyndale and Waternish are both in the north of Skye but Bracadale and Minginish are in the south. They are the areas we need to look at.

With respect to the Parish of Bracadale, the First Statistical Account of 1791–99 states, 'There are no considerable lakes or rivers. There are no remarkable mountains within the parish; but a considerable ridge of very high and lofty hills run betwixt this parish and the parish of Strath.' In case of doubt, the Parish of Strath is described as being bounded '[o]n the west by the parish of Bracadale' and that, in the Parish of Strath:

> on entering the Bay of Scavaig, the spectator is struck with the rugged outline presented by the spiry and serrated peaks of the lofty Cuillin. On landing, he finds himself surrounded by rocks denuded of every vestige of vegetation. As he advances, a valley, enclosed by mountains of the most precipitous character, opens to the view, thus encircling and forming the dark lake of Coir-Uisge.[11]

Cosmo Innes described the Parish of Strath as follows:

> It is bounded on the west by the Coolin (or Cuillin) hills, 3000 feet above sea level, and stretching from the head of Loch Scavaig on the south to the head of Loch Sligachan on the north. It has numerous lakes and at its west end north from Loch Scavaig are the lake of Coiruisge (or Coriskin), studded with green islands and surrounded with steep rugged rocks, and the famous spar cave of Strathaird.[12]

Thus Loch Coruisk together with the eastern slopes of the rugged Black Cuillin ridge are in the Parish of Strath and, for the purposes of the 1611 charter, the Cuillin were not in the Parish of Bracadale. This stands in stark contrast to Drummond Young's assertion that 'it is reasonably clear that the Cuillins lie within the parish of Bracadale'. And this is quite important since, in deciding what is *habile*, '[l]ands possessed in an adjoining parish would not necessarily or usually be held to fit the description, especially if . . . the principal subjects were described as lying in a different parish'.[13]

So what about Minginish? Well, unlike Bracadale and Strath which are parishes, Minginish is a large and vague description of the central part of the Isle of Skye and nothing can be said for certain as to whether the Cuillin are in Minginish or not. But it probably does not matter because the 1611 deed also says something very important about how much land was granted.

Remember the four *unciates* in Bracadale and four unciates in Minginish? An *unciate* is a medieval unit of land assessment equivalent to an *ounceland* or, in the Highlands of Scotland, a *davoch* which is, in turn, an extent of land capable of yielding an ounce of silver in annual rent. Such an area is the equivalent today of around 200 acres of grazing or 50 acres of arable land. MacLeod was granted four of these in both Bracadale and Minginish – a maximum extent therefore of 1,600 acres of grazing land or 400 acres of arable ground or a mixture of the two. In 2000, MacLeod was putting 23,000 acres of land up for sale. How can 23,000 acres of the Cuillin be conceivably contained within a maximum grant of 1,600 acres?

The vast bulk of the Cuillin is bare rocky precipitous mountain waste. As we have seen from our friend Cosmo Innes, this kind of feudal grant was typical of the time – waste ground and mountains were of no value and were not included in feudal grants of the period. As Cosmo Innes pointed out:

> In truth, the arable – the cultivated land of Scotland, the land early appropriated and held by charter – is a narrow strip on the river bank or beside the sea. The inland, the upland, the moor, the mountain were really not occupied at all for agricultural purposes, or served only to keep the poor and their cattle from starving. They were not thought of when charters were made and lands feudalised.[14]

And, as the historian Skene also observed, 'The great mountain ranges and the groups of larger hills either formed deer forests or lay waste and within their bounds were shealings (*sic*) or summer pasture attached to farms . . .'[15]

The 1611 charter is very specific. It does not convey some vague description of land, mountainous or otherwise. It conveys four *unciates* of land in Minginish and four *unciates* of land in Bracadale and these *unciates* are agricultural land which would have been leased to the tacksmen of the Clan MacLeod. No tacksman of any clan would have paid good silver money for a lease of precipitous wastes. A later deed of 1931 actually spells out the place names contained in the 1611 deed. These are all to the west of the Cuillin around Loch Eynort and Loch Harport (see Figure 6). This extent of land is more than sufficient to account for the eight *unciates* that were granted.

This all suggests that, in fact, there are questions about whether the deed is *habile* – questions which neither Alan Menzies nor James Drummond Young even bothered to explore. But it also raises a more fundamental question which I said I would come back to. Can prescription even be entertained in the first place? If the Cuillin may be beyond boundaries identified in his title (such as the boundary of the Parish of Bracadale), then not only is his title not *habile*, prescription itself is not even allowed.

The fact that there is such a significant discrepancy between the area of land explicitly and unambiguously granted and that which was being put up for sale should have alerted the CEC's legal advisers to examine the case law rather more closely and, in particular, to probe carefully the question of whether prescription is, in fact, available as a means of asserting ownership in the first place.

As Rankine points out, '[T]he peculiarity of a bounding charter is that no amount of possession under it of a corporeal subject beyond the limits can enable the possessor to vindicate the ownership thereof.'[16] A parish boundary is sufficient to make a charter bounding and, as we have seen, the Cuillin were not actually within the Parish of Bracadale. But there is another aspect to the 1611 charter that should have given Mr Menzies and Mr Drummond

Young some pause for thought and that is the extent of land that was described – the eight *unciates* or, at maximum, 1,600 acres.

John Rankine, who wrote the authoritative volume on the laws of landownership, makes it clear that a measurement of extent (the eight *unciates*) cannot of itself define a bounding charter[17] and this would be the end of the matter were it not for a case that went before the outer house of the Court of Session in 1905. This concerned land next to the Union Canal in West Lothian. The North British Railway Company claimed that their title included ownership of a further acre of land beyond the 4 acres that it expressly admitted. A Mr Robert Brown disagreed and took a case against the railway company, claiming that this acre belonged to him. The company's title contained no bounding description but simply this 4-acre stated extent. In the original judgement, Lord Ardwall opined that:

> It appears to me, therefore, that I am entitled to read the disposition by the light of the final measurement and settlement to which the disposition itself refers me, and without which the description in the disposition of the land conveyed is defective and unsatisfactory. I accordingly have arrived at the conclusion that the defenders' title is a bounding title under which they cannot acquire, by prescription, any land in excess of the subjects actually conveyed.[18]

The North British Railway Company appealed the decision to the Inner House but it was upheld. Lord Kyllachy opined that:

> There is nothing in the title in the way of description which seems capable of being read as covering any larger area than that contained in the measurement given. There is nothing in the title here to which any larger extent of ground than is contained in the measurement can be ascribed. It is by measurement alone that any description is given.[19]

And Lord Stormonth-Darling concluded that:

> And by consequence while such measurement may not in strictness constitute what is called a bounding charter, it ne-

cessarily, at least, constitutes a limitation in gremio of the title – a limitation per se sufficient to exclude any ascription to the title of a possession substantially in excess of the measurement.[20]

This observation is worth noting carefully. It is saying plainly that, even where a title does not contain a description of the boundaries, a stated measurement (whilst in itself not bounding) may be taken to exclude the remedy of prescriptive possession beyond the stated extent. MacLeod was granted 1,600 acres of Minginish and Bracadale and, in 2000, was trying to sell 23,000 acres. Beyond an appeal to the United Kingdom Supreme Court, this 1905 decision is binding on all future cases. It is clear, therefore, that significant doubts exist over whether any prescriptive rights can be claimed at all beyond the 1,600 acres or so contained within MacLeod's title. If this is, indeed, the case, then MacLeod's title cannot rest on possession or prescription.

It is also worth pointing out that grants of land by the Crown are treated differently from grants from one private individual to another. In a case before Lord Cockburn in the Court of Session in 1846 concerning the foreshore at Portobello, where the Crown challenged a 30-foot encroachment on to the foreshore, the noble lord granted interdict against the encroachment and made the important observation that:

In considering all of this, we must never lose sight of the principle that royal grants must be strictly construed. 'Law,' says Lord Stowell, 'interprets the grants of the Crown by other rules than those that are applied to grants by individuals. Against an individual, it is presumed that he meant to convey a benefit with the utmost liberality that his words bear. It is indifferent to the public in which person an interest remains, whether the granter or the taker. With regard to the grant of the Sovereign it is far otherwise. It is not held by the Sovereign himself as private property, and no alienation shall be presumed except that which is clearly and indisputably expressed.[21]

So, where does all this get us? Royal grants must be strictly construed. In the absence of a bounding charter, a declared extent is nevertheless capable of excluding prescription to any area substantially in excess of that extent. MacLeod's only claim to secure ownership is through prescription which requires a *habile* title but there is little evidence of this and plenty to suggest that there is no prescription possible. And, yet, Mr Drummond Young drew on no facts or evidence of the extent of the 1611 title, no facts or evidence as to the *habile* nature of it and no evidence as to whether, in this particular case, prescription was even available as an option given the huge discrepancy between the stated acreage and the area marketed.

Suddenly, Mr MacLeod's title begins to look rather more questionable.

Meanwhile, as the debate raged in the media and politicians competed with each other to see who could be most outraged, the case was causing something of a stir in the Registers of Scotland. If the mountains were sold, the Keeper would have to make an important decision. The land would be registered in the new Land Register and, unlike the old Register of Sasines, this involves the Keeper validating the title and providing indemnity for any defects that may later appear. Naturally, the process involves a careful check of the title and, if the Keeper is not satisfied, she may withhold indemnity from all or part of the land to be registered. 'We will need to handle this with kid gloves' is how one exchange of emails referred to the impending registration. In the event, no application for registration was made as the Cuillin were never sold. We do not know, therefore, what the Keeper would have made of the claims of ownership and her position today remains that 'the sufficiency of the title of MacLeod of MacLeod to include the main part of the Cuillin will be addressed on receipt of any application for registration'.[22]

The reality of the Cuillin is this. MacLeod was never granted the land in 1611. In all likelihood, the land was part of a large common used, probably very infrequently, for hunting and perhaps some summer grazing. As the centuries passed, MacLeod appropriated the mountains possibly by a private mutual agreement with the neighbouring Mackinnons and Macdonalds. The Crown never asserted its interests and the law of prescription allowed MacLeod to claim ownership. MacLeod does not own the Cuillin. No amount of legal finessing can disguise the fact that his claim rests on the corrupt principle of prescription which, when examined according to the relevant legal principles, falls apart. If you or I had claimed ownership of a porcelain vase, a car or a sum of money in such a manner, we would be charged with reset.

So ingrained has become the belief born of centuries of the sort of clever legal manoeuvring outlined earlier in this book that few people in 2000 thought to stop and think about the fiction that was being perpetuated. The few who did (Alan Blackshaw, Brian Wilson, Alasdair Morrison, John Farquhar Munro, myself and others) were left gasping in astonishment at how the untroubled legal mind could find titles '*habile*' and confirm millions of pounds' worth of land on the basis of some receipts for woodcock shooting. The Crown Estate Commission treated the public, politicians and media with contempt and could not move fast enough to distance itself from any suggestion that their duties might require them to investigate thoroughly. The ease with which the Commissioner, Ian Grant, and his staff dismissed such suggestions when questions were raised over the legitimacy of an aristocrat's title stands in stark contrast to the enthusiasm with which they have pursued others such as the people of Selkirk when they had the temerity to suggest that the salmon fishings in the Ettrick belonged to them (see Chapter 14).

One final twist in this story, in fact, is that the CEC should never have been involved in the case in the first place. In 2000, its Head of Scottish Estates admitted that, in the absence of any good title in MacLeod's name, 'the Cuillin would be allodial land and would remain part of the hereditary possessions of the Sovereign in right of the Crown – that is, in my view, and subject to legal advice, it would be part of the Crown Estate.'[23] This is not actually the case and reflects a long history of the CEC's failure to recognise that it does not administer all Crown rights in Scotland. It only administers the 'property, rights and interests under the management of the Commissioners'.[24] Since the Cuillin has never been managed by the CEC, it does not form part of the Crown Estate.[25]

But, if the CEC does not administer the Crown rights in the Cuillin, who does? The answer is a quaintly named body based in

Edinburgh, the Queen's and Lord Treasurer's Remembrancer (QLTR). Part of the Crown Office and Procurator Fiscal Service, the QLTR administers three Crown rights – matters of bona vacantia, ultimus haeres and treasure trove. All three of these are based on the common law principle relating to ownerless goods – namely, that which belongs to no one becomes the king's. The Scotland Act vested these Crown property rights in Scottish Ministers and it is they, therefore, who hold title to the Cuillin – a fact that the CEC finally admitted five years later.[26]

In any event, John MacLeod was clearly relieved at the CEC's conclusions and issued a statement:

> I am glad that the rest of the world now knows beyond a doubt what has always been known on Skye, that the Black Cuillin are part of the heritage of MacLeod. The Crown Estate's investigation has shown my confidence in that thought to be well founded, and it is a great relief to hear that public statements made beforehand by others, which questioned my personal integrity in putting the Cuillins on the market, have been proved groundless.[27]

The Scottish Office, in their statement claimed that:

> This has been a worthwhile exercise. It is the first occasion on which such a claim of ownership has been subjected to this kind of scrutiny. The conclusions highlight the fact that any meaningful challenge to such claims of ownership will only come through legislative change rather than interpretation of existing Scots law.[28]

The message is clear. Eight centuries of property owners making the laws of property will not be overturned by the loyal servants of the Crown seeking legal opinion from a Queen's Counsel as to the validity of an aristocrat's title.

Had Wilson not been a minister in the Scotland Office, it is doubtful whether the Crown Estate Commission would ever have paid any attention to the concerns being raised. Scotland has suffered from too many lawyer politicians, such as Donald Dewar and Jim Wallace, whose instincts are caution, timorousness and inaction when faced with any challenge to the established order. Both could have, if they had wished, challenged MacLeod's title. They could have initiated a process which would have affirmed the land as Crown land. Instead, Jim Wallace meekly attended a meeting of the Scottish Landowners' Federation and told them proudly that he had no plans to interfere in the 'private ownership' of the Cuillin.

Had a successful challenge been mounted, what might have been the impact beyond the specific case of the Cuillin? Perhaps not a great deal since there must be few landholdings that rely on an original Crown grant. In most cases of long family ownership, successive generations have used any number of opportunities to grant the next one a title in a more definitive manner than previously, complete with a plan and with prescription to fill any gaps. But it would have been a wake-up call in terms of the process of land reform. It would certainly have caused much rummaging around in charter chests by the landed aristocracy to check their titles and who knows what might have emerged from that process once they attempted to register them under the far more stringent conditions of the new Land Register?

Simple Fraudulent Misrepresentation

Scotland's Crown lands

When Robert the Bruce defeated Edward II at Bannockburn in 1314, he achieved his goal of securing the Crown of Scotland for himself. Of course he had been crowned at Scone in 1306 but only after that sunny but bloody day in June could he exercise his power free of the threat from England. As monarch, Bruce was vested with ultimate power over the whole of the realm of Scotland. He had the power to grant and revoke feudal grants and had access to the Crown lands reserved for the king to provide him with an income. In the twelfth and thirteenth centuries, this land – the Crown demesne – was extensive and included a network of over a hundred royal hunting forests.

From 1200 to around 1650, the monarchs of Scotland were actively engaged in the granting of feudal charters. These could be revoked at will and were seldom heritable. After 1746, a whole raft of feudal powers and obligations was swept away, including heritable jurisdictions and military service obligations, and the security of vassals in their property was substantially increased. From then until 24 November 2004, the ultimate owner of all land in Scotland outwith the Northern Isles remained the Crown but with far fewer real powers. From 1746, the possessors of feudal charters were entitled to sell or grant their land to whomsoever they pleased without the need for the superior's consent and, from this time on, land began to assume the character of property as opposed to administrative and judicial powers.

Traditionally, the Crown lands of Scotland were administered by the Baron Court of the Exchequer based in Edinburgh to whom all the revenues were paid. In 1832, however, the administration of, and revenues from, most of Scotland's Crown lands moved south to London where they remain today. Since then, the revenues of the Crown Estate in Scotland have been paid to the Treasury in exchange for the Civil List and thus the monarch no longer has any role in the administration of Crown lands.

The Crown lands of Scotland consist of a range of property rights and interests that were retained by the Crown. It is a historic estate with many elements dating back to the very earliest days of the Scottish kingdom and consists of a wide range of disparate interests ranging from ancient possessions such as Edinburgh and Stirling Castles, rights to gold and silver, the seabed, foreshore, rights as ultimate heir to ownerless property, treasure trove, oysters and whales.[1] These different property rights are today administered by different government bodies.

First of all the property, rights and interests that went south in 1832 (and which have been managed by a range of bodies since then) were, by 1961, administered by the then Commissioners of Crown Lands. In 1961, the Crown Estates Act transferred the administration of these property rights to a new body, the Crown Estate Commission (CEC), often known today (incorrectly) as 'The Crown Estate'. It is 'charged on behalf of the Crown with the function of turning to account land and other property, rights and interests' and 'the property, rights and interests under the management of the Commissioners' is known as the Crown Estate.[2] These rights and interests include the seabed, most of the foreshore, agricultural estates, salmon fishings, rural agricultural estates, urban property and gold and silver.

Secondly, a number of other Crown property rights are administered by the Crown Office in Edinburgh by the Queen's and Lord Treasurer's Remembrancer, a position that is held by the Crown Agent and which is under the direction of Scottish Ministers. The QLTR administers three distinct Crown rights. The first is treasure trove, and all antiquities found in Scotland are claimed by QLTR. Failure to report and hand over treasure trove is an offence and one of the initiatives taken in recent years has been an agreement with eBay not to permit the marketing of antiquities found in Scotland that have not been reported. The second is bona vacantia – literally 'ownerless goods'. These consist of the assets of dissolved companies (land, buildings, cash and equipment), the assets of missing persons and lost or abandoned property. The amount of such property has increased in recent years thanks to increased computerisation in Companies House and the introduction of computerised land registration. All claims of land where no owner can be found must be reported to QLTR who can claim it for the Crown. The third right is that of ultimus haeres – literally 'ultimate heir'. When a person dies without leaving a will and has either no blood relatives or none who can be easily traced, their estate falls to the Crown.

Finally, Scotland's royal castles, palaces and abbeys – the ancient possessions of the Crown which include such iconic properties as Edinburgh Castle, Stirling Castle, Linlithgow Palace, Brechin Cathedral, Holyrood Park, Argyll's Lodging and Dunfermline Palace – are owned by Scottish Ministers. Twenty-six such properties were the subject of transfers from the CEC to Scottish Ministers in 1999 although it is unclear why this took place since they never formed part of the Crown Estate in the first place.[3]

At this point, it is worth drawing attention to the confusion that has been caused by the incorrect use of terminology by the CEC in recent years. The Crown Estate is, as is made clear in the legislation, an estate of property, rights and interests in Scotland which comprise the Crown lands of Scotland. It is a type of public property and has always been so. Ownership of this land and related property rights and interests is and always has been vested in the Crown in Scotland. The CEC, on the other hand, is a statutory body charged under the Crown Estate Act of 1961 with the administration and management of this estate and the associated revenues. The confusion arises in two forms. The first is that the CEC has rebranded itself as 'The Crown Estate' (the organisation) which is easily confused with 'the Crown Estate' (the property rights and interests which it administers). This confusion is then compounded by frequent statements from the CEC that it owns, for example, the seabed. Here are two instances:

As the owners of most of the seabed throughout the UK, we have amassed a wealth of experience and a bank of knowledge that I believe will prove crucial if the fledgling renewable industry in Scotland is to fully realise its potential.[4]

And:

In Scotland The Crown Estate own and manage around half of the foreshore and almost all of the seabed out to the 12 nautical mile territorial limit.[5]

These claims are incorrect, a fact which Roger Bright, the Chief Executive of the CEC, clarified in evidence to the Treasury Committee of the UK Parliament in March 2010, 'The Act gives us all the powers of ownership, although we are not owners in our own right.'[6] As we shall see, this confusion is at the heart of an important debate over the future of the Crown Estate in Scotland.

There is a long history of antagonism between communities – particularly coastal and marine communities – and the CEC. These have flared up from time to time in the form of legal actions over, for example, the rights of salmon farmers in Shetland, moorings in Rothesay and salmon fishing rights in the River Yarrow at Selkirk. The property rights and interests of the Crown Estate are a form of public land which are defined by Scots law, situated in Scotland but administered by what is, in effect, a commercial property company based in London. In many ways, it is no different from the many absentee landowners in Scotland with whom the only contact people have is a demand for rent.

Many such contemporary cases have pitted ordinary local people against the legal might of the CEC. In Selkirk, for example, a determined campaign waged by local people succeeded, after twelve years of wrangling, in having control of the fishings returned to the common good of the burgh as an ancient part of the burgh commons. But this campaign took twelve years of local voluntary effort to achieve a position where the historical truth was finally admitted by the CEC. One person close to the campaign characterised the CEC approach as including 'delay, attempts to split us up, simple denial of incontrovertible evidence, superciliousness, distortion, taking things out of context, abrogation of previous agreements and simple fraudulent misrepresentation'. This determination by the CEC to assert their interests stands in stark contrast, as pointed out earlier, to their attitude over the sale of the Cuillin.

In Rothesay, local boat owners have historically moored their boats in Kames Bay and other locations around the Island of Bute. In recent years, however, the CEC has demanded that all moorings be licensed with them and that anyone wishing to moor their boat on the seabed should obtain a £70 annual licence. Residents of Rothesay, however, argue that their royal burgh charter gives them the right to moor boats and that the CEC has no authority in the matter. After an attempt at legal action was dropped by Argyll and Bute Council, the Port Bannatyne Moorings Association was formed. It agreed to collect rents from boat owners at a 50 per cent reduced fee and hand these over to the CEC. Many boat owners, however, refused to join the association and to pay the licence fee. As a result, the Moorings Association refused to hand over their fees unless the CEC took action against unlicensed moorings. The CEC responded by raising an action in the Court of Session to affirm its right to rents from the seabed. In June 2010, the Court of Session found in favour of the CEC.[7]

In Stirling, the local community council has been campaigning to overturn an agreement struck between Stirling Council and the CEC whereby CEC are being paid to transfer the King's Park, an ancient possession of the Crown, to a new public trust. This was in contrast to the twenty-six other ancient possessions of the Crown in Scotland noted above that had been conveyed by the CEC to Scottish Ministers in 1999, immediately prior to the establishment of the Scottish Parliament for no consideration, including part of the ancient possessions of the Crown in Stirling – the King's Knot. The central issue here was that the CEC insisted on treating the King's Park as a 'rural estate' rather than as an ancient possession of the Crown which it clearly is, having been a royal hunting forest.[8]

It is quite notable how, in case after case, the CEC is willing to throw vast amounts of money in lawyers' fees at intimidating and challenging local communities in the highest court in the land over cases which communities have no realistic hope of defending. This stands in stark contrast to the one recent occasion when the CEC was asked to take action in the public interest – namely, to investigate the legitimacy of John MacLeod's claims to own the Cuillin. In this case, the CEC could not run away quickly enough.

As if to rub salt in the wounds, the Crown Estate Act forbids us from questioning anything that the CEC do.

> The validity of transactions entered into by the Commissioners shall not be called in question on any suggestion of their not having acted in accordance with the provisions of this Act regulating the exercise of their powers, or having otherwise acted in excess of their authority, nor shall any person dealing with the Commissioners be concerned to inquire as to the extent of their authority or the observance of any restriction on the exercise of their powers.[9]

In other words, shut up – it's none of your business.

In 2007, Highland Council, Highlands & Islands Enterprise (HIE), Comhairle nan Eilean Siar (the local authority for the Western Isles), Shetland Islands Council, Orkney Islands Council, Argyll and Bute Council, Moray Council and the Convention of Scottish Local Authorities published a report calling for a whole-sale review of the Crown Estate in Scotland.[10] In 2010, the Treasury Select Committee launched an inquiry into the administration and expenditure of the Crown Estate. In its final report, it recommended a full review of the powers and functions of the CEC, expressed concern over their monopoly position over the seabed and questioned the rationale for having so many bodies involved in the marine environment. The report devoted a chapter exclusively to Scotland in which it recommended better relations with the Scottish Government and highlighted the frustration felt by many organisations over how the CEC operates in the country. Above all, the report criticised the CEC for putting commercial interests ahead of its wider public interests.

Not surprisingly these worthy recommendations failed to generate much excitement. But what did spark a debate was the factual observation that the CEC does not own the seabed. To those who had taken an interest in this topic, the facts were clear. As the Scottish Law Commission noted in 2003:

The constitutional aspects of the Crown and the management of the Crown Estate are reserved matters. However, the Crown's prerogative functions are not reserved nor is property belonging to the Crown. The Crown's interest as proprietor of the fore-shore and sea bed and the public rights held by the Crown in trust for the public are therefore not reserved.[11]

The week before the report was published, the papers were full of reports on the new marine energy leases in the Pentland Firth. The SNP government was extolling the benefits to Scotland of developments which, in Alex Salmond's words, had the potential to make Scotland the Saudi Arabia of marine renewable energy. But, if the CEC did not own the seabed, why was it involved and why was all the revenue from this lucrative industry heading south to London leaving Scottish Ministers to meet all the costs of planning and regulation of the industry? For politicians, it was a wake-up call. For years, they had been seduced by the lobbying of the misnamed 'Crown Estate', read press releases of how it owned the seabed and been advised that all matters to do with the CEC were reserved and, well, it was all too complicated.

Following the SNP's 2011 Scottish election victory, Alex Salmond argued that he wished to see the powers of the CEC devolved to Scotland. Despite wide support for the proposal (including robust recommendations in an inquiry report from the House of Commons Scottish Affairs Committee), the UK Government refused to include such a measure in the Scotland Act 2012 which implemented the proposals of the Calman Commission.[12]

But this need not be the end of the matter. The Crown rights in the seabed and foreshore are a public asset and, as the Scottish Law Commission noted, are not reserved to Westminster. These marine rights could quite easily be administered by Scottish Ministers or local authorities by simply abolishing all Crown property rights in the foreshore and seabed and transferring them to Scottish Min-sters.

The CEC is playing a significant role in the development of marine renewable energy through its exercise of the property rights of the seabed but has no accountability to either the Scottish Parliament, Scottish Ministers or the local government in whose area the seabed is located. It is within the gift of the Scottish Parliament to rectify this situation and ensure that the development of marine renewables, an industry worth billions of pounds, provides the maximum economic benefits to some of the most fragile coastal communities in Scotland.

In November 2009, I sat on a panel discussing a film of the John McGrath play *The Cheviot, the Stag and the Black, Black Oil*. I had never seen the film version and it was interesting because it included fascinating material at the end about the oil industry. There were interviews with homeless couples, American oilmen and with that giant of north-east politics, the late Bob Middleton. This mini-documentary reinforced the central message of McGrath's play – namely that the people, having failed to wrest any meaningful control over land for centuries, were about to be taken for a ride again as big corporations took control of North Sea Oil. It was powerful stuff.

How ironic, then, that, just as the next marine bonanza opens up in the Pentland Firth and elsewhere around the Scottish coast, those calling the shots over Scotland's valuable public land are not Scottish Ministers accountable to Parliament but a group of unelected Crown Estate Commissioners in London whose attitude to Scotland is illustrated by the fact that their Scotland report is listed under 'regional inserts' to their annual report on the CEC website.[13]

Scotland's marine environment is public land and part of Scotland's Crown lands. It should be administered and managed in Scotland by democratically accountable local and national government. Given the resistance of the UK Treasury to any such move, however, it remains open to the Scottish Parliament to force the issue by abolishing all Crown property rights in Scotland and leaving the CEC with nothing left to manage.

From Lord Leverhulme to Lord Sewel

Community ownership of land

Community landownership and community buyouts have been the story of landownership in Scotland over the past fifteen years and have been the main reason land reform was such an issue for the incoming Labour government in 1997 and during the early years of the Scottish Parliament. There have been huge changes taking place, in particular in the north and west Highlands, and community buyouts have given long-term hope and confidence to many communities who badly needed it. This chapter tells the story of community landownership in Scotland, recent events and what it might mean for the future.

Although not regarded as ownership in the modern sense of the word, the earliest forms of land tenure were essentially communal. Such systems persist today in many parts of the world and, although they have been viewed with hostility by many development agencies in the past, they have proved remarkably resilient despite decades of neo-liberal reforms. It is interesting to note that the 2009 joint winner of the Nobel Prize in Economics was Professor Elinor Ostrom in recognition of her work on the governance of what academics call common-pool resources. These can include things like pasture, forests, water and fisheries. This is not the place to go into the extensive literature about commons – suffice to say that they have always played a significant role in resource management and, as efforts to regulate deforestation or overfishing by means of conventional markets show, they will continue to have an important role in the management of land.[1]

The first thing to say, therefore, is that, whilst community ownership has been fashionable over the past ten years, it is not new. As earlier chapters have demonstrated, Scotland has a long history of common land. If anything is new, it is private ownership. As discussed earlier, however, the concept of common land differs from community-owned land. In the former, it is the character of the particular land in question (irrespective of how the ownership is framed) that bestows upon it the quality of common land. Community ownership, on the other hand, is a quality of the owner, not the land, and reflects characteristics of the landowner.

In this sense at least, community landownership is relatively new. Its origins lie in the Chartist Land Plan, the National Land Company, the Commercial Land Company, the land leagues and the cooperative and labour movements of the nineteenth and early twentieth centuries.[2] They lie too in the failure of previous generations to resist the rise of an absolutist property regime as land became increasingly commodified as a financial and political investment. Elsewhere in Europe, after 1789, land became the basis of a peasant society with its attendant structure of credit banks, co-ops, small-scale landholding and local municipal commons. As a consequence, when radical opinion in Britain turned to the land question as it did in the latter part of the nineteenth century, it made little headway except at the economic margins in the Highlands and Islands. Lloyd George's budget of 1909 was the closest Britain came to full-scale land reform and it failed. Apart from state intervention in the form of the small landholders' legislation and by the Board of Agriculture and Forestry Commission, there was no thought given to community-based solutions for the best part of the twentieth century. There were two exceptions.

In 1918, Lord Leverhulme bought the Isle of Lewis and, a year later, Harris. At the time, the islands were in a state of civil unrest with numerous land raids by ex-soldiers recently returned from the First World War. They were demanding that Leverhulme's farms be broken up and rented out as smallholdings. Leverhulme at first refused to meet the crofters' demand to break up the farms but later changed his mind and, in a generous gesture, offered the whole of his Lewis and Harris estate to the inhabitants of the island as a gift. The crofting landward districts turned down his offer of outright ownership due to the very specific problems that crofters faced when they became sole proprietors under the then prevailing crofting legislation. However, the Stornoway Town Council voted to take up the opportunity and, in 1923, the Stornoway Trust was created by Deed of Trust passed in Parliament.[3]

So was born Scotland's first large-scale community-owned estate and it still exists to this day. The rest of Lewis and Harris was divided into lots and Leverhulme transferred them to a series of different companies each with names, such as Lewis Island Crofters Ltd, Uig Crofters Ltd and Pairc Crofters Ltd, that sounded rather as if they were community owned. Shares in these companies were then sold and the estates became private hunting estates.

The other significant and often forgotten initiative was in Glendale in the north of the Isle of Skye which was the home of the prominent land reformer John Macpherson who was one of a number of Glendale crofters who had fought for the land rights of crofters. He and his fellow tenants had argued that the 1886 Crofters Act did not go far enough as it left them as tenants of a landlord. Instead, he and the Glendale martyrs argued that they had a historic right to full ownership of the land. The Congested Districts Board acquired the 20,000-acre estate in 1904 and, in 1908, individual crofts were sold to the 147 crofting tenants who agreed to be part of the scheme. As part of the deal, they had to renounce their status as crofting tenants. The common grazings was transferred to the crofters collectively as common property held as pro indiviso shares attached to each of the owner-occupied crofts and was to be paid for in instalments over fifty years. As a result of this unique arrangement, crofters have been able to sell their individual holdings together with their share of the common grazings. It is not therefore community ownership in the normal sense of the term where there is one collective legal entity that owns the property.

For almost seventy years after the Stornoway Trust took over the Parish of Stornoway, practical moves to extend community ownership were virtually nonexistent although mention should be made of feuars' organisations across Scotland which had emerged as early as the eighteenth century and which continued to develop sporadically.

Historically, outwith burghs, there was no established legal entity that could hold title to land on behalf of the community apart from parish councils. If a landowner wished to gift or sell land to a village, it was not immediately apparent in whose name the property should be held. He would be happy enough granting individual feus to villagers but a vehicle was needed to hold title to land to be used by all the inhabitants. Such land would typically be a village green or amenity land in the village and was frequently associated with the new planned villages that emerged in Scotland in the eighteenth and nineteenth centuries. The answer was to be found in providing the feuars with a collective identity as Feuars' Committees. Land was gifted or sold to the committee of feuars of the village who collectively took title. Feuars' Committees exist in Peterhead, Fraserburgh, Denholm and Letham. An interesting description of the function of the Feuars' Committee is provided on the website of the Feuars of Letham:

> When George Dempster, Laird of Dunnichen Estate, created the village of Letham in 1788, he soon realised that some form of administration was needed as the village grew. He then founded the Feuars' Committee, a unique organisation with the villagers themselves electing and serving on the committee. Early roles included administering the common land and buildings, such as the bleaching ground, school and mill. The Feuars' Committee still exists today and the history pages demonstrate how, through the passage of time, the committee has changed whilst retaining its original aim. The aim of the Feuars' Committee was, and indeed still is, to manage for the 'common good'.[4]

In recent years, similar committees have been set up to take ownership of common land in and around housing developments. A good example is the Alnwickhill Proprietors' Association in Edinburgh.[5] More often, in the past, however, the institutional memory has faded and property which was granted to a Feuars' Committee has been absorbed into the property of the local authority or the perception has developed that they own it.

In the 1970s and 1980s, there were also some acquisitions of common grazings by crofters in Skye at places such as Geary. But, these and the small-scale urban initiatives aside, community ownership fell out of fashion until June 1992 when some crofters in Assynt noticed some small planes flying across their crofts at low level. One of them – a seaplane – landed on the beach and out stepped a titled family and an Iranian gentleman who had come, it transpired, with a view to buying the estate. They were promptly informed that since the whole estate was under crofting tenure there was little to be gained from owning it. Following a champagne picnic on the beach, the party got back into the plane which promptly got stuck in the soft sand. One of the crofters finally managed to extricate the aircraft and the strange visitors took off. Such bizarre goings-on are symptomatic of all that is wrong with land dealings in too many parts of Scotland. It served as a useful wake-up call to the Assynt crofters, though.

The North Lochinver Estate in Sutherland had been sold by Edmund Vestey in 1989 to a Swedish company for £1,080,000. In 1992, they went bust and the liquidator put the estate back on the market. At a meeting of the Assynt branch of the Scottish Crofters Union on 6 June 1992, it was resolved to do everything possible to resist the sale by the use of crofting legislation. Weeks later, at a public meeting, it was proposed that the crofters should attempt to put in a bid for the estate. Judged by some to be 'bordering on the lunatic',[6] it was an inspired idea which, for the time, was audacious in the extreme but which heralded a new era in landownership in Scotland (see Plate 4). The efforts of the crofters of Assynt caught the public imagination and they bought the estate in February 1993.[7]

What marked the Assynt case out, however, was that, for the first time since the late-nineteenth-century land agitations, ordinary people had organised a political campaign to take over land and had won. No government scheme or philanthropic landlord was involved. Assynt was a game changer – a taboo had been broken. It could no longer be assumed that land could be bought and sold without at least some active interest in the outcome by those whose lives would be affected by it. But the crofters of Assynt were also being influenced and, to some extent inspired, by events elsewhere. On the Isle of Eigg, there had been a growing antagonism between the landowner, Keith Schellenberg, and the residents. Further south, on the Isle of Gigha, eviction notices had been served on inhabitants by the liquidators of the bankrupt crook, Malcolm Potier. These events led to a debate in the House of Commons on 4 June 1992 initiated by the Argyll MP Ray Michie who expressed particular concern about the situation on Gigha.[8] Thus, by the time that the crofters in Assynt had launched their campaign to buy their land, the issue had become centre stage politically.[9] The government's response, however, was predictable. This is what Lord James Douglas-Hamilton had to say:

> I understand why the hon. Member is so interested in the circumstances of the sale, but it is essentially a private matter which I am sure will be resolved by those concerned. Highland land use has long been a particularly difficult and sensitive issue. Some appear to believe that all land in the Scottish Highlands should be subject to a more or less compulsory purchase regime, under which a corporate body such as Highlands and Islands Enterprise had powers of purchase or direction. That power would be available if a corporate body believed that the land was being misused or neglected. The Scottish Office is opposed to that approach. We believe that it is interventionist in character and that it assumes that corporate bodies are in a better position to determine how land should be used than those directly involved. We believe that land matters should be dealt with on the basis of consultation and mutual co-operation. We are confident that the future prosperity of the Highlands and Islands is best served by the removal of anti-competitive rules.[10]

From 1992, there was not only a growing awareness of the issue but an increasing resolve to do something about it. The question was what? In May 1992, John Major had won the UK general election somewhat against expectations and the Tories had gained a seat in Scotland. The mood in Scotland was particularly gloomy as a consequence. The travails on the west coast therefore served to reinforce a sense of powerlessness in the face of what many electors saw as an illegitimate government and engendered a sense of excitement that, even in the absence of any political assistance, ordinary people could make crazy dreams come true.

As the prospects for devolution were put on hold, it became evident that land reform was something that had to be tackled. Labour were, by now, committed to setting up a Scottish Parliament and attention began to be focused on what exactly might be done about dysfunctional landowners. Meanwhile crofters on the Borve and Annishader Estate on Skye followed Assynt and bought their 4,500-acre estate though, this time, membership was not, like

Assynt, restricted to crofting tenants but open to all residents within the boundaries of the estate. The island of Eigg remained in the headlines and so too did a succession of failed businessmen on the peninsula of Knoydart where the community were anxious about their future in an uncertain land market.

The lead-up to the 1997 election, therefore, was characterised by a focus on the land question that had been absent for eighty years. Even Michael Forsyth, the Conservative Secretary of State for Scotland took an interest. He could hardly avoid the debacle unfolding on the Isle of Eigg which had been sold to a mysterious German artist, Marlin Eckhard Maruma, for £1.6 million. Soon the islanders were in open revolt, the global media was covering the ongoing saga and the *Scotsman* newspaper covered each twist and turn extensively. Michael Forsyth was a right-wing free marketeer. One of the most divisive figures in Scottish politics, he was not an obvious land reformer but some of us at the time recognised a politician with some sympathy for the folk on Eigg who simply wanted to be allowed to take more control of their own affairs. In his short term in office as Secretary of State, he visited Eigg and Assynt and was impressed. Speaking to reporters after his helicopter trip to Eigg he was clearly moved:

> Frankly, I was rather appalled by the description [the residents] presented of an island whose infrastructure is crumbling and which is suffering from serious neglect. The present situation is pretty shocking and is not sustainable. The islanders have a right to a degree of security.[11]

Forsyth's interest became a small footnote in a bigger drama although he did secure the passing of the Transfer of Crofting Estates Act of 1997. This was as far as he was prepared to go, however, and he opposed proposals to extend the scope of the act to privately owned crofting estates. On 1 May 1997, Tony Blair and the Labour Party won a landslide election victory which ended eighteen years of Conservative government and brought a Scottish Parliament a step closer. It was a long-standing opponent of devolution, Brian Wilson, who made the next historic move in securing the agreement of Highlands and Islands Enterprise to set up a Community Land Unit (CLU).[12]

The CLU provided both technical assistance and financial support to any community in the HIE area that wished to explore the possibilities of community ownership. With a dedicated staff and a budget of millions it was soon active in encouraging and facilitating a growing number of community buyouts across the HIE area. By 2000, there were 144,000 acres of land in community ownership. In the ten years that followed, this increased to 420,000, almost a threefold increase. The CLU was a critical initiative but, on its own, could not provide the impetus for this kind of dramatic expansion. The key was not the CLU and it was not the land reform legislation, which was still four years away. The key was money. If communities were to acquire large tracts of land or even modest tracts of land, they would need the funds to do so. On 25 January 2000, Brian Wilson announced the establishment of the Scottish Land Fund with a budget of £10.78 million. Not to be confused with another body with the same initials, the SLF was set up in February 2001 and ran for five years before being wound up in July 2006. The fund was part of the new fifth lottery body set up by Labour, the New Opportunities Fund, and had a dedicated committee based in Scotland that made all decisions on funding. (I was a member.) On a day-to-day basis the fund was administered by HIE.

The SLF dealt with 739 enquiries over the life of the programme and 316 applications for funding. In the five years of its operation between 2001 and 2006, the SLF awarded 250 grants totalling £13.9 million to 188 community groups in rural Scotland to acquire, develop and manage land. It was the SLF and the funds it made available that drove the expansion in community ownership.[13] The SLF was replaced by the Growing Community Assets fund which, in its first year funded seventy-four projects to the tune of over £23 million, including £2.25 million towards the acquisition of the South Uist estate. This fund closed for applications in August 2008 but re-opened on 30 June 2010.

It has been a popular misconception that community buyouts have been supported with 'public' money or with 'taxpayers'' money. This has been a particular refrain of the critics of community ownership. But it should be pointed out that the bulk of the funding for acquiring land has been from the Scottish Land Fund which is the proceeds of the sale of lottery tickets. If people don't like what the lottery spends its money on, they are under no obligation to buy a lottery ticket – I never have.

The other confusion which arose in the early days of the SLF and which is linked to the above was the idea that the community right to buy (introduced in the 2003 Land Reform Act) was linked to the Scottish Land Fund when, in fact, they were two distinct processes. This confusion came to a head over the purchase of the Newtonhill woods on the outskirts of Inverness. With much fanfare and a ministerial visit, the community body was given the right to buy and made an application to the Scottish Land Fund which promptly turned it down, thus demonstrating its independence.

In June 2012, a new Scottish Land Fund was established with £6 million of Scottish Government funding to run for three years. Since this is financed by taxpayers' money rather than lottery funds, this new tranche of cash will be subject to rather greater scrutiny and may well become rather more politicised than the previous lottery-run programme.

Community landownership in Scotland, 2012

Property	Owner	Acres	Date of Acquisition
South Uist Estate	Stòras Uibhist Ltd	93,000	2006
Stornoway Estate	Stornoway Trust	69,400	1923
North Harris Estate	North Harris Trust Ltd	62,500	2006
Galson Estate	Urras Oighreachd Ghabsainn Ltd	48,380	2007
Glencanisp and Drumrunie Estates	Assynt Foundation Ltd	44,578	2005
North Assynt Estate	Assynt Crofters' Trust Ltd	20,570	1993
Knoydart Estate	Knoydart Foundation Ltd	16,771	1999

Community landownership in Scotland, 2012—contd

Property	Owner	Acres	Date of Acquisition
West Harris Estate	West Harris Crofting Trust Ltd	16,255	2010
Melness	Melness Crofters' Estate Ltd	12,522	1994
Forest of Birse	Birse Community Trust Ltd	9,000	1999
Eigg	Isle of Eigg Heritage Trust Ltd	7,263	1997
Borve and Annishader Estate	Borve and Annishader Township Ltd	4,502	1993
Gigha	The Isle of Gigha Heritage Trust Ltd	3,694	2002
Little Assynt Estate	Culag Community Woodland Trust	2,940	2000
Bhaltos	Bhaltos Community Trust Ltd	1,800	1999
West Ardhu and Langaull	North West Mull Community Woodland Company Ltd	1,708	2006
Lochbay Grazings	Trustees for Common Grazings Committee for Lochbay Township	1,566	1980
Abriachan	Abriachan Forest Trust Ltd	1,322	1998
Dùn Coillich	Highland Perthshire Communities Land Trust Ltd	1,100	2002
Ardmore Township	Clerk and Members of Common Grazing Committee for Ardmore Township	1,003	1980

Table 9: this table lists all the community landownership
bodies owning property of over 1,000 acres in extent

Source: Author's own data

Around 425,000 acres of land across Scotland are now owned by
community organisations of one sort or another (see Table 9). This
represents the single most significant change in landownership in

Scotland although it is geographically restricted to the Highlands and Islands. Remarkably, less than 1 per cent of all community-owned land is located outwith this region. The reasons for the difference include the relatively larger scale pattern of landowner-ship in the Highlands and Islands, the economic vulnerability of many communities to absentee landlordism, the prevalence of crofting tenure and the strong sense of historical grievance at the impact of the Highland Clearances. In practical terms, the availability of technical and financial assistance through the CLU has been vital and is unavailable outwith the HIE area.

From being a novel and almost revolutionary idea in the early 1990s when the crofters of Assynt and islanders on Eigg were struggling to wrest control of the land they lived on from the dead hand of absentee landlordism, community ownership is now a mainstream concept although it remains firmly a predominantly rural phenomenon and one still rooted in the north and west.[14]

Can community ownership be sustainable? Despite some routine difficulties, the story to date is of success. In Gigha, Knoydart, Eigg and other places, communities are regenerating, school rolls are increasing, housing stock is being upgraded and expanded, popula-tion is on the increase and, according to one islander on Eigg, 'the spectre of full employment' has returned. In that sense, the project has been an undoubted success. But it is also clear, particularly in the aftermath of the crisis in public finances that further expansion cannot rely on generous grants from the lottery or even from the limited public funds available from the new Scottish Land Fund established in 2012. In Chapter 30, I make a suggestion as to how this problem might be solved but meanwhile, in 2012, there is a distinct sense that the community ownership bandwagon has come to a halt as the funding wheels have ground to a halt.

Is community ownership actually the solution in many cases? I am convinced that it is but there is a danger that community ownership is seen as *the* answer when actually it is just one of a number of answers. In 1999, I observed that:

In the widely-publicised cases of Eigg and Knoydart, the con-cerns of the community were focussed on the uncertainty with

which they contemplated a future in which anyone from anywhere could buy the whole estate. The factors which led to the
situation in which Eigg and Knoydart found themselves were:

- an unregulated market in land
- the scale of the holding on offer (together with the Edwardian and Victorian infrastructure)
- the lack of obligations on any prospective purchaser.

It was against this background that the communities concerned concluded that the only way forward lay in taking the
estates into community ownership in partnership with others.
That was the appropriate response in a situation where they were
powerless to do anything else. Communities bought the land
because of the failure of the system to provide anything other
than an international speculators' lottery.

Proposals to entrench the community right to buy as a
legislative right when land comes to be sold, whilst they may
provide the right solution in some circumstances, do therefore
implicitly treat the symptoms of the problem rather than the
circumstances which brought the situation about. If such large
estates as Eigg and Knoydart did not exist, if those who owned
them were many in number and were resident, indigenous folk,
the problem would never have arisen in the first place.

In other words if measures are taken to secure a smaller-scale
pattern of landownership involving resident landowners in a
market which is regulated (even modestly) then the kinds of
crisis which paralysed Eigg and Knoydart for so many years
would simply never have emerged.

The community right to buy is a proposal born out of an
acceptance of the current division of land and the unregulated
market. It is a proposal which demands a lot of communities
dissatisfied with the status quo. It is a measure which treats the
symptoms of the problem rather than its underlying causes.[15]

And therein lies a problem for many community-owned estates
today. If the most appropriate solution is a diversity of forms of
tenure, is the fact that Knoydart or Gigha or South Uist are now
still owned by one large-scale landowner (albeit under community

control) any better than what it replaced? What happens now if a young family want to purchase a plot of land for a house or a cooperative business wants to buy land for a factory or an investor wants to acquire some mineral rights? In many cases, answers are being found to these questions but it has not always been easy. Certainly community ownership must not simply perpetuate ad infinitum large-scale landownership. It must be responsive to the need to diversify landholdings and allow the community to grow.

Finally, what is community ownership? So-called community ownership today, in fact, comprises a number of distinct models of ownership, not all of which are strictly community. The earliest acquisitions by Assynt, Eigg and Knoydart stand out as different.

The Assynt Crofters' Trust is a company not a trust and membership is restricted to crofting tenants on the estate. Other members of the community have no say in its activities.

The Isle of Eigg Heritage Trust owns the Isle of Eigg and is a company limited by guarantee with no share capital. It has three members, namely the Isle of Eigg Residents' Association, Highland Council and the Scottish Wildlife Trust. The Residents' Association has four seats on the Board of Directors, with the Council and the Trust having two each. Collectively they appoint a ninth member, the independent Chair. The resident community on Eigg therefore exercises direct influence in the Trust through their Residents' Association.

The Knoydart Foundation is also a company limited by guarantee and has five members – namely, the Knoydart Community Association, Highland Council, the Chris Brasher Trust, the John Muir Trust and the neighbouring Kilchoan Estate.

Ironically, because of the narrow and inflexible definition of community contained in the Land Reform Act, none of these buyouts would have been able to take advantage of it, had the legislation been in place at the time. In recent years, more communities have adopted a more inclusive structure with membership of the company open to all adult residents who live on or adjacent to the estate. However, the new legislation also imposes something of a straitjacket on community bodies. Whereas before they could have constituted themselves as a cooperative or a trust or a partnership, now they are obliged to follow the tightly defined structure of the Land Reform Act. In time, such a structure may prove not to meet the needs of every community and yet there is no flexibility to change.

The Highland historian, James Hunter, has documented the emergence, growth and flourishing of Scotland's community land movement in a recent book, *From the Low Tide of the Sea to the Highest Mountain Tops.* He concludes the work with this observation: 'Today, you can stand on any one of more that 500,000 acres in the Highlands and Islands and, on asking some local person who owns that acre, get the answer, "Us." In years to come, this question needs to produce that same response when it is posed not on any one of 500,000 acres but on any one of millions.'[16]

Community ownership has transformed the future of the western Highlands. It has been a revolutionary movement supported and guided by some very talented individuals and has now formed a representative body, Community Land Scotland to promote and expand community landownership. It will endure but the challenge is not only for it to flourish and expand, it is to become an accepted way of doing things outside its north and west heartlands. Only when it becomes as normal in Dundee or Possil as it is in Dunvegan or Pairc can it truly be said to have represented a paradigm shift.

Those Who for Our Sake Went Down to the Dark River

The rise of the heritage landowner

The not-for-profit sector encompasses a diverse range of organisations concerned with social, community, recreational and environmental goals. The term does not imply that such organisations don't make a profit – it simply reflects the fact that any surpluses that are made cannot be distributed to members as they would be in a conventional shareholding structure. Instead, they have to be used to further the aims of the organisation. The history of that part of the sector concerned with community has been covered in the previous chapter and here I want to take a particular look at the emergence of environmental, heritage and recreational organisations as players in Scottish landownership – I call them the heritage landowners.[1]

The emergence of heritage landowners is closely associated with the wider land reform movement of the late nineteenth century and with the question of access in particular. Increasing numbers of people were heading to the hills for recreation but were denied access to huge swathes of the countryside managed as sporting estates. This created a powerful grievance among the public and, in the walking and climbing clubs that were beginning to form, there emerged some prominent advocates of the freedom to roam who allied themselves with prominent figures from the Land League to campaign for the abolition of the oppressive trespass and game laws. James Bryce was the Liberal MP for Aberdeen South and a determined supporter of access to the hills. In 1884 he introduced the Access to Mountains (Scotland) Bill which was reintroduced every year until 1914, failing on every attempt. In 1892, he summarised the case:

> All I ask to-night is to bring forward the grievance and suffering caused to the people of Scotland, and in a lesser degree to the people of other parts of the United Kingdom, by their exclusion from their right to enjoy the scenery of their own country, and to seek healthy recreation and exercise on their own mountains and moors. The grievance, no doubt, is greatest in Scotland. It is not too much to say that all over the Highlands the hills are completely closed. The Counties of Ross and Inverness are half occupied by deer forests, and I think there are ten counties altogether in which deer forests exist. They cover large portions of the Counties of Sutherland, Argyll, and Perth, and extend into several other counties.

He cited the American millionaire:

> who has joined deer forest to deer forest, and formed a sort of enclave of wilderness in the Counties of Ross and Inverness, stretching almost from sea to sea for nearly 40 miles. Along the borders of this wilderness an army or cordon of ghillies is stationed to carry out the orders of the proprietor, and so strictly are these orders carried out that when the pet lamb of a tenant strayed within the boundary the animal was seized, and proceedings were taken against the tenant.

And concluded that:

> [t]he time has come when we must assert what we believe to be the paramount rights of the nation. If anyone says that is dangerous to the rights of property, I will answer by saying that the real danger comes from the selfish and reckless, and even perverse and spiteful, use of the rights which the law has allowed. If there is any danger to property, it is because persons have declined to recognise the reasonable and equitable limitations within which those rights ought to be exercised.[2]

Despite the failure of these bills, outdoor recreation continued to grow in popularity. Amenity groups were set up and campaigns were launched to establish national parks and, in 1931, The National Trust for Scotland was established. Its genesis lay two years earlier in 1929 when the 500-acre Loch Dee estate in Galloway was offered to one of these amenity groups, the Association for the Protection of Rural Scotland which had been established in 1926. The Association was not constituted to own land and thus declined the offer. The possibility then emerged that it might be taken on by The National Trust which raised such hackles in Scotland that a separate body, The National Trust for Places of Historical Interest or Natural Beauty in Scotland (NTS), was established by Act of Parliament on 1 May 1931. Despite the fact that the trust was dominated by the aristocracy, the outdoors movement welcomed its formation and saw it as a vehicle for the fulfilment of their ambitions. They did not have to wait long. In 1935, Lord Strathcona put the Glencoe hunting estate in Argyll up for sale. For the mountaineers and walkers this was their Shangri-La and Arthur Russell, Percy Unna and Logan Aikman, who were active members of the Scottish Mountaineering Club and the NTS, set about raising the funds to acquire the estate. They were successful and, two years later, added the Dalness estate. As a forerunner of things to come, they then set up the Mountainous Country Fund in the NTS to which mountaineers enthusiastically donated money and which, over the next thirty years, became the main vehicle for the acquisition of another 60,000 acres of mountainous land from Arran to Torridon.

Sir Nicholas Soames' Three-Tier Mahogany Buffet

Land and heritage tax exemptions

In 1998, the comedian Mark Thomas cleverly drew attention to the existence of the little-known Conditional Tax Exemption Incentive. This is an arrangement whereby owners of buildings, land and artefacts of outstanding cultural or scientific value, can be exempted from inheritance tax if the new owner agrees to look after it, allows the public access to it and, if a painting or similar moveable object, undertakes to keep it in the UK.[3] Until 1998, the system of public access was somewhat compromised by the public not being able to know what artefacts were subject to the scheme and in his inimitable style, Thomas and friends provided hours of good telly in their attempts to see Sir Evelyn De Rothschild's Gainsborough and Sir Nicholas Soames' 'three-tier mahogany buffet with partially-reeded slender ballister upright supports'. As a result of the publicity, Gordon Brown announced in the1998 Budget that the rules would be tightened up and that a new website would provide details of the various assets.

There are currently sixty-six properties across Scotland that have Conditional Tax Exemption. The scheme was designed to secure public benefits in terms of access and conservation of land and buildings. In many cases, there are obvious and tangible benefits. On the Island of Ulva, off Mull, a host of advice, assistance and facilities is provided for visitors which might not otherwise be made available. Robert Balfour, a past convenor of the Scottish Landowners' Federation, owns a valuable moss in Fife and undertook to conserve it and maintain a public footpath in exchange for a modest tax break of a few thousand pounds when he inherited the estate in 1986.

Others, however appear to be of limited value. The undertakings by the owners of the Altyre Estate, for example, allow for 'pre-arranged access for groups arranged by recognised wildlife organisations for up to 25 days each year', over 2,500 acres, and access is also available for scientific work 'save as might be prejudicial to the natural heritage interest'.[4]

In return for the tax exemption, the Earl of Airlie allows the public to walk in his woods all year round and to follow the 'Policies Walk' from 2–5 April, 3 May, 17 May–6 June, 2 August and 30 August between 10 a.m. and 3 p.m. We are informed by Her Majesty's Revenue and Customs that, during 2010, John Grant of Rothiemurchus kindly allows access to the Rothiemurchus section of the Cairngorms National Nature Reserve, including the Munro, Braeriach, 'throughout the year by rights of way and permissive paths'.[5]

John Christie of Lochdochart Estate is equally obliging. He allows the general public to:

> take access through the designated lands, following estate roads and tracks on low ground and enclosed areas, for the purpose of hill-walking on the higher ground at all reasonable times. In particular access through the designated lands will always be available to walkers and climbers seeking to climb Ben Challum and Beinn nan Imirean during daylight hours.[6]

Mr James Priestly of Headbourne Worthy, near Winchester, owns the Invergeldie Estate in Perthshire and, bizarrely, in return for not having to pay inheritance tax, he has agreed 'not to encourage public access' to the south-west slopes of Ben Chonzie above Comrie. Over the remaining exempt land, he undertakes to 'permit the public to wander at will on open hill and moor, except that during the period from 12 August to 30 September each year, access to land away from public rights of way and from estate tracks may not be granted'.[7]

Charles Fforde on Arran has agreed to 'take the steps to secure reasonable access to the public and to publicise that access as outlined on the map'.[8]

This is all most generous and might even be of some value to the public were it not for the fact that, on 25 February 2003, the Queen gave royal assent to the Land Reform (Scotland) Act, Part I of which provides the public with responsible access over virtually all of Scotland. What might once have been a concession negotiated in return for a tax break is now a statutory right. Why then do so many landowners continue to avoid paying tax in exchange for letting us walk on their land? Why, indeed, is one landowner effectively being paid *not* to encourage public access?

Scottish Natural Heritage (SNH) is the adviser to Her Majesty's Revenue and Customs on the scheme in Scotland. Why has it not advised the taxman that the provision of access can no longer be regarded as a legitimate undertaking in order to avoid paying inheritance tax? According to SNH, all undertakings must contain provisions for public access to meet the requirements of the Capital Transfer Act 1984 and there are no cases in Scotland where conditional exemption has been given solely to secure public access to land.[9] But this still begs the question why the 1984 act has not been amended to take account of the new access arrangements in Scotland. Why should anyone be exempt from paying tax for allowing the public to do what they have every legal right to do even if it is only in partial fulfilment of conditional exemption undertakings?

Meanwhile, I'm a bit of a fan of the paintings of Alessandro Turchi, l'Orbetto, and discovered that there is a painting attributed to his school located somewhere in the Scottish Borders for which the owner is granted an exemption. Not only this but there are another 463 paintings, books and pieces of furniture available for the public to view. I have no idea where all these treasures are but they are available for public viewing on twenty-five weekdays per year from 17 May to 18 June. This is a bit of a problem if you are working, as most of the population are, and would have to take a day's holiday. Still, hey ho, a helpful lady from the National Galleries of Scotland told me that they run bus tours to see the collection for £12 a head. I think I shall go on this summer mystery tour.

The early success of the NTS in acquiring mountain property was due to the increasing frustrations of hill users over the issue of access and the continuing absence of any measures such as national parks to provide any effective protection to scenic landscapes. It also demonstrated that, where government failed to act by way of intervening in the land market to secure public benefits, ordinary people could instead. This then established the rationale for future interventions by conservation bodies and explains why their expansion was so dramatic in the 1980s and 90s.

Some of the concerns of the growing outdoors movement were addressed in the immediate aftermath of the Second World War with the introduction of town and country planning and the establishment of national parks (though landowning influence stopped these being established in Scotland). One interesting development, which was a forerunner of things to come, was the establishment of the National Land Fund by the Labour chancellor, Hugh Dalton in 1946.

Concluding his historic Budget speech, he began with a gentle gibe at Winston Churchill:

> Hugh Dalton: Finally, I have a word to say about the land . . . In 1909, 37 years ago, David Lloyd George introduced a famous Budget. Liberals in those days sang the 'Land Song' – 'God gave the land to the people'. I think that the right hon. Member for Woodford used to sing that song.
>
> Mr. Churchill: I shall sing it again.
>
> Mr. Dalton Then I hope for the right hon. Gentleman's full support in the proposals I am about to make. The strains of that song have long since died away. But much land has passed, since then, from private into public ownership and 't is the declared policy of the Labour Party that much more should so pass, and that the principle of the public ownership of land should be progressively applied.

He then went on to announce the establishment of a £50-million fund – to be called the National Land Fund – to be used to acquire land across the UK.

> The Fund might well be used to help such bodies as The National Trust, the Youth Hostels Association, the Ramblers' Associations and many other such societies, whose purpose is not to make profit but to open the country to the people and to facilitate recreation, open air sport, and physical fitness . . . There is still a wonderful, incomparable beauty in Britain in the sunshine on the hills, the mist adrift across the moors, the wind on the downs, the deep peace of the woodlands, the wash of the waves against the white, unconquerable cliffs which Hitler never scaled. There are beauty and history in all these places. It is surely fitting, in this proud moment of our history, when we are

celebrating victory and deliverance from overwhelming evils and horrors, that we should make through this fund a thankoffering (*sic*) for victory, and a war memorial which, in the judgment of many, is better than any work of art in stone or bronze. I should like to think that through this Fund we shall dedicate some of the loveliest parts of this land to the memory of those who died in order that we might live in freedom, those who for our sake went down to the dark river, those for whom already 'the trumpets have sounded on the other side'. Thus let this land of ours be dedicated to the memory of our dead, and to the use and enjoyment of the living for ever.[10]

The fund was used in Scotland to acquire the Rowardennan Estate on Loch Lomond but little else. By the 1950s, the fund's purpose had been emasculated by the Conservative government and, in 1957, the then Chancellor, Peter Thorneycroft, raided £50 million from its £60 million balance. It then fell into abeyance until 1977 when, following a critical report by the Commons Expenditure Committee, its remaining assets were given to the National Heritage Memorial Fund established in 1980. It has continued to fund the acquisition of land but not for the purposes Dalton envisaged. Instead, the principal beneficiaries have been environmental bodies such as the RSPB, the John Muir Trust and the NTS.[11]

In the three decades after the war, very little land was acquired by heritage bodies despite the existence of the National Land Fund. It was not until the early 1980s that the modern pattern of heritage ownership began to take shape. In February 1986, the RSPB bought 5,300 acres of Upper Glen Avon in the Cairngorms. This marked a change in emphasis for the RSPB and for conservation landholding policy. Since 1958, the RSPB had been involved at Loch Garten with Operation Osprey and it bought 1,500 acres of land there in 1975. The RSPB owned other land but in small parcels, usually in critical areas for bird breeding. The purchase of Upper Glen Avon signalled a new interest in the conservation management of extensive habitats and, at the time, this was the largest acquisition of land by a conservation body since the NTS bought Ben Lawers in 1950. It marked the beginning of

the recent expansion in conservation ownership.[12] Shortly after-
wards, in 1988, the bird charity acquired the 21,000-acre Forest
Lodge Estate which now forms part of the Abernethy Forest
Reserve. At the time, according to the RSPB, this was the largest
single area owned by a voluntary conservation body anywhere in
Europe.

The National Heritage Memorial Fund contributed £500,000 to
the acquisition and has since spent almost £12 million in support of
land acquisition in Scotland, of which £11 million was for the
purchase of Hopetoun House and Dumfries House and £900,000
was for acquisitions by the RSPB of land at Loch Garten,
Abernethy, Wood of Cree, North Hoy and Loch Gruinart, by
the NTS at Loch Lomond and by the John Muir Trust (JMT) on
Knoydart. This latter body was formed in 1983 with a focus on
wild land and stimulated largely by dissatisfaction with the management record of the NTS on its mountainous properties.

During the 1980s and 90s, amid growing concerns about nature
conservation and amenity in key parts of the country, a wider range
of voluntary bodies including the Royal Society for the Protection
of Birds, the Scottish Wildlife Trust and the John Muir Trust
began acquiring ever larger areas of land. Some of these acquisitions involved hunting estates, the most prominent among them
being the 30,000-hectare Mar Lodge Estate in the Cairngorms.
This controversial acquisition helped to re-ignite a debate about
landownership in Scotland. Were such areas of national and
international conservation and recreational importance adequately
safeguarded by the unregulated international market in land? The
answer, according to the voluntary bodies, was patently no but, not
being keen to be drawn into a political debate about landownership, they instead adopted a strategy of acquiring as much of this
land as was possible. Soon other prominent hunting estates, such as
Glenfeshie, came on the market. This was followed by more public
debate but, in this case, no successful intervention.

The story of Glenfeshie is a microcosm of the concerns that were
raised more widely about the failure to protect land of high
conservation value. The existing mechanisms of Sites of Special
Scientific Interest were failing as they simply prevented obvious
damage – a list of so-called potentially damaging operations was

cited for each one. There was no obligation on the owner to manage such areas to the standard needed to conserve and enhance the often-degraded environment.

Glenfeshie had been offered to the Nature Conservancy Council in 1967 for £100,000. Sensibly, they decided to accept the offer but it was then blocked by a senior civil servant from the Scottish Office called George Pottinger who claimed that the NCC already owned too much land in the Cairngorms. Pottinger was later jailed for corruption in a scandal involving the architect John Poulson. The estate was bought by Lord Dulverton for £105,000. In 1988, it was sold to a Wiltshire businessman, whose company was registered in the Cayman Islands, for £2.6 million. Again the NCC were blocked from purchasing it by the government. In 1994, the estate was on the market again for £4–5 million and was bought by a secretive charity, Will Woodlands Ltd, for £4.7 million. By now, there was widespread concern over the environmental degradation and the decline in the native Caledonian pinewoods. Yet again, the government vetoed any involvement by, what was by this time, Scottish Natural Heritage. In 1998, it was sold for £6 million to a Danish businessman and then finally, in 2001 to another Danish businessman, Flemming Skouboe, for £8.5 million. He remains the current owner. All told, for an estate which was, until recently, in environmental decline, it yielded a handsome 11.6 per cent tax-free return in capital growth – so much for loss-making sporting estates.

Understandably, environmental organisations stood on the sidelines gasping in amazement at the continued failure to afford proper protection to this large part of the Cairngorms National Nature Reserve which could have been acquired in 1967, sparing half a century of conflict and a level of public subsidy probably well in excess of that sum. It was these kinds of cases that convinced organisations such as the RSPB and the JMT that it was probably best if they took a more proactive role to acquire land if they could.[13]

In 1994, the Heritage Lottery Fund was established to distribute income from the National Lottery and this gave a further boost to land acquisition by voluntary bodies. Among its most prominent grants were the £10.5 million given to assist in the acquisition of the Mar Lodge Estate in the Cairngorms and the £1.4 million towards the acquisition of Glen Finglas by the Woodland Trust. In 1996, I highlighted the fact that conservation bodies owned over 330,000 acres of Scotland, that, in the period 1980 to 1995, this area had grown by 197,500 acres and that, if this rate of increase continued, they would own 10 per cent of Scotland by 2010. Not surprisingly, it has not turned out that way. The rate of acquisition has slowed down although the total area under the ownership of heritage groups is now over 480,000 acres and their key landholdings are outlined in Table 10.

Heritage landownership in Scotland, 2012

Organisation	Acreage
The National Trust for Scotland	192,000
Royal Society for the Protection of Birds	125,858
John Muir Trust Ltd	59,938
The Scottish Wildlife Trust Ltd	28,283
The Woodland Trust Ltd	20,995
Clan Donald Lands Trust	19,459
The Church of Scotland	14,841
Trees for Life Ltd	9,785
The Borders Forest Trust Ltd	3,168
Plantlife International – The Wild-Plant Conservation Charity Ltd	3,058
RSFS Forest Trust Co. Ltd	3,014
The Hebridean Trust Ltd	340
Total	480,739

Table 10

Source: Author's own data

Who is best qualified to look after Scotland's wealth of fine landscapes and internationally important wildlife sites? The voluntary conservation bodies have taken it upon themselves to do the job that government has failed to do. In doing so, however, they have unwittingly become caught up in a wider debate. Not only is such expansion a tacit admission of failure on the part of government, it is also an implicit criticism of the system of private property rights which has contributed to the threats to wildlife, scenery and wild land in the first place.

But, by becoming landowners in their own right, conservation groups have, arguably, merely perpetuated the very system they seek to cure. The principal reason for this growing acquisitiveness is that these organisations take the view that the most valuable land for birds or wild land or whatever it is that they exist to protect is vulnerable if left exposed to the open private market in land. History bears them out on this point as we shall see but it puts such bodies in an awkward position. For years, apologists for land-owning interests have denied that the ownership of land confers power. But conservations groups deploy that same power to secure the protection of the environment – power that, by extension, has been responsible for much of the environmental degradation which has taken place in these areas. So conservation groups have ended up exploiting the very power which they have recognised as lying at the root of the problem.

Matters came to something of a head in 2000 with the proposed sale of the Cuillin followed shortly afterwards by the purchase of Ben Nevis by the John Muir Trust. How long could the gravy train last? Was it appropriate that such bodies should go on buying vast tracts of land? Some, such as the Woodland Trust, are not even under any form of democratic control by their members. Conservation groups are now immensely powerful players in certain parts of the country – for example, in Sutherland and Caithness (RSPB), the Cairngorms (RSPB) and on Skye (JMT).

Most are sensitive to this situation and have put in place arrangements to involve local communities in the management of their estates. Others, such as the Scottish Wildlife Trust on Eigg, are involved in sharing power in the ownership of land. As to the future, most organisations appear to be as acquisitive as they have ever been and little thought has been given to what kind of alternative strategies might be available to achieve the same ends. The large organisations are now significant businesses with a large workforce and it is naive to think that they are going to simply wind down if and when it is judged that birds or wild land enjoy proper protection. On the contrary, conservation groups have a vision of how they would like things to be and owning land allows them to put this into practice. In 1997, I wrote the following and don't have any reason to alter my view thirteen years later:

> We need to make that power more accountable to the wider public interest through a fundamental review of property rights. We need to distribute that power more widely and we need to integrate conservation with wider land use policies. We need to spread the ownership of land use problems and in so doing generate more lasting solutions. Conservation should be seen as an engine of economic and cultural regeneration in the remoter parts of this country and not something to be run by outside elites. Unless one wants the country to be run by a benign ecological dictatorship, then local interests must be given more responsibility, authority and accountability over land use.[14]

Tartanry, Royalty and Balmorality

The rise of the hunting estate

During the early 1980s, I worked as a stalker's ghillie on a hunting estate in Angus (see Plate 10). At the time, I considered such places and practices perfectly normal but, as a result of the myriad of rich experiences gained over those years, I now see why, in the words of Glasgow geographer Hayden Lorimer, 'racial, patriarchal, colonial and class structures were crucial determinants in the bounding and politicising of Highland nature'.[1] The work was straightforward but the cultural practices were out of the Edwardian period. Where you stood, the doors you did not go through, the people you did not speak to – these were all aspects of class differentiation which were entirely new to me. What was worse, the whole glen was infused with such malfunctioning social norms and the insidious power struggles between the landowners, the tenants and the visiting public. Times have changed (a bit) since then but it was an eye-opener into the world of landowning hegemony in Scotland for me.

Hunting estates loom large in any analysis of Scottish land-ownership on account of their extent and the conspicuous con-sumption that this form of landholding represents in a region of Scotland where the land issue has been so prominent. There are around 340 such properties covering around 2.1 million hectares of land – over 50 per cent of all privately owned land in the region (see Figure 7). The typical estate ranges in size from 5000 to 8000 hectares.[2]

There is a long tradition of hunting in Scotland going back to the very first arrivals of people after the ice retreated. As the Scottish nation developed, hunting was widely enjoyed both as an everyday activity in pursuit of food and as a recreational activity by the nobility. Many of the forest laws that were enacted in medieval times were designed to protect and conserve game species. Prior to the seventeenth century, however, there was no relationship between game and landownership. Outside of the royal hunting forests, everyone was free to hunt game and to claim the fruits of their endeavours. Subsequently, however, and culminating in an act of 1621, game was converted into an exclusive right of property not by claiming ownership of wild animals which are still legally *res nullius* or 'belonging to no one' but by effectively excluding all but landowners from the right to kill them. This remains the legal position today. Landowners have the rights to game not by any specific rights to the quarry but through the power to prevent anyone else from hunting it. Rights to game have thus become a valuable part of landownership and, as a result, cannot be separated from the land. Salmon, being part of the *regalia majora* or 'Crown rights', are a real exception and can be held independently of the land.

Not only are exclusive rights to game of relatively recent origin but the exclusive dedication of large areas of land to hunting dates back only to the second half of the nineteenth century, following a marked decline in the sheep farming economy. This coincided with rising levels of wealth in the south of Britain and the growing passion for the sport of deerstalking and other hunting activities. Technical progress in the design of the rifle and the penetration of the railway also contributed in opening up the Highlands to the tourist.[3]

This prompted a rapid growth in the leasing of land for deer forests by wealthy individuals from the British landed and mercantile classes.[4] Queen Victoria herself lent her own imprimatur to the process when her husband Prince Albert first leased Balmoral Estate on Deeside in 1848 and later purchased it in 1852. There followed a rapid expansion in the process of 'afforestation' and, as one writer put it:

> Everybody who was anybody in 1850 wanted a Highland sporting estate. There were plenty of takers in the Victorian world of burgeoning industrial capitalism – an emergent class of nouveau riche, redolent with competitive snobbery, desperate to emulate a traditional land-owning aristocracy.[5]

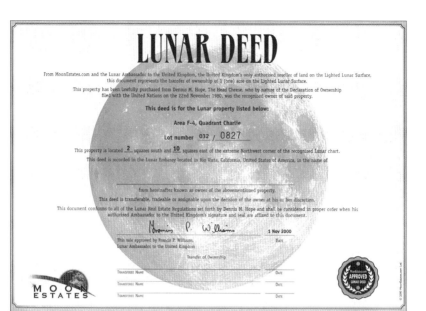

1. Moon deed

2. Common Chest of Wittenberg of 1522 in Luther House, Wittenberg

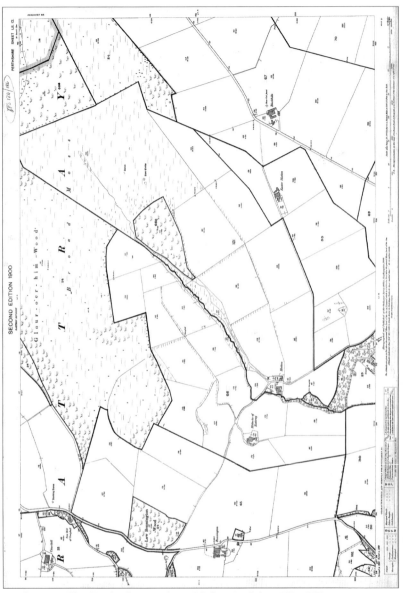

3. Valuation Office (Scotland) map: 1/1250 OS sheet Perthshire LII.15 NE
(National Archives of Scotland IRS124/184)

4. Allan MacRae, Chairman of the Assynt Crofters' Trust, celebrating the acquisition of the North Lochinver Estate by the Assynt Crofters' Trust (© John Paul Photography)

5. Newspaper advertisement for the Cuillin (*Scotsman Property Weekly* 30 March 2000)

6. The First Raid on Alyth Hill (Walla Mollison, Alyth)

7. The Second Raid on Alyth Hill with Councillor Matt Crighton cutting the fence closely observed by the Alyth Constabulary (Walla Mollison, Alyth)

8. Rockall as unclaimed territory. Photographed from HMS *Vidal*, 17 September 1955, the day before its formal annexation (National Archives ADM 1/25906 © Crown copyright)

9. Affixing the plaque annexing Rockall to the Crown, on 18 September 1955 – from left to right, Lieutenant Commander Desmond P. D. Scott, Corporal A. A. Fraser and James Fisher (National Archives ADM 1/25906 © Crown copyright)

10. The author and Brandy, a Highland garron, in Glen Esk (© Andy Wightman)

11. Kinross Town Hall and library (part of the common good of the burgh of Kinross) in a state of dereliction, June 2006 (© Andy Wightman)

SCOTLAND.

OWNERS OF LANDS AND HERITAGES
17 & 18 VICT., CAP. 91.

1872-73.

RETURN

I.

OF THE NAME AND ADDRESS OF EVERY OWNER OF ONE ACRE AND UPWARDS IN
EXTENT (OUTSIDE THE MUNICIPAL BOUNDARIES OF BOROUGHS CONTAINING
MORE THAN 20,000 INHABITANTS), WITH THE ESTIMATED ACREAGE,
AND THE ANNUAL VALUE OF THE LANDS AND
HERITAGES OF INDIVIDUAL OWNERS;

AND OF THE NUMBER OF OWNERS OF LESS THAN ONE ACRE, WITH THE
ESTIMATED AGGREGATE ACREAGE AND ANNUAL VALUE OF THE
LANDS AND HERITAGES OF SUCH OWNERS IN EACH COUNTY.

II.

A SIMILAR RETURN FOR MUNICIPAL BOROUGHS CONTAINING MORE THAN
20,000 INHABITANTS.

Presented to both Houses of Parliament by Command of Her Majesty.

EDINBURGH: PRINTED BY MURRAY AND GIBB,
PRINTERS TO HER MAJESTY'S STATIONERY OFFICE.

1874.

C.—899.]   [Price 2s. 3d.

12. Return of Owners of Lands and Heritages, Scotland, 1872–1873

Daily Scottish Mail

FRIDAY, JANUARY 24, 2003

40p

WHISKY GALORE
Forty bottles of malt
must be won by 6pm
See Page 41

I've spent £67,000 on plastic surgery
See Pages 24 & 25

'It seems Zimbabwe and Scotland share the same goals and ambitions when it comes to land reform'
Robert Mugabe's official spokesman yesterday

LET THE GRAB BEGIN

SCOTLAND'S land laws were ripped apart by MSPs yesterday as they passed the most far-reaching rural reforms for generations.

The Land Reform Bill was nodded through by five to one, enshrining the right of state-

By **Eddie Barnes**
Scottish Political Editor

backed individuals to force private landowners to sell them their land.

Opponents described the measure as a 'Mugabe-style land-grab', claiming it

Turn to Page 4, Col. 1

13. *Daily Mail* front page, 24 January 2003

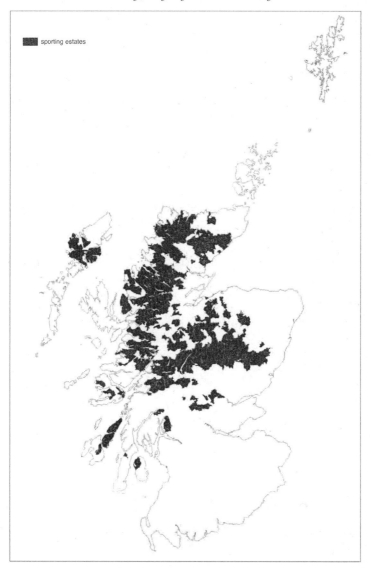

Figure 7: Distribution of sporting estates

Source: Author's own data

This nouveau-riche class of emergent landed proprietors bui[ ] lodges and houses, pushed roads into the glens, constructed path[ ] for the passage of hunters and ponies (to extract deer carcasses[ ] built boundary fences, devised and implemented new game man[ ] agement techniques and passed new laws to embed the new regim[ ] by entrenching hunting rights. As a consequence, a triumphar[ ] new cultural formation took hold – the Highland sporting estat[ ]

Prior to 1811 there were only six or seven deer forests activel[ ] managed for hunting. By 1873, the number of estates had risen t[ ] 79 and, by the end of the nineteenth century, there were betwee[ ] 130 and 150 deer forests covering 2.5 million acres – a vast outdoo[ ] playground for the upper strata of British society. Despite a modes[ ] contraction after World War I, mainly as a consequence of th[ ] acquisition of land by the Forestry Commission, deer forest[ ] extended over 2.8 million acres in 1957. In 2002, the extent c[ ] hunting estates, incorporating not only deer forests but all lan[ ] used primarily for hunting including grouse moors, stood at ove[ ] 4.5 million acres of land.[6]

The extent of deer forests and hunting estates, 1883–200[ ]

Year	Acreage
1883	1,709,892
1898	2,510,625
1904	2,920,097
1913	2,958,490
1957	2,800,000
2002	4,550,327

Table 11

Source: Scottish Land Enquiry, 1914, Orr, 1982, and author's own data

The sporting estate phenomenon has attracted much attentio[ ] over the years from critics and adherents alike, both of whom hav[ ] sought, in various ways, to challenge or uphold the hegemony [ ] hunting estates in the Highlands. During their genesis, the proces[ ] of afforestation was physically resisted in many parts of th[ ] country.[7] Gaelic culture at that time was still prevalent acro[ ] the Highlands and Islands and it repeatedly failed to understand the new dispensation and its accompanying game laws which were alien to older indigenous traditions. This cultural alienation is evident in the Gaelic proverb which asserts that 'everyone has a right to a deer from the hill, a tree from the forest, and a salmon from the river'. Such a view forms part of a wider belief system which has consistently found it difficult to reconcile the fact that 'the fish that was yesterday miles from the land was claimed by the landlord the moment it reached the shore'.[8] It is important to understand that the Highland Clearances were, at this time, still in living memory and, whilst the development of hunting estates was merely the next stage of the transition to a capitalist system of landholding, the emotions that the Clearances had evoked were, in many senses, rekindled by the spread of this hunting vastness.

The hunting estate remains the dominant landholding framework in the Highlands and Islands and, since its genesis, has resisted any attempt at reform bolstered by a political climate that has taken little serious interest in its affairs. The British upper classes and, now, a much wider sector of society are passionate about hunting. Ownership of a Scottish hunting estate is the epitome of the hunting lifestyle, allowing for the enjoyment of exclusive hunting rights over large areas of country. This conspicuous consumption of leisure is thus intimately bound up with the ideology of landownership and the sanctity of property rights. Any challenge to the hegemony of the hunting estate attracts equally passionate defence. As the former editor of the *Daily Telegraph* and keen hunter Max Hastings wrote:

> The delusion is widely held in Scotland . . . that the Highlands are a paradise in a state of natural grace, which might more properly be held in public ownership. The Scots must be told again and again until they start to believe it, that their hills are in reality intensively and expensively managed by private landowners, almost all of whom incur huge financial cost in doing so, which would have to be made good from the public purse if they were not there.[9]

It is worth exploring this claim in some more detail since Highland hunting estates are almost universally claimed by their adherents to be uneconomic enterprises. This argument is frequently deployed in defence of the hunting estate regime in terms of the beneficial impacts that the net inflow of funds from external sources brings to some of the most fragile parts of rural Scotland. In the absence of any official data on the economics of estates, it is difficult to quantify such impacts. However, one estate did recently publish financial information that, in addition to providing some specific data, demonstrated how such information can be used to convey very specific messages.

The estate concerned is the Letterewe Estate in Wester Ross. It covers 32,000 hectares of roadless wild country and has, for a long time, been one of Scotland's most famous deer forests. The estate was acquired by the Dutch businessman Paul van Vlissingen who was also an active conservationist.[10] Conscious of the debates in Scotland on land matters since he purchased the first part of his estate in 1978, he, unusually among his peers, sought to take an active part in these debates. One way in which he did this was to publish a ten-year management plan for Letterewe in September 1998.[11]

The plan outlines the management objectives – 'the natural development of wild land, its flora and fauna in all its interrelationships' – and argues that the owners see the estate as a 'valuable wild land asset to be loved', rather than as 'a producer of income'. The plan was launched at a press conference in September 1998 against the backdrop of the political debate on land reform in Scotland and van Vlissingen made a number of comments on the prospects of land reform.

What makes the plan interesting is its presentation of the estate as a benevolent institution which incurs heavy operating deficits and which finances scientific research and provides other 'local support'. To reinforce this message, the plan includes a summary of the estate's finances (excluding scientific research and 'other local support') as follows:

- Present estimated market value   £8,000,000
- Average annual income   £250,000
- Yearly out-of-pocket loss   £120,000
- Loss of income on asset value at 7%   £560,000
- Total loss of income to owners per annum   £680,000

Such a financial presentation reinforces the view of sporting estates as benevolent institutions in which losses are inevitable and significant financial inputs are made to the local economy. But interestingly the figures imply more than the usual simple annual revenue losses and suggest that investment income foregone on the asset value – that is the income the owner would have received if it were invested elsewhere – represents a further benevolent contribution to the local economy. On this basis, the total 'loss of income' to the owners is a breathtaking £680,000 per annum.

It is impossible to analyse the revenue any further – for example, is the private consumption of the estate for holidays and hunting paid for in these accounts? However, what the figures do *not* reveal is that the underlying asset – the land – has undergone significant capital appreciation. On the basis of the purchase price of the estate, which was bought in different parcels since 1978 for a total of £3,405,000, and a current value of £8,000,000, the property has grown in value by 7.8 per cent per annum. In 1999 alone, such growth would yield a capital appreciation of £624,000, a figure which outperforms the opportunity cost of investment elsewhere and which is more than sufficient to finance ongoing annual operating deficits.

Letterewe, far from being a loss-making concern, has actually performed handsomely and, against such a scenario, annual losses are not inevitable trading losses but the price paid for the consumption of non-market benefits. Further complications in interpreting the nature and scale of the financial performance are introduced if one attempts to include potential tax liability since the core part of the estate is owned by Clyde Properties NV, a company registered in Curaçao, a tax haven in the Netherlands Antilles. Letterewe's finances are typical of the sporting estate sector and recent research has confirmed that revenue losses for an average estate are in the order of £40,000 per year, the average estate being approximately one quarter of the size of Letterewe.[12]

The reality for most estates is that they are owned to provide tangible benefits to the owner by way of a place to relax, enjoy holidays and undertake a range of leisure pursuits. The 'loss' incurred in doing so is, in fact, the cost of leisure. Despite this, capital returns can be gained from estate ownership. As one leading estate agent wrote recently in an in-house magazine for owners of Bentley cars:

Be your interests fishing, shooting, walking or golf, or simply to identify an ideal environment to raise your family in an increasingly uncertain world, Scotland has the best to offer. As an investment, owning Scottish property, particularly a quality sporting or residential property, has generally proved very rewarding with significant long-term capital gain being achieved in many cases. Of late, such property investments have proved safer and considerably more rewarding than many other investments. As these properties are in short supply, they will continue to prove a sound investment in years to come.[13]

Just as starvation in Africa will not be sorted out by pumping aid relief money in, nor will the structural problems of the sporting estate economy be overcome by an equally misguided policy of relying on a stream of external subsidies from the various maverick characters who regularly find themselves the proud owners of a Highland sporting estate.

The sporting estate in reality is an indulgence for wealthy people who like hunting. They are uneconomic because they were never designed to be economic. No rural development programme anywhere in the world advocates the sale of land to a few wealthy individuals who will then 'support' the rural economy by injecting cash from outside which will, in turn, support a few jobs. Nobody in any serious development agency, if given a blank sheet of paper, would design such an economy for the Highlands. As James Hunter observed when it was suggested that landowners might feel threatened by the developing debate about landownership:

The more they feel threatened in my view the better. They need to feel threatened and they should feel threatened because there can be no future in Britain in the 21st century for a rural economy dependent on tweedy gentlemen coming from the south to slaughter our wildlife. That is not the way to run the Highlands and Islands.[14]

At the same time, others were beginning to vent their frustration with the treatment of the sporting estate. In 1994, the Scottish Landowners' Federation secured the abolition of sporting rates on land in Scotland. The move was portrayed by government as bringing Scotland into line with England but enraged not only critics of sporting estates but also the independent chairmen of Scotland's rating valuation tribunals who, in a report to the Scottish Office, made no secret of their anger. 'Sporting estates,' the document explained, 'like to describe themselves, when it suits them as being part of a sporting industry. In fact they are part of an inefficient trade which pays inadequate attention to marketing their product, largely because profit is not the prime objective.' It continued, 'These sporting estates change hands for capital sums which far exceed their letting value and which are of no benefit to the area, and are often bought because there are tax advantages to the purchaser, not necessarily in the UK.' Dismissing the argument that sporting estates provide employment and should therefore be freed of the rates burden, the chairmen's report points out that:

> [t]he local staff are poorly paid, their wages bearing no relation to the capital invested in the purchase price, and it is not unusual to find a man responsible for an investment in millions being paid a basic agricultural wage. Many of the estates use short-term labour during the sporting season, leaving the taxpayer to pay their staff from the dole for the rest of the year. Estates can in many cases be deliberately run at a loss, thereby reducing their owner's tax liability to central funds elsewhere in the UK.[15]

In 2002, the results of a study into sporting estates was published and showed that, of a sample of 218 estates:

- 39% of legal titles are held in the name of an individual or individuals;
- 23% are held by trusts;
- 21% by companies registered in the UK;
- 16% by companies registered offshore.
- 50% have been owned by the current owner or their family for 25 years or less;
- 20% have been owned by the current owner or their family for 26 to 50 years;
- 30% have been owned by the current owner or their family for over 50 years.

- 66% are owned by absentee-owners (defined by principal place of residence).
- 39% of estates were obtained by inheritance
- 61% of estates were purchased.[16]

The hunting estate, as currently constituted is something of an anachronism. It was created in a very different era and yet has persisted despite increasing questions over its contemporary validity and role. Partly as a consequence of the changing political, economic, environmental and social context, however, it is hard to see how it can survive unaltered for very much longer. New thinking is needed to explore how the long- and well-established sport of hunting can be integrated with other forms of recreation without the necessity for the exclusive proprietorial framework of hunting estates.

In European terms, it is also notable that the investment made by public and voluntary associations in mountain huts, footpaths and other aspects of the recreational infrastructure in many countries is difficult to foster in Scotland where the land resource is held in large privately owned hunting reserves. Indeed, currently, much of the footpath infrastructure and accommodation in mountain areas is far inferior in its extent, range, quality and management to almost everything that other countries in Europe have to offer. Mountain accommodation in particular is struggling to cope with the demands being placed upon it.[17]

To develop such a strategic approach it will be necessary to challenge the hegemony of the sporting estate and to conduct a more informed and critical appraisal of its role in the outdoor recreational economy. This is not necessarily to suggest that it has no role but it is evident that the personal attitudes and motivations of the 340 or so sporting-estate owners has been and continues to be somewhat different from those who see an alternative future for the 2.1 million hectares of land in question.

A strategic view of the future needs to acknowledge that hunting and other forms of outdoor recreation are desirable and legitimate forms of land use which should be developed within a new framework which seeks to optimise land use, increase investment and broaden the base of decision making and accountability over land use in the Highlands. Arguably, the current sporting-estate regime does not do this for a range of economic, social and environmental reasons – namely:

- it is not driven by rational economic criteria in its management and does not even maximise the potential income from hunting;
- it has fostered an elitist social formation which has contributed to the dislocation of local communities and culture;
- it has been responsible for restrictions on access and environmental degradation;
- at best, it tolerates other recreational activities rather than embracing and developing them and represents an opportunity lost in terms of the full exploitation of alternative recreational activities;
- high capital values associated with the consumption of status and leisure have precluded alternative approaches to the management of the Highland hills.

The purpose of any alternative approach would be to achieve optimum recreational land use from Highland hills by putting in place a framework of ownership and control within which all forms of recreational land use were developed and promoted. This would involve looking at each activity and seeking to develop its strengths, manage its impacts and meet its needs for the future.

Such an approach might aim to achieve the following specific objectives:

- ecological restoration and management of the wild nature experience for hillwalkers and hunters – wildness is currently part of the hillwalking experience but has been eroded for walkers by bulldozed tracks and the use of mechanised vehicles;
- pro-active management of hillwalking economy in terms of huts, lodges and trails – along the lines of those in countries like Norway – designed to attract more participants and achieve dispersal of impacts throughout the Highlands and Islands;
- retention of wealthy hunters who can own lodges and lease hunting as part of the wider distribution of hunting opportunities;

- self-employment of gamekeepers who also act as guides and nature wardens;
- improved game management, particularly of red deer, through licensing schemes.

This envisions a future for the region that places recreational land use at the heart of economic development and environmental enhancement. Central to such a future is that areas such as the Mamores and the Cairngorms would be vested in community land trusts and where recreational development would be overseen by the community but implemented by private enterprise.

This would involve alienating land for fixed developments, in particular hunting lodges and other forms of accommodation. The kind of substantial wealth possessed by many prospective sporting-estate owners could be captured by offering them not a sporting estate *en bloc* but the opportunity to buy the lodges, where much of the money is spent, and by selling them long leases of five to ten years of the hunting rights which would be vested in the local community. Meanwhile not-for-profit organisations could be franchised to develop and promote trails, guidance and information. There would be substantial reforestation to improve the environment and to diversify the recreational experience for both hunters and other users.

Gamekeepers could become self-employed or employees of private hunting businesses that purchase or lease licences from the community. They could become more multi-skilled in other forms of recreation and in environmental management thus developing a highly skilled and trained hunter/mountain guide/naturalist capable of integrating a range of disciplines that are currently sectoral. This would also extend the work season for individuals.[18]

Such an alternative vision for the future does, of course, raise questions about the mechanics of achieving it. This is a vexed question but it is interesting to note that elements of an alternative way forward have already been proposed.[19] In particular the idea of community-owned hunting estates working in partnership with private individuals owning hunting lodges has already come to fruition in one case – that of the North Harris Estate. In 2003, the community successfully purchased this 22,228-hectare hunting estate in the Outer Hebrides in partnership with a businessman who purchased the most expensive assets – Amhuinnsuidhe Castle and the salmon fishing rights.

The current climate for land reform suggests that it might become easier in future to challenge some of the shibboleths that have been erected both by protagonists and antagonists of the sporting-estate regime. So far, however, only a relatively limited set of land reform measures has been put forward which tend to deal with the more acute symptoms of the current system and division of land. A more radical approach would be required to achieve even a modest change in the pattern and character of Highland sporting estates.

It is abundantly clear, for example, that the current unregulated market in sporting estates is one important reason for the inflated values of such holdings. Wealthy interests from around the world are bidding against each other and forcing up prices. A reduction in value of estates as a result of more regulation would be a good thing if, for example, capital previously committed to purchase no longer simply transferred to the previous owner but was available for investment in infrastructure.

In order to achieve the kind of changes imagined above, the critics of the hunting estate might have to put aside their prejudices about hunting, fishing and shooting – unless, of course, they are adopting a moral standpoint in relation to blood sports – and they need to accept the benefits that the hunting economy can bring. Equally, those advocates of the status quo need to recognise that sporting estates are a product of their time, that the wider community has legitimate interests in wild places, that hunting as a recreation should be the subject of public policy interventions just as other recreations are, and that the sporting estate, as it is currently constructed, is an anachronism.

The sporting regime is not an inevitable fixture in the Highland landscape and could very well be a transient phenomenon. Hunting estates persist as the dominant feature in the division of land in the Highlands and Islands but the proprietorial grip over how the Highland landscape is ordered and fashioned is weakening.

I Want the Assurance That I Will Not Be Evicted

Farming and the agricultural tenant

On 3 February 2003, around one hundred tenant farmers across Scotland received eviction notices ordering them to quit their farms. It was the culmination of a hectic few weeks of such notices being served. On a day of particularly severe winter weather, every effort was made to deliver the legal papers. Some farmers, forewarned of the move, battened up their letterboxes but to no avail. These tenants all leased land by means of limited partnership tenancies, a legal device which had been constructed by lawyers to prevent tenant farmers enjoying security of tenure. The draconian activity was provoked by the fact that the next day, the fourth, an amendment was to be tabled in the Scottish Parliament to a new agricultural holdings act that would give such tenants security of tenure and the right to buy their farms if they should ever come up for sale. The amendment was necessary to protect tenants against further eviction notices issued between that date and the passing of the act.[1]

The Agricultural Holdings (Scotland) Act of 2003 is one of the unsung successes of the land reform programme introduced by the Scottish Parliament. It provides a number of important benefits to tenants including a right to buy when the farm is sold, rights to diversify land use, rights to assign the tenancy and improvements to compensation arrangements when a tenant leaves the farm. George Lyon MSP was one of its architects and, in the debate that passed the act, he had this to say:

> For too long, tenant farmers have played the game with the deck stacked against them. Until now, the landlords have held all the

aces in negotiations. The bill waters down dramatically the powers of landowners and their factors. Those powers must be watered down, because landowners have seriously abused the provisions of the Agricultural Holdings (Scotland) Act 1991. The partnership tenancies created by that act were nothing more than a legal device that left tenants with no security and at the mercy of landlords, who could kick them out at any point during the partnership agreement.

Write-down agreements robbed tenants of the value of their investments and, to rub salt into the wound, the tenants usually ended up paying rent on their own investments. Post-lease agreements were designed to allow landlords to dump their responsibility for repairs, renewals and provision of fixed equipment on tenants.

The use of Queen's Counsel and expert witnesses in rent arbitration meant that the cost of arbitration for tenants was prohibitive. The most recent rent arbitration that was carried out on Arran, of which the minister might be aware, cost £12,000. If a landlord has to balance that cost over 60 farms, because the precedent is set when the rent goes up, the cost is affordable, but if an individual tenant on a three-year rent review has to spread the cost of £12,000 over three years, it is a no-brainer – they do not do it.

I believe that the actions by landlords and factors that I have described drove a coach and horses through the 1991 act and left tenants powerless to fight for a fair and just deal. I hope that the bill will end that abuse. It will shift the balance of power back to tenant farmers and will be fundamental in ensuring the future of the tenant farm sector. The creation of two new tenancy vehicles and the provisions allowing diversification should reinvigorate the tenanted sector and act as a further spur to rural development.[2]

In no other land use is the struggle between the landless and the landed so marked and of such long standing as agriculture. People have always been farmers out of necessity and farming requires land. Any analysis of farming is likely therefore to shed much light on land relations.

For most of Scotland's history, famers have not owned the land they farm. They have been tenants of a landlord. When feudalism was imposed, when the lands of the church were appropriated and when the commonties were divided, the peasant got nothing and the lord got the lot. With the security of property, the lord could borrow and invest whilst the peasant could not. The lord could plan for the future and bequeath his land. The peasant had an insecure lease and no right to bequeath. Towards the end of the nineteenth century, this became political and nowhere more so that in the crofting districts of north-west Scotland.

The Agricultural Holdings (Scotland) Act of 1883 provided compensation to outgoing tenants for improvements they had made to their holdings. But, for many of Scotland's tenants, this was a modest concession in the face of landed power. By this time, crofting tenants had begun to organise land raids and rent strikes in protest at their situation and the Napier Commission was established to examine their grievances. From the outset, it became clear that the stakes were high.

In the first few minutes of taking evidence in Braes on Skye on Tuesday 8 May 1883, the first witness examined was Angus Stewart, elected by the crofters in the district to present evidence to the Commission. But before he could do so, he wanted assurances that what he had to say would not lead to him being evicted by the landlord. 'I want the assurance that I will not be evicted,' he said, 'for I cannot bear evidence to the distress of my people without bearing evidence to the oppression and high-handedness of the landlord and his factor.'

Having secured this assurance from Lord Macdonald's factor, Stewart continued:

> The principal thing that we have to complain of is our poverty and what has caused our poverty. The smallness of our holdings and the inferior quality of the land is what has caused our poverty; and the way in which the poor crofters are huddled together, and the best part of the land devoted to deer forests and big farms. If we had plenty of land there would be no poverty in our country. We are willing and able to work it.[3]

Over the course of the next six months, testimony was heard across the Highlands and Islands and at hearings in Edinburgh and Glasgow, ending on 26 December 1883 in Edinburgh.

In their report, the Commissioners concluded that:

> [t]he crofter of the present time has through past evictions been confined within narrow limits, sometimes on inferior and exhausted soil. He is subject to arbitrary augmentations of money rent, he is without security of tenure, and has only recently received the concession of compensation for improvements . . . The crofter belongs to that class of tenants who have received the smallest share or proprietary favour or benefaction, and who are by virtue of power, position or covenants, least protected against inconsiderate treatment.[4]

And:

> the severance of the labouring classes from the benefits and enjoyments of property (certainly one of the elements of civilisation, morality, and public order), and their precarious and dangerous condition as dependent on capital and mere recipients of wages, is a question which engages the reflection of those who reason, and those who govern. There is a general desire that the labouring man in every sphere of activity should be invested with a greater share of substantial possession, and be attached by deeper and more durable ties to the soil of his country.[5]

The subsequent Crofters Act of 1886 went a long way, considering the politics of the time, towards alleviating the suffering of the crofters. As Hunter observed, 'By the standards of an age accustomed to regarding landed property and private contracts between landlords and tenants as inviolable, even sacrosanct, the Crofters Act was a measure so radical as to be little short of revolutionary.'[6]

But, for all its revolutionary flavour, it was still a response to only the most visible and, to some extent, politically threatening section of tenant opinion across Scotland. There was nothing in the act for those who were landless and it was restricted in its scope, as mentioned earlier (see Chapter 10), to the seven counties that Napier and his Commissioners had visited. Crofting tenants in the rest of the Highlands simply vanished as a result over the next thirty years. This did not go unnoticed by the newly energised crofting community, however, who had already set up the Highland Land Law Reform Association in Fraserburgh in 1883 to fight for land reform. Two years earlier, 6,000 tenants and crofters in the north-east met in Aberdeen and established the Scottish Farms Alliance, later the Scottish Land Reform Association. It sought land reform, security of tenure and the abolition of primogeniture, hypothec and entail.[7]

The common interests of the crofting tenants of the north-west Highlands and of the north-east and Lowlands of Scotland failed, however, to emerge as a united force and, as a consequence, reform was limited to the north and west. The year 1886 was a turning point according to Ian Carter, the leading historian on the north-east. The prospects of securing tenants' rights had never been better. There was a mass organisation and much evidence of the sort that had been presented to the Napier Commission but:

> [i]t was not to be. Northeast peasants could not mobilise sufficient political muscle to force the Liberal government to give them the same legislative protection that Highland peasants were to enjoy. The reason for this inability was not lack of numbers. It was the failure of northeast peasants clearly to realise and represent their own class interest . . . Capitalist farmers were allowed to present themselves as the representatives of all farmers, to pursue their sectional interest under the guise of pursuing farmers' general interest . . . When the Pentland Act finally did reach the statute book in 1912 it gave too little protection and was much too late. The northeast peasantry had been irreparably penetrated; as a class it was dead.[8]

Two things are notable in this observation. The first is that there is a world of difference between a tenant farmer on an insecure lease and a farmer who owns their own farm. By successfully creating the impression that all farmers share a common interest, capitalist farmers (both tenants and owners) ensured that the fate of the small tenant was sealed. The second is that there was then and remains today a continuing demarcation between the so-called Highlands and Islands (which in fact omits much of the Highlands in Perthshire and Aberdeenshire, for example) and the rest of Scotland. The failure of the north-east crofters was a signal that a line had been drawn.

That legacy was all too obvious when the Scottish Land Enquiry Committee's report was published in 1914. In it is contained evidence of a beleaguered and insecure tenantry.

> It is reported by a leading solicitor with extensive knowledge of the South-East of Scotland for example, that the practice prevails of letting farms to applicants whose political opinions are the same as those of the landlord. In a recent case the question was put to the applicant: 'What are your politics?' As a rule it is unnecessary to ask the question as the agent or the proprietor have already made discovery; and it is common knowledge throughout the rural districts that, on the majority of estates, farmers of Liberal politics are careful not to intrude their political opinions.[9]

In the words of one tenant:

> As a matter of fact, every farmer knows of dozens of cases, past and present, of harsh legal robbery in the shape of confiscation of tenants' improvements. The argument that there are very many Scottish lairds who treat their tenants justly, is the same argument as was advanced in favour of slavery, and many people then seriously argued that because in the main, masters treated their slaves very well, therefore slavery should not be abolished. The two cases are similar. No conscientious man will take advantage of bad laws, but that is no reason for having bad laws. Most people will admit that the land laws are wrong when the following things are not only possible, but are, and have been actually done, and that not seldom
>
> (1) Confiscation of a tenant's improvements.
> (2) Raising rent on a tenant's improvements.

(3) Eviction of a tenant who has improved and sunk capital in permanent improvements, and re-letting the farm to a new tenant at a higher rent.

(4) Eviction of a tenant because he enforced his rights re ground game, heather burning, etc.

(5) Eviction on capricious grounds.

All these are obviously unjust, and with an absentee landlord they are very present dangers to all tenants, and militate against anything but a hand-to-mouth style of farming, good for neither landlord nor tenant, nor the country at large.[10]

In 1949 tenant farmers finally won the right to secure tenancies which could be bequeathed to their successors and these tenancies, now governed by the Agricultural Holdings (Scotland) Act 1991, still account for over 80 per cent of all farm tenancies in Scotland.

The debate today is a continuation of earlier debates about land tenure. In particular, over the past fifteen years, there has been a growing tension between landlords and tenants. This has arisen in part because the success of the 1949 act means that agricultural tenants now have such security that turnover of tenanted land is low and there is limited scope for new entrants into agriculture. Prior to the 2003 act, the only forms of formal farm tenancies permitted within the legislation were either a seasonal let of less than one year or a secure tenancy.

Moves to introduce more flexible tenancy arrangements formed the core of the 2003 act which, as well as allowing for shorter tenancies, also provided tenants under a secure tenancy the right to buy their farm if and when it was put up for sale. This measure provoked heated debate as many tenant farmers wanted an absolute right to buy at any time. As a consequence, tenant farmers are now represented by their own organisation – the Scottish Tenant Farmers Association which emerged from the Scottish Tenant Farmers Action Group set up in 2001 to respond to the new tenancy proposals. This initiative was born out of a growing frustration with the ability of the main farmers' union, the National Farmers Union Scotland, to represent the interests of the tenanted sector adequately – a direct parallel with the trap into which peasant farmers in north-east Scotland fell in the 1880s.[11]

The percentage of farms that are tenanted, 1940–2008

Year	Percentage
1940	68.7
1950	60.2
1960	48.8
1970	43.2
1980	42.1
1990	37.9
2000	32.0
2008	28.2

Table 12

Source: Scottish Government

The proportion of tenanted land has been inexorably on the decline since the early twentieth century (see Table 12). There are two main reasons for this. Since the First World War, a number of large agricultural estates have been sold and split up, adding to the owned acreage. In recent years, however, the reduction has been more as a consequence of landowners taking farms 'in hand', whereby they are no longer tenanted and are managed directly by the landowner. No statistics are kept on the background of owned farms so it is impossible to know the balance between farms owned by a farmer and farms now back in the hands of a landowner.

The 2003 Agricultural Holdings Act allowed tenants with a secure agricultural tenancy to register an interest in their land and, if and when it was to be sold, to have a right to buy it. At the time, tenant farmers' groups wanted to go further and obtain an absolute right to buy but this was never going to happen. Limited though it is, the 2003 act has been a success in terms of the right to buy. In land reform terms, it has the great virtue of being simple in contrast to the community right to buy (see chapter 27).

A four-page form is filled out and this is then submitted not to civil servants and ministers but to the Keeper of the Registers of Scotland. The Keeper is required to follow a few simple steps to ensure the application is in order and has no powers of discretion to decide whether farmer A deserves the right and farmer B does not. Within a predictable timetable, the tenant farmer has their right registered. The only grounds for refusal are if the application does not conform to specific terms in the act – for example, the land to be registered is not held under a qualifying agricultural tenancy. Such refusal can easily be rectified by submitting an amended application correcting such deficiencies.

In practice, any tenant farmer whose holding qualifies under the act can, if they wish, obtain a registered interest. They don't have to make any case for sustainable development, demonstrate serious intent to do anything or submit their case for consideration to a panel of civil servants to take months to determine. Aside from the fact that the right to buy is only available when the land is to be sold, this act is much more in line with real land reform as being enacted in places such as South Africa.

The evidence of success is there for all to see in the Register of Community Interest in Land (Agricultural Tenants) where, as of 31 January 2013, there were 1,148 successful registrations covering around 500,000 acres of land.[12] This compares with a mere 37 successful registrations under the community right to buy covering less than 10 per cent of the land registered by tenant farmers (see Chapter 27).

But beyond the issue of tenancies and their future lies the vexed issue of agricultural support. The Common Agricultural Policy (CAP) accounts for around 40 per cent of the European Union budget and political attempts to curb this spending have foundered in the face of vested interest for many years. Overproduction, butter mountains, set-aside and headage payments are just some of the grossly expensive and wasteful consequences. In June 2003, the latest incarnation was introduced by the European Union – the Single Farm Payment (SFP). Given that public support is an integral part of agricultural economics, new entrants to farming – young people with fresh ideas and energy – have a legitimate claim to a share of that support, perhaps even a greater claim in order to get them established. But the me, me, me attitude which prevails in the upper echelons of farming politics precludes this possibility.

For decades, farmers have essentially been the architects of their own support packages. The Scottish NFU has been run by people with the time and money to do so and these are by and large the larger farmers with the staff and the resources to devote their time to lobbying Brussels, London and, latterly, Edinburgh. The crofter, the struggling tenant and the average family farmer have neither the time nor the resources for much of farming politics. The result is a package of support that has been skewed towards the larger and wealthier farms, which has, in the process, increased land prices by capitalising the value of grants and subsidies and which has enabled those who have land and capital to obtain more land and capital at the expense of those who really need it.

The result is a crisis. Land values are too high, there's little or no land to let, support is concentrated in the hands of the already well-to-do and the public has very little say in the whole matter. One reason for the crisis is that money from outside has been attracted in to farmland, drawn by tax incentives that have led to land value inflation. Why else do dairy farms, for example, sell for £1 million when dairy farmers are making a loss?

The current support system, the so-called Single Farm Payment is, as we shall see, something of a misnomer. Introduced to Scotland in 2005, the SFP replaced a range of production subsidies that previously existed. The SFP is decoupled from production which means that the subsidy that farmers receive is no longer linked to how much food they produce. Instead, farmers receive a sum of money which relates to how much they got in the past (2000–2003). Critically, however, they do not need to do any farming to receive these funds. Moreover, the funds are not tied to land and can thus be bought and sold by farmers. Any farmer can sell their entitlement (the terminology used is itself revealing) to another farmer who need only have 3 hectares of land and need not do any farming to receive the subsidies.

The Scottish Government website which explains the background to the Single Farm Payment Scheme (SFPS) has the following to say about it:

> The SFPS is not 'money for nothing'. In return for their SFP, farmers/crofters must maintain their land in Good Agricultural and Environmental Condition (GAEC) and respect regulations relating to public, animal and plant health, environmental protection and animal welfare. Many non-market benefits are secured by this subsidy. Rural communities, in some of the most

remote areas, where alternative land uses or job opportunities are scarce are sustained. The skills offered by farming families and the business opportunities they help, generate a healthy rural economy which in turn benefits the wider rural economy. And, the maintenance of high nature value areas, habitats, and landscapes benefit the general public and the tourist industry.[13]

The Cabinet Secretary for Rural Affairs and the Environment, Richard Lochhead, who is in charge of agriculture, said something rather different to Parliament on 10 June 2009:

> Farmers in Scotland receive more than £430 million each year through the single farm payment. The payments are based on support that was received in a reference period, which means that any link between the size of the payment and the farmer's economic need or the public benefits that he delivers is at best accidental and at worst non-existent. A quick analysis illustrates the case for change. At parish level, the highest payments in Scotland average £650 per hectare, and the lowest payment is £3 per hectare. At individual field level, the highest payment in Scotland is £3,950 per hectare, whereas the lowest is 6p – not £6, but 6p – per hectare. That situation is clearly unsustainable.[14]

After decades of trying to reform the CAP, we still have a system that is crude, unfair and illogical. Lochhead went on to announce an inquiry to be chaired by Brian Pack which produced its first report in December 2009.[15] So where does all the money go? A number of people have asked that question over many years.[16] It has taken persistence and the new freedoms afforded by the Freedom of Information Acts to find out exactly where the money goes. The Scottish Government now publishes the information on its website.[17] Of the £591 million paid in farm subsidies in 2009:

> 10% – £59.2 million went to a mere 182 farmers or 0.95% of the total number
>
> 20% – £118.3 million went to a mere 538 farmers or 2.77% of the total number
>
> 30% – £177.5 million went to a mere 1032 farmers or 5.3% of the total number

During the twelve years from 2000 to 2011, the top fifty recipients of agricultural subsidy received £230,600,000 – an average of over £4.6 million per farmer. The amount received by the top fifty increased from £22 million (2008), to £24 million (2009), to £27.6 million (2010) and to a staggering £35 million in 2011. Among the top fifty are some of Scotland's wealthiest landowners including the Earl of Moray, Leon Litchfield, Earl of Seafield, Lord Inchcape, Earl of Southesk, the Duke of Buccleuch, the Earl of Rosebery and the Duke of Roxburghe (see Table 13).[18]

The recipients of the 50 largest farming subsidies, 2000–2009

	Farm Business	Public Subsidy 2000–2009
1	G Barbour & Co.	£8,553,490.76
2	Ross Bros	£7,471,753.86
3	J & T F Macfarlane Ltd	£6,386,898.29
4	Genoch Mains Farms	£5,399,036.85
5	Moray Estates Development Co.	£5,377,315.70
6	Kevan Forsyth	£4,898,816.33
7	William Hamilton and Son (No 2)	£4,674,668.94
8	John C McIntosh	£3,963,146.23
9	J C Innes & Sons	£3,874,754.77
10	J R Graham Ltd	£3,816,892.37
11	L G Litchfield Bowland Farms & Tulchan	£3,796,184.55
12	Cullen Farms/Seafield	£3,640,542.48
13	IAN WHITE LTD	£3,375,673.13
14	Stracathro & Careston Ests Ltd	£3,356,348.60
15	Dalmahoy Farms	£3,337,148.15
16	Glenapp Estate Company Ltd	£3,326,154.45
17	Mr A J Duncan (A Firm)	£3,151,446.94
18	Lour Farms	£3,093,010.10
19	Southesk Farms	£3,045,727.03
20	Glenmore Properties Ltd	£2,998,934.88
21	Wesley Gracey	£2,965,471.14
22	G Mcdougal (Bassendean) Ltd	£2,958,281.66
23	Iain Service & Co. Ltd	£2,942,136.43

The recipients of the 50 largest farming subsidies, 2000–2009—contd

	Farm Business	Public Subsidy 2000–2009
24	Faccombe Estates Ltd	£2,910,433.42
25	Dunecht Home Farms	£2,904,864.96
26	Charles M Kirkpatrick	£2,886,312.91
27	Auchencheyne Ltd	£2,849,394.88
28	Sunwick Farm Ltd	£2,834,824.42
29	Mr R McBride & Son	£2,786,323.28
30	RSPB	£2,770,759.18
31	Strathmore Farming Company	£2,762,600.74
32	BQ Farming Partnerships Ltd	£2,748,999.86
33	Mr W J Henderson & Sons	£2,736,180.59
34	Auchtydore Farms	£2,729,513.37
35	Aucheneck Estate	£2,691,139.29
36	Klondyke Farms Limited	£2,688,839.76
37	M/S A S & H M McGimpsey	£2,688,259.05
38	OLD HALL FARMS	£2,672,567.70
39	Backmuir Trading Ltd	£2,612,324.97
40	John Wight & Sons	£2,605,228.82
41	R & N Barclay	£2,579,473.90
42	James H Fowlie (A Firm)	£2,548,685.12
43	John A Wallace & Sons	£2,533,273.62
44	Rosebery Estates	£2,504,030.65
45	W L & J Anderson	£2,499,945.55
46	Balbirnie Home Farm	£2,490,661.88
47	Auchmacoy Estate	£2,456,434.48
48	Hugh Gordon (A Firm)	£2,418,760.81
49	Balgonie Estates Ltd	£2,363,222.53
50	John A Cameron & Son	£2,231,942.87

Table 13

Source: Scottish Government

The recipients of the five largest subsidies in 2009 were:

- **Frank A Smart & Son Ltd** Torphins, Aberdeenshire £1,208,468.34
- **G Barbour & Co.** Crocketford, Kirkcudbrightshire £1,056,296.26
- **Ross Bros** Strichen, Aberdeenshire £1,049,792.28
- **Glenmore Properties Ltd** Craigellachie, Banffshire £1,038,124.52
- **William Hamilton & Son** Stonehouse, Lanarkshire £892,385.35

The biggest recipient of a Single Farm Payment in 2009 was Frank A Smart and Son Ltd of Easter Tolmauds Farm, near Torphins, in Aberdeenshire. Mr Smart collected £1,208,468.34.[19]

Glenmore Properties Ltd is owned by the Strathdee family and was the recipient of £1,038,124.52 in 2009. This company is based in Speyside and, according to its website, owns a portfolio of thirty-nine farms throughout Moray, Aberdeenshire and the Highlands. One farm it owns is the Hallowood, Trove and Barmuckity Farm to the south-east of Elgin which it acquired in 1991 for £300,000. Since then, it has sold eighteen housing plots and six properties for a total of £1.3 million. It received improvement grants of £25,200 from Moray District Council in 1993. In March 2009, another twenty-four plots of land with full planning permission were being advertised at a total guide price of £2,935,000. A 10 per cent discount was available for completing the sale by the end of the month.

Another big winner has been AM Ejendomme APS, a Danish company that owns the Balnacoil Estate in Sutherland. Its wholly owned subsidiary, Balnacoil Farming Ltd, has received £1,145,477.08 in Single Farm Payments since the estate was purchased in October 2006 despite it being a sporting estate and having no livestock.

On 1 December 2011, the Scottish Government announced that 14,300 payments (75% of payments) had been made that that week, injecting over £335 million into the rural economy. Richard Lochhead said, 'The single farm payments are vital for Scotland's farmers and I'm delighted that, once again, over 70 per cent of applicants will receive their payments in the first 15 days – providing a boost not just for farmers but also the whole rural economy.' It is not clear whether he thought that Glenmore Properties was one of the farmers who needed such a boost but he nevertheless sent the company a cheque for a staggering £1,354,830. Between 2000 and 2012, this company has received a total of £6.9 million of public money, including £6.3 million in Single Farm Payments, in return for which it was not obliged to do any farming. Big farmers always swing policy in line with their vested interests. But, if farming support is to be fair in future, there are strong arguments to restrict subsidy to one farm per farmer. The reason Mr Strathdee gets so much is because he owns thirty-nine farms!

It's a racket. A farmer with 100 acres can go to auction and buy SFP entitlements at around twice their annual value, lease some marginal land producing nothing for £5 per hectare, pocket the annual payments and do nothing. They can then enjoy a yield of 20–30 per cent return on capital. They are the so-called 'slipper farmers' and they have attracted the ire of the National Famers Union itself who, in their submission to the Pack Enquiry pointed out:

> That the current system also allows a small number of producers to remain eligible to receive SFP while delivering little in the way of active production causes much anger amongst active farmers. NFU Scotland believes that there needs to be a solution to this problem that prohibits individuals in these circumstances from receiving SFP.[20]

It gets worse though. Since the SFP entitlements are classed as an intangible asset, those farmers operating as companies (and that includes Frank A Smart & Son Ltd and Glenmore Properties Ltd) can write off the cost of acquiring them against their income. It took me a while to grasp this but you can write off against tax the cost of acquiring an entitlement to public subsidy! So, not only does the hard-working taxpayer fork out to pay these subsidies in the first place, he or she then forks out again to make up for the tax foregone when the cost of acquiring more subsidy entitlement is deducted from the farmers' tax bill!

The growing scandal was highlighted by Brian Pack who, in his interim report, criticised what he called 'armchair farmers':

> [B]ecause payments are made in relation to entitlements and not the land itself, a farmer who was active in the reference period could potentially have rented out or sold their good quality land and then rented poorer quality land that required little management to meet cross compliance requirements and still claim their Single Farm Payment whilst not actively farming.
>
> Clearly, if the direction of travel is towards a system where agricultural support needs a strong and robust rationale, the current system is lacking. It is hard to justify support to agriculture whilst the current system allows payments to armchair farmers.[21]

In his report, he publishes a startling map that shows most of the support going to the wealthiest parts of the country with the biggest farms and biggest landowners.[22] This is precisely the danger with payments based on areas of land – those who have the most, get the most. As Pack and his colleagues found when they visited Brussels:

> During our visit to Brussels, various Commission officials, including Mariann Fischer Boel, expressed their concern that area-based direct payments were increasing land values and rents. They were concerned that the EU was on a vicious cycle with a SFP designed to support farm incomes causing rent/land values to increase resulting in reduced farm incomes requiring ever greater SFPs, and so on.[23]

Trading of entitlements is verging on the criminal. These are public subsidies and no one should be 'entitled' to them, far less be in a position to simply give up farming and sell what, in effect, is a public allowance.

The Scottish Crofting Federation made a strong critique of the system in their submission to Pack which is worth quoting in full.

For whoever has, to him shall more be given; and whoever does not have, even what he has shall be taken away from him' Mark 4:25. The whole argument of paying more (because of volatile markets) to those with the highest ability to produce for the market is weak. This simplistic model is highly inequitable and will not lead to the objectives we should be seeking for Scottish agriculture. There is no justification for providing unfettered support at the highest rates to those with the most advantage to earn a fair wage from the market.

We think that it is not going to be acceptable to the public that those with the best quality land and therefore the best ability to operate in the market receive the highest support from the public purse regardless of how their practices driven by wealth creation impact on the public heritage, whilst those managing huge areas of some of Scotland's finest landscape and biggest carbon deposits in a sustainable manner are supported the least.[24]

Current financial support from the EU ends in 2013 but whether a new deal can be agreed by then is doubtful. In any event, it is clear that a new system (which will probably include a ceiling on individual annual payments of €300,000) will be phased in over a period of ten years. This means that the gravy train for Scotland's largest landowners and farmers will be running well beyond 2020.

The challenge remains to provide a system of support that benefits the environment, helps young farmers, invests in the rural economy and is equitable. For half a century, large landowners and farmers have swallowed up billions in public subsidy whilst those on the margins continue to struggle. Current SFPs are a fixed pool of funds which are based upon historic entitlements. Already there is plenty evidence that the biggest and strongest are attempting to appropriate more than their fair share, and thus funding, like land, is becoming more concentrated in the hands of fewer and fewer farmers.

Crofting, however, has not only the question of agricultural subsidies to fret about. The future of crofting itself is in something of a crisis and it is to that we will now turn our attention.

A Highly Unsatisfactory Guddle

Crofting and the Scottish Parliament

The complaints of the crofters have already been alluded to in the previous chapter. Crofting tenure was introduced in 1886 through the Crofters Holdings (Scotland) Act. It provided security of tenure, the right to judicially reviewed rents, the right to bequeath tenancy and the right to compensation for permanent improvements to all crofters in the seven crofting counties of Shetland, Orkney, Ross and Cromarty, Caithness, Sutherland, Inverness and Argyll. It was a radical piece of land reform legislation pushed through in extraordinary political circumstances, the impacts of which have been profound for many areas in the Highlands and Islands.

Crofting land consists of individual crofts tenanted by crofting tenants organised into townships which collectively share a large area of common grazings. There are 17,936 crofts with an average size of 8 acres and, of these, 4,287 are owned and the remaining 13,649 are tenanted. It is estimated that there are between 10,000 and 12,000 crofting households which are home to 33,000 people.[1] There are around 1.2 million acres of common grazings. The tenure system, therefore, covers a total of around 1.3 million acres of land or about 7 per cent of Scotland.[2]

The 1886 act which set this whole system up, however, was a piece of legislation which was criticised both at the time for making no provision for the landless cottars and subsequently for having retarded the development of a more economic and efficient agricultural economy. The security it offered to agricultural tenants, however, has ultimately proved to ensure its one great contribution to the rural economy – namely, that it has retained populations in some of the most inhospitable regions of Scotland whilst other more fertile and productive regions now lie empty.

Crofting developed as a system of land tenure inside the existing system of Highland estates. The crofting community today, therefore, consists of crofters with their individual crofts held on an annual tenancy from their landowner together with an area of common grazings. Whilst crofting legislation defined the crofter as an agricultural tenant with statutory rights, it did nothing to redefine the role of landowners other than to constrain their rights. The tension that persisted between crofter and landlord together with the developing confidence of the crofting community were eventually to inspire the event which, as much as anything, catapulted landownership back on to the political agenda in the 1990s – namely, the takeover of the North Assynt Estate by the Assynt Crofters' Trust in February 1993 (see Chapter 15). In 1997, the then Secretary of State for Scotland, Michael Forsyth, secured the enactment of the Transfer of Crofting Estates (Scotland) Act 1997 which provided the power for crofting communities to take over a landlord's interest in government-owned crofting estates.

Crofting reform was then taken up as part of the land reform agenda that was adopted by the Scottish Executive in 1999. In particular, a crofting community right to buy was to be created. This would allow crofting communities on privately owned land to buy out the landlord's interest and the proposal enjoyed strong popular support within crofting circles. However, when, in July 1999, the Executive published their White Paper on land reform, there was no mention of the crofting right to buy. Internal memos circulating later that summer show how determined the civil servants were to delay such a measure which, it was claimed, was complex, time-consuming and tricky to draft. The decision was made not to include any crofting measures in the bill and it took insistent lobbying from Brian Wilson, the Minister of State at the Scottish Office, and others to reverse this decision. On 24 November 1999, Jim Wallace, the Minister for Justice, announced that the crofting right to buy would, after all, be included in Land Reform bill which was eventually published in February 2001 and passed in January 2003. This early skirmish proved an omen of things to come and perpetuated a certain suspicion that civil servants were less than enthusiastic about crofting matters.

Whilst the crofting community right to buy was welcome – though it has proved inordinately complex to implement due to the onerous burdens on the community[3] – moves to reform crofting tenure itself were becoming confused. Aware of the need for further reform, the Scottish Executive launched a consultation on a new crofting bill in March 2006. Despite being broadly popular, it contained measures that legitimised the free market in crofting tenancies whereby crofters sold their tenancy on the open market for inflated prices. There was a real danger that, were this to continue, the entire crofting system, which is based on a regulated system of tenancy, would collapse. Such was the outcry that these provisions were dropped from the final legislation passed in 2007. But what the controversy highlighted was a fault line that had been developing for some time. In a nutshell, it is in the economic interests of one class of crofters to aspire to ownership of their croft in order to take advantage of entry into the free market in land. However, for another class, who still value the coherence that crofting has delivered to otherwise economically fragile communities, the regulated tenancy is all that prevents the rapid decline in the community solidarity that an open market would lead to. As Brian Wilson pointed out recently, 'In reality, since the late 1960s, the whole thrust of the debate has been to erode the system of tenure and "normalise" it into one that is based on individual ownership.'[4]

This remains a hugely controversial issue and is what lay behind the appointment of a Committee of Inquiry on Crofting chaired by Professor Mark Shucksmith.[5] In their report, the Committee identified a number of themes to the contemporary debate over crofting reform.

First, there is the balance struck by crofting legislation and regulation between the interests of crofting, crofters and crofting communities . . . Second, there is also the debate between those who see the future of crofting in terms of agriculture and amalgamation of holdings, on the one hand, and those who see its future in terms of non-agricultural sources of income and

occupational pluralism on the other. Third, there is the difference in view between those who see the future of crofting in an
Irish-style model of individualised owner-occupation and those
who advocate a more collectivised model of community-owned
estates and crofting tenants. Finally, there is a debate between
those who see the future of crofting as lying in the hands of
others (a recurrent argument has been that crofters lack the
necessary ability) and those who advocate crofters themselves
taking responsibility for the future of crofting and crofting
communities.[6]

The Shucksmith report contained recommendations that would
tackle absenteeism and the threat of the free market by way of new
regulations. By this time, the SNP government was in charge and it
faced the same vociferous debate on these proposals when it sought
to incorporate them into the draft Crofting Reform (Scotland) Bill
2009. Once again, the crofting interest had split between those
who, this time around, opposed tighter regulation and wanted to
see a free market and those who did not. As I write, quite whether
the bill, as it is currently drafted, will do either terribly effectively
is a moot point.

The product of 1886 has evolved into a complex and, many
would argue, highly unsatisfactory guddle. It has undoubtedly
succeeded in retaining populations in some of the most fragile parts
of the UK but it remains open to question whether it can survive
the decline that has taken place in many areas and the pressures to
respond to the free market. James Hunter, the historian, gave
evidence to the Rural Affairs Committee of the Scottish Parliament
on 20 January 2010 and, as an illustration of how cumbersome the
system had become, presented them with a hypothetical example of
the kind of regulatory complexities faced by the Crofters Commission today:

Suppose (and the family circumstances here are entirely ima-
ginary) that I, a history professor in Dornoch, am left the
tenancy of a croft in South Uist, say, on the death of my father.
Once upon a time, I could only have staked my claim to the croft
by living on it. Now I don't have to. So I tell myself that it will be

nice to retire one day to the family croft – or, even if I never get round to so doing, it will be equally nice for my daughter to have that opportunity. So I retain the tenancy – which costs me just £15 a year in rent.

But in South Uist there are young folk in search of crofts. So the Crofters Commission, looking to assist them, starts absentee proceedings against me. I have good lawyers and those proceedings go on for ever and a day – until, in the end, I agree to assign the tenancy of my croft to someone else. However, I'm now looking to get the best offer for my tenancy and, crofts today being in demand, this comes, not from a young person in South Uist, but from an aspiring crofter in Surbiton.

The Commission, whose powers in this matter are entirely negative, can – and do – veto the chap from Surbiton, but they can't force me to sell my tenancy to even the most deserving individual in South Uist. So I'm left to come forward with nominee after nominee until, tiring of this charade and now wholly at odds with the Commission, I decide to exercise my purchase rights and buy the croft from the landlord (as crofters have been entitled to do since 1976) for fifteen times the annual rent – being £225.

This all takes forever – just as it takes forever, all over again, when the Commission, as it's entitled to do, now decides to force me, as the landlord of what's both a vacant (in law) and unoccupied (in fact) holding, to place a tenant on my croft. (The present Bill will change the definition of a purchased croft but will leave non-resident owners of those crofts open to being forced by the Commission to let their crofts.)

Since I've belatedly seen the light, or simply become fed up, I agree to let or sell my croft to a South Uist twenty-year-old – let's call him Iain – who assures both me and the Commission that he's determined to make a go of crofting. Unfortunately, one year into his occupancy of the croft Iain loses his job in South Uist and gets another in Glasgow where he marries and settles down.

Five years on, the Crofters Commission gets round to inquiring once more into absenteeism in South Uist and writes to Iain asking when, or if, he intends taking up residence on his croft.

He replies that he intends eventually to retire there, just as I once did, and the Commission, still looking to help aspiring crofters in South Uist, starts proceedings against him . . .

All of this will have taken many years, occupied many hundreds of man-hours at the Commission, cost the public purse a small fortune and achieved precisely nothing.[7]

It is this kind of ludicrous situation that the latest legislative efforts seek to address.

Crofting is clearly facing its biggest crisis in many years. Successive attempts to reform the tenure system have generated minimal consensus and led to an increasingly polarised debate within the crofting community. How this will be resolved remains to be seen but it is worth taking the time to read a remarkable and informative case study of the crofting community of Camuscross on the Isle of Skye which was written by Iain MacKinnon and Susan Walker and published in August 2009. In a fascinating thirty-five-page analysis of crofting in the community, the authors highlight the strengths of the crofting tenure system if it is properly administered and the weaknesses if it is not. In conclusion they state:

Opposition to the previous Crofting Reform Bill (leading to its drastic last-minute revision) was necessary to bring into stark relief the differing priorities of Government and crofters. Nearly five years have elapsed since then. As our report makes clear, the stress to the integrity of the crofting system has not slackened in that time. If, in this latest reform process, our Scottish Parliament fails to bring about meaningful legislative change to support hard-pressed crofting communities it will be a failure for all the political parties. It will mean that our political system has undermined the efforts of communities like our own to retain the social, cultural and agricultural spirit of crofting.[8]

Planting Forests Is a Sure Way
to Grow Rich

Trees are political

Scottish forestry owes a debt to Scotland's aristocratic landowners. It was landowners such as the Duke of Atholl, the Duke of Argyll and the Marquis of Breadalbane who began to adopt the principles of good forestry practice and manage their woodlands for productive timber. By 1800, any significant extent of the native forests of Scotland had long since disappeared and, along with the principles of good agriculture, the principles of silviculture began to be studied and adopted by progressive Scottish landowners.

Until the First World War, it was the large mixed-land-use estates, such as Cawdor, Atholl and Argyll, that were responsible for managing the bulk of Scottish productive forests. This was not due simply to the fact that such estates dominated the countryside but to the fact that, in Scots land law, all trees belong to the landowner. Tenant farmers who farmed over 90 per cent of the available land might perhaps have considered adopting the agroforestry practices of their French and German counterparts but they would have quickly stumbled upon the hard reality of the law. As a consequence, those who had responsibility for the stewardship of the vast majority of Scotland's land never had the opportunity to engage in forestry or woodland management since any reward for their exertions would have belonged to their landlord.

It took the trauma of the First World War to bring about change. The extensive felling of forests across the UK to support the war effort left the country denuded of trees and timber imports were vulnerable to enemy attack. There was an imperative to increase the security of supply and so, in 1917, the Acland Committee recommended that the UK should plant 1.7 million acres of forests of which two thirds should be established within thirty years. This was a job primarily for the state and so, in 1919, the Forestry Commission (FC) was set up as the state forestry service. It was hugely successful and had achieved over 80 per cent of its targets within twenty years although, in 1922, a parliamentary committee recommended it be abolished. It survived for much of the twentieth century because, despite bouts of hostility towards it, landowners actually liked the Forestry Commission as it provided two useful functions. Firstly, it underpinned a market in the acquisition of land and this helped many proprietors, especially those in the Highlands of Scotland, to remain solvent by selling off large tracts of land for planting. Secondly, it provided the legitimacy for seeking financial support for private sector forestry in the form of grants and tax reliefs. This was designed, in theory, to support the private sector to contribute their share of a national timber reserve. Early schemes such as the Forest Dedication Scheme were successful in delivering this goal and provided an incentive for private owners to manage their woodlands for the sustainable production of timber. Tax reliefs which recognised the long time horizons involved in forestry were also available and it was the manipulation of these reliefs in the 1960s by a new breed of forestry 'investors' that began the controversial growth in investment forestry of the 1970s and 1980s.

The Forestry Commission meanwhile continued to expand its estate to an all-time peak of 1,976,928 acres of Scotland in 1981. The Conservative governments in power from 1979 to 1997 were, at times, keen to privatise the FC and, although they never achieved this, they set in motion a programme of land disposal which was continued under every government since including all Scottish governments. Today, the FC estate is 1,648,193 acres in extent and accounts for less than half of the total woodland cover though over half of the timber production. Contrary to popular belief, the estate is not actually owned by the Forestry Commission but by Scottish Ministers and, in recent years, a succession of reviews has focused the FC on delivering a much wider range of public benefits than it has ever before been tasked with, including intensive recreational development such as mountain biking trails and the development of renewable energy from biomass, hydro and wind.

As the FC estate was being sold off in the 1980s, the government, at the same time, was keen to boost the private sector and it is this steady expansion that accompanied the decline of the public sector that has been one of the more significant features of the changing pattern of landownership in Scotland over the past thirty years.

Until 1988, when the availability of tax incentives was abolished, a high proportion of forest owners were high-rate taxpayers who invested in forestry in order to be able to offset expenditure against other sources of income. This was the era of Terry Wogan, Cliff Richard and Shirley Porter who were able to avoid tax by buying up land to afforest. The environmental and political outcry that accompanied this culminated in an *Observer* magazine exposé on St Valentine's Day in 1988. The front page screamed, 'Exposed – the tax ploys of the rich and famous' and, inside, Geoffrey Lean and George Rosie wrote, 'Planting forests is a sure way to grow rich, if you are rich already. Through tax relief and grants, the taxpayer will cover up to three-quarters of your costs without expecting any of your profit.'

It was a bonanza for the forestry profession and, as a forestry student in the early 1980s, I was among the vociferous opponents of these developments, which earned me a degree of enmity from my colleagues. I thought, reasonably in my view, that, if there were millions of pounds available for forestry investment, it should go to the farmers and crofters of Caithness rather than celebrities from London. This would have contributed towards the social goals of forestry which had been prominent in the 1940s and 50s. To many in the forestry industry, however, this sounded too much like socialist forestry even though I was still advocating giving money to private landowners! It was, therefore, a source of some delight when, in the 1988 Budget, Nigel Lawson abolished all tax reliefs for forestry and shockwaves went through the forestry world as this scam came to an end.

During the 1980s, controversy raged over planting in the so-called Flow Country in Caithness and Sutherland and on Sites of

Special Scientific Interest such as at Creag Meagaidh in Inverness-shire. Conservation groups and many Liberal and Labour politicians were calling for a halt to tax-avoidance forestry and for the focus to be more on integrating farming and forestry, benefitting local communities and restoring native woodlands.

The generous grants and tax reliefs led to rapid changes in landownership. Since the abolition of such incentives and their replacement by direct grants, existing landowners, many of whom are not high-rate taxpayers, are benefiting to a greater degree although there is still a significant involvement from external investors. During the 1990s, the grants on offer remained substantial with a number of landowners in receipt of over £1 million in public subsidies.

Although very small schemes receive higher payments, for those above 25 acres, a flat rate was payable. This meant that, for particularly large schemes of new planting, it was possible to end up making a surplus on the expensive process of afforestation and this was exploited by a number of investors in the early 1990s. Historically, it had been impossible to obtain any information on how much grant aid was paid to whom and, as recently as May 1994, the FC responded to queries about grant payments by claiming that such matters were confidential even though they involved substantial sums of public money. In 1995, it released, for the first time, a list of those in receipt of sums of over £1,000.[1]

Remarkably, the Forestry Commission did not have the power to refuse an application on the grounds that it was too expensive and, in one case in the early 1990s when the local community were against half of an extensive planting scheme, the Forestry Commission failed to persuade the landowner to amend his application. To people's astonishment, the government could only refuse an application on silvicultural grounds and were, in effect, held to ransom. The scheme went ahead at a cost of £2 million and involved the eviction of the only farming family left on the estate. This scandal prompted calls for reform and, within a few years, grant budgets and individual awards had been capped and funding schemes had become more targeted. Today, private investors remain prominent in forestry ownership with some wealthy individuals and timber processing companies in particular expanding their holdings in Scotland.[2] Since forestry remains outside of the tax system, investment in growing and mature forests remains popular among wealthy investors seeking a shelter from capital gains tax liabilities.

The precise ownership structure of private forestry remains something of a mystery. Unlike most other European countries, which not only consider the ownership of forests to matter a great deal but collect and publish extensive data on the subject, the Forestry Commission collects minimal information on forest holdings and publishes nothing. There is no forestry equivalent of the agricultural census and therefore no information on the current pattern of private ownership of woodlands and forests in Scotland despite the important influence government incentives have had on ownership patterns.

A first attempt to analyse forest ownership was made by Sandy Mather in 1987. The extent of new-investor forestry was underlined by the finding that traditional landed estates accounted for less than half of the private forest area compared with over 90 per cent in the 1960s. Corporate interests accounted for 20.5 per cent of private forest holdings with pension, insurance and other financial institutions such as Electricity Supply Nominees and the Midland Bank accounting for 44 per cent of such corporate lands. Mather observed that:

> there has been no stated policy towards ownership structure. Whether by design or by default, the state has exerted an influence of fundamental significance for the structure of forest ownership through its choice of policy instruments. Whether by design or default, the state has facilitated the expansion of financial ownership of forests in Scotland.[3]

The UN Economic Commission for Europe (UNECE) collects and publishes data from 56 members states on forest ownership. Many countries, such as Sweden, not only report on the pattern of forestry ownership, but on the gender, age and residence of owners. The UK, by contrast, provides no data on the demographics, gender or residency of forest owners. The Scottish data supplied to the most recent UNECE survey was based upon a UK sample survey conducted in 1977. In an attempt to do rather better than this, I undertook some research for the Forest Policy Group. The results are quite revealing:[4]

Of the 67% of Scotland's forest area that is privately-owned:

- 91% is owned either by landed estates or by investment owners,
- 55% is owned by absentee landowners and,
- 32% is owned by people who live outside Scotland.

Scotland's forest resource is thus dominated by the state, landed estates and forestry investors. This contrasts with other European countries where a significant proportion is owned by individual resident owners, farmers, co-operatives and municipalities.

In comparison to the rest of Europe, Scotland has by far the most concentrated pattern of private forest ownership dominated by large holdings and by far the lowest proportion of the population involved in owning forests. A detailed comparison with eight European countries (Austria, Belgium, France, Hungary, Latvia, Lithuania, Norway, Poland and Slovakia) reveals that whereas 55% of forest holdings in Scotland are larger that 50ha, the equivalent European figure is 1.6%. Conversely, whereas 60% of European forest holdings are smaller than 1ha, the Scottish figure is 6.3% (see Figure 8).

Not only do the citizens of other European countries have a far greater stake in their forests but they also own much of the forest industry. For example, Metsäliitto is a Finnish producer co-operative owned by 130,000 Finnish forest owners. It is Europe's largest wood producer, has a turnover of €8.4 billion and employs 30,000 people. Metsäliitto was established during the 1930s following land reforms which saw 51% of the country's forest area pass to individual land owners. In Sweden, 51,000 forest owners, owning 36,000 forest properties, own Södra, a company operating timber processing and pulp and paper plants.

For Scotland's forest economy to fulfil its true potential, the ownership, governance and use of the nation's forests must be in the hands of local people and businesses to reflect local and regional priorities rather than the demands of financial investors and the large-scale timber-processing industry.

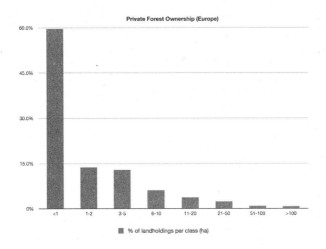

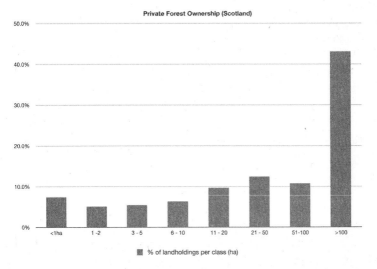

Figure 8: The pattern of private forest ownership in Europe and Scotland

Source: Wightman, 2012. Forest Ownership in Scotland

Some important reforms have been made to broaden participation in forestry. Community ownership of woodlands has expanded with over 200 community groups across Scotland owning or managing woodlands.[5] There have been important recent reforms to the law on trees and land tenure. The Land Reform Policy Group (LRPG) recommended in their final report in 1999 that there should be new legislation to 'give rights for secure tenants to plant trees, to cut and sell timber, and so to derive an income from farm woodlands integrated with their agricultural business'.[6]

And so, in 2003, the Agricultural Holdings (Scotland) Act was passed which, among other things, provided that 'for so long as the tenancy continues to have effect, the right to cut timber from any trees planted on the land by the tenant on or after the coming into force of this section; and any such timber belongs to the tenant'.[7] This might seem quite unimportant but it ended a law going back to the days of the medieval royal hunting forests. It is an example of the kind of radical reforming land law that was the hallmark of the first Scottish Parliament between 1999 and 2003 and which has made a real difference to tenant farmers across Scotland with a number of successful schemes promoting agroforestry and restoration of woodland pasture.[8]

I Will Not Allow House Prices to Get Out of Control

The new property-owning democracy

The largest group of landowners in Scotland are those who own the 2.5 million owner-occupied houses across the country, predominantly in urban areas. In 1900, the majority of Scottish households rented substandard one- or two-roomed houses from private landlords. In 1970, the majority rented their home from the local council. Today, over 62 per cent of homes are owner-occupied. The increase in owner-occupation has been particularly notable in recent decades as a result of the sale of council housing introduced by the Conservative government in 1980 when owner-occupation was below 40 per cent.

Not always thought of in discussions about landownership, housing is not significant in terms of the pattern of landownership across the country but is hugely significant in terms of its impact on the economy as a whole. The dramatic increase in house prices leading up to the credit crunch was due to the Labour government's policy of low interest rates which persuaded people to borrow cheap money and bid up the price of housing to levels beyond that which could reasonably be serviced by incomes. Home ownership is an extremely tax efficient form of investment with no capital gains tax paid on windfall gains from sale. As a consequence, a speculative bubble grew as house prices rose to levels increasingly outwith the reach of those on average earnings and key workers such as nurses, police and teachers. A crash was inevitable and should give pause for thought to those who believe that the rise in homeownership represents an unquestioning good for society and the economy.

Recent research shows a growing gap between the poor and the wealthy with the personal wealth held by the wealthiest 1 per cent rising from 17 per cent of the national wealth in 1991 to 24 per cent in 2000. Britain as a whole is moving back towards the levels of inequality in wealth and poverty last seen more than forty years ago.[1] At a total value of £3.51 trillion, housing is the single greatest source of wealth for UK households[2] and, before house prices started to fall during the period 2008–2010, the wealth of many owner-occupiers was rising faster in the value of their homes than through their earned income. For such households, these increases represent a tax-free gain at the expense of those in society who own no property and pay full taxes out of their earned income.

The boom in house prices in recent years is, in fact, a boom in land values. The cost of a house itself – the building materials and labour – has changed little over the years. Instead, as every estate agent knows, the value of a house is down to location, location, location and the growing number of asset-rich homeowners is a direct consequence of the willingness of successive governments to hand over the rise in value of land (which is a direct proxy for a growing economy) to those who own a house on it. This is illustrated in Figure 9 which shows the value of an identical house, in similar neighbourhoods but in different parts of the UK. All prices are relative to a £150,000 house in London. The difference in the price to be paid is the difference in land value.

The capture of land values by a wealthy class of property owners has been achieved largely through borrowing. In November 2012, the total UK personal debt stood at £1.42 trillion. Of this, 89 per cent or £1.264 trillion was debt on property.[3] This compares with the total UK national debt which, in December 2012, stood at £1.114 trillion.[4] The borrowing on houses is therefore 12 per cent greater than the total UK debt even after all the bank bailouts.

Much of this borrowing is secured on the value of land which represents anything from 30 to 80 per cent of the value of a house depending on the location. Around 43 per cent of all mortgages in the UK are interest-only and the owners are, in effect, no more than tenants since, if they cannot pay the interest, they are left with nothing.

Figure 9: Diagram showing the difference in price of an
identical house across the UK

Source: Nationwide Building Society

A number of years ago I stayed for a week in a hunting lodge in
the Highlands. In a large wicker basket next to the fire was a supply
of newspapers. One day, in this basket, I found what turned out to
be copies of papers relating to a board meeting of one of Scotland's
leading housebuilding companies. They contained a number of
evaluations of land acquisitions around the Central Belt of Scotland and revealed that the main source of profits for housing
developers is land values which can rise by tenfold once planning
permission has been secured. The capture of rising land values by
developers and homeowners represents a massive transfer of wealth
from the poorest in society to the wealthiest.

Forget the traditional landed classes. It is the UK's growing
middle classes who are the new lairds, appropriating billions of
pounds of land value secured against record levels of borrowing.
All this money needs to be paid back and those same people will
also have to pay the increased taxes necessary to pay the national
debt. More and more people are now learning the hard way that the
prosperity that so many politicians have so irresponsibly led us to
believe can be achieved on the back of rising house prices is an

illusion that will have to be paid for by generations to come. Forget your inheritance – here's some debt instead.

The dispossessed younger generation has taken to the Internet to make its views known.[5] In one such website (www.pricedout.org.uk), Kate John, its volunteer press officer, observes, 'Whenever you read a newspaper, it's "Oh no, house prices have fallen" or "Good news, house prices recovering". But who really benefits from rising house prices?' Having saved diligently for years to put down a deposit to buy a house, she found that all her savings could be wiped out by a mere one month's rise in house prices.

All this represents a serious threat to social cohesion and will lead to growing resentment between the generations as the ability of the younger population to support a growing older population will be seriously compromised. According to David Willetts, the Conservative MP, the pinch will come in 2030 as the burden for providing pensions and care to the post-war baby boom generation will fall on a smaller, poorer and badly housed younger generation who will be faced with working longer, paying higher taxes and receiving fewer services.[6] Between 1995 and 2005, for example those aged twenty-five to thirty-four saw their wealth fall whilst that of those aged fifty-five to sixty-four tripled on the back of inflated residential land values.[7]

In his first Budget, Gordon Brown made the following commitment:

> For most people, the acquisition of a house is the biggest single investment that they will make. Homeowners rightly expect their investment to be protected by sensible policies pursued by Government. I am determined that as a country we never return to the instability, speculation and negative equity that characterised the housing market in the 1980s and 1990s.
>
> Volatility is damaging both to the housing market and to the economy as a whole, so stability will be central to our policy to help homeowners. We must be prepared to take the action necessary to secure it. I will not allow house prices to get out of control and put at risk the sustainability of the recovery.[8]

He failed. In many parts of Scotland, the ratio of average house prices to average earnings is over ten to one.[9] The answer to the boom and bust of the economy as a whole can be found by eliminating property bubbles which lead to excessive borrowing. To do this, it is necessary to adopt new ways of dampening rising land values. These might include extending capital gains tax to main homes or introducing land value taxation – an idea that will be discussed further in Chapter 30.[10]

But achieving a more stable and fairer housing market also requires new mechanisms that do not rely on the speculative activity of volume housebuilders which represents a classic case of market failure – as prices rise, production fails to keep up with demand but as prices fall, builders retreat and output collapses. A business model built on profits from land values to finance the building of homes is crazy and it is worth reflecting on how things can be done differently. A recent pamphlet on the housing crisis from the think tank Compass reminded us that the former New Town Development Corporations 'purchased land at agricultural prices and provided infrastructure with Treasury bond finance, issued planning permissions and used the resulting uplift in land value to repay the loans'.[11] This, and alternative models from other countries in Europe, such as Denmark, where banks and lenders share risk with owners, is the way forward. Unless some radical thinking is done, the future looks grim.

With MPs and MSPs making significant capital gains on property acquired using their allowances, the question of housing affordability takes on a new and rather more pointed relevance in British democracy.[12]

As Charles Moore recently wrote in the *Daily Telegraph*:

The promise of liberal capitalism is that people are free to share in and accumulate the rewards of their labours, and that this, in turn, will help those rewards increase. For millions of people, this is now not happening. Every expectation of intergenerational security on which bourgeois life thrives is blocked. With the public purse as empty as the voters' pockets, no political party can see the way through this. Ministers, bankers, Parliament have all failed, while looking after themselves comfortably in the process. So the conditions are ripe for a new politics of grievance and anger. Which is where revolutions begin.[13]

Three Score Men with Clubs and Staves

The struggle to protect common land

Ask any lawyer about common land in Scotland and they will probably say that there is none left.[1] Until a few years ago I would probably have agreed with them since, as related in the first few chapters of this book, Scotland's history is a history of the appropriation of common land into private ownership. In particular, the division of Scotland's commonties looms large in any study of the commons and it is frequently asserted that there are no commonties left. This is undoubtedly due mainly to the extensive public record of division under a series of seventeenth-century acts allowing for the commonties to be divided among neighbouring landowners. Search the catalogue of the National Archives of Scotland and you will find 888 records relating to commonties including 345 beautiful plans. The geographer Ian Adams undertook an extensive study of Scotland's commonties in 1967 and documented the fate of as many as he could in 1971 in his *Directory of Former Scottish Commonties*.[2] The title is misleading, however, as we shall see.

Seven distinct types of common land can be identified in Scotland:

- Crown commons
- Greens and Loans
- Commonties
- Scattalds
- Common mosses
- Runrig lands
- Burgh commons (common good land)

As Cosmo Innes, already quoted, said, 'Looking over our country, the land held in common was of vast extent.'[3] And Tom Johnston claimed that by:

> adding together the common lands of the Royal Burghs, the common lands of the Burghs which held their foundation rights from private individuals, the extensive commons of the villages and the hamlets, the common pasturages and grazings, and the commons attaching to run-rig tenancies, we shall be rather under than over estimating the common acreage in the latter part of the sixteenth century, at fully one-half of the entire area of Scotland.[4]

It is difficult to verify this figure since Johnston provides no precise definition of common land. The claim is not sustained by what we know of the extent of commonties and burgh commons which has been established through historical research and, in the case of commonties, by the maps of recorded divisions. Most probably, Johnston is including in this figure the extensive areas of land over which peasants exercised common use which, in 1500, was very probably around half the country. But only a small part of this would come to be defined as any one of the seven categories of common mentioned above as feudal titles swallowed up historic patterns of use without a murmur of protest.

Commons are not the same as the community-owned land we have become familiar with in Scotland in recent years where communities have bought estates, forests and other types of property. What gives community-owned land its distinctiveness is that membership of the landowning body is open to everyone in the community. The land itself could easily be – and, indeed, formerly was – in private ownership. Commons on the other hand are distinctive because their status reflects a historic quality of the land itself and an assembly of user rights vested in the public.

For centuries the ordinary people of Scotland have had rights over land which have evolved through practice, tradition and habitual use. Historically, prior to feudalism, most land was in a sense common. However, as feudalism evolved, rights were eroded and marginalised as the strength of feudal property law swept across the country.

Ian Adams and Robin Callander have carried out the most detailed analysis of commons history in Scotland and characterise the various types as follows:[5]

CROWN COMMONS

These were commons held directly by the Crown and thought to have their origins in the once extensive royal hunting forests. Most were eventually feued by the Crown and those that survived suffered from increasing encroachment. An act of 1828 allowed for the division of Crown commons between adjoining landowners.

GREENS AND LOANS

Greens are small areas of common land usually closely associated with villages and can be found across Scotland in places such as West Linton, Dirleton, Udny, Aberlady and Carstairs.[6] They provided a public place for markets, for milking cows, bleaching linen and a range of other communal activities. Historically, they had either been gifted by local landowners or were simply the surviving communal ground of a former *fermtoun*. Most of these greens belong to the inhabitants of the village although title has often been assumed by the local authority. Very little systematic research has been carried out into greens in Scotland in comparison to England and Wales where a formal and active system of registration is in place and any land on which a significant number of inhabitants have indulged in lawful sports and pastimes for twenty years, as of right, can be registered. There are thought to be about 3,665 registered greens in England and Wales.[7]

Loans are linear routes to and from an area of common ground or other public place. Unlike rights of way which are on private land but over which the public has a right of access, loans are themselves common land. A particular type of green is the grazing stance situated along old drove roads and this is often associated with loans. One famous stance is opposite the Potarch Inn on

Deeside. Others can be found in Glen Clova – now a car park, with picnic tables, managed by Angus Council – in Falkirk – where the remnants of the Falkirk Tryst stance is now the site of a fair in the summer and the rest is a golf course and housing – and in Alyth – where the Market Muir was the meeting point for drovers coming down from the north.

SCATTALDS

Scattalds are found in Shetland and are the equivalent in Udal law to the commonties in feudal tenure. They could be divided under the 1695 commonties legislation. Historically there were at least 127 scattalds in Shetland and 15 or more of these survive today.[8]

COMMON MOSSES

Common mosses provided essential livelihoods to local people through the gathering of peat for fuel. They were invariably associated with commonties and could be divided by the 1695 act. But the act also recognised the practical difficulties involved in dividing mosses and allowed for them to be excluded.

> And where mosses shall happen to be in the said commonties, with power to the said lords to divide the said mosses amongst the several parties having interest therein, in manner foresaid. Or in case it be instructed to the said lords that the said mosses cannot be conveniently divided, his majesty, with consent foresaid, statutes and declares that the said mosses shall remain common, with free ish and entry thereto, whether divided or not.[9]

This exception in the act resulted in many mosses being left out of divisions and surviving as independent commons. Once a moss had been left out of a division, it could never then be divided in future. Many are thought to still survive but again, many will have subsequently been lost by encroachment and illegal appropriation. Balerno Common in Midlothian is a good example of an extant commonty. Consisting of two areas – Red Moss and Bavelaw

Marsh – it was excluded from the commonty division of 1768. The whole area is a Site of Special Scientific Interest and the Scottish Wildlife Trust manage part of it as a nature reserve.[10]

Rigs were narrow strips of cultivated land. They formed the predominant method of farming in pre-Improvement times that was known as 'runrig'. By a separate act in 1695, rigs could be divided in a similar manner to commonties. As Callander points out:

> Originally, many areas of runrig, together with their shared hill ground, were held by two or more proprietors. Each owned a number of rigs which were interspersed with the rigs of the other owners and each owner had an undivided share in the ownership of the common hill. The common hill was thus a commonty and the runrig lands equivalent to a commonty on arable land.[11]

Since runrig lands were more valuable, their division proceeded apace and it would be futile to expect any to have survived centuries of intensive agricultural use.

COMMONTIES

As note earlier, it is frequently claimed that Scotland's commonties have disappeared. This indeed is implicit in the title of Ian Adams' *Directory of Former Scottish Commonties*. In fact, they are not all defunct. There are actually around ninety commonties in Scotland for which there is no apparent record of division.[12] They are spread over twenty-five of Scotland's thirty-four counties and range in size from a few hectares to over 2,000 hectares (see Figure 2). Many of these need further research and investigation. Some are known to have survived as noted later in this chapter. At least one, the Rynacra Commonty on the flanks of Schiehallion, survived until 1926 when it was eventually divided (see Figure 10).

As the communal use of all these commons declined, many were quietly appropriated by neighbouring landowners through encroachment and with fences being moved, loans ploughed and stances enclosed. Very little systematic investigation or recording has been carried out into these important local commons. As a result, time is running out to identify and assert public rights over them. It is vital that efforts are made to identify and assert the public's rights over these commons. Lack of awareness of Scotland's commons has prevented this happening and has also led to the ease with which they can surreptitiously be appropriated by powerful interests.

The remainder of this chapter explores a range of surviving commons. It has accumulated on a rather ad hoc basis over the past few years and in no way represents anything approaching a systematic survey or synthesis. The field is ripe for much further digging. Nothing noted here is common good (for which, see the next chapter) or land that is in community ownership but not common land (see the distinction made earlier).

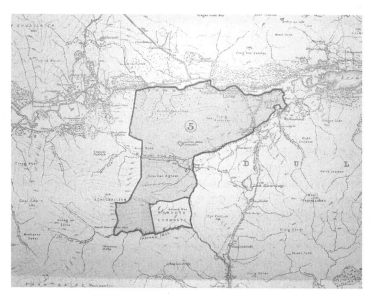

Figure 10: Rynacra Commonty, Perthshire

Source: Sales particulars of the Breadalbane Estate, 1920

CARLUKE

Of the ninety or so commonties across Scotland for which there is
no record of division, one is in the Parish of Carluke. In Ian
Adams' *Directory*, it is noted as follows.

CARLUKE

Unidentified common

In 1839 86 acres remained in the parish as undivided common.[13]

This information was derived from the *New Statistical Account
of Scotland* which was, until Adams' work, the most systematic
enquiry into the extent of commonties in Scotland. I noted this
along with others of interest and promptly forgot all about them.

In May 2005, I was doing some routine research on landownership in Lanarkshire and was examining a Land Certificate for a 123-
hectare forest to the north of Carluke. The map showed an area
coloured yellow and, although it was not immediately relevant to
what I was interested in, I had a look in the description of the
property to see what this related to. The description reads as follows:

> Subjects lying to the north of Yellowshields Road, Carluke edged
> in red on the Title Plan, being 122.6 hectares in measurement on
> the Ordnance Map; Together with (One) a heritable and irre-
> deemable servitude right of access for foot and vehicular pur-
> poses over the road tinted brown on the Title Plan. (Two) right
> of common grazing on the hill of Commonty tinted yellow on the
> Title Plan and (Three) servitude right of way'. . .

This is as exciting as it gets reading title documents! Here, in the
new Land Register, in 2005, with a full state-backed guarantee of
title is delineated on a modern Ordnance Survey map a commonty.
Clearly this owner has only a right of grazing on the commonty and
thus their right is a mere servitude. But there will be others who
have property rights in the commonty – those who, were they to
petition for a division, would be entitled to ownership of part of the
commonty.

Those entitled to a share of a commonty when it was divided
were the heritors (landowners) in the parish. Historically, in rural

Scotland, that amounted to not very many people. In some cases, one landowner owned the whole parish – in which case, the commonty was extinguished since it was no longer the undivided common property of a number of heritors. In the Parish of Carluke in 1840, there were fifty-four heritors. Virtually everyone else was a tenant. In normal circumstances, each heritor would have a share in any division. Indeed, in all probability, there was a division of a much larger commonty and this 86-acre piece of land is a remnant, possibly a moss, which was excluded. And this is where things begin to get interesting since, in the Parish of Carluke, there are now many more heritors. The majority of householders own their own home and are thus owners of land, albeit small bits. Indeed, in the town of Carluke alone, there were 5,388 households in 2001 of which two-thirds are owner-occupiers. There are therefore somewhere in the region of 7,000 individuals with a claim to a share in the commonty assuming that, on average, there were two names on each title deed. It would be impractical to make such a division and thus the most appropriate vehicle for owning the common is some for of trust or community company.

A few months after this discovery I contacted Carluke Parish Historical Society who knew nothing of the commonty or, indeed, what a commonty was. But even more interesting facts were yet to emerge. The commonty is in the middle of what was then the UK's largest wind farm, Black Law, owned and operated by Scottish Power. Indeed, it is surrounded by wind turbines on all sides but none are on the commonty itself. This transforms the potential of a piece of windy moorland from being essentially worthless to rather lucrative. But the good folk of the Parish of Carluke are not sharing in the bonanza that has been created for the handful of landowners on whose ground the fifty-four turbines are situated since they were not aware of its existence and so could not enter into any negotiations.

When I contacted Scottish Power to ask why no turbines had been planned for the commonty, I was told that they knew all about it, that all existing leases specifically exclude the commonty and that they had not sought to develop it because they were uncertain as to who would legally be in a position to sign the lease. In 2012, however, the Carluke Development Trust decided to attempt to resolve the uncertainty by claiming ownership and registering a title to the land.[14] How many more commonties lie undetected across Scotland? There's no clear answer but at least the process of land registration is beginning to uncover them. What remains to be done is to increase awareness among communities so that they can reclaim their historic land rights.

ALYTH

Not all commonties have lain unnoticed. In the town of Alyth, on the eastern border of Perthshire, a debate over commonty rights has been raging for over a hundred years. The Parish of Alyth contained three commonties – the Forest of Alyth Commonty, the South Commonty and the North Commonty – as well as the runrig lands of Aberbothrie and Bardomy. The Forest of Alyth Commonty extended to 7,946 acres to the north of the town and is still named as such on the Ordnance Survey map. The South Commonty of Alyth was 364 acres in extent and lay to the south-east of the town and the North Commonty of Alyth or Hill of Alyth Commonty consists of several hundred acres.[15]

The Forest of Alyth Commonty was divided in 1792 after seventy years of legal and physical dispute. The Court of Session records that:

> The people of Blacklunans and Bleaton, in a numerous body, accompanied with Mr Smith's Tenants of West-forest came and . . . they proceeded to pull down a part of the pursuer's Mill of Drumturn and Mill Dam, threatening to destroy it wholly; which they probably would have done, had they met with any resistance to irritate them further. And some time thereafter when the pursuer was about to erect his summer sheilings as usual, for his beastial, in the middle of his ordinary pasture, these people turned out a second time. In greater numbers than before, about three score men, with clubs and staves, and other weapons; and before the sheiling was finished, after abundance of abuse of language bestowed upon the pursuer and his servants, who were at work thereat, they razed it to the ground, and as the pursuer had been informed, made a bon-fire of the timber, after he and his servants were forced to withdraw.

This was to be the first in a series of instances of resistance to the division of commonties in the parish. The South Commonty was divided in 1858 after eighty years of legal wrangling. The inhabitants of Alyth were left with 6 acres of the common as a market stance and this remains today on the south side of the town. The North Commonty or Hill of Alyth Commonty was initially to be included in the south common division but was dropped from that process to be dealt with separately. In 1812, a summons was raised for the division of the Hill of Alyth. Sir James Ramsay of Bamff was particularly anxious to see a division and wrote in a memorial that:

> it is of infinite consequence that as much of the hill as possible should be obtained at this place. It is quite in sight of the house of Bamff, and in its present appearance it is an object of all others the most dreary and repulsive.

But the process stalled and, by 1843, the Hill of Alyth was noted as still being a commonty in the *New Statistical Account of Scotland*. Since then, no further actions have been raised to divide the commonty and it therefore remains a commonty to this day – except that some wholly underhand and nefarious land deals have been done. In 1925, the Reverend James Meikle wrote, 'The upper part is common and the old feuars of Alyth had the right of pasture and of cutting turf. The boundaries have been encroached upon on several sides, the encroachments being known in tradition.' This was an early warning of things to come.

At this point, it is worth stressing that there were two quite distinct interests in the Hill of Alyth. The first was a servitude right – a right of use – which was enjoyed by certain feuars in the town who typically had rights of 'feal and divot, stone and mortar and pasturage' over the common. The owners of such rights would have no right to a share of any division. The second interest was a right of property – that is to say, those landowners who, in the event the commonty was divided, would be eligible to a share in the division. In 1925, this would come to only a modest number, including the lairds of Airlie and Bamff, but, later in the twentieth century, all those who owned property in the parish including homeowners would be entitled to be party to any division.

A Non Domino

Most land transactions are straightforward. Harry sells land to Sally. Before Sally buys it, her solicitor checks that Harry does in fact own it, that there are no outstanding creditors and that there are no onerous burdens or restrictions on the title. Houses, farms and shops are sold in such a way every year. But Harry can also sell land to Sally that he does not own and that no one appears to own. He can do this by granting her an *a non domino* disposition – literally, a disposition 'from someone who is not the owner' and if no one raises any objections, then Sally will become the owner ten years after the title is recorded provided that she can demonstrate open, peaceable and continuous possession. She becomes the owner through our old friend prescription. Two of Scotland's leading property lawyers describe it as follows:

> It sometimes happens that someone notices that a piece of ground is unoccupied and apparently abandoned. Using prescription, it is possible to acquire ownership. What happens is that the person gets a friend to grant to him a gratuitous disposition of the land and the disposition is recorded'. . .[16]

Eilean I Vow is a small island in the middle of Loch Lomond in the narrow north end between Inveruglas and Ardlui. In the middle sits an ancient ruined castle, a former stronghold of the Clan MacFarlane who lived in it until 1697. In 1784, the chief of the clan MacFarlane sold all his land to pay off debts but it is not clear whether Eilean I Vow was included. On 29 September 1994, Anne Squires granted an *a non domino* disposition to her husband Dennis Squires (the Squires own the Ardlui Hotel). Three years later, on 28 August 1997, a Mr Douglas Laurence McFarlane from Bo'ness claimed to have tried unsuccessfully to trace ownership of the island and recorded an *a non domino* disposition from himself to himself.[17] Then, some years later, the Clan

MacFarlane Society realised what had happened and claimed that the island belonged to the clan. In August 2006, Mr McFarlane told *The Herald* newspaper, 'Come next August, we'd be looking to sell the island for £1 million. I think that's a fair price.'[18] August 2007 was a critical date as it would then be ten years since the recording of the deed and, provided he could show possession and if the Squires could not, Mr McFarlane might be in a position to assume full ownership. The Clan MacFarlane Society were predictably aggrieved and, on 2 November 2006, Sheena Laura Mac-Farlane, the wife of the Clan Society's Vice President, added to the claims by recording an *a non domino* disposition in favour of the Clan MacFarlane Charitable Trust. Quite where that leaves everybody is a little unclear![19]

Until recently, such chaos was commonplace. In recent years, however, *a non domino* titles have been brought into disrepute. Some people have used the facility to try to obtain land by stealth and, in one case, a speculator presented an *a non domino* disposition for a house in which the owner was actually living. It is an area fraught with danger, and in recent years the law has been tightened up.[20] A legal case in Aberdeen ruled that an *a non domino* disposition in the form of Harry to Harry as in the case of Mr McFarlane does not even satisfy the basic requirements of being *ex facie* valid. These can, therefore, no longer be accepted for recording. Section 43 of the Land Registration etc. (Scotland) Act 2012 provides a new statutory basis for these dodgy deeds. The issue is further complicated by the fact that, for such a deed to be competent to found prescription, it must not betray its *a non domino* character. This is what, in my view, renders the Airlie deed, cited on p. 283, invalid. But, if the deed appears to be otherwise normal, how is anyone to know that it is in fact *a non domino*? That is a good question and can lead to lengthy legal battles over valuable land.[21]

Why is such a piece of legal trickery still allowed? Well, it is worth observing that the wailing and gnashing of teeth over the practice is somewhat synthetic since this is exactly how much of Scotland was rendered into private ownership over the centuries. The facts that more people own property today, that the new Land Register is more transparent, that land is so much more valuable and that knowledge of the law is more widespread all mean there is greater awareness and scrutiny of any potential abuse compared to the secretive world of the seventeenth and eighteenth centuries. But we are still faced with the fact that *a non domino* deeds are allowed to form the basis of ownership. ∤

In some cases, this is legitimate. Where, for example, a farm has been owned for generations but a small or even a modest parcel of land has no clear title, the owners should be able to rectify the deficiency and generate a marketable title. Where, though, land has no clear owner, things become a bit trickier. In strict law, no land has no owner. If land belongs to no one, it falls automatically to the Crown and no one should be able to get hold of land by an *a non domino* deed. This was recognised by the Scottish Law Commission in their recent report on land registration and the subsequent Land Registration etc. (Scotland) Act 2012 (which provides a new statutory basis for this nonsense) even admits (in section 43(1)) that such deeds are, in all respects, invalid.

If *a non domino* dispositions are used to claim ownership of land which genuinely does not have an owner, then, naturally, one has to ask whether this is legitimate. Is this, in fact, not simply the latest manifestation of the legalised theft doctrine that has been developed and applied so successfully by Scotland's landowners down the ages? How much land is being claimed this way is difficult to ascertain. The Keeper was unable to provide any figures on the extent of land over which she withheld indemnity, although as I remarked on p. 122, such cases are commonplace. By definition, this is all land that the alleged owner cannot demonstrate that they own. So why should a system of public registers of land allow them to gain title? All such land should either fall automatically to the Crown and put up for public auction.

In 1923, the Earl of Airlie sold a number of farms adjoining the commonty but included as part of them portions of the commonty itself even though he had never owned them. In title deeds, the seller of land is supposed to state upon what basis he has acquired the land so that a continuous chain of ownership can be established. In the title deed for the farm of Loyalbank, the Earl of Airlie merely states that the portion of the commonty extending to 218 acres is 'presently occupied and possessed by the said George Cromar Whamond and others'. . .' George Whamond was the tenant to whom the farm was being sold. He was a tenant of the Earl of Airlie and owned nothing and yet here is the Earl of Airlie citing his possession as evidence of ownership. All the farms were sold 'without warrandice, express or implied', meaning that no guarantee was being given as to the ownership of the land in question.[22]

Fears grew that an encroachment had taken place but little was done until 1948 when a fence was erected across the commonty and passions were roused. The Town Council, which had initially approved the fence, now took up the case and began a correspondence with the Earl of Airlie's solicitors, Mackenzie and Kermack. They admitted in a letter of 3 March 1949 to Provost David Sim that:

The Hill of Alyth was Common to the adjoining proprietors and while no actual division has been judicially made, recognised areas have been for a considerable period attached to the Farms, *ex adverso* the Hill. The portions of the Hill attached to the Farms belonging to the Lord Airlie . . . were sold along with these farms but no warrandice express or implied was granted as regards these areas.

The Earl of Airlie therefore simply grabbed the commonty and sold it to his tenants without the approval of the other parties with commonty rights. These titles are defective in law since only a judicial division can provide legal ownership of any part of a commonty. The 1695 act is the 'only competent mode of division of a commonty'.[23]

Nevertheless, Provost Sim sought legal advice and was informed that:

There is no doubt whatsoever that the Hill of Alyth is a commonty. The titles of Bamff Estate confirm this, as do the titles of the lands which originally belonged to the Earl of Airlie, but which now belong to various proprietors of other grounds surrounding the commonty.

The commonty has never been divided . . . I would add that the views I have expressed are most emphatically confirmed by the Edinburgh Agents for the Earl of Airlie.[24]

Meanwhile the townspeople were getting fed up and, on 24 July 1949, conducted a symbolic exercise of their rights on the commonty (see Plate 6). According to the report in the *Perthshire Advertiser* of 27 July 1949:

About 500 of them climbed the hill on Sunday and, working in small parties, cut divots round the bases of a 600 yard stock fence, most of which collapsed. In this way they exercised their right to 'fuel, feal and divot' (peat, moss and turf). A leaflet issued by the Commonty Defence Committee states, 'The hill of Alyth Commonty has been fenced for the first time. The fight to retain the hill for the people is not one for Alyth alone. We have fought for our country and our own hill commonty as our predecessors did in the cases of the Reekie Linn and Jordanstone.'

The following Friday, a dedicated few made another excursion on to the hill and, this time, raised the stakes by cutting the fence (see Plate 7). The *Perthshire Advertiser* carried the story the next day.

In spite of warnings by the police, an Alyth councillor, a member of the Alyth Hill Commonty Committee, yesterday carried out his threat to cut part of the fence on the hill of Alyth. By doing so he earned the promise from the police that he would be charged with 'malicious mischief.' Around 30 people were charged following a demonstration, in which 500 Alyth people cut down the fencing because they believe the hill to be common land. The question of the hill was raised in the House of Commons on

Thursday. The Secretary of State for Scotland said he was aware of the situation at Alyth. He repeated an answer given at Perth in February of this year that the question whether any rights were being infringed by the erection of fencing could only be decided by a court of law, and he had no right to intervene.

As before, however, nothing came of this flurry of correspondence or the unrest on the hill. Locals, however, were very active in asserting the commonty during this period. A number of town councillors and feuars wrote to the Rt Hon. Arthur Woodburn, Secretary of State for Scotland in March 1949. In their letter, they complain of the inordinate expense of taking their case to court. They point out that 'Historians such as Mr Thos Johnston, Mr Cosmo Innes and others also warn us of the danger of becoming subject to landowner made laws, supported in the past by lawyers who have lent their knowledge and abilities to the highest bidder.' They go on to point out that '[t]housands of acres of Common land in the surrounding district have been enclosed by landowners in the operation of the law of prescription simply because the people were afraid or couldn't afford to contest them'.[25]

My own investigations in the surrounding countryside bear this out with at least two other commonties that have simply been divided up in the past 30 years and sold by owners who have no title. In one case, the Keeper of the Registers of Scotland has added a note to the effect that 'Agent aware granters apparently only have title to rights in pasturage.' In other words, they only have a right of use and not of ownership. Nevertheless, this lawyer saw fit to draft and submit for recording a deed that conveyed ownership. Without legal intervention either by court action or legislation to prevent such theft, this situation will continue.

In 1977, the Earl of Airlie's trustees made another, even more blatant disposal of another 54 acres to Ramsay of Bamff and 52 acres to the owner of Westfield Farm. The deed is quite brutally honest about the whole affair. It claims that the 106 acres of the Hill of Alyth being sold form part of the Lands and Baronies of Lintrathen, Alyth and Cortachy, which had been granted to the trustees in 1901, but admits that:

the said subjects known as the Hill of Alyth are not referred to by name in the particular description of the said Lands and Baronies . . . and that we as Trustees foresaid and our predecessors as proprietors of the aforesaid lands have never claimed the said subjects as part of our or their property but that it can be construed from the titles of the said Lands and Barony that the said subjects may be included therein.[26]

In other words the commonty is not ours to sell but here it is anyway! Such a deed is known as an *a non domino* deed (for a full discussion on the term *a non domino*, see pp. 278–80). But, as Scotland's two leading conveyancers observe, 'a disposition *a non domino* must not reveal that the disponer is not the owner, or it will lose its potential status as a foundation writ'[27] because it would be invalid *ex facie*.[28]

As has been clearly stated by a number of authorities, the commonty was never divided and, to that extent, still exists. It has, however, purportedly been sold. How competent those trans-actions are in the light of the admissions made of non-ownership is a very interesting question. As recently as 1998, FPD Savills marketed a part of the commonty for sale as part of Westfield Farm. In the sales brochure, they specifically drew attention to the Hill of Alyth and stated, 'The sellers acquired title from previous heritable proprietors to Hill of Alyth without warrandice. The purchaser will be given title to the hill on the same terms.'

Despite frequent upwellings of concern in the community, no legal challenge has ever been made to those farmers who gained parts of the commonty in their title. The topic continues to excite debate in the pages of the local newsletter, the *Alyth Voice*. Murdo Fraser MSP, who lives in Alyth, wrote a long exposition on the topic in the September 2007 edition. In it, he argues that the current landowners may well have acquired good titles through prescription. In fact, this is doubtful since the original deeds were quite plainly defective. He also claims that the reason the law of prescription was introduced was to prevent land lying idle and unused. This is piffle. Such thoughts were a million miles away from the framers of the legislation in 1617 who were concerned solely to create a legal device that could be used both to clarify conflicting titles and to fabricate some semblance of legality to the lands they had stolen from the Church. And here on the Hill of Alyth, the Earl of Airlie, in 1923 and later in 1977, is doing exactly the same thing!

Events took an interesting twist in May 2007 when Scottish Ministers acquired the disputed hill on behalf of the Forestry Commission for the mouth-watering sum of £2,295,000. Given that half of this ground did not legally belong to the previous owner, there appear to be some questions to be answered as to why such a vast sum of public money was thought appropriate to be spent on the purchase of stolen property. Indeed, it appears that the Forestry Commission knew nothing of the history of the hill prior to acquiring it and only learned about it during the first public meeting it organised in Alyth to discuss how to manage the hill. When a local resident wrote to the Forestry Commission pointing out the fact that the hill was still a commonty and that locals held rights over it, the Area Land Agent replied that 'we are not prepared to devote resources to this complicated and, potentially, fruitless quest'.[29] Given that the land was acquired as part of the Woodland in and around Towns Initiative, it is a pity that no one thought to ask the local community about their existing rights first.

Anyhow, since the good folk of Alyth have, so far, been the victims of all this barefaced land-grabbing, perhaps Alex Salmond might make it all up to them by giving them back their commonty.

BIRSE

The Parish of Birse on Deeside is home to a remarkable and vibrant local community business, Birse Community Trust, which was established in 1998. It has, over the past decade, forged a national reputation for rural development and has acquired a wide range of property rights for the benefit of the inhabitants. The most interesting for the present discussion is the 9,000-acre area known as the Forest of Birse Commonty which occupies the high ground in the south-west of the parish. In 1999, after years of research and patient negotiation, the Trust managed to secure the ancient rights over the whole of the Forest of Birse Commonty. Like many such initiatives, it had its roots in the local history research being carried out by one of the residents, in this case Robin Callander. In the course of undertaking documentary research and speaking to the older members of the community, he learned of a history of disputes over the commonty ranging from physical violence all the way to cases in the House of Lords. Crucially, his research uncovered the fact that there was still a set of ancient rights to use the commonty. This included the rights to manage the native pinewoods.

Over a period of four years and in the course of much legal debate and tough negotiations with the two landowners who owned the solum and the sporting rights in the commonty, the embryonic Trust managed to secure these ancient rights to be managed for the common good of the inhabitants of the parish. This was the catalyst for an ongoing programme of development which has reached the stage where the Trust now owns a whole range of property across the parish. The rights to the pinewood, for example, could now be administered to support a number of local businesses including the three unique nineteenth-century water-powered woodworking mills, all now owned by the Trust.

The Forest of Birse Commonty is an instructive example of the potential of common land rights in the modern day. They are not some archaic relic of the past but an important part of the future for many communities across Scotland.[30]

COMMONTY IN ABERDEENSHIRE

At what point does one begin to get angry about the way in which common land has been quietly appropriated by powerful interests? Personally, it happened several years ago when I learned of the fate of one of Scotland's commonties. What follows has been anonymised in order to avoid the risk of any liability to any party in what turned out to be a delicate situation.

A small commonty, only a few acres in extent, stood on the edge of a village. It was fenced off and the Council had, for as long as the villagers could remember, burnt the gorse whins every year when they died back. The site was a former drovers' stance. The land was valued by local people for recreation. A badgers' set had been there for at least fifty years and larks, linnets, yellow buntings, blackbirds, thrushes, curlews, mallards and stonechats all nested there. In the late 1990s, the farmer – let's call him Mr Fraser – who owned the adjoining farm removed the metal fences and, over a five-week period, proceeded to spray and bulldoze the land. The locals protested but to no avail. When challenged, the farmer simply replied, 'Prove to me that it is not my land.' A prominent firm of housebuilders then submitted a planning application for executive houses. This was approved and the developer acquired the site for £1.1 million – not bad for a small corner of land which, until then, had been maintained by the Council, used by local people and cost the farmer nothing at all.

The houses are now all built and the new owners have laid out pretty lawns where the badgers' set used to be. No linnets or stonechats sing above the whin anymore and BMWs sit atop the site of their former nests. My correspondent – let's call him John – had challenged the Council on whether, in fact, the commonty was owned by the farmer or not. They told him, correctly, that who owned the land was no concern of the planning process and that they were quite entitled to assume that the developer had made the appropriate checks about who owned the site. John then started a letter-writing campaign to raise awareness of the issue. At one point, he was offered several thousand pounds to desist. He didn't and asked me to investigate.

It turned out that Mr Fraser had acquired the farm some fifty years ago from a prominent public institution that had owned it since 1753. There is no record of the commonty ever having been divided. In a map of 1869, the land is shown as common. When the first deed in almost 200 years was drawn up for the sale to Mr Fraser, the land was described as:

> [a]ll and whole the town and lands of [name of farm], with the miln thereof called [name of miln], milnlands, multures and knaveships of the same, together with the houses, biggings, yards, tofts, crofts, outsetts, insetts, muirs, marshes, commonties, parts, pendicles and pertinents of the same whatsoever.

The deed included a plan which showed the commonty within the boundaries. No one in the village was aware that his title included such a claim to the land since none of the usual mix of village residents had thought to examine his title deed in the Registers of Scotland in Edinburgh. How silly of them. And so another small part of Scotland's historic commons disappeared under brick and tarmac aided and abetted by a system of land registration that allows the rich and powerful to grab what they like and leaves the ordinary folk blissfully ignorant and disenfranchised. The poor indeed have no lawyers.

THORNHILL

From a lost common to a recovered one. Thornhill is a small village in Perthshire. A small 9-acre piece of land known as the North Common has been used since time immemorial by the inhabitants of Thornhill for pasturage and recreation. No one thought too much about legal matters until, in April 1989, a local farmer – we will call him John Smith – recorded a deed in the form of an *a non domino* disposition to his son – we will call him Arthur. An *a non domino* disposition is a transfer of property granted by a person who has no title to it (see pp. 278–80). Anyone who records a deed of this nature can, after ten years of open, peaceable possession with no judicial challenge, acquire full ownership (see Chapter 5). This caused some ill feeling in the village as not only was the North Common regarded as belonging to the people, but John had, on a previous occasion, successfully acquired a field within the village by means of an *a non domino* disposition.

Mr Smith snr. claimed to have recorded the deed in order to flush out the true owner and said that he would be happy to relinquish his title if issues to do with drainage and fencing could be sorted out. Stirling District Council agreed to enter into negotiations with Smith snr. on behalf of the community council but stalemate ensued. The Council was wound up in 1996 but its successor eventually secured an agreement in 1998 whereby title to the common was transferred to the North Common Trust and the land was, at last, in safe hands.

But it was a close-run thing. Had another year passed, Arthur would have been in a position to claim prescriptive rights founded on an *ex facie* valid title and possession that had been held openly, peaceably and without judicial interruption for ten years. Why had it taken so long? Most obviously, a small community is not in a position to deal with such issues and lacks appropriate sources of impartial advice. But it does illustrate, even where such a land grab was identified early on, how difficult it can be for communities to assert their rights. Had Mr Smith been rather more circumspect, then Arthur, and not the North Common Trust, would now own the common.

One interesting idea did emerge out of this case, however. One of the local campaigners, Tom Cunningham, realised that, if the North Common had no distinct title – and remember that John Smith's objective in all of this was to flush out one if it existed – then a candidate for having a title and certainly a better one than Mr Smith's would be the successor to whoever once owned the land when it was part of a big estate. At some point in the past, all the farms and indeed much of the village, with the exception of the church and manse, would have been owned by the local estate who would have had a possible claim to title of the common. The estate was the Kings Boquhapple Estate which had been sold off in 1922 by Captain Home-Drummond-Moray. Were the villagers to have acquired the title to that estate – which, after investigation, would almost certainly contain very little – they could have mounted an insurmountable challenge. It would have entitled them to, in effect, mop up perhaps a number of miscellaneous bits of ground that appeared to be ownerless.

At the same time, though in a different context, this same idea was appealing to me. I was intrigued by the activities of a Mr Brian Hamilton, dubbed in the press the Raider of the Lost Titles (for more on this, see pp. 336–38). He specialised in buying up old estate titles and sifting through them to see what was there. It worked like this.

Suppose Lord Blinny owned the 20,000-acre Blinny Estate which contained a number of farms, villages and woodlands. It had been in his family since 1760 but, in the depression between the wars, he sold the whole lot at a roup in 1925. This was not uncommon across Scotland. Lord Blinny, however, retained the mansion house and some superiorities. His son is still alive and lives in Australia. I approach him and ask if I can buy the Blinny Estate. He tells me that it was all sold years ago – he sold the mansion house five years ago and the superiorities were abolished by the Abolition of Feudal Tenure Act. Yes, I say, but I would still like to buy it. What about £100? If you insist, he replies. And so I instruct my lawyer to draft a deed selling me the Blinny Estate. The deed will narrate all the parcels that have been sold and, according to Lord Blinny, there is nothing left. He may well be right. But what if there is something left, some morsel, some ancient right, perhaps a piece of common land that was never sold? For £100, I play lucky dip. If any disputes come up like that over the North Common, I now have the title that will perhaps secure me ownership. As a strategy, it has much to commend it and more communities should adopt it.

Other commons in Scotland exist in Denholm, Yetholm, Crichie, Balerno, Bowden and Gifford.[31] Many more await publicity, discovery, identification, assertion and protection. It should be noted that it is not only private interests that have encroached on common land. Amongst the key historical users of common land have been the Scottish Gypsies or Travellers who comprise Scotland's oldest indigenous ethnic minority community. Their patterns of occupation necessitated a detailed understanding of land rights and, for centuries, they travelled the country, resting up in traditional commons such as old grazing stances and drove roads. During my own childhood, I recall seeing Travellers along the roadside in the Highlands and encamped by the river. As the years went by, their numbers dwindled. Lay-bys were dug up or blocked off. Sites that had been used since antiquity were extinguished on the orders of some bureaucrat in a local authority office or by the unauthorised actions of the local landowner.

A separate and distinct group of Travelling people are the showmen or travelling show and fairground families. They too have a long history and tradition of travelling around the country putting on fairs and shows on common land and land set aside for that purpose. Indeed, the majority of fairs held in Scotland trace their origins back to charters and privileges granted in the medieval period and usually associated with Scotland's burghs. For example, the Links Market in Kirkcaldy has been going since 1302 and claims to be Europe's longest annual street fair, running for a mile along the Esplanade.[32]

Contrary to much media comment, community ownership of land in Scotland did not start with the purchase of the Island of Eigg and other community buyouts. Far from being a new idea, it is in fact a very old idea dating back to the earliest origins of the Kingdom of Scotland. Commons are a valuable part of our history and culture. The challenge today is to identify, assert and restore this valuable inheritance before it is lost as part of the land grabbing that continues to this day under the direction and protection of Scotland's laws of prescription.

23

All Property of a Burgh

Scotland's common good

I grew up and went to school in Kinross. Then, it was the county town of Kinross-shire and a burgh. There was an annual agricultural show and a lively folk festival. My father travelled to work in Edinburgh on the train and I remember being one of the first people to walk along the then unopened concrete M90 motorway. There was a fine town hall and library (now in a state of dereliction – see Plate 11). I now realise that the town I grew up in was a special place partly on account of its sense of civic identity and that was down to the fact that we governed ourselves through an elected town council.

Speak to any councillor from most local authorities about Common Good Funds and they may raise their eyes, draw their breath or mutter mild obscenities. Mention it at a public meeting and you will probably trigger an animated discussion. Pore over any number of local newspapers in Ayr, the Borders, Fife or Angus and you will read the occasional story about how the fund is being spent – or misspent. Visit any town in Scotland and you will come across names such as Market Muir, Market Street, Muirton, Links and Green. These all denote forms of common land such as all burghs in Scotland owned at one time. And this property still exists. It still belongs to the people and forms an important part of their cultural heritage. It is also a significant resource for regenerating local communities. But, since 1975, this land has been subsumed within the new local authority structures and assets that should have been carefully stewarded for the benefit of the inhabitants of the former burghs have, instead, been lost, neglected and, in many cases, misappropriated.

Burghs in Scotland were established by feudal charters which gave them powers and land. As early as 1491, legislation was passed to provide protection for the Common Good Funds but, as we saw in Chapter 8, the funds were seriously depleted by municipal corruption. On 15 May 1975, town councils, which had been in place for centuries, were abolished by the Local Government (Scotland) Act 1973 and replaced by a system of district and regional councils. These, in turn, were replaced by the current unitary authorities in 1996. However, although the town councils were wound up, their Common Good Funds were to be preserved for the benefit of the inhabitants of the burgh. That duty now falls to Scotland's thirty-two local authorities. Moreover, the burghs themselves were not abolished. Burgh charters remain live legal documents which confer legal powers and still represent the founding title to much heritable property. A recent Court of Session case involving moorings in Rothesay, for example, was founded on rights conferred in its royal charter.

Common Good Funds are the assets and income of the former burghs of Scotland (see Appendix for a full list of such burghs). They represent a substantial portfolio of land, property and investments and, by law, continue to exist for the common good of the inhabitants of the former burghs. This property and the funds associated with it are an important part of the cultural heritage of many towns across Scotland and provide significant resources for the economic, social and environmental development of these communities.

Robin Callander describes the common property of burghs as follows:

the property rights and privileges of use held by the burgh or its feuars were the burgh commons. These did not represent a single type of common land, but might encompass the full range of Scottish commons: commonties, common mosses, runrig lands and common hill land, greens and loans. These areas and other rights, like fishing privileges, were not always held exclusively by the burgh, but might also be shared in common with the owners of land outside the burgh's boundaries.[1]

Today, clues to the existence of such land is found in place names such as Burgh Muir and Market Muir but, until recently, many people had forgotten about common good or they regarded it as of historic interest only. The situation is further confused by the complex legal situation surrounding common good. Indeed, the only time most members of the public are likely to have been made aware of common good property is when a dispute has arisen and court proceedings have begun as happened in Port Seton (1997), Mussel-burgh (1982) and Burntisland (1993). In the south of Scotland, however, there is still an awareness of the burgh commons since they are central to the common ridings ceremonies. These have their origins in the very real need for burghs to inspect their boundaries to check that no neighbouring landowner had encroached upon them.[2]

In recent years, however, the increasing number of cases arising around Scotland has awoken communities to their common heritage. Typically these have related to plans to sell off land in towns and campaigns have been mounted to stop them. During 2004, I began receiving phone calls from people in places such as Ayr, Musselburgh, Oban, Cupar, Kinross and Peebles. They told me of their concerns about land sales, about record keeping in local government and about financial irregularities. I decided to investigate further and, in April 2005, I wrote to all of Scotland's thirty-two local authorities asking them to provide me with details of all land and property held in Common Good Funds. Together with James Perman, a chartered accountant from Largs who had spent years investigating common good in his hometown, we published a report with our findings in November 2005.[3]

What we discovered was a poor understanding of what common good was, poor record keeping and financial irregularities. Of Scotland's thirty-two councils, eleven supplied no information, failed to reply or denied they had any common good. Those that did reply supplied information that was often patchy and incomplete. What we also uncovered were some very dodgy deals reminiscent of the kinds of maladministration that was uncovered by the 1833 report of the Municipal Corporations Inquiry (see Chapter 8).

In June 2003, the journalist Bob Shields reminisced about the office of Secretary of State for Scotland which had just been abolished as a full-time post.

It looks like I'll never be the Secretary of State for Scotland

It's not the kind of job most schoolboys would fantasise about. But then most schoolboys didn't walk from Ayr's Belmont housing estate to Ayr beach, every sunny day of the holidays. The route took you from one of Scotland's newest council estates past some of the oldest and most elegant homes douce Ayr had to offer.

Bouncing our ball down a street called Chapelpark Road, me and my pals were stunned into silence when a sleek, chauffeur-driven black Rolls-Royce, pennants flying from both wings, slipped past us then turned into a gravel driveway and out of sight.

Convinced we had seen The Queen, we couldn't wait to tell our parents of our exciting experience. So imagine my disappointment when my report of this royal sighting didn't even merit my dad diverting his concentration from the Sporting Life.

'That would be Wullie going home for his tea,' he said from behind the racing pages.'

'Who's Wullie?'

'Wullie Ross. He's the Secretary of State for Scotland.'

Of course, I hadn't a clue what that meant. But I ran round to tell my pals our royal sighting wasn't royal after all.

There was much debate about what a Secretary of State for Scotland actually did. But we reckoned he probably got to see Ayr United for nothing. Maybe even free pies. A chauffeur-driven Rolls AND free admission to Somerset Park? That was good enough for me.[4]

We do not know whether Willie Ross was given free admission to Ayr United games or whether he enjoyed free pies. We do know, however, that Willie got free common good land. In a deed recorded in the Register of Sasines for the County of Ayr on 19 March 1953, the provost, magistrates and councillors of the royal burgh of Ayr sold 'one rood, one square pole and fourteen and thirty-nine decimal or one hundredth square yards or thereby' of land to 'Major William Ross, Member of Parliament for the Kilmarnock Division of Ayrshire'.

The deed was signed by Willie Ross and witnessed by Malcolm MacPherson, MP for Stirling and Falkirk, and Willie Hamilton, MP for West Fife. On behalf of the provost, magistrates and councillors of the royal burgh of Ayr, the deed was signed at a meeting held at Ayr on 9 March 1953 by Councillor Adam Hart, Councillor Andrew Young Crawford and Town Clerk Robert Cunningham Brown and sealed with the Common Seal of the royal burgh of Ayr.

The quarter acre plot of land at what is now 10 Chapelpark Road formed part of a 16-acre parcel of land purchased by the Council in 1947 which was – and the remaining portions which form Corsehill Park are – common good land for the benefit of the inhabitants of the royal burgh of Ayr.

Willie's plot was sold by feu disposition. The provost, magistrates and councillors conveyed the land under the following feu burdens:

- there should be erected within 18 months of entry a private dwelling of not less value than £3000 with details to be approved by the Council, and to be maintained as a private dwelling and used for no other purpose
- the Council bind themselves to ensure that other feus granted and fronting onto Chapelpark Road would contain the same £3000 condition
- there shall be erected boundary walls four and a half inches thick and five feet high with nine inch butts at ten feet centres

In consideration of the feu, Willie Ross might have been expected to pay a sum of money – he was not. The only financial consideration was a £15 annual feu duty.

Never mind free pies – this transaction, therefore, amounted to a free gift of common good land owned by the burgh to Willie Ross upon which to build the elegant home at the end of the gravel driveway into which the young Bob Shields observed the 'sleek, chauffeur-driven black Rolls-Royce, pennants flying from both wings' make its dignified entrance.

One of the problems in discussing common good is the confusion and lack of clarity as to what exactly it is. Its historical origins are clear but, even in 1975 when the town councils were abolished, it was obvious that not everyone knew what was and what was not common good or kept appropriate records. Further reform of local government in 1996 compounded the confusion and, with the turnover of staff in the intervening years, much knowledge and understanding has inevitably been lost.[5]

For many years, the question was rather confused by the fact that the leading legal case on the topic was not actually about the definition of common good but about whether such land could be sold and, specifically, whether land owned by a burgh was inalienable. The case involved the Market Muir, a large area of open ground currently situated behind the County Buildings in Market Street, Forfar. Under the terms of the burgh charter, markets were authorised on the land for eight particular days. For the rest of the year, the inhabitants of the town had used it for all sorts of games and pastimes including shinty, cricket, football and quoits. The Town Council, however, wished to lease the ground for a more regular agricultural market which would deny the public the right to enjoy such pastimes and a local doctor, Dr Murray, took out an interdict against the magistrates. In 1893, Lord McLaren upheld Dr Murray's complaint and concluded that common good land could not be alienated where it had been dedicated to a particular use by the burgh's charter, had been dedicated to that use by the Town Council or where evidence could be shown that the public had made use of the land since time immemorial.

The resolution of this question has unfortunately led many people to mistakenly believe that this case was about what defines common good when, in fact, it only settled the question of common good that could not be alienated. The question of definition was settled fifty years later in Banff.

Duff House is a fine Georgian mansion house in Banff designed by William Adam for the Earl of Fife. In 1906, the Duke of Fife wrote:

> I propose to ask the towns of Banff and Macduff to accept from me as a free gift the mansion of Duff House and that portion of the park immediately surrounding it, covering an area of about one hundred and forty acres. This would include the gardens, stables, two lodges and the rod fishing along the land comprised in the gift. I offer this gift with absolutely no restrictions as to the manner in which it is to be developed and managed, as I am convinced that the corporations of the two towns will know how to act for their material advantage, as well as for the recreation and well-being of the community.[6]

The house was conveyed in 1907 and, in 1909, the property was leased to a company called Duff House Ltd who assigned the lease, in 1913, to Duff House Sanatorium Ltd who, in 1931, changed their name to Ruthin Castle Ltd. By 1940, the business was making a loss and the company was wanting a way out of their ninety-nine-year lease. They found it by reference to the Town Councils (Scotland) Act 1900 which stated that '[a]ll feus, alienations or tacks for more than five years of any heritable property of the burgh, or vested in the Council, so far as forming part of the common good' were to be made by public roup. No such auction had taken place in 1909, however, as the Councils had simply entered into a private bargain with their predecessors. Ruthin Castle Ltd, therefore, argued that their lease was null and void and wrote to the Councils renouncing their lease on these grounds. The Town Councils, reluctant to see their tenant walk away from their ninety-nine-year commitment, argued that the house was not common good and that the provisions of the 1900 act did not therefore apply. In the court action that followed, the Court of Session initially upheld the Councils' view that it was not common good but Ruthin Castle Ltd appealed and were successful. Lord Wark concluded, 'There was in the end no dispute between the parties that all property of a royal burgh or a burgh of barony not acquired under statutory powers or held under special trusts forms part of the common good.'[7]

This was an important ruling and, in the absence of any contrary decision by the House of Lords or the UK Supreme Court, remains the highest judicial authority on the question of what defines common good. It has been most recently cited in another Court of Session opinion in the case of the harbour in Greenock. Lord Drummond Young noted that:

Common good is a category of property held by burghs prior to 1975, and by the various forms of local authority that have existed since that date. In its original form, it comprised all property of a royal burgh or a burgh of barony not acquired under statutory powers or held under special trusts. It was thus the ordinary property of a burgh, held for the general purposes of the community. It is owned by the community, and the town council or other local authority is regarded in law as simply the manager of the property, as representing the community. Typically, the common good included public buildings such as churches and the municipal chambers, the streets of the burgh, public open spaces and markets. It might also include lands, houses and other forms of property. In a coastal burgh, the harbour would typically form part of the common good. In this connection, it should be recalled that the burghs of Scotland were commercial in origin; that applied both to the older royal burghs and to the more recent burghs of barony created by private landowners, of which Greenock was an example. Consequently commercial property such as markets and harbours was an important part of the common good.[8]

So there we have it and, lest there be any doubt, Lord Wark's comments formed the gist of a Scottish Parliamentary written answer in 2006:

Campbell Martin (West of Scotland) (Ind): To ask the Scottish Executive what constitutes a common good asset and how such assets differ from property or land owned by a local authority.

Mr Tom McCabe: The Common Good originated as revenues from properties belonging to the early Burghs of Scotland. The Common Good, as these revenues were then termed, is of great antiquity and there is no equivalent in English local government although the term remains current in Scotland. Essentially, the Common Good denoted all property of a Burgh not acquired under statutory powers or held under special trusts.[9]

The way to establish whether property falls within the definition is to examine the title deeds. If the land has been gifted or sold to the Town Council before 1975 then it is common good. The only two exceptions are if it was acquired using statutory powers or if it was held in a special trust. This will usually be obvious from the title which will reveal whether the Council is using powers under any of a variety of acts to do with housing, sanitation, water or education, for example. If the property is held by a trust, then this too should be immediately obvious.

Having dealt with the question of definitions, the next issue that arises is how local authorities account for the common good in their burghs. From the annual accounts of a local authority, it should be possible to find out how much any Common Good Fund is worth and how it has been managed in any year. Many accounts do reveal this information but, of Scotland's 196 burghs, only 132 featured in the 2005 accounts of Scotland's thirty-two councils. The number rose to 144 in 2009 (see table on p. 302). The quality of reporting varies considerably and, on examining some of the accounts published by Scotland's local authorities, one might be forgiven for thinking that matters are still pretty unclear. Take the burgh of Hamilton, for example.

The Hamilton Ahead initiative is a major regeneration project being carried out in Hamilton town centre. Over 80 per cent of the finance for the project is being obtained from the sale of land held in the Hamilton Common Good Fund. As at 31 March 2009, a cumulative total of £53,618,000 had been generated from the sale of land held in the Hamilton Common Good Fund account. But the total assets of the Hamilton Common Good Fund stood at £3,159,000 on 31 March 2009 including £2,823,000 of fixed assets.

There is thus a discrepancy of around £50,795,000 between the receipts from land sales and the fixed assets value of the Common Good Fund.

The land sales receipts have been spent redeveloping Hamilton town centre and so the value of the redevelopment should be included in the value of the Common Good Fund. It would be very wrong to sell £53 million worth of land from the fund and not end up with at or around that figure in the redeveloped value. In 2005, I asked the Deputy Chief Executive of the Council, Mr Archibald Strang, for an explanation. He stated in a letter of 13 October 2005 that:

> The Hamilton Ahead initiative uses the sale of Hamilton Common Good assets as a source of funding to finance developments that provide benefit in line with the principle of the Common Good Fund. However, as these assets are managed or maintained by other resources of South Lanarkshire Council, they appear on the balance sheet of the Council and not the Common Good Fund.[10]

But you can't do this. The assets of the Hamilton Common Good Fund, the proceeds of the sale of Common Good assets and the assets acquired using the Common Good Fund belong – legally – to the Hamilton Common Good Fund.

Interestingly, the list of common good assets provided by the Council did include the retail park, the Asda superstore and the cinema which are all part of the redevelopment and which are leased on long leases by the fund. But they don't appear in the accounts – why not? If I were an inhabitant of Hamilton, I'd want to know what happened to all this money. The good citizens of Hamilton should be told who authorised this raid on their common wealth.

Across Scotland, similar stories of misappropriation can be told and, although reporting has improved in recent years, in too may cases it still remains unclear what assets are held and how much they are worth. Parliamentary petitions have prompted debate in Parliament[11] which has resulted in guidance being issued by the Scottish Government to the effect that, '[f]or councils to fully maximise the potential of their assets, they must hold accurate records of the assets they are responsible for. This would include those assets held for the Common Good.'[12]

The Local Authority (Scotland) Accounts Advisory Committee then published revised accounting guidelines in December 2007.[13] These required all councils to have published full inventories of all assets of Common Good Funds by 31 March 2009. So I wrote to all of Scotland's councils in May 2009 and asked them again to provide me with a list of all the heritable and moveable assets held by the Common Good Funds they administer.

The results are an improvement on 2005.[14]

	2005	2009
Common Good Funds	132	144
£ value reported	£1.42 billion	£2.5 billion
No. land assets reported	766	1,610

The figures above show that there was an increase in the number of reported Common Good Funds from 132 in 2005 to 144 in 2009. The reported value of the Funds rose from £1.42 billion to £2.5 billion and the total number of individual property assets rose from 766 to 1,610.

There remain ongoing problems, however. Many councils are only beginning to get to grips with constructing an asset register. Fife Council, for example, which administers twenty-five Common Good Funds, was criticised in an audit report for not having a complete and comprehensive record of all assets and for failing to ensure that all the rental income was received. Like other councils, it is working to improve matters. But this is just the beginning of what needs to be done.

Common good assets form a central part of the history, heritage, culture and identity of communities across Scotland. Over many decades, however, their significance has been lost, their status diminished, their role forgotten and their fate increasingly inse-cure. We should be aiming to expand the portfolio of such property to promote regeneration in Scotland's towns and cities. It is now apparent that thirty years after the abolition of town councils, Scotland's towns and villages have lost much of their identity, cohesion and self-belief. Common good assets can play a part in recovering civic identity and prosperity.

It is self-evident that those best positioned to take a view on the best interests of the inhabitants of a burgh are the inhabitants themselves. This should be done through open, transparent and democratic debate and yet they have no such avenue to do so. Instead the local authority determines this question. This is no longer sustainable.

There are literally hundreds of millions of pounds floating about in the form of previously unaccounted-for assets, undervalued assets and underused assets. This wealth belongs to local people and not to the Council. It should be used to begin a process of civic renewal and physical regeneration, to deliver wealth and prosperity and to give back to towns across Scotland some self-respect, belief and power to improve the welfare of their community.

For this to happen, town councils need to be restored. Scotland, like the rest of the UK, is poorly represented at the local level. If you travel through Belgium, the Netherlands or Germany, you'll see that local democracy is evident in well-maintained town halls, civic identity and real power for citizens.[15]

In 2008, I cycled through Europe and stopped in the beautiful town of Wittenberg, home to one of the most influential political figures in Europe – Martin Luther. The Reformation that he inspired was motivated by the avarice, greed and corruption of the Church but Luther's revolution was as much political and economic as it was theological. In the wonderful Luther Museum I was astonished and delighted to see, in a corner of one of the rooms, a beautiful large wooden chest with a complex array of locking mechanisms (see Plate 2). In 1522, a Wittenberg church order established the common chest into which went the expropriated ecclesiastical endowments of the old church together with the tithes. The proceeds were used to finance a welfare system that gave interest-free loans to artisans, provided for poor orphans and supported the education and training of poor children. It is hard to comprehend how radical an idea this was five hundred years ago. The idea spread rapidly so that, by 1523, common chests had been established in, among other places, Augsburg, Strasbourg, Regensburg and Nuremberg.

At about the same time, the residents of Edinburgh, Jedburgh, Fraserburgh and Musselburgh were being systematically defrauded by corruption and nepotism leading in many cases to bankruptcy.

We now have the opportunity to reverse centuries of decline in the civic life of Scotland's 196 burghs by returning to them their property and real powers to better the lives of their citizens. The Common Good Fund is there for the common good of the inhabitants of the burgh. There are no other statutory restrictions on it. It is a free fund which could be used to build wealth and prosperity in a new municipal enlightenment. Let's say goodbye to the property speculators and developers who have blighted so many towns, to the centralised politics of unitary authorities and to the despair and decay of the past. It's time for Scotland's burghs to be given back to the people.

24

Let for a Penny a Year

The strange case of the Edinburgh common good

Having carried out a wide-ranging investigation of common good land across Scotland and been involved in advising communities in places such as Musselburgh and Ayr, I decided to take a closer look at my hometown of Edinburgh. A number of people had alerted me to irregularities in the Common Good Fund and initial correspondence with the Council reinforced doubts about record keeping and probity. In February 2006, a report on the Common Good Fund was due to come before the Executive Committee of the Council. I contacted my Local Councillor Michael White and we met to discuss the issues. At that time, he served on the Scrutiny Committee which was entitled to 'call in' any decisions made by the Executive for further scrutiny. We agreed that this was the best course of action in relation to the February report and I agreed to submit a report outlining my concerns. The Scrutiny Committee met on 27 April and I highlighted a range of problems including the facts that the fund assets had not been properly recorded or accounted for in the past twenty-five years, the management and administration was flawed and the residents of the city were losing out since the fund had ceased distributing any grants some years earlier. One of the most serious concerns was over the Waverley Market.

The Waverley Market is a site of 1.68 acres at the east end of Princes Street in Edinburgh just beside the Balmoral Hotel. The former market site is now occupied by the Princes Mall shopping centre. The story of how this, the most valuable asset of the City of Edinburgh Common Good Fund, has been administered and managed is a tale of confusion, incompetence and betrayal of the rights of the citizens of the city.[1]

In 1766, with finance from the Common Good Fund, the Town Council purchased 34 acres of land to the north of the Nor Loch from the Trustees of Heriot's Hospital. This was to be the site of Edinburgh's New Town. The Waverley Market developed as a fruit and vegetable market on the site of what is now Waverley Station and moved north to its current position after the railway was constructed in 1844. There, the market flourished until it relocated again in 1938 to what is now the Fruitmarket Gallery on Market Street. From 1938, the Waverley Market was used as a venue for a wide variety of events. It hosted cattle shows, dog shows, car shows and Ideal Home shows. In 1972, the Offshore Theatre Company premiered *The Great Northern Welly Boot Show* with Billy Connolly at the Edinburgh Festival Fringe. The old market was demolished in 1973 and the site then lay undeveloped until 1982, whilst being rented to the Chamber of Commerce for use as a car park.

By 1979, plans were well advanced to develop a shopping centre on the site and the favoured option was for a leaseback arrangement whereby the Council would lease the site to a developer for a period of 125 years. The developer would then construct the shopping centre and lease it back to the Council once it was complete. The Council would then sublease the individual retail units. Under this arrangement, the developer paid for the construction of the centre but received a rent of 6.5 per cent of these costs from the leaseback to the Council. Any rental yields the Council received over and above this would be shared, with the Council retaining the first £1.4 million and the remainder being split equally between the parties.

In March 1982, a 125-year lease was granted by the City of Edinburgh District Council to Reed Publishing Pension Trustees Ltd and Reed Pension Trusts Ltd who built the new shopping centre. In April 1988, the centre was complete and the Council leased back the new shopping centre. In November 1989, after most of the units had been let, the Council agreed to extend its principal lease to Reed from 125 years to 206 years and, at the same time, both Reed and the Council sold their respective interests to Letinvest plc and Speciality Shops plc. The rather complicated leaseback deal was now at an end and in its place was a much simpler arrangement. The Common Good Fund still owned the ground and Letinvest and Speciality Shops leased the site now with a shopping centre built upon it. In 1990, the Council reported in the Notes to the Balance Sheet that:

Following the sale of the Waverley Market Complex, the free proceeds after repayment of debt, were utilised by the Council in creating a Property Development Fund which, together with the interest thereon, amounted at the end of the year to £4,249,744.

But the deal had its critics, with Councillor Donald Gorrie commenting that the 'whole Waverley Market story was one of continued blunders'. It had, in fact made a £900,000 loss since the Council had already written off accumulated debts for the site.[2]

In 1998 the lease was sold for £21.3 million to Scottish Metropolitan Property plc. In 2005, it was then sold again – first for £40.5 million to Continental Shelf 274 Ltd and PM Limited Partnership and then for £37.6 million to PPG Metro Ltd, a company owned by the Scottish businessman David Murray. The annual rental roll stood at £2.3 million.

At this stage, it is worth remembering that, throughout the development of the Waverley Market, the Council freely admitted that the site was an asset of the Common Good Fund. In 1982, the Notes to the Common Good Accounts reported that:

A major property owned by the Common Good Fund is the Waverley Market Site on Princes Street and since this is now being redeveloped as a speciality shopping centre there is no longer any rent income from its use as a temporary car park.

The development was also promoted as lucrative. In a report from November 1979, the director of estates wrote that:

Even on the most pessimistic view possible . . . net income to the Council will be not less that £500,000 per annum with growth linked directly to the increasing values in Princes Street. It is appropriate to draw to the Committee's attention the fact that the site is held on the Common Good Account which enables the

District Council to make more flexible use of any funds engendered than would normally be the case.[3]

In the Council's own Financial Appraisal, prepared in 1981, the
value attributable to the site is 50 per cent of the realisable
development value. In other words, whatever the value of the
completed shopping centre, half of it was attributable to the
location value of the site which was owned by the Common Good
Fund. The Common Good Fund, as the owners of the solum or
site, would, had things been organised differently, have received
half of the £37.5 million paid for the leasehold interest by David
Murray and be in line for some 50 per cent or so of the annual
rental income – £2.3 million in 2005. One might assume, therefore,
that the Common Good Fund would receive a significant boost
from the Princes Mall development. As already noted, the Council
secured over £4.2 million from the sale of its leaseback interest in
1989. But this was credited to a property development fund and
not to the Common Good. The capital was used to invest in other
land and property across Edinburgh which should be held by the
Common Good Fund but is not.

And what about the lease of the site to PPG Metro? Well, since
1982 when the lease was signed, the Common Good Fund of the
City of Edinburgh has received the grand total of 23p for one of the
most valuable pieces of real estate in Edinburgh since the site is let
for a rent of 1p per year (if asked). By the end of the lease in 2188,
the Common Good Fund will have earned £2.60 (if asked) and
precisely nothing if not asked. As a result of this incompetency, the
Common Good Fund lost both the revenue and the capital value
inherent in perhaps its most valuable asset.[4]

In 2005, the Council continued to include the Waverley Market
in the accounts as an asset of the Common Good Fund. Following
my revelations in 2006, however, the Council's response was to
claim in 2008 that:

Waverley Market ceased to be an asset of the Common Good and
its inclusion on the asset register and balance sheet of the Fund
in 2005 was an error. Acts of the Council in 1937 and 1938
transferred the fruit and vegetable market from Waverley Mar-

ket to premises in East Market Street. In effect the then Council substituted the East Market Street premises for the Waverley Market premises, and with it the common good status. Accordingly Waverley Market ceased to be part of the common good at the time of the transfer of the fruit and vegetable market to East Market Street.[5]

The Council are claiming here that the inclusion of Waverley Market as a common good asset in 2005 'was an error'. This is based upon the claim that the 1937 and 1938 acts transferring the market functions to East Market Street resulted in the transfer of the common good status. This is a fairy story. In 1983, an exchange of letters between the Director of Administration and the Director of Finance in relation to VAT liability for the shopping centre construction confirmed that the site was common good. The letters confirm that the site was freed from any statutory market obligations in 1933 but that the loss of these rights had no impact on the common good status since that was derived from the fact that the land had been purchased by the Common Good Fund in 1766. The Director of Administration even suggests that forthcoming private legislation could be used to remove the site from the common good as had been done with the markets and slaughterhouses in 1967.

The Waverley Market is part of the Edinburgh Common Good Fund because it was acquired by the Common Good Fund as part of the land assembly of the First New Town in the late eighteenth century. Nothing that has transpired since alters that.

It was intriguing to note that, in a survey of common good assets I undertook in 2009, the City of Edinburgh Council provided me with a spreadsheet containing the details of 120 parcels of land and property in the Common Good Fund. Imagine my surprise when there, in line 95, are the words 'Waverley Bridge – 1.68 acres – value £1'.[6] So it is part of the Common Good Fund after all! In which case, what's happened to all the money?

A final twist in this particular tale is that, in December 2006, the Scottish Law Commission published a report and a draft bill designed to provide for the compulsory and automatic conversion of all leases of over 175 years' duration (which still have over a hundred years left to run) to full ownership.[7] David Murray's company has a lease of 206 years in duration (it was originally 125 years but was extended to 206 years in 1989). In November 2010, the Scottish Government introduced the Long Leases (Scotland) Bill to Parliament. It contained the Scottish Law Commission's recommendations and would, as drafted, have converted the Waverley Market lease to full ownership with compensation payable of around 42p to the City of Edinburgh Council. The Bill failed to become law before the Scottish Election in May 2011 but was re-introduced in January 2012.

During the passage of the Bill, I and others attempted to persuade MSPs to exempt Waverley Market and other possible common good assets from the provisions of the Bill but failed to make much headway until May 2012 when The Scottish Government agreed to extend the unexpired portion of the lease from 100 years to 175 years for commercial leases. The Long Leases (Scotland) Act became law on 7 August 2012 and, by coming into effect in 2015, by which time the Waverley lease will have 173 years left to run, means that the Waverley Market lease will not convert to ownership.

The Common Good Fund of the Royal Burgh of the City of Edinburgh dates back to the days of the founding charters of the Canongate, Holyrood and Edinburgh itself. Over the centuries it survived corruption, nepotism and bankruptcy. It financed the land acquisition of the New Town – Princes Street, George Street and all the other public spaces in the New Town belong to the Common Good Fund. Until 2007, annual grants were made to community groups to help finance the installation of disabled facilities. The history of the Common Good Fund in the twentieth century is a history of decline. In 1904, the annual income of the fund was around £2 million at today's prices but, in 2009, it made a loss of £510,000.

The campaign to recover the millions of pounds that rightly belong to the citizens of the Royal Burgh of Edinburgh goes on.

Problems Rarely Arise with Land in Private Ownership

Land Reform in the twentieth century

Land reform is the process of redistributing power over land by means of redistribution, land tenure reform, market reform and taxation policy. It is an important part of the social and economic policy of many countries around the world from those emerging from colonialism to those of the former Eastern Europe moving to a mixed economy.

The high point of land reform in Scotland until recently was the period 1880–1920 and the reforming Liberal administrations who introduced the Crofters Act of 1886, set up Committees of Inquiry into land use, introduced the radical 1909 Budget with its famous land tax and later extended crofting tenure throughout Scotland with the Small Landholders Act of 1911. Tom Johnston's philippic *Our Scots Noble Families*, published in 1909, captured the essence of much radical opinion at the beginning of the twentieth century as quoted earlier in the Introduction.

Not until the establishment of the Scottish Parliament was there to be such a sustained effort to reform landed power. In the postwar years, there was the nationalisation of coal and of the planning system but, as discussed in Chapter 10, the fundamental architecture of landed power remained unaltered and it was not until twenty years later that the land question again came to the fore.[1]

The 1970s were an important period in the evolution of political ideas about landownership. John McEwen's book *Who Owns Scotland*, first published in 1977, advocated the complete nationalisation of rural land in Scotland and this statist approach was very much in tune with thinking in the British Labour Party at the time. This period also saw the rise of the Scottish National Party and the creation of the Scottish Labour Party both of whose work on the land question broke new ground in their rejection of the nationalisation approach. There was partial feudal tenure reform in the Land Tenure Reform (Scotland) Act 1974 and there was the beginning of land registration with the Land Registration (Scotland) Act 1979. The *West Highland Free Press* was founded in 1972 and its priorities are summed up by the Gaelic slogan on its masthead: '*An Tir, an Canan, 'sna Daoine* – The Land, the Language, the People'. During the following thirty years, it broke the taboo that had kept stories about landed power out of local papers and regularly ran stories which informed people, for the first time, about the activities landowners and their agents were up to.

Timeline of land reform

Date	Reform
1449	Leases Act
1491	Common Good Act
1503	Feuing Act
1560	Reformation
1617	Register of Sasines Act
1617	Prescription Act
1832	Reform Act (Scotland)
1833	Burgh Police (Scotland) Act
1835	Municipal Corporations in Scotland Report
1873	Return of Owners of Lands and Heritages
1886	Crofters (Scotland) Act
1909	Lloyd George's People's Budget
1910	Inland Revenue Survey of Land in GB and Ireland
1911	Small Landholders (Scotland) Act
1949	Agricultural Holdings (Scotland) Act
1974	Land Tenure Reform (Scotland) Act
1979	Land Registration (Scotland) Act
6 November 1996	House of Commons Debate Land Ownership (Scotland)
1 May 1997	Labour win the General Election
12 June 1997	Isle of Eigg Heritage Trust take title to Isle of Eigg. Brian Wilson MP establishes Community Land Unit.

Timeline of land reform—contd

Date	Reform
31 October 1997	Lord Sewel announces setting up of the Land Reform Policy Group
February 1998	Land Reform Policy Group publishes 'Identifying the Problems'
29 April 1998	House of Commons Debate Land Reform (Scotland)
September 1998	Land Reform Policy Group publishes 'Identifying the Solutions'
5 January 1999	Land Reform Policy Group publishes 'Recommendations for Action'
8 July 1999	Land Reform White Paper published
3 May 2000	Abolition of Feudal Tenure (Scotland) Act
8 March 2001	Leasehold Casualties (Scotland) Act
2 February 2001	Land Reform draft bill published
February 2001	Scottish Land Fund established
27 November 2001	Land Reform (Scotland) Bill introduced in Scottish Parliament
20 March 2002	Land Reform Stage 1 debate in Scottish Parliament
23 January 2003	Land Reform (Scotland) Act passed by Scottish Parliament
26 February 2003	Title Conditions (Scotland) Act
12 March 2003	Agricultural Holdings (Scotland) Act
2004	Tenements (Scotland) Act
14 June 2004	Community Right to Buy comes into force
28 November 2004	Feudal tenure abolition takes effect
31 May 2012	Land Registration etc. (Scotland) Act 2012
24 July 2012	Land Reform Review Group established

Table 14

By the end of the seventies, although McEwen and many others still advocated outright nationalisation of land, most radical opinion was beginning to move towards ideas of community ownership and more pluralist private ownership in association with an enhanced role for public ownership. John McEwen had produced the facts, the nationalists and the Left had developed the ideas and writers such as James Hunter, John Prebble and Ian Carter had published a substantial body of historical information and analysis which challenged more conservative interpretations of Scottish history.[2] The radical theatre company 7:84 was also touring the country with its satirical polemic *The Cheviot, the Stag and the Black, Black Oil.*

The election of a Tory Government in 1979, however, and the failure of the devolution referendum that year put paid to any action on land reform for a decade. But then, in the early 90s, civic Scotland stirred.

In 1989, Edmund Vestey, the owner of over 90,000 acres of land in Sutherland and Wester Ross, sold the 21,300-acre coastal crofting lands north of Lochinver to a Swedish company, Scandinavian Property Services Ltd. In 1992, this company went into liquidation and the land agents John Clegg advertised the estate for sale in seven separate lots. The whole estate was under crofting tenure and the prospect of the thirteen townships having seven new landlords appeared ludicrous. A public meeting was held and it was agreed that the crofting tenants should mount a bid for the estate.

This was a radical move which quickly captured the imagination of the public. The Assynt Crofters' Trust was led by a group of charismatic and astute crofters who orchestrated a brilliant campaign of public relations and remained one step ahead during a difficult few months when events could easily have gone against them. At one point, the crofters made it clear that, if the estate was sold to anyone else, they would collectively use their individual statutory rights to acquire individual crofts and transfer them to the Trust. Such a possibility concentrated the minds of the liquidator and events moved quickly to a deal in December 1992. The Assynt Crofters' Trust took ownership of the estate on 1 February 1993 (see Plate 4).

From this moment on, the land question assumed an entirely new dimension. No one had previously considered the possibility that tenants on a landed estate would have the courage and resolve to play the land market and win. From then on a number of communities in the Highlands and Islands – Eigg in 1997, Knoydart in 1999 and Gigha in 2002 – managed to negotiate the acquisition of substantial estates and a transformation took place in the possibilities for resolving conflicts over landownership.

On 22 September 1992, as the Assynt crofters were in the thick of negotiations and fund raising, John McEwen, whose book had done so much to keep the flame of land reform alight, died – three days short of his 105th birthday. A small group of his friends formed the Friends of John McEwen and, on the first anniversary of his death inaugurated the John McEwen Memorial Lectures on Land Tenure.[3] The role of these was to provide well-reasoned, authoritative and groundbreaking presentations on land tenure in Scotland and, in the process, to build momentum for land reform and bring the topic into the mainstream of political debate. A series of high-profile lectures from 1993 until 1999 complemented the action taking place in Assynt, Eigg and Knoydart and ensured that land reform enjoyed regular exposure in the media. Donald Dewar himself, in the fifth lecture in 1998, highlighted the role the lectures had played in helping prepare the ground for the political action that was to follow.

Scottish land reform even made an impression on the international stage. In 1995, I attended the UN Commission on Sustainable Development in New York with Bill Ritchie, a crofter in Assynt and one of the founders of the Assynt Crofters' Trust. At the plenary session in the presence of hundreds of representatives from over fifty countries, Bill managed to ask one of a handful of questions to the panel which included a high-level UK civil servant. How was it, he asked, that the UK government had been emphasising the importance of people in developing countries being given more ownership and control of land and resources upon which they depended when, in places like Assynt, land could be bought and sold, above the heads of local people, by faceless foreign corporations at hugely inflated prices? The poor man had no answer but it generated a huge amount of interest among delegates, many of whom came up afterwards to engage in animated discussion about land rights across the world!

These events all contributed to a growing expectation that, when the government eventually changed and fulfilled its commitment to deliver a Scottish Parliament, land reform would be a priority.[4] And this civic activism combined with the political commitment of key figures in the Labour Party, such as Donald Dewar, Brian Wilson, Calum MacDonald, John Sewel and Sam Galbraith, meant that, when Labour won the 1997 General Election, they were ready to act.

The Labour Party manifesto for the 1997 general election included a pledge 'to initiate a study into the system of land ownership and management in Scotland'. On 31 October 1997, Lord Sewel, the Minister for Agriculture, Environment and Fisheries in the Scottish Office, gave a speech at the Rural Forum AGM and Conference in Oban and launched the government's discussion paper 'Towards a Development Strategy for Rural Scotland'. For a whole generation of people at that conference, what Lord Sewel had to say was a breath of fresh air after almost two decades of Conservative government. In an intelligent and insightful speech, Lord Sewel, who had thirty years' experience studying rural communities and rural development, announced plans for greater involvement by local people and greater democratisation in rural services. The really newsworthy element, however, was the plan to establish a Land Reform Policy Group (LRPG), comprising civil servants from the Scottish Office and Forestry Commission and one external adviser, Professor John Bryden, and chaired by Lord Sewel. Its remit was 'to identify and assess proposals for land reform in rural Scotland, taking account of their cost, legislative and administrative implications and their likely impact on the social and economic development of rural communities and on the natural heritage'.[5] The first thing to observe about this remit is the restriction of the inquiry to 'rural Scotland' in contrast to the manifesto pledge. This was subsequently to frustrate efforts to extend the provisions of the community right to buy (see Chapter 27).

Over the course of the next eighteen months, this group launched two consultation papers, 'Identifying the Problems' in February 1998 and 'Identifying the Solutions' in September 1998. In January 1999, the group's final report, 'Recommendations for Action', was published. It covered a wide range of topics, including law reform, land reform legislation, countryside and natural heritage, agricultural holdings and crofting. The proposals ranged from the creation of national parks to a review of the law of the foreshore and seabed. They included landmark legislation such as the abolition of feudal tenure and providing tenant farmers and crofters with the right to buy the land they worked. The recommendations also included embryonic ideas on the community right to buy.

The period from February 1998 to the establishment of the Parliament in July 1999 witnessed an unprecedented debate across Scotland on the topic of land reform which continued for much of the term of the first session of Parliament as a series of bills was published, debated and passed by the new legislature. The letters pages and columns of the newspapers were full of the hopes, fears and questions of land reformers, landowners and others seeking to make sense of the unfamiliar, and seemingly extreme, ideas that were all being developed at once.

The stakes were high with land reformers expecting radical changes and landowners fearful of what might happen. By early 1998, following their crisis meeting (see Chapter 10, pp. 115–16), the SLF had engaged PR consultants and was in the early stages of changing its name. Landowners had an image problem as a consequence of their uncritical acceptance of the way land was held in Scotland and their resistance to change. The media thrives on controversy and the debate over land reform provided plenty good copy. So when, in April 1998, the SLF were reported to be considering an apology for the Highland Clearances, the press, radio and TV had a field day.[6] Commentators such as Brian Wilson and Jim Hunter stepped in to pour scorn on such an idea. In fact the SLF were not considering any such apology and it had never been discussed. One journalist had merely suggested to the convener that the SLF should apologise and was told that, if it was an issue, then it might certainly be considered but would have to be discussed fully first.

That was all there was to it but the media response was indicative of the rather excitable atmosphere at the time. It is worth remembering that this was a remarkable time. Eighteen years of Conservative government had come to an end and, with it, the comfortable certainties of landowning interests. A Scottish Parliament was in sight, the House of Lords appeared to be on the brink of extinction and land reform, a topic which had been taboo for so long, had now become mainstream. The worst fears of some landowners were, they thought, about to be realised and land reformers, such as Brian Wilson, who had been campaigning for thirty years on the issue, were finally beginning to see results.

Over its twenty pages, the LRPG's first report, 'Identifying the Problems', posed a wide variety of questions. However, it contained little analysis or context. On the one hand, this allowed for a flexible and varied response but, on the other, with little in the way of rationale or analysis, it was difficult to know how to respond.

At its October crisis meeting the previous year, members of the SLF listened in gloomy silence to a paper from their Director Maurice Hankey entitled 'Your Land is their Agenda'. In it, he painted a scenario in which the Scottish Parliament would legislate for the break-up of big estates and the abolition of feudal superiors, where tenants would be given a right to buy, community owner-ship would be promoted, succession law reformed and upper limits set on the amount of land any individual could own. No doubt this was partly designed to stimulate the membership to take possible reforms seriously but it was also, in the absence of any intelligence as to what the Labour Government was really thinking, a plausible scenario. Such ideas had been widely floated over the previous decade or so and all were perfectly possible.

The response from the SLF to the LRPG's paper was, in fact, quite muted. Whilst strongly opposed to any controls on absentee landowners and foreign landowners, the Federation welcomed the consultation paper and supported its general approach. It cleverly suggested that many of the problems were merely perceptions generated by the media and that, in reality, the problems that did exist were confined, by and large, to the western Highlands where only 8 per cent of the SLF membership owned land. With no research background to inform the LRPG, it was difficult to refute this assertion. In response to the questions 'What specific examples are there of problems due to private ownership and what would be suitable remedies?', the SLF stated bluntly, 'Problems rarely arise with land in private ownership.'!

A total 361 responses were received which, for a government consultation exercise, is remarkable. Of these, 326 were available – and remain available – for public inspection.[7] From a detailed analysis of the responses, 27.6 per cent were against land reform and, of these, 91 per cent were from landowners and their agents. The percentage of responses in favour of land reform was 47.8% and 26.4% were uncertain. Excluding landowners and their agents, 81.2% were in favour of land reform and only 4.2% against, with 24.6% undecided.[8]

The land reform agenda was clearly going to affect landowners who, understandably, were distinctly unenthusiastic about the line of questioning being pursued. But the necessity of pursuing it was forcefully put by a confidential submission from one rural resident.

This submission is confidential because I prefer it not to be made available for public inspection. The submission contains no information that is genuinely confidential. However, I see limited benefit in making some of my views in this submission more widely available.

It appears that relatively few people take the trouble to inspect the submissions made available from public consultations and that those people are usually acting on behalf of particular vested interest groups. My recent experience suggests I can express my views more freely in this submission . . . if they are not readily available to some of those vested interests.

In the last few months, my views on land reform have cost me what I considered two valuable 'lifechances' (LRPG 2.1). This has resulted from individuals who support the status quo taking action to influence the decisions of others they know, so that opportunities were closed off . . .

[T]he crucial point I am making from my personal experience is that the LRPG should not underestimate the profound influence in many parts of rural Scotland still, of the need to avoid your views 'offending' estate owners, their factors, lawyers and other agents.

The inhibiting influence of this 'estate culture' can perhaps be imagined in the area where I live . . . [where] circa 95% of the entire area is held by 15 estates covering more than 500 square miles . . . [and] should add to a sense of their influence on both the development of the area and the lives of individuals in the area.

I appreciate that the LRPG's proposals will not be directly tackling this concentrated pattern of estates, or the culture of vested interests that goes with it. However, I hope that the LRPG will remember in considering the 'liberating effect' of their proposals, that in many parts of Scotland there can still be a personal cost for publicly supporting land reform.

This is a sobering message considering that the LRPG case for land reform opens with this claim: 'Land is a key resource. The lifechances of people living in rural areas depend on how it is used. All too often in the past, the interests of the majority have been damaged by the interests of the few who control that resource.' This particular response exposes the fact that life chances are not only dependent on how land is used but also, more fundamentally, by the pattern of landownership. Given the growing tendency to emphasise the importance of how land is used over how it is owned – a frequent and repeated insistence of landowners and their agents – it is worth being reminded of the real power dynamics at play. Sadly, for those of us who entertained the notion that land reform was going to deal with the underlying problems, this response also very astutely identifies that the LRPG had no intention of tackling the concentrated pattern of landownership.

Over the summer of 1998, the LRPG worked hard to absorb the representations that had been made and develop ideas about what problems were relevant to its remit and how they could be resolved. Brian Wilson MP had been invited to deliver the McEwen lecture in September. At the time of being invited, he was a Minister of State in the Scottish Office. He had been present on the Isle of Eigg in June 1997 to witness the Isle of Eigg Heritage Trust take ownership of the island and had been responsible for setting up the Community Land Unit within Highlands and Islands Enterprise. But, in July, he had been moved to the Department of Trade and Industry and an opportunity presented itself to invite Donald Dewar in his place. The occasion was also used to publish the next of the LRPG's papers, 'Identifying the Solutions'.

This paper was in marked contrast to the open-ended questions of the 'Problems' paper. It contained seventy detailed proposals complete with costs, pros and cons and the legislative and administrative implications. Interested parties could now get stuck in to well-defined suggestions of how to move forward. Donald Dewar talked about creating new opportunities, about increasing diversity and about letting local people have a far greater role in decision-making about land. He also talked for the first time about creating a new community right to buy whereby communities would be able to acquire the land when it came on to the market. And he made a very revealing remark.

> I wish to be absolutely clear that I regard this right as an essential prerequisite of land reform. The problems must be overcome and the right must be established. I am determined to find the most effective way of giving communities a right to buy the land where they live, and time to put together the necessary bid. It would go further than any other step to change the whole atmosphere surrounding the land ownership argument, it would provide the essential backdrop against which the other changes would be seen, and it would do much to empower the people who work on and live on the land, giving them real rights, and a real say over their own destiny.[9]

Shortly after his speech, the consultation paper, 'Identifying the Solutions', was published and everyone was invited to submit their views on the proposals by 30 November 1998. The proposals included the community right to buy. But how was this to be a genuine consultation when Dewar had only minutes previously stated that this was an essential prerequisite and that he was determined it would happen? We live in a democracy and consultation is meant to be part of a system of improving the way in which we are governed. Some are cynical about such exercises but Dewar himself had, during his lecture, stressed the importance of seeking people's views and achieving as much of a consensus as possible. Yet here he was telling people that, in effect, it didn't matter what they thought and that he was determined that this was going to happen anyway. That, indeed, is often the way of such exercises but it is unusual to have it made explicit! The failure to consult on this important policy properly perhaps explains why it subsequently ran into so much trouble (see Chapter 27).

The enthusiasm to engage with the process was confirmed though by the receipt of 848 responses to the proposals. Landowners contributed 234 responses and, at 29 per cent of the total, were the single largest group. They were followed by individuals who submitted 222 responses – 28 per cent of the total.[10] When combined with salmon proprietors and land agents, the proportion of responses from landed interests was 44 per cent.

Responses this time around were far more focused and structured than they had been to the first paper because people were responding to clear proposals as opposed to open questions. Landed interests were overwhelmingly hostile to the vast majority of the proposals though there was a touching naivety in one of the respondents (number 355) who wrote, 'It is our feeling that the present system of land tenure in Scotland has served us well over the years . . . maybe some changes are due to bring us into the 21st century.' And another (number 734) declared, 'I am at a complete loss to understand why there is a need for land reform in rural Scotland.' Landowners were opposed to increased community involvement in land. 'I don't propose to tell the local baker how to run his business and he has no business telling me how to run mine' was typical of the sentiment.

From this opening cynicism towards the overall vision, the tone is set in most landowner replies for an even more cynical and reactionary response to many of the detailed proposals. SLF members had been issued with response sheets with blank spaces to be filled in next to each proposal which probably explains the prevalence of many instinctive, hasty and reactionary handwritten answers. The fears of being under attack from an uninformed urban population and of an agenda driven by misinformed land reform activists are evident and, in some cases, are built into a virulent and personal attack on Lord Sewel and land reformers. Many responses highlight the same concerns suggesting that a briefing had been issued. They argue that:

- land reform is not popular – less than 1 per cent of the population see it as a priority;
- only 346 responses were made to the first paper – hardly the display of support that politicians claim;
- the LRPG is unqualified to investigate such issues as it lacks anyone with practical experience of landowning, farming or land management;
- land reform is driven by a naive and ignorant urban population and by a handful of bad experiences in the Highlands;
- compensation should be given for loss of feudal superiorities.

In a typical response, all these points are made by way of a preamble to engagement with the individual proposals themselves. There were, however, a small but significant number of both conservative and progressive landowners who presented intelligent and reasoned arguments for both the status quo and for reform.

Finally, land agents in general opposed much of what was on offer but in more moderate and tempered tones. The bulk of responses from crofters were handwritten one-page replies in response to attendance at one of the public meetings that had been organised by the Scottish Office and were concerned exclusively with crofting matters. Tenant farmers were almost all from Arran and Strathspey and often related bitter tales more reminiscent of the Napier Commission in the 1880s than modern Scotland in the 1990s.

The speed that events then took is quite remarkable. The closing date for responses was 30 November 1998 and over 450 (56 per cent) were actually received later than this although they were dated 30 November. In the busy month of December, the responses were apparently digested and analysed and a final report, 'Recommendations for Action', was launched shortly after New Year on 5 January 1999. Before the launch, though, the spin doctors were hard at work.

On 3 January 1999, the main headline on the front page of the *Scotland on Sunday* newspaper screamed, 'Rogue lairds to have their land sold off – abolition of the feudal system a radical move against abuses by absentee owners'. 'Absentee lairds,' it reported, 'who mismanage their estates will be forced to sell their land to the state under radical new plans to be announced this week.' And continued:

> Sources close to the Scottish Office stressed ministers believed the new powers will rarely, if ever, be used and hoped that the threat of compulsory purchase would be enough to convince poor landowners to change their ways . . . Few people had expected the government to be quite so radical in formulating ideas for land reform.

It was a classic piece of spin designed to fortify the 'radical nature' of the Land Reform Policy Group's proposals which were to be launched two days later. It provoked outrage from land-owners. 'This idea sparks feelings of absolute horror in me. It is a recipe for total disaster', fulminated Graeme Gordon, ex-Convenor of the SLF.[11]

On 5 January 1999 in Bute House, Donald Dewar unveiled the final recommendations of the LRPG. Invited to the event were 'around 40 representatives of interested bodies and individuals who have made a contribution to developing the recommendations'. I didn't receive an invitation but had been asked by various news-papers and TV to provide reaction to the announcement. I felt that this would be useful for the public, many of whom knew little about the topic beyond what they read in the papers and, if the story that *Scotland on Sunday* had just run was correct, then some background analysis would be just what the media needed. I explained that I was not invited to the event but supposed that I could hang around outside on Charlotte Square and speak to them afterwards. It was obvious, though, that if I wanted to say anything sensible, I'd need to hear what was said so I asked a friend who runs a press agency in the south of England to ask the Scottish Office for a press pass for his 'Scottish correspondent'. This was duly granted and I got in the door. Climbing the grand stairs of the Georgian interior of the official residence of the First Minister of Scotland, I passed the civil servant who had directed the whole land reform process on her way down. A brief look of astonishment crossed her face as we passed and, when she got to the foot of the stair, I heard her sharply ask a colleague, 'What's Andy Wightman doing here?' Things were getting interesting. I headed to the back of the crowded room and huddled with the rest of the press pack on the floor.

Given the people the Scottish Office had indicated would be there, I was surprised to see the Duke of Buccleuch, various other landowners, land agents and representatives from the Scottish Landowners' Federation. The establishment were having a day out. No wonder I hadn't been invited. Eventually, Donald Dewar came in and made his speech. A whole raft of proposals was announced and it was clear that Labour meant business. Undoubtedly this was a historic occasion but there was nothing about plans to confiscate land. During questions afterwards, I asked him about this. He looked at me disdainfully and confirmed that there were no such plans.

On the way out, I bumped into the Duke of Buccleuch[12] and we had a brief and pleasant chat during which he opined that 'everyone should have the right to buy in the Highlands'. This rather surprised me and afterwards I realised that his views echoed those of a century earlier when the Lowland aristocracy was quite content to see what, by the standards of the day, were radical reforms to crofting law implemented in 'the north' to calm dissent and thus prevent the agitation spreading further south.

I duly spoke to the TV cameras and confirmed that the *Scotland on Sunday* story had turned out to be a classic piece of spin. There were to be no powers to confiscate land. Indeed, Dewar had been at pains to assure landowners that they had nothing to fear from the plans. There were no plans to punish rogue lairds and nothing was said in the proposals about absentee landowners – good or bad. And the abolition of feudalism has absolutely nothing to do with either bad lairds, abuses of ownership or absenteeism! But by this time, the spin had produced the desired result among the general public and the following day's papers were full of sensational claims on either side of the debate. This was followed by reports in the *Scotsman* on 25 January that Prince Abdul Aziz al-Thani, a member of the ruling family of the Gulf state of Qatar, had bought the Newmiln Estate in Perthshire for £2.3 million. According to the report, this gentleman would now be subject to the government's proposals to check up on absentee landlords in Scotland and faced having his land seized if he mismanaged it. Prince Abdul, of course, need not have worried about anything of the sort.

This all suggests that the politics of land reform, as Dr Ewen Cameron, a Highland historian at Edinburgh University, observed in 2001, 'represent the pursuit of what is least disruptive, the minimum possible reform to retain support and to argue that promises have been fulfilled whilst alienating the fewest and committing the least possible amount of public money'.[13]

Feudalism was the first to go. On 11 February 1999, the Scottish Law Commission published a draft bill to abolish feudal tenure.

'Our proposals offer a fresh start for the new millennium,' said Professor Kenneth Reid, the lead commissioner on the project. 'No country with any interest in the state of its laws would wish to carry forward such a system into the next century. It is an embarrassment.'[14] Parliament was quick to act and, less than a year after its first sitting, passed the Abolition of Feudal Tenure etc. (Scotland) Act 2000 on 3 May 2000.

The new Scottish Executive lost no time in pressing on with their proposals. Within a week, it had published the Land Reform White Paper containing detailed proposals on the public access and community right to buy proposals. On 24 November 1999, the new Parliament held its first debate on land reform and this laid out the basic positions of the various political parties on the topic.[15]

Over the following five years, a series of legislation was debated and passed, including:

- Abolition of Feudal Tenure etc. (Scotland) Act 2000
- National Parks (Scotland) Act 2000
- Leasehold Casualties (Scotland) Act 2001
- Agricultural Holdings (Scotland) Act 2003
- Land Reform (Scotland) Act 2003
- Title Conditions (Scotland) Act 2003
- Tenements (Scotland) Act 2004

With the exception of the Tenements Act, all this legislation was passed between 1999 and 2003, during the first session of the new Parliament. It was a busy period of drafting, consulting, amending, taking evidence and debating a wide range of issues many of which had never been debated in such a public manner. All kinds of individuals and organisations, who had never before taken any active part in the political process, submitted written evidence and were called as witnesses. For those who were interested in promoting land reform, it was a wonderful opportunity to engage with the parliamentary process for the first time – or at least in a far easier way than had previously been the case when long trips to London had been necessary.

For the landowners, however, it was a challenge. In the past, their numbers had included members of the House of Lords and, as we saw in Chapter 10, they were used to a level of access to ministers that was never afforded to the representative bodies of much of the rest of civic society in Scotland. It was an uncomfortable experience for the representatives of the SLF who found themselves in the unfamiliar situation of answering tough questions from elected representatives about their position on land reform.[16]

The impact of some of this legislation is explored in later chapters but it's worth exploring what happened next to the land reform process. If the first Parliament (1999–2003) was concerned with getting legislation on the statute book, the second (2003–2007) was focused on bringing the various measures into effect and implementing them. In August 1999, the Scottish Executive published a 'Land Reform Action Plan', setting out the programme for implementing the recommendations of the LRPG. This was followed by a series of twelve progress reports, the last of which was published in August 2003.[17] Lord Sewel had stated, 'These present recommendations are therefore by no means the final word on land reform; they are a platform upon which we can build for the future.'[18] This begs the question, what has happened to the platform and where is the second tranche? For the past five years or so, there's been a vacuum. The land reform programme, so painstakingly put together and implemented between 1997 and 2004, has apparently vanished. Has everything been done? Is land reform finished?

In 2007, a new administration was elected to govern Scotland – the Scottish National Party. Its manifesto contained nothing about land reform despite the real enthusiasm of many of its members for it and the extensive amendments that Roseanna Cunningham MSP tabled during the debates on the Land Reform Bill. The party had also set up the Scottish Land Commission which published its 'Public Policy Toward Land in Scotland' in November 1997, an initiative which they saw as complementary to the work of the LRPG.[19]

Instead of seizing the opportunity to move land reform forward to the next stage, the SNP administration has shown a distinct lack of enthusiasm. Aware of the silence in their manifesto, in September 2007 I prepared a paper entitled 'Land Reform: An agenda for the 2007–2011 Scottish Parliament' which I sent to all MSPs.[20] In it, I proposed six topics for possible further work. They were:

- common good
- review and extension of the community right to buy
- reform of the arrangements governing Crown Land in Scotland
- land value taxation
- reform of succession law
- right to buy for tenant farmers.

All these were areas where work had already been done or was underway. The Scottish Law Commission, for example, was working on a bill to reform succession and this was published in April 2009. In December 2006, a detailed and comprehensive review of the Crown Estate in Scotland had been published by the Crown Estate Review Working Group which consisted of six local authorities, COSLA and HIE.[21] In February 2007, I had published a detailed twenty-three-page review of the community right to buy highlighting problems and making recommendations for improving the way the act was framed.[22]

I was particularly interested in how the SNP would respond since they were in government and in a position to take matters forward in a way the other parties were not. After a series of hopeful emails, everything went cold and nothing further happened. And nothing ever did happen. In June 2009, Roseanna Cunningham, the Minister for the Environment ruled out any review of the Land Reform Act.[23] Despite having the opportunity to make a significant contribution to land reform, the Scottish government effectively killed off the land reform agenda. Why this happened is not entirely clear. Certainly, the SNP had their hands full running a minority administration and struggled to achieve a number of their key manifesto commitments. But that does not explain why a party, which for all of its history had campaigned for land reform and which had taken an active part in the land reform debates of the two previous parliaments, suddenly decided that there was nothing for it to do. Some have suggested that since the SNP holds a number of marginal SNP/Conservative rural constituencies such as Perth and Kinross and Angus, it was reluctant to rock the boat of wealthy farmers and landowners. Others have pointed to the fact that many politicians genuinely felt that land reform had been completed.[24] Either way, the result has been that the momentum and radical edge present in the first Parliament has disappeared.

In their manifesto for the 2011 Scottish election, the SNP promised to establish a Land Reform Review group to review land reform legislation to date and to advise on "other improvements which we will legislate on over the course of the next five years".[25] On 24 July 2012, at a Scottish Cabinet Meeting on the Isle of Skye, Alex Salmond announced the setting up of this group which will publish its conclusions in April 2014. The Group's remit is to identify how land reform will:

- Enable more people in rural and urban Scotland to have a stake in the ownership, governance, management and use of land, which will lead to a greater diversity of land ownership, and ownership types, in Scotland;
- Assist with the acquisition and management of land (and also land assets) by communities, to make stronger, more resilient, and independent communities which have an even greater stake in their development; and
- Generate, support, promote, and deliver new relationships between land, people, economy and environment in Scotland.

Whether this Group succeeds in its remit and whether this latest "review" stimulates any radical change remains to be seen. The history of land reform is littered with fine statements and rhetoric from would-be reforming politicians who, when the time comes for action suddenly lose their reforming zeal.

Little More Than an Instrument for Extracting Money

Land tenure reform in Scotland

As has been pointed out earlier, land tenure is concerned with the rules of the game and landownership is about the players. One can criticise individual landowners all one likes but the responsibility for changing the system rests with the public and those we elect to Parliament. For decades, however, as this book has made clear, that legislature was composed of the same powerful interests that stood to benefit from this selfsame legislation. Indeed, there is a good argument to suggest that everything enacted before the Equal Franchise Act of 1928 is up for re-negotiation. Instead, what has happened is a partial reform of land tenure that attempts to modernise the system but does not challenge the assumptions underpinning it such as the law of prescription.

Land tenure reform is a topic that has, until recently, been the preserve of lawyers and academics. The public has not taken much interest in it although the abolition of feu duties in 1974 is familiar to many homeowners of a certain generation. As the opening remarks in the Scottish Law Commission's 'Report on Land Registration' make clear:

Land registration law is law that is as important as it is incon-spicuous. Indeed, to non-lawyers it is so inconspicuous as to be invisible: few even realise that it exists. There is no harm in that. Much law is like plumbing: useful but unexciting and seldom thought about except when it goes wrong. Visible or invisible, it is important.[1]

Much the same could be said about all aspects of land law but, as I try to argue in this book, if land reform is wanted and if it is to succeed, there is no alternative – the public must have a far better grasp of land tenure than they do now. Despite some valiant efforts, there is little evidence that the system is becoming more widely understood although the legislation enacted by the Scottish Parliament has helped to raise the profile.[2]

The process of reforming law on most topics is undertaken by the Scottish Law Commission. Technically, their job is not to reform the law – though that can be the effect of their work – but to recommend ways of simplifying, updating and improving the law of Scotland. It takes its instructions from the government of the day and works on the basis of four-year programmes of law reform. (It is currently working on the eighth programme 2010–14.) During the past few years, the Commission has published the following important property law reform proposals:

Date	Topic	Report number
1990	Report on Succession	124
1990	Report on the Passing of Risk in Contracts for the Sale of Heritable Property	127
1997	Report on the Law of the Tenement	162
1998	Report on Boundary Walls	163
1998	Report on Leasehold Casualties	165
1999	Abolition of the Feudal System	168
2000	Jurisdiction under the Agricultural Holdings (Scotland) Acts	177
2000	Report on Real Burdens	181
2003	Report on Law of the Foreshore and Sea Bed	190
2003	Irritancy in Leases of Land	191
2006	Conversion of Long Leases	204
2007	Sharp v Thomson	208
2009	Succession	215
2010	Land Registration	222

This is an impressive list of reform and the work of the SLC has contributed hugely to building a more modern and straightforward system of property law. The majority of the above reports have been implemented by means of legislation or other measures.

Despite the apparently dry nature of many of these subjects, the reports often make for fascinating reading. As one would expect of reports from some of the best legal minds in the country, they are written with precision and logic as well as a degree of flair, style and good humour. In its 2010 report on Land Registration, for example, the authors write, 'The 1979 Act's brevity means that on numerous issues it is simply silent. Of course, no legislation succeeds in covering everything. There are always holes. But the 1979 Act is a Swiss cheese.'[3]

The most significant outstanding matters yet to be dealt with are the law of the Foreshore and Sea Bed and the law of Succession. Before dealing with them, let's look at the topics that have already been dealt with.

Land tenure reform to date

The abolition of feudal tenure was, for many, the major flagship piece of land reform legislation and followed a discussion paper published by the SLC in 1991 and a final report published in 1999.[4] It had been a goal of reformers for generations – a major report was published in 1966 and this was followed by a government commitment to act in 1969 and 1972[5] – but only modest progress had been possible in 1974 when feu duties were abolished and existing ones could be redeemed. To most people, this was feudal abolition and the fact that a further act was required in 2000 came as something of a surprise. But feudal tenure is a system whereby owners of property owe obligations and duties to a feudal superior and one of those (and by far the most obvious) was the obligation to pay an annual feu duty. Examine any feudal title and it will be replete with conditions restricting the use of the property and requiring the superior's permission for all sorts of alterations to these burdens. Such consent was often only given in return for payment of a sum of money. As the Scottish Law Commission observed in their 1999 report:

> From the point of view of social policy the main reason for recommending the abolition of the feudal system of land tenure is that it has degenerated from a living system of land tenure with both good and bad features into something which, in the case of many but not all superiors, is little more than an instrument for extracting money.[6]

During the consultation on the feudal abolition bill, representations were received from all over Scotland complaining of the arbitrary and often vindictive exercise of feudal powers. Complaints from the Island of Arran were particularly impassioned with local businesses and households often held to ransom by feudal demands. Local families were having to pay hundreds of pounds to establish bed-and-breakfast businesses and companies were being thwarted in their desires to change the use of buildings. The feudal system was being used as a form of private planning control fifty years after planning was democratised.

It had long ago become clear that the feudal system had ceased to serve any useful purpose – in contrast to its useful role in eighteenth- and nineteenth-century urban Scotland (see pp. 14–16) – but the lack of time in the Westminster system for Scottish legislation precluded reform. With the advent of the Scottish Parliament, the topic went straight to the top of the agenda. The SLC report and draft bill on feudal abolition was published in February 1999 and within ten months of the Parliament taking up its powers, it was on the statute book. The Queen gave her royal assent on 9 June 2000.

The act wastes no time in getting to the point. In Section 1 it boldly states, 'The feudal system of land tenure, that is to say the entire system whereby land is held by a vassal on perpetual tenure from a superior is, on the appointed day, abolished.'[7] That appointed day arrived on 28 November 2004 and Professor Hector MacQueen of the *Scots Law News* published a brief intimation of death on his blog.

Tenure: Peacefully, at home, after a long illness bravely borne, at midnight 27 November 2004, Feudal (Feudalism), in approximately his 881st year (birth never registered and all documentation lost). Sadly missed by a wide circle of conveyancers, title raiders and barons, who found Feudalism a lucrative source of status and revenue throughout his long and utile life. The body has been donated to the National Archives and the Registers of Scotland for the furtherance of legal-historical research. A memorial service will be held at Scone Abbey, near Feudalism's supposed birth-place, at either Whit or Martinmas, to which all superiors and vassals are warmly invited. Donations for a monument in the form of a pyramid topped with a crown, to be erected at Holyrood, where Feudalism's last rites were performed, may be sent to the Queen's and Lord Treasurer's Remembrancer, Crown Office, Edinburgh. An elegant obituary by Professor George Gretton may be found in the pages of the November 2004 issue of the Journal of the Law Society of Scotland.[8]

The Title Conditions (Scotland) Act 2003 also came into force on the same day. Recognising that it is useful to have certain burdens in titles relating to matters such as the management of common areas and the preservation of amenity, this Act codifies and restricts what is now acceptable as a burden in a title. These two acts make the whole process of owning property clearer and fairer. But there was more.

Those who believe that land reform is of relevance only to rural areas should take a look at the Tenements (Scotland) Act 2004. It too helped to reduce the potential complications arising out of the ownership of common areas. Tenements form over a quarter of Scotland's housing stock and include office blocks and large houses that have been divided into flats. I know from personal experience how stressful the process of organising common repairs can be. The Tenements Act is a major step forward in making life for tenement dwellers more straightforward when it comes to maintaining the fabric of people's houses.

Finally, the problem of leasehold casualties, where payments are due at certain events from the holders of a long lease, came to the fore as a result of the activities of the so-called 'Raider of the Lost Titles' (see pages 336–38). These were abolished by the Leasehold Casualties (Scotland) Act 2001.

These are the principal land tenure reforms to date. But a number of topics await action – namely, succession, foreshore and seabed, leasehold reform and land registration. Succession is dealt with in Chapter 28 but let's have a look at the others.

Foreshore and seabed

The law of the foreshore and seabed may seem somewhat arcane but it is a vital public space which is becoming more and more significant for marine renewable energy, minerals and leisure uses. The

Scottish Law Commission published a report in 2003 proposing a number of important reforms that would clarify the law and allow for a better-integrated framework for management. The report has sat on the shelf gathering dust as there seems to be no one with sufficient interest to take things forward. This is a pity since the consultations on the SLC proposals revealed significant problems:

> The consultation responses we received confirmed dissatisfaction regarding the management of the sea bed. In particular, the tension between the [Crown Estate] Commissioners on the one hand and harbour and local authorities on the other was evident. There were calls for an end to commercial charges for use of the sea bed and for more local control over its use, particularly within harbour areas. However, the question whether the Crown should continue to have full ownership of the sea bed and foreshore and should be able to charge grantees for the exclusive use of the sea bed for such purposes as fish farms, harbour works and permanent moorings is outwith the scope of our remit, which is to advise on reforms which would clarify, and bring consistency to, the existing law.[9]

Indeed this dissatisfaction was further underlined when the Commission moved on to discuss harbours:

> There is a general view that it is anomalous that a port authority has no absolute right of control over the sea bed and moorings within the area for which it is administratively responsible. There is considerable hostility towards the Crown Estate Commissioners and their management policy which seeks to maximise commercial gain from the use of its marine estate.[10]

Such matters may be outwith its remit, but we can't have a sensible debate on them if we don't sort out the law that underpins them. The report also highlights the real conflict there is between long-established public rights over the foreshore and suggests that popular recreational activities such as beachcombing should be put on a statutory footing. It recommends that valuable common law rights of the public should be given statutory protection and that

Raider of the Lost Titles

Following the launch of the final report of the Land Reform Policy Group on 5 January 1999, I was asked to write a story for the *Sunday Times* on Scotland's twenty worst landowners for publication on 10 January. I can normally turn out a story pretty quickly but this was a bit of a challenge for three reasons. Firstly, the timescale was tight for a major feature. Secondly, I don't like this populist style of journalism where deficiencies in the system of landownership are pinned on individuals in order to create hate figures. Moreover, the underlying angle was that such 'bad landlords' were going to be targeted when, by this time, it was clear that nothing of the sort was going to happen. Thirdly, by naming and shaming individuals, the article would have to be what newspaper editors call 'legalled' – subjected to a line by line analysis by the paper's lawyers to minimise the risk of legal actions by those named – and that would be tedious.

I needed the money, though, and couldn't refuse – so who to choose? There were some obvious choices but I ended up stuck for number twenty until I remembered the controversy over the so-called 'Raider of the Lost Titles'. This concerned a Mr Brian Hamilton who, as a mature student, took a course in land economy at the University of Aberdeen and discovered an interest in, and a talent for, understanding the complexities of old titles. He acquired a knack of buying up feudal estates – superiority interests in land – and exercising the perfectly legal rights associated with them. One example was a house that had been feued to the old Aberdeenshire county education authority with a feudal condition that it be used for education purposes. When Grampian Regional Council decided to sell the schoolhouse as a private residence, it should, by right, have returned the ownership to the former owner. It didn't and so, when Hamilton bought the former superior's interests, he was able to invoke them and seek the return of the property or compensation.

Hamilton was smart and was perfectly within his rights even though his methods were regarded as distasteful. Alex Salmond initiated a major debate on the topic in the House of

Commons on 6 November 1996 and outlined the string of cases of perceived abuse that Brian Hamilton had effected. He argued that 'Brian Hamilton has profited by many hundreds of thousands of pounds from his feudal speculation, and left lives and nerves shattered in his wake. The law is a mess, but the Government have done nothing to tackle the problem'.[11]

Sir Hector Monro, for the government, argued that Hamilton's activities were reprehensible. But, conscious of the publicity surrounding the case, he was keen that his fellow landowners in the Scottish Landowners' Federation were not tarred with the same brush:

> Such behaviour is very different from that of those who happen to have owned feu titles for very many years; when a building changes use, by law it must fall back into the ownership of the person who gave the original feu. That is different from the position, which the hon. Gentleman rightly outlined, of a company or individual searching out feus and buying them up, and putting the current owner of a house in an impossible position.[12]

It took Brian Wilson MP, who had personal experience of the miseries inflicted by feudalism on Arran in his constituency, to point out the flaw in focussing such criticism solely on the poor Mr Hamilton. He argued that, in fact, there was no real difference between Hamilton and other feudal superiors who had held their estates for decades:

> I want to draw a distinction between the activities of the newcomers to this field, such as Mr. Brian Hamilton, and the traditional exercisers of those powers. It is a racket waiting to be exploited. It is just as bad for the people who live under the Seafield, Lovat and Arran estates of this world, which have silently and perniciously exploited these powers for many years.[13]

In the rush to print, I found myself caught up in the odium felt for Mr Hamilton and wrote:

> Brian Hamilton is not a typical Scottish laird. Dubbed the 'Raider of the Lost Titles' he does not own vast acres of land

but is a former North Sea welder from Surrey who knows the feudal system inside out and has made a considerable profit by exploiting it, most recently by invoking leasehold casualties in the village of Boghead in Lanarkshire.

He has amassed a fortune by buying up feudal super-iorities and demanding that his vassals (mainly home-owners) pay thousands of pounds in payment under ancient clauses in title deeds or face losing their property. Defending his actions by blaming incompetent solicitors who failed to observe the small print in old titles, he is said to have left lives shattered.

Response: I am being tarred and feathered in order to save other people's faces – incompetent lawyers. We all purport to live by the law and if people expect other people to obey the law then they should do so themselves.

A few years later once all the fuss had died down, I met Brian Hamilton in the National Archives of Scotland. We got to know each other and had a number of enjoyable chats about the more arcane elements of land law. He is now a respected dealer in barony titles to whom all Edinburgh lawyers turn for advice. His misfortune was to have been buying superiority estates rather than ordinary estates and to have been a new-comer rather than old money.

Brian Hamilton actually did land reform a favour by highlighting the anachronism of the law and he was directly responsible for the fact that, three months after the debate, Donald Dewar instructed the Scottish Law Commission to review the law relating to leasehold casualties which were subsequently abolished in 2001.[14]

I now regret having written what I did. Whilst I would not have done what Hamilton did, he was unfairly pilloried for doing nothing different from what other feudal landowners have been up to over the centuries – namely, exercising his legal right. Such shortcomings are the fault of society and not of landowners. As Churchill said, 'We do not want to punish the landlord. We want to alter the law.'

the law of prescription, which, as we have seen, has been used to appropriate land, should not be used to extinguish public rights. It also says useful things about harbours and ports. This is all important stuff that is very much in the public interest and it should be acted upon before we find that rights we have taken for granted are one day extinguished through failure to follow through on these important recommendations.

Leasehold

In December 2006, the SLC Report on Conversion of Long Leases was published.[15] This proposes to allow all tenants holding a lease that was granted for more than 175 years and which still has over a hundred years to run to convert their tenancy into full ownership. A long lease or tack is similar in many respects to a feu which is, in reality, a perpetual lease. This is why leasehold has remained rare in Scotland in contrast to England where it is commonplace. Many long leases run for hundreds of years and the 999-year lease is not uncommon. They originated in the nineteenth century when much of Scotland's estates were entailed and thus could not be feued. The alternative was to lease it and this is precisely what took place in villages and towns across Scotland. In the particular case of common good land, there is often a prohibition on alienating land without the approval of the courts and so burghs decided to lease it instead. This was a potential problem in at least one case – the Waverley Market in Edinburgh, where the tenant has a 208-year lease (see Chapter 24). In 2012, the Scottish Parliament passed the Long Leases (Scotland) Act which implemented the recommendations of the Scottish Law Commission. The Waverley Market is exempt from conversion due to amendments made during the passage of the Bill.

Land registration

In February 2010, the Scottish Law Commission published a 600-page report on land registration.[16] Its aim is to completely replace the 1979 Land Registration Act – the one that is regarded as a 'Swiss cheese'. The principal reason for the proposal, which comes after three separate discussion papers, is that much of the law on land registration has evolved as a result of practice over the past twenty years and this is unsatisfactory for a system that purports to secure title to assets worth billions of pounds. The report, therefore, makes recommendations on areas of uncertainty in the law and on ways to streamline the law – including topics such as record keeping, completion of the register and indemnity. Again, this is a vital piece of work which will help to answer the question of who owns Scotland and provide greater clarity to both owners and to the public.

The Land Registration Bill was introduced to Parliament on 1 December 2011 and became law on 10 July 2012. Despite the welcome modernisation of the technical aspects of land registration law, the Scottish Government refused to consider changes that would address some of the concerns raised in this book. These included reform of *a non domino* titles, a system of registration to protect common land, a ban on registration of owners in offshore tax havens and free access to the Land Register for the public. The Act thus provides a modern technical framework for convyancing and land registration. What it fails to do is to extend this to a modern system of land information.[17]

Prescription

A central theme of my argument in this book is that the historical construction of land law has favoured the few at the expense of the many. Unfortunately, there's not a great deal that can be done about this in terms of restitution but plenty can be done to ensure that this situation is not perpetuated. Some of the measures that would help to achieve this are outlined later in this book but one is perhaps best discussed here and that is the law of prescription.

As we have seen, prescription was introduced in 1617 to legitimise in the eyes of the law the theft of Church lands. It was intimately bound up with that other significant act of 1617, the establishment of the Register of Sasines, and both were designed by the nobility to defend and protect, as far as possible, their ill-gotten gains. Over the centuries since then, prescription was used to appropriate further acreage from the common good as evidenced by the Duke of Argyll's statement that the principle of prescription provided the foundation of 'a very good deal of the property held by Members'.[18]

Lawyers are fond of their metaphors and the ones deployed in relation to prescription are particularly revealing. They talk about prescription as the means by which possession ripens and matures into ownership and of how it is a cure for a defective title as if it is some fine wine or maybe even a Swiss cheese. Funnily enough, they have never seemed to call it what actually is – legalised theft.[19] For theft is what prescription legitimised and, as argued earlier, if any ordinary citizen was found to be in possession of stolen goods, they could be charged with reset.

In 2005, I received an email from one of Scotland's most eminent experts in the field of property law. I had put to him some queries about a particular piece of common land that a neighbouring landowner had encroached upon and had, apparently, successfully appropriated to his holding. What, I wondered, did the law of prescription really say about all of this. Today, prescription is regarded as a device that can be deployed to legitimise that which is legitimate. For example, it can be deployed to provide protection to a purchaser where the documents in the legal record are vague but where the validity of one's title is not in doubt. But it can also – and this is where I was in for a surprise – be the basis for transferring ownership from one person to another.

The expert kindly provided me with an example. Suppose I own a farm of 100 acres and you own an adjacent farm. There is a muddle about the boundary with your farm. Your title and mine both include a certain half an acre. In fact, my title to it is good and yours is not. Nevertheless, it is you who possess the half-acre because you plough and sow and reap it. After ten years of this, ownership would pass from me to you. So prescription can transfer ownership. Of course, the requisites must be met. There must be true possession. This must be stressed since often possession is clear – for example, when a farmer ploughs and sows and reaps a piece of land – but often possession is fuzzy and hard to prove. The possession must be *nec vi, nec clam, nec precario* – literally 'not by force, not secretly, not with licence' or, as in the 1973 Prescription and Limitation act, 'openly, peaceably and without any judicial interruption'. And there must be an apparent title in the Register.

Call me naive but this astonished me. It seemed wrong. How could one person get hold of another person's land in such a way? But then it struck me that this has been the game all along, only it is our commons that were lost and the gentry were perhaps rather more obliging and mannerly when it came to encroachment on neighbouring private proprietors. In recent years, prescription has been relied upon by, for example, John MacLeod to claim the Cuillin and landowners in Perthshire to claim a commonty (see Alyth in Chapter 22).

What does this all mean?

Land tenure reform is a significant element in any wider package of land reform since it provides the opportunity to revisit the fundamentals of how land is owned. This is of particular importance now that we have a Scottish Parliament and the public have the opportunity to make more effective use of the legislative process. It is no coincidence that its arrival ushered in a period of sustained land law reform, since Westminster simply never had the time to undertake these kinds of changes and thus property law stagnated. In future, there will be more property law reform. Reading the list of those who submitted comments to the various SLC discussion papers, it is clear that public engagement in reform has, thus far, been restricted, by and large, to the legal profession. Scotland's laws of land tenure and ownership belong to all of us and it is to be hoped that, in future, a wider range of interests in civic society take the opportunity to have their say too. Failure to do so may mean that opportunities to improve the law are missed and that the historical tendency for the law to favour the haves over the have-nots continues.

Bureaucratic Nit-picking and Fine Legal Arguments

The community right to buy

As outlined in Chapter 25, the community right to buy (CRTB) was first put forward as an idea by Donald Dewar in his 1998 McEwen Lecture when he said that he was determined that such a right would be created. It formed part of the final report of the LRPG and was then the subject of a legislative process leading to its incorporation in the Land Reform (Scotland) Act 2003. The right to buy came into force on 14 June 2004 and provides opportunities for communities in rural Scotland to apply to register an interest in land and property. Once such an interest is approved by Scottish Ministers, it is entered on the Register of Community Interests in Land held by the Registers of Scotland.[1] The effect of the registration is to provide the community with a right to buy the registered land if and when the owner decides to sell it – or, more accurately, a right to try to buy the registered land since the landowner may subsequently withdraw it from sale.

During the passage of the legislation, there was extensive debate about the scope of the legislation including how to define a community, how to define rural, how to define the land for sale and what procedures to follow. It rapidly became clear that this was going to become a complex piece of legislation hedged around with conditions, constraints and discretionary powers of application.[2]

Although initially, the right was to apply only to areas of 'special importance' in rural Scotland and the community was defined solely as those living or working on the land in question, the right now applies to any land in rural Scotland – defined as land outwith settlements of over 10,000 population – and the community comprises all adults on the voters' roll living in defined postcodes. The legislation requires that a community body is set up and that it conforms to certain conditions. Any application for registration must be submitted before the land in question is put up for sale although there are procedures for late registration which demand stiffer compliance with the range of criteria to be satisfied before Scottish Ministers will consent to placing the land on the register. Once registered, the community must wait until it is put up for sale and must then conduct ballots and present further evidence to Scottish Ministers as to why they should be allowed to buy the land.

It is often claimed in the media that places such as Eigg and Gigha were acquired as a result of the Land Reform Act. They were not. The community-right-to-buy provisions of the Land Reform (Scotland) Act 2003 only came into force on 14 June 2004 and Eigg and Gigha were bought long before that (1997 and 2002 respectively). In fact, the take-up of the legislation has been quite limited.[3] As of 1 May 2012, there were 142 applications to register land of which:

- sixty-two had been registered
- thirty-three had been activated
- forty-six had been deleted and
- one was pending a decision.

This overstates the volume of registrations since some communities withdrew and then resubmitted applications. Furthermore, some community bodies have had to submit multiple applications because the land they wished to register is in separate ownerships. Taking this into account, a total of seventy-seven community bodies have applied to register an interest of which thirty-three have secured a registration and nine have succeeded in acquiring land.

A total of 44,698 acres have been acquired under the act by the nine communities:

Community	Acreage
Assynt	44,578
Machrihanish	1000
Bute Forest	397
Comrie	90
Crossgates	29
Duisdale	3
Neilston	0.5
Catrine	0.5
Silverburn	0.2

(Note – Assynt comprised three separate applications.)

Of the 300,000 acres of land that have come into community ownership by whatever means since 1 July 1999, 46,098 acres or 15 per cent has been acquired using the powers of the Land Reform Act. Of the forty-six deleted applications:

- fourteen were refused by Scottish Ministers
- thirteen were withdrawn by the applicant
- seven registered interests were deleted after the community body failed to conclude a purchase within the prescribed period of six months
- five were refused due to the discovery of option agreements over the land
- four were deleted following a successful legal challenge by the landowner
- two withdrew after securing a purchase of the registered land outwith the terms of the act and
- one was refused because another community body was granted the right to buy over the same registered interest.

The cost to the taxpayer for the sixty-six successful registrations was £719,936 or £10,908 per registration.[4]

If you take the time to examine the Register of Community Interests in Land, you will be struck by the number of documents and correspondence. Looking closer, the complexities of the legislation also become clearer.

For example, a community body called Lochwinnoch Community Buyout Group (LCBG) registered an interest in the former Struthers lemonade factory in Lochwinnoch. It was given the right to buy but then the landowner withdrew it from sale leaving all their efforts in vain. A number of communities have gone through the whole process only to find that the landowner, unbeknown to them but possibly in response to the knowledge that an application was in the offing, had entered into negotiations with a potential buyer and agreed an option to purchase at some unspecified future date. In such circumstances, Scottish Ministers are bound to refuse the application.

When the idea was first put forward, the Land Reform Policy Group stated the measure 'would greatly empower communities' and 'would effect rapid change in [the] pattern of land ownership'.[5] Most privately owned land in Scotland has never been exposed for sale privately or openly for over a hundred years. It is estimated, for example, that at least 25 per cent of estates of over 1,000 acres have been held by the same families for over 400 years.[6] Even in parts of Scotland where turnover is higher such as the Highlands, over 50 per cent of private land has never been exposed since the Second World War and 25 per cent was not exposed at any time in the twentieth century.[7] The CRTB might be better described in such circumstances as the right to buy for the great-grandchildren of the community and it is hard to see how the proposal enjoys the advantages attributed to it. In particular, it is far from clear that the legislation empowers individuals or communities since no community is likely to be empowered by speculation that, at some point in the future, they might be able to take over control of the land.

Nine successful acquisitions in five years do not represent a rapid change in the pattern of landownership. The Act is failing for five main reasons:

1. The legislation is a complex and bureaucratic minefield with numerous obstacles all of which have to be negotiated expertly and exactly if an application is to be successful. Much of the complexity is a necessary consequence of the fact that the act has to deal with processes of property law, respect human rights and ensure that the powers contained in

the act are not abused. But, given that registration is essentially a speculative endeavour – the actual right may never arise or may be refused when the time comes or the land may be withdrawn from sale – which is unfamiliar to communities and given the policy aims of land reform, it is desirable that any community with the desire to make an application should be able to do so with the minimum of effort.

2. The act gives Scottish Ministers – and, in practice, this means civil servants – substantial discretionary powers. The extent and significance of these powers confer by far the greatest empowerment not on communities but on Scottish Ministers who sit in judgement of the necessity, worth and value of a community's aspirations. Excluding administrative obligations such as sending letters to people, Scottish Ministers have over twenty separate discretionary powers under the act all of which can be exercised in a fashion that is exempt from any appeal and which have been incompetently discharged in a significant number of cases to date (see next point).

3. The administration of the act has been woeful. In one case, a community waited a full two months only to be told that the application did not make it clear that the land shown on their map was the land they wished to register. Such a claim should have been obvious within a matter of days of receipt but, in this case, the landowner's lawyers had pored over the application and noted possible technical breaches of the law which they made clear they might challenge in the courts. Fearful of facing legal action, Scottish Ministers buckled and invented bizarre reasons for refusal which were not applied to other cases where breaches were far more obvious but where there was not the same fear of legal challenge.[8]

In another case, Kinghorn Community Land Association wanted to register an interest in land to the west of the town which had formerly been part of their burgh common since 1605 but which had been sold off by corrupt Town Council officials. Because the land was held in separate ownerships, the community were obliged to submit eighteen separate applications. All maps were prepared to the same standard but all omitted the vital grid reference. The omission should have been noted upon receipt by the Scottish Executive but was not. As a result, one landowner mounted a legal challenge against three of the plots of land on the basis that there was no grid reference on the map. It was successful and the registrations were then deleted.

Of registered applications to date (1 May 2012), on this one criterion alone (inclusion of the grid reference on the map), fifty-one out of the ninety-five registered interests – fully 54 per cent – were, in fact, incompetent and could, as a result, have been successfully challenged by any landowner.

4. Much of the decision making continues to be taken within an excessively legalistic context with civil servants constantly taking internal legal advice and constantly looking over their shoulders in anticipation of potential legal challenges – not by communities, it might be added, but by landowners. This has introduced a clear discriminatory element in the whole process whereby, if there *is* any aspect of an application that may be open to challenge from the landowner, Scottish Ministers would rather reject it than accept it. In these circumstances, applications involving a hostile landowner are less likely to be accepted. Whilst this may, in some cases, be viewed as protecting the interests of the application – they can make a further application that may overcome the alleged deficiencies although by this time it may be too late – it is clear discrimination. To make matters worse, Scottish Ministers can take as long as they like to reach the key decisions that they are required to take. Section 37 (19) states, 'Any failure to comply with the time limit specified in subsection (117) above does not affect the validity of anything done under this section.'

Community bodies have also to take certain actions and decisions within statutory time frames but they, unlike Scottish Ministers, are provided with no such comforting subsections that allow them to take more time if they need to. If they fail in their statutory obligations, their interests will be extinguished. The balance is wrong here. Scottish Ministers and bureaucrats can take months but communities, who do not have the same resources of full-time staff, legal advice and money, have to jump and jump fast or all is lost.

5. Landowners have a number of ways in which they can simply circumvent the right to buy. Where communities have submitted competent bids, they have found that landowners have done secret deals in the background which have frustrated their aspirations. In some cases, landowners have simply withdrawn the land from sale following the right to buy being granted. There are numerous opportunities for landowners to frustrate the aspirations of communities. The legislation offers several technical obstacles. Turcan Connell, an Edinburgh legal firm that has successfully frustrated the ambitions of communities, stated in a recent briefing:

> If a landowner wishes to prevent an application being registered, it is far more fruitful to scrutinise an application to see if it complies with the statutory requirements. He should not necessarily rely on the thoroughness of the Civil Servants. In the first application by the Seton Fields Community Company, [Ministers] declined to register because the plan was not properly incorporated into the application. The second application was declined in 24 hours because the application referred to a non-existent paper apart as a definition of the postcode areas . . . By these means, the landowner can use any gaps between prohibition letters to conclude missives of sale of the land.[9]

They go on to refer to another application which was overturned on appeal because the community body had failed to note that there was a standard security over the property. As with the poor of 300 years ago with whom Cosmo Innes had such sympathy, the ordinary citizen today faces an uphill struggle to exercise rights contained in an act that is supposed to empower them. Instead, communities are faced with the prospect of well-paid lawyers scrutinising every detail to try to coerce weak civil servants into running for cover in fear of a possible legal challenge.[10]

The failure of the legislation can be explained in a number of ways. Its genesis was as part of a flawed process – Dewar was committed to the proposal before there had been any consultation. The Land Reform Policy Group were working at great speed and failed to analyse the situation properly in order to devise appropriate solutions. During the legislative period, the concern of the drafters was to cover every eventuality and, where this could not be done, to implant ministerial discretion.

The civil service was instinctively conservative about the whole project and, indeed, about land reform as a whole. When Brian Wilson MP was Minister of State in the Scottish Office, he decided that the best way to advance community ownership would be by setting up a dedicated unit of specialists with a budget to support communities along the way. By doing so, he intentionally circumvented the Scottish Office civil service. Before the 1997 election, Wilson had been invited to visit the Island of Eigg to join the celebrations of them taking title to the land on 12 June. During the weekend following the election victory, it occurred to him that the visit to Eigg could now be converted into a ministerial visit (he was now a Minister of State in the Scottish Office) and an opportunity to launch a new policy initiative. Two days before the event, he phoned Chief Executive of Highlands and Islands Enterprise Iain Robertson and secured his enthusiastic support for setting up a Community Land Unit which, since 1997, has assisted hundreds of community groups across the HIE area. Had he pursued this in the normal manner by instructing his civil servants to explore the idea, he knew there was a real chance that the initiative would be watered down, delayed and otherwise obstructed by all sorts of objections.

My own experience of this came much later after the Scottish Parliament had passed the Land Reform Act on 23 January 2003. An important element of the CRTB was defining what land would be eligible to be registered. This was to be the subject of secondary legislation but Scottish Ministers had proposed that a threshold of 3,000 people be used. This would mean that all land in settlements with a population larger than this could not be registered and the citizens of towns such as Eyemouth (pop. 3,300) and Banff (pop. 4,640) would be unable to take advantage of the new law.

Allan Wilson was one of the ministers piloting the bill through Parliament and he had expressed support for looking again at the threshold to enable as many communities as possible to take advantage of the right to buy. I was of the view that the threshold should be abolished and that all land, urban and rural, should be eligible.[11] Knowing that a final decision on the threshold would be taken after the act was passed, I contacted the minister urging him to raise the threshold from 3,000 to 10,000 and he agreed to meet me. On 18 March 2003, I made my way up a long narrow staircase to a small garret room above the Scotch Whisky Heritage Centre at the top of the High Street. To my surprise, I found a tray with biscuits and a flask of tea and Allan Wilson sitting at a table on his own. For those unfamiliar with etiquette in such matters, ministers never meet anyone officially without a civil servant present to take notes, advise on points and ensure an efficient follow-up of anything that is agreed at the meeting. Where were his civil servants, I asked. 'Well,' he explained, 'if they were here, we would make no progress. You see, they don't want to raise this threshold and I'm having difficulty persuading them. I want to talk about what we should do.'

I was astonished but, on reflection, not surprised. The next day he sent me an email:

> Our chat yesterday has already proved VERY useful and has helped shape my thinking and now hopefully, others. I would like to keep up the dialogue on a confidential basis outwith the usual channels so to speak given the nature of our discussions. It is VERY important that I don't come out with half-baked propositions or that officials are prematurely advised of what I propose. In that context this mailbox is the best means of confidential communication until Parliament is dissolved at the end of next week, after which I can be contacted on [email supplied].

With Parliament dissolving on 27 March for the May election, we had agreed that a commitment in the Labour Party manifesto was the best way to ensure that the threshold was raised since it would then be more difficult for the civil servants to block it. Thus the Scottish Labour Party fought the 2003 election with a commitment to make further moves to extend the benefits of community landownership to urban Scotland.

> Labour is proud to have introduced the right for communities to buy the land where they live and work. This will bring direct benefit to rural communities. In a second term we will see through the important measures in the Land Reform (Scotland) Act and take further steps to extend the benefits of community ownership to urban Scotland.[12]

The consultation paper issued in August 2003 proposed the higher threshold of 10,000 and this became the new, higher threshold on 15 June 2004, when the CRTB came into force.[13]

The Land Reform Act has frequently been cited as one of the successes of devolution and a measure which, had the Scottish Parliament not been established, would never have reached the statute book. This latter observation is undoubtedly true. With the lack of parliamentary time at Westminster for Scottish legislation and the hurdle of the House of Lords, even in their present form, it is inconceivable that such an act would have been passed. It is interesting though to compare the CRTB with the other land reform measure introduced by Parliament – the agricultural tenants' right to buy contained within the Agricultural Holdings (Scotland) Act 2003. This provides tenant farmers with a similar conditional right to buy their farm if and when it is put up for sale by the landowner. Like the CRTB, a tenant farmer has to register their interest in order to take advantage of the right to buy. Unlike the CRTB, however, the tenant farmer's right to buy involves a fairly simple process and the completion of a fairly simple form. As a result, on 31 January 2013, there were 1,148 registered interests from tenant farmers compared with 95 from communities across Scotland.

Too often contemporary politics is constrained by its loss of faith in political ideology and principle. Instead, it operates by responding in a managerial kind of a way to pressure from civil society. The Land Reform Policy Group is a classic case. Civil society and a few individual politicians had been pressing for land reform for a long time. Government responded by setting up a group of predominantly civil servants to develop a programme of reform which could be presented as radical and effective but did not, in fact, change matters a great deal. It was an exclusive process of policy development which ignored history, ignored the overseas experience – not only in Western Europe but also in Latin America and Africa – marginalised dissent and suppressed criticism of its assumptions.

One critic claimed:

> Concepts such as community involvement, participation, and empowerment are not a particularly new set of ideas. They have been trucked around the developing world for the last 30-odd years by experts in the World Bank and United Nations agencies with little real success. This muddled thinking on community has now entered the minds of the wise persons who title themselves the Land Reform Policy Group. However in hitching themselves to the community of place banner they have done so with little research, knowledge or understanding of the social land movement and its 150 years of organised effort. Such an opportunistic, narrow and exclusive approach to social landownership is not good enough nor strategic enough to enable Scotland-wide policy to be developed.

Moreover:

> However the institutions of government, political structures and delivery mechanisms are not particularly participatory, gender sensitive, inclusive or empowering.
>
> This new agenda is driven from above through centralised Public agencies and distant bureaucracies which operate to narrow Ministerial directives and managerial instructions that are locked firmly within the grip of civil service administrative rules and regulations. The term given to this type of participation is institutionalised participation, in which the State and its Agencies both decide and determine what the policies and the permitted actions will be. It is the hegemony of the State and its Agencies and is nothing less than elegant power dressed up as citizen's participation.[14]

Interestingly, despite the fact that ministers have continued to refuse any review of the effectiveness of the legislation, it has been the subject of an inquiry by a working group from the Home Office and the Office of the Deputy Prime Minister that looked at how a community right to buy might be formulated in England. In its 'Final Report', the group came to a number of conclusions about how relevant the Scottish model might be for England. Among these were:

> **Extent of Application:** It seems more equitable and consistent with the neighbourhoods (*sic*) policy of offering opportunities everywhere if a community right to buy in England applied to both urban and rural areas.
>
> **Complexity:** The complexity of the Land Reform (Scotland) Act 2003 is a major disincentive to community groups . . .
>
> **Type of Community Body:** In Scotland the community body had to be a particular kind of organisation (company limited by guarantee). This had proved to be restrictive . . .
>
> **Promotion and Profile:** Awareness had been a problem in Scotland as the Scottish Executive has not publicised the new powers . . .
>
> **Centralised vs. Localised Approach:** The Scottish precedent is highly centralised with a great deal of Ministerial consent built into the Act. Such a centralised approach would be unsuitable and undesirable in England and we need to avoid a bureaucratic system. It was agreed that the process should be as simple as possible, reducing the need for central Government intervention.[15]

It is quite remarkable that the Home Office in London has spent more time and effort reviewing the effectiveness of the community right to buy than has the Scottish Government. In particular it is notable that the English approach was to integrate a community right to buy with other policies aimed at regenerating urban areas. In Scotland, by contrast, due to the arbitrary definition of rural by reference to the population of settlements with those under 10,000 classed as rural and those above as urban, the community right to buy is applicable to the 'rural' settlements of Tranent, Shotts, Lanark and Cumnock but not available in 'urban' Stranraer, Inverurie, Forfar or Galashiels. Why should this potential be restricted to places like Killin and Tobermory? Community businesses, leisure facilities, amenity ground, allotments, play parks and community centres are just as important in Pilton, Easterhouse, Niddrie and Govan as they are in Kelty, Alva, Invergordon or Lesmahagow.

I have been arguing ever since 1997 that we should abandon this artificial distinction between urban and rural. Bill Aitken, the Tory MSP, was quick to dismiss the idea back in 2003 describing it as 'totally unworkable in urban areas'. 'I can't', he went on, 'imagine that too many people in Easterhouse, for example, would be willing to form a community group with a view to staging a buy-out of their houses and land from Glasgow City Council.'[16]

Well, that is exactly what Glasgow Housing Association was set up to do and is exactly what many community enterprises in urban areas have done and are attempting to do with the support of the Scottish Government. So why the difference in treatment? Despite persistent requests to extend the right to buy to urban areas and to some of the poorest communities in the country who could benefit, ministers have consistently refused to do so. Another block came on 25 February 2010 during Question Time in the Scottish Parliament.

> **Bill Kidd (Glasgow) (SNP):** To ask the Scottish Government whether it will consider extending the community right-to-buy provisions in the Land Reform (Scotland) Act 2003 to urban areas.
>
> **The Minister for Environment (Roseanna Cunningham):** There are no plans at present to do so, but I am aware of a developing debate in urban areas, particularly in relation to derelict land.
>
> **Bill Kidd:** Why has land reform been confined to rural areas and not extended to urban areas, considering the large areas of dereliction in our towns and cities that could usefully be developed for community use?
>
> **Roseanna Cunningham:** The original intention of the 2003 act was to remove barriers to sustainable development within rural communities, so it is defined as being about rural land reform and therefore rural right to buy, and is confined to communities

of less than 10,000. The feeling was that the lives of people who live and work in large towns and cities are not constrained in the same way as those of people in the country. After all, it is easier for urban dwellers to choose to move homes or jobs; people in rural areas do not have the same kind of choices, unless they change their entire way of life. Therefore, there was considered not to be the same rationale for a community right to buy in the urban context.[17]

The failure of the community right to buy to deliver on its two promised aims – to greatly empower communities and to effect a rapid change in the pattern of land ownership – has led to calls from a number of quarters for a review of its effectiveness. In June 2006, Rhona Brankin, the minister responsible at that time, said there would be a review later that year.[18] In January 2007, Sarah Boyack, the then minister, stated that ministers were committed to reviewing the 2003 Land Reform Act 'during 2007'.[19] Labour lost the election in May 2007 and, in July 2009, the next minister, the SNP's Roseanna Cunningham, said, in response to a First Minister's Question:

> The Land Reform (Scotland) Act 2003 has only been in effect for a relatively short period of time and we are continuing to monitor the community right to buy provisions. If there is evidence that the provisions are not working as Parliament intended then a review of the act will be considered.[20]

Why so much reticence? In particular, why did the SNP government not do more to shake things up? Why did it take until July 2012 before setting up a Land Reform Review Group?

In the final debate on the Land Reform Bill on 23 January 2003, Roseanna Cunningham moved Amendment 208. Under the heading 'Duty on Ministers to report on diversity of land ownership', this read as follows:

> Ministers shall report to the Scottish Parliament at least once every four years on –

a) the extent to which the exercise of the rights conferred by this Act has contributed to the diversity of land ownership in Scotland; and

b) measures they are taking to encourage greater diversity of land ownership by the further exercise of those rights.

And she said in the chamber:

Amendment 208 is fairly simple and straightforward and its effect should be obvious to all members. It would require the Executive – whomever it might comprise – to produce a report every four years on the diversity of land ownership and what it is doing to address the concentration of land ownership. I have previously reminded the chamber of the current land ownership pattern in Scotland. The bill's title shows that the bill is intended to bring about change. A report once a parliamentary session is not too much to ask for our monitoring of the change that the bill will bring about (*sic*).[21]

The amendment failed but the minister at the time, Allan Wilson, agreed to do this. A commitment was given in August 2003 but, to date, no such report has ever been published.[22]

The community right to buy is a complex, legalistic piece of legislation that provides numerous opportunities for bureaucratic nit-picking and fine legal arguments. This keeps bureaucrats and lawyers in business but does nothing to empower communities. Such a situation has greatly diminished both the radical intent of the act and its practical utility. What should have been a straightforward process of delivering tangible benefits to communities has turned into a time-consuming and impenetrable process of micro-management by officialdom.

In a response to the Land Reform Draft Bill, the Caledonia Centre for Social Development wrote:

We have grave reservations about the democratic credentials and scope for popular participation in land issues when so much of the detailed decision-making on key aspects of this so-called community right is in the hands of Ministers in central Government. In our experience this is a recipe for obfuscation, strife, and distrust. It also raises serious questions about the transparency of the whole process. Far better, in our view, would be to vest much of this decision-making in local fora which could take evidence and take decisions in public.[23]

It is a source of some regret to note that, twelve years later, sadly, these reservations have been borne out.

Undermining the Whole Fabric of Scottish Family Life

The law of succession

When an owner of land dies, the law of succession determines what happens to his or her property. As I pointed out in the introduction, land law is not always easy bedtime reading and succession is no exception. However, if people in Scotland wish to exert meaningful influence over how their country is owned, they need to do some homework – so on we go with the lesson.

Lord Stair, in his 1681 Institution of the Law of Scotland argued that:

> [t]he expediency of primogeniture is partly public and partly private. The public expediency is that the estates of great families, remaining entire and undivided, they, with their vassals and followers, may be able to defend their country against sudden invasions . . . The private expediency is for the preservation of the memory and dignity of families, which, by frequent division of the inheritance, would become despicable or forgotten.[1]

Prior to the Titles to Land Consolidation (Scotland) Act 1868, primogeniture ruled and, on death, land passed automatically to the eldest son. Females were completely disinherited unless there were no male heirs. From 1868, however, it became possible to bequeath land to whomsoever the owner chose but, if they left no will, the rules of primogeniture continued to apply. The Succession (Scotland) Act of 1964 abolished primogeniture so that now owners can still bequeath to whom they wish but, if they die without leaving a will, the next of kin will inherit equal shares. The 1964 act also regulates the so-called legal rights that children and spouses can claim by right regardless of the wishes of the deceased. These entitle a surviving spouse to one third of the deceased's estate if the deceased left children or descendants of children or one half if there are no children. These legal rights, however, apply only to moveable property.[2]

What this means today is that, if the deceased leaves a will, they are free to pass on their estate to whomsoever they wish. They can, if they are so minded, disinherit their family completely and hand it all over to the proverbial cat and dog home. If they do, however, the children and spouse have legal rights to claim a portion of the moveable property but not the heritable property – land and buildings. If no will is left, the estate is inherited by strict rules which effectively share it among a surviving spouse and children.

One thing that has remained constant, however, is that children have no legal rights to inherit property. They never have had and they still don't. This marks Scotland out in comparison to our European neighbours[3] and it was not until the Enlightenment that thinkers such as Adam Smith published powerful denunciations of an institution that was regarded as retrograde and a barrier to economic progress. In *The Wealth of Nations* in 1776, Smith wrote:

> Laws frequently continue in force long after the circumstances which first gave occasion to them, and which could alone render them reasonable, are no more. In the present state of Europe, the proprietor of a single acre of land is as perfectly secure of his possession as the proprietor of a hundred thousand. The right of primogeniture, however, still continues to be respected, and as of all institutions it is the fittest to support the pride of family distinctions, it is still likely to endure for many centuries. In every other respect, nothing can be more contrary to the real interest of a numerous family than a right which, in order to enrich one, beggars all the rest of the children.[4]

Forget feudalism or other aspects of landed power, the one factor that has sustained such a concentrated pattern of private landownership has been the law of succession and, in particular, the continuing division between heritable property and moveable property. This has meant that progressive reforms to provide legal rights for spouses and children to a share of a deceased's estate have never been extended to land. Despite a long history of calls for reform, the one change that would have – and still could – transform the pattern of landownership has been blocked by the vested interests of landowners. In 1914, for example, the Scottish Land Enquiry Committee recommended reform:

> We also recommend that the law of primogeniture should be abolished and that the rules of succession applicable to moveable estate should also apply to heritage. This would involve that heritage would be subject to the same legal right of the children, widow and widower to a share of the estate . . . as in the case of moveable estate.[5]

The twentieth century also witnessed growing demands to redress the historic discrimination against women who, until 1964, could be left destitute and on the streets even in cases where the deceased husbands had significant wealth. After a few modest reforms, the Mackintosh Committee reported in 1951 and recommended that the law of primogeniture should be abolished, that the distinction between male and female succession should be abolished and that the distinction between moveable and heritable should be abolished for intestate succession. The Faculty of Advocates, the Scottish Land and Property Federation and the Court of the Lord Lyon all opposed change. Landed interests argued that the abolition of primogeniture and the blending of heritable and moveable property would 'disrupt the Scottish familial social system and be detrimental to the interests of agriculture and the landed interests generally'.[6]

In 1964, when Parliament eventually got round to doing something about the law, the opposition continued in the House of Lords where the Earl of Perth, Duke of Buccleuch and assorted other members of the aristocracy spoke out against the tide of modernity. 'I strongly object to the passing of legislation which will force these ancient families, humble though they may be – families of long descent, much respected in the countryside, and a social asset – to put farms on to the market,' argued Lord Saltoun.[7]

Lord Haddington concurred:

Its object, apparently, is to make a more just and more equitable distribution of estates in the event of intestacy. But I see little justice in forcing a family to sever what might be a long connection with a property, be it large or small; and that is what is bound to happen in many, indeed in most, cases by the provisions of this Bill. By assimilating heritable property, which from time immemorial has passed under the law of primogeniture, with moveable property and dividing it equally among the intestate's next of kin, you are striking at the very roots of Scottish traditions and undermining the whole fabric of Scottish family life.[8]

The nobility tried to exempt all landholdings of over 3 acres, all country estates generally and specific landed rights such as fishings but the act of 1964 largely followed the recommendations of the Mackintosh Committee and implemented significant change for which Lord Craigton, Minister of State in the Scottish Office explained the need in the House of Lords debate:

As the Mackintosh Report points out, our present law of heritable succession belongs to the Middle Ages, when its rules of primogeniture and male preference were admirably suited to the feudal state of society in which they were evolved . . . It was quite clear that rules intended to avoid a subdivision of feudal holdings are inappropriate to a world in which the feudal obligation is no longer a factor . . . I now turn to Clause 8 which affects intestacy and which is, in my opinion, one of the most important provisions of the Bill, especially because of the almost complete predominance of small intestate estates. Under our present law, the spouse of a person who dies intestate can claim a share of the moveable estate by way of jus relictae, but has no claim to the ownership of the heritable estate. The significance of this emerges when one remembers that in the vast majority of cases where there is any heritable estate at all it consists solely of the family dwelling-house. The unfortunate widow has now in fact no right to the house in which she has lived, possibly for many years and, unless she can make some arrangement with her husband's relatives, she may, quite literally, find herself out on the street.[9]

Radical though this was, however, the act preserved the status quo in circumstances where a landowner made a will, and although spouses and children were to be entitled to a share of the moveable estate, there was no right to land and property. The net effect of this is that land and property continue to be inherited, by and large, by eldest sons since that is the wish of the deceased. Bearing in mind that until the early twentieth century, over half of Scotland was entailed and that over half of Scotland even today has been held in the same family for at least a hundred years, the chances of women and children obtaining any meaningful stake in landownership through inheritance remains a distant prospect. It is a prospect, it might be added, which is the source of much bitterness in many landed families though it is seldom articulated in public.[10]

Since 1964, further proposals have been made by the Scottish Law Commission who published a report and a bill in 1990. It argued that legal rights should cease to distinguish between heritable and moveable property and that children and spouses should enjoy the right to defeat any attempt to disinherit them of land. Predictably, the Scottish Landowners' Federation and the National Farmers Union Scotland continued their opposition to any legal rights over heritable property. They pointed out that many landowners wished to leave their estate to one child or grandchild in order to preserve a viable unit for the benefit of all those who lived and worked on it. They felt very strongly that the owner of land should be left free to choose as he or she thought best.[11]

But the Commission pointed out that the results of perpetuating the distinction are often arbitrary and unprincipled. If the deceased owned land as an individual, they argued, it is heritable property and thus immune from a claim but, if he or she owned shares in the company that owns the land, then these are treated as moveable and the children and spouse can claim a legal share. The Commission thus concluded:

> We cannot believe that it is right that the distribution of property on death should depend on such distinctions and considerations. We recommend that, in relation to the legal shares of spouse and issue there should be no distinction between heritable and moveable property.[12]

Nothing was ever done with these proposals, however, and it took ten years until the whole question was re-opened after devolution by the increasing changes in family structures such as divorce and co-habitation. Some of these were addressed in the Family Law (Scotland) Act 2006. But it was not until 2007 that the Scottish Law Commission published its latest discussion paper which was followed by a report and bill in April 2009.[13]

Once again, the Commission is arguing for the distinction between heritable and moveable to be abolished. They also, however, float the idea that adult children – those over the age of eighteen – should no longer be entitled to any legal rights. This would represent a dramatic change in succession law but, whereas providing legal rights over heritable property provides an effective way to reduce the concentrated pattern of ownership of land, restricting this right to dependant children negates such objectives entirely since few landowners will die before their children are eighteen.

True to form, the landed interests continued to oppose this reform and the National Farmers Union Scotland (NFUS), the Scottish Rural Property and Business Association (SRPBA), the Scottish Estates Business Group (SEBG) and the legal agents of choice for the landed classes, Turcan Connell, all argued strongly that agricultural land, landed estates and agricultural businesses should be excluded from the deceased's estate for the purposes of legal share. The response from the SRPBA and the SEBG argues that all rural land, buildings and houses should be excluded from any claims for a legal share in order to avoid 'fragmentation of the estate' and to avoid the forced sales of mansion houses leading to 'a closure of the business as a whole'. Turcan Connell believe that estates and farms should, where the deceased wishes, continue to be passed on to one individual and that all farms, landed estates and historic houses and gardens should continue to be excluded for any claim on the estate of the deceased.[14] All other respondents to the earlier consultation, it should be noted, saw no reason for an exception to be made for this one particular type of business property. The Commission also reiterated the arbitrary consequences it had highlighted seventeen years earlier.

However, in the 2007 discussion paper which preceded their recommendations, the Commission made a remarkable admission. It asserted that the legal rights to heritable property would raise difficulties where the deceased is 'anxious that only one child should inherit his or her business'. 'This is particularly acute,' it claimed, 'in relation to agricultural property where it is traditional for the farm to be left to the child who will work the farm: this prevents the fragmentation of the estate.' 'We have immense sympathy with these concerns,' it continued.[15]

Why should what is 'traditional' have any bearing on what is in the public interest? Why did the Commission have immense sympathy for those who did not want to see fragmentation of estates but not with the bulk of the Scottish population who want to see effective land reform? The reason would appear to be that the Commission 'had the benefit of comments on an early draft from representatives of the Scottish Estates Business Group'.[16] Why was such a group given such privileged access to the Commission's thinking at such a formative stage in their deliberations? Why is a group of twenty heads of the wealthiest families in the country, including the Duke of Roxburghe, the Duke of Argyll, the Duke of Atholl, the Duke of Buccleuch and the Duke of Westminster, being given preferential treatment over the hundreds of thousands of other families in the country and over the thousands of children and spouses of landowners and farmers who stand to be disinherited if these few get their way?

All this opposition to the redistribution of land is a touch odd. Why is there so much opposition to a measure that does not affect members of the landed class since they will be dead when it takes effect? Succession should be as much about the public interest as the private interest. If it is thought desirable to reduce the concentrated pattern of landownership in Scotland, succession reform is the best way to ensure this happens as the triggers that will deliver it are certain – everyone dies. The usual arguments about preserving the integrity of businesses and landholdings are a fig leaf for the preservation of landed privilege. Plenty of other types of business manage perfectly well in multiple ownership so why can't land?

Fragmentation is not a problem – it is an aspiration. We *should* be fragmenting land. If folk want to enjoy the supposed benefits of managing 250,000 acres together they are free to do so by co-operating. Moreover, a farm can still be run efficiently if owned by four brothers and sisters – they merely need to co-operate and manage it as a single entity. It is the scale of management that produces efficiencies not the scale of ownership.

Of course, the 2009 report from the Commission did not cave in to the vested interests of the landed classes but it appears that it is still difficult for politicians to avoid being seduced by the arguments of landed power. The Scottish Government has announced that it will be taking forward consultations on the proposals[17] but, remarkably, the SNP minister responsible still appears to believe that landowners' concerns should take precedence over the imperative of land reform. In the government's initial response to the Commission, Fergus Ewing MSP argued that:

> In considering this further, we will want to take account of the fact that the farming and land owning communities have ongoing concerns about legal shares for children coming out of the whole estate and the impact this might have on the continued operational viability of land holdings.[18]

This is quite remarkable. After 800 years of feudalism, entail and primogeniture, with the most concentrated pattern of private landownership in Europe and with a land reform programme that aspires to achieve a rapid change in the pattern of landownership, an SNP government minister is thinking about the interests of the landowners before the interests of women, children, the landless and Scottish society.

The division of land is a matter of public policy and not private vested interests. It cannot be right that the wishes of those who have departed this world should be promoted as a means of sustaining the institution of landed power. It remains to be seen whether such considerations will play any part in the debate to come in the Scottish Parliament and whether Scotland's politicians are able to recognise the huge benefits that would flow from succession law reform if land is allowed to be distributed more equitably across society.

Their Unjust Concealing of Some Private Right

Secrecy in Scottish landownership

In the *Sunday Times* Rich List of 1995, the Duke of Buccleuch was listed at number thirty-three and said to be worth £200 million. Following the publication of the list, the Duke of Buccleuch wrote to Philip Beresford, the compiler of the list, as follows:

Dear Sir,
Much as I would like to be No. 33 in your chart of the richest 500, I fear I am there under false pretences.

As you rightly mention the calculation is based upon a hypothetical valuation of works of art. What you may not realise is that if I were to sell items in the collection, 80% of the proceeds would go straight to the Treasury. This is because 80% was the rate applicable to my father's estate when he died in 1973.

My worth on that score should therefore be reduced from £200m to £40m and as I own no shares in Buccleuch Estates Ltd., I might find myself level-pegging with Gordon Baxter and Sean Connery.

Can you please take this into account next time?

In recent years the top rate of inheritance tax was reduced to 40% but even this would affect the positioning of many others whose worth is based upon art collections.

  Yours faithfully
    Buccleuch

There are a number of interesting things about this letter. One of them is Buccleuch's claim that he owns no shares in Buccleuch Estates Ltd. The Duke of Buccleuch is frequently identified as being the largest private landowner in Scotland, owning over 260,000 acres of land across the UK. Of course the name on the title deeds is Buccleuch Estates Ltd but what most people have always believed is that this is simply a family company. But here is the late Duke claiming that he has no shares in the company. So, if the Duke of Buccleuch owns no shares, who does and does the current Duke have anything to do with the company that bears his name?

At first glance, Buccleuch Estates Ltd appears to be a conventional limited company with directors and shareholders. In fact, it is the ultimate parent company for a string of other companies including Buccleuch Properties Ltd which holds property worth £88 million, including land in Granton.[1] Buccleuch Properties Ltd is, in turn, the parent company of companies such as Buccleuch Property (Kettering) Ltd, Tarras Park Properties (Germany) Ltd, Buccleuch Property (Moscow) Ltd and a slew of joint ventures in Cyprus, Luxembourg, Russia, Germany, Ireland and the UK.

This global empire is all ultimately owned by Buccleuch Estates Ltd. So who owns Buccleuch Estates Ltd? The answer is that it is wholly owned by a nominee company, Anderson Strathern Nominees Ltd, a company whose total paid-up share value is £4, whose shareholders are four Edinburgh lawyers and whose total assets amount to £4. The company has been dormant since its incorporation in May 1992 and it owns 100 per cent of Buccleuch Estates Ltd, a company with total assets of £275 million and a turnover of £64 million in 2008.

The purpose of Anderson Strathern Nominees Ltd is thus merely to hold the shares of Buccleuch Estates Ltd on behalf of others. Who those others are remains a mystery though it might be reasonable to presume that the directors of the company know who they are. The directors are:

- the tenth Duke of Buccleuch and twelfth Duke of Queensberry KBE DL
- the Duchess of Buccleuch and Queensberry

- Jane, Duchess of Buccleuch
- the Earl of Dalkeith
- Lord Damian Scott
- Lord John Scott
- PJ Scott Plummer DL
- JRK Glen (chief executive).

Despite the Duke of Buccleuch being chairman and director of Buccleuch Estates Ltd, he owns no shares in the company. Neither do any of the other directors. It is impossible to ascertain what interests they have in the 260,000 acres of land under their control across the UK or the extensive commercial property interests stretching from Edinburgh to Germany. Instead, the entire operation is owned on paper by a dormant company worth £4.

What may, at first glance, appear straightforward – the Duke of Buccleuch owns Buccleuch Estates Ltd – is, in fact, far less so. The true details of who owns land in Scotland are very often unavailable as individuals hide behind nominee and offshore corporate structures. The title may be clear but the beneficial ownership – those exercising real control – is frequently unknown. Whilst this poses obvious questions about whether the public have the right to know who really owns property, it also raises issues about financial reporting, taxation and national security.

Two days after the September the 11th attack on the World Trade Center in New York, a retired British civil servant stood up to make a presentation to the Cambridge International Symposium on Economic Crime – a discreet gathering of high-level policy makers, taxation specialists and money-laundering specialists. Andrew Edwards, a former deputy secretary to the UK Treasury, made his presentation to a session on taxation and money laundering. In it, he argued that 'tax evasion, money laundering and economic crime of all kinds are symbiotically linked in a social ecology which is shamefully prevalent'. And he went on to highlight how the lack of transparency in disclosing beneficial ownership of land, companies and trusts allows international criminals to commit economic crimes and launder the proceeds of illegal activities.[2]

Edwards had warned of this before. In the 'Quinquennial

Review of Her Majesty's Land Registry in England and Wales', he observed that owners can register their property in any name they choose as long as they are not attempting to defraud others. Most typically, this involves recording their title in the name of a private company in an offshore jurisdiction or in the form of a trust set up in any jurisdiction they please. Either way, the true identity of the beneficial owner is concealed and there is no way for the public to ascertain who really owns the land. Edwards argued:

> In these days when economic crime and money laundering have become major issues for the world economy and society, and when property assets are a significant vehicle for holding the proceeds of crime, the fact that the Registry neither records on the Register nor knows who the true owners of property are becomes ever harder to defend.
>
> There must be a strong case, therefore, for including in the Register details of the true or beneficial owners of registered properties where these differ from the nominal owners.
>
> Current money laundering legislation requires solicitors carrying out regulated financial business to verify the identity of their clients. Perhaps surprisingly, however, this requirement does not extend to conveyancing transactions.
>
> The disclosure of such information on the Register, and the index of true or beneficial property owners that the Land Registry could compile from it, would be invaluable for law enforcement, regulatory and tax authorities, as would similar information on ownership of private companies. Without such information, the transparency of land registration must always be seriously qualified.
>
> The existence of the requirement would itself do something to deter the unscrupulous from putting the proceeds of crime into property assets.[3]

These arguments, whilst being advanced in the context of the Land Registry, apply equally to Scotland. There is no obligation on property owners to reveal their true identity when they record titles in the Registers of Scotland. This means that the public registers of landownership fail to disclose who really owns Scotland. Andrew

Edwards was prompted to make his recommendations by concerns over criminal activity and money laundering. But there is also the much wider issue of tax avoidance to consider. The beneficial owners of nominee companies, trusts and offshore companies don't pay their fair share of inheritance tax, income tax and capital gains tax like the rest of us since the Inland Revenue faces two problems. Firstly, it hasn't a clue who is behind such structures and, therefore, can't chase them and, secondly, even if they identify those involved, they have limited jurisdiction in Panama, Grand Cayman and Liechtenstein.

Andrew Edwards' recommendations in his 'Quinquennial Review' of 2001 appeared in the Land Registry's '10-Year Strategic Plan' for 2003–2013. A joint consultation would be undertaken with government 'on the issue of including on the Land Register details of the true or beneficial owners of registered properties'.[4] In February 2010, I asked the Land Registry what progress it had made with this and was told that a new strategic plan was adopted in 2008 and it contains no reference to the question of beneficial ownership.

An indication of the scale of the problem is illustrated in Table 15.

Foreign and beneficial ownership of privately owned rural land in Scotland, 2012

Ownership	Acres	%	Cumulative %
Offshore Company	727,634	4.63%	4.63%
Foreign Individual	197,175	1.25%	5.88%
Trust	2,132,127	13.56%	19.44%
Nominee Company	417,179	2.65%	22.10%

Table 15
Source: Author's own data

These figures are underestimates since they are based only on what I have been able to ascertain from a limited sample. A fuller analysis would involve many weeks of research. In particular, the scale of ownership by nominee companies is a vast underestimate since it takes time and money to identify the beneficial owners of companies and I have only included three known cases.[5]

It is clear from these figures that over 22 per cent and perhaps as much as 25 per cent of the privately owned rural land in Scotland is held in some form of offshore or beneficial ownership where, to varying degrees, the beneficiaries are unknown and tax is being avoided.

The tax issue has already caused concern within the Inland Revenue. In 2002, the Court of Session ruled in a judicial review brought by Mohamed al-Fayed against the Inland Revenue.[6] Al-Fayed had negotiated what was called a forward tax agreement with the Inland Revenue whereby, in order to save the Inland Revenue the complexities of calculating his tax liability on income from abroad, he paid an agreed sum each year, from 1998 to 2003, of £240,000. The Inland Revenue, however, came to the view that this figure was not a fair reflection of Mr al-Fayed's tax liability and terminated the agreement in 2000 which led Mr al-Fayed to seek judicial review. He lost the action, curiously enough, because the court ruled that the Inland Revenue had no statutory powers to enter into such agreements which were, in its view, ultra vires.

Three events had led to the termination of that agreement. One related to the evidence given at the Neil Hamilton libel trial which began in November 1999. At the trial, al-Fayed had accused Hamilton of accepting cash in return for asking parliamentary questions. Another related to the tax affairs of the Harrods group. And the third issue related to Mr al-Fayed's Highland estates. These are owned by a company called Bocardo Société Anonyme, a company registered at Aeulestrasse 38, 9490 Vaduz, in Liechtenstein, and Ross Estates Co., a company registered in Ireland whose ultimate parent company is Tane Fount Société Anonyme which is again registered in Liechtenstein.

The Court of Session judgement spells out the facts:

On 2 July 1999, Mr W S Lockyer, Inspector of Taxes, Wick wrote to Mr Alan Carmichael of SCO [Special Compliance Office], Edinburgh to notify him of the progress of an investigation by Wick Office into the ownership of certain Scottish estates. This was the Who Owns Scotland? project. In this letter, Mr Lockyer gave certain information that the investigation had brought to light concerning the affairs of the Al Fayed family. Liaison continued between Wick office and SCO Edinburgh on the matter during the rest of 1999.[7]

The Who Owns Scotland? project was stimulated by the publication of my book, *Who Owns Scotland* in 1996 which alerted the Inland Revenue to the possibility of tax avoidance by certain landowners. The fact that a book by an independent author was the impetus for the Inland Revenue project is quite astonishing. That their subsequent investigation was one of three events that then led them to terminate a forward tax arrangement is more than enough evidence in support of the need for far greater transparency in the beneficial ownership of land and property. It reinforces the proposal by Andrew Edwards that beneficial ownership should be disclosed and this one case alone has probably secured several millions of pounds in extra tax for the Treasury. How much more could be recovered if we knew who really owned all of Scotland?

In an investigation undertaken in 2003, I estimated that the annual loss of tax revenue was around £72 million.[8] However, that was based on an analysis of fewer than 500 rural estates and it excluded urban property. In total, across Scotland, the losses may run into many millions more. Although this is not a huge sum of money in terms of public finances, the principle that all owners of land should pay tax is important. Arrangements whereby the wealthy can avoid tax whilst the poor must pay have no place in a fair society. Moreover, it is important that the public know who really owns their country.

Despite ongoing concerns, no Scottish Government has been willing to tackle this problem. Perhaps in the fallout of the banking crisis and the calls for tougher crackdowns on offshore tax havens, some action will be taken at a UK level. Perhaps even Andrew Edwards' recommendations will eventually be implemented.

Meanwhile, it is worth recalling that, in 1617, the Register of Sasines was established and the act opened as follows:

Our sovereign lord, considering the great hurt sustained by his majesty's lieges by the fraudulent dealing of parties who, having alienated their lands and received great sums of money for that, yet, by their unjust concealing of some private right formerly made by them, renders subsequent alienation done for great sums of money altogether unprofitable, which cannot be avoided unless the said private rights be made public and patent to his highness's lieges.

In 2010, the Scottish Law Commission published its 'Report on Land Registration'. In the Introduction, the Commission states that:

There are sometimes calls for the law to require owners of land to disclose their identity, or for this requirement to apply to those who own more than a certain amount of land. This idea does not need new legislation: the law has required this ever since the Registration Act 1617. It is not possible to acquire ownership of land in Scotland – whether a thousand-hectare estate or a flat in a city – without registration, and registration requires the disclosure of the identity of the acquirer. Secret ownership has been impossible in our law for almost 400 years.[9]

In making this claim, the authors are technically correct. Any recorded title discloses the owner's identity which is to say the name of the owner. But the point that is being missed here is that a nominee company, a Trust or an offshore corporation, whilst a 'legal person' and capable of being the 'owner', is not a real human being and, in dealing with landowners, it is legitimate and indeed necessary to be able to identify the person or persons who have ultimate control of the 'owner' where it is a company or Trust. The SLC argument is a legal nicety.

Buccleuch Estates Ltd and Bocardo Société Anonyme own land in Scotland but there remains no way of discovering who these organisations really represent. In 2012, the Scottish Government rejected any measures to provide such disclosure in the Land Registration etc. (Scotland) Act 2012. It is to be hoped that the Land Reform Review Group will recognise the validity of the argument and urge Scotland's politicians to support full transparency.[10]

We Do Not Want to Punish the Landlord

Land values and land value taxation

For most investors, a return of 300 per cent is beyond their wildest dreams but, for many landowners, this is eminently achievable without even putting in any investment. Don Riley is a commercial property developer and landlord in London. As the Jubilee Line Extension (JLE) was being constructed during the 1990s, he noticed that property prices in Southwark were rising. So, he set off on his bike and began to map out what was happening. His conclusions were startling. He found that the £3.5 billion invested in the JLE by the taxpayer had resulted in a £13.5 billion increase in property values along the route.

On reflection, this is not surprising since individuals and businesses will generally (all other things being equal) like to be close to public transport hubs especially in a congested city like London. What is surprising, however, is that the public and politicians seem content to sanction this direct transfer of wealth from the taxpayer to private landowners. What is more surprising is that politicians and the public never seem to stop and wonder whether there's a better way to pay for such large-scale and expensive public infrastructure projects. If £3.5 billion of investment delivers £13.5 billion appreciation in the value of property, why were the landowners not asked to contribute 25 per cent of their capital gains which would have paid for the railway in its entirety?

There are three main reasons why they weren't. Firstly, we have forgotten the simple truth that, as an economy grows, so do land values. It was not offices or pubs that were increasing in value in Southwark, it was the land on which they stood because this land was close to the railway stations. Location, location, location is not some lazy shorthand of estate agents – it is reality. Secondly, we have failed to appreciate that rising land values represent the capitalisation of the economic activity of the community at large. If there were not millions of people living in London, working in London and travelling across the city, there would be no demand for the best land and no value in it. Thirdly, the UK is so infatuated with the idea of property as an investment that we have forgotten what it is that delivers high property prices and it is not bricks and mortar – they depreciate. It is, in fact, the rising value of land.

In the past, this was well understood by politicians such as Winston Churchill.

If a railway makes greater profits, it is usually because it carries more goods and more passengers. If a doctor or a lawyer enjoys a better practice, it is because the doctor attends more patients and more exacting patients, and because the lawyer pleads more suits in the courts and more important suits.

At every stage the doctor or the lawyer is giving service in return for his fees. Fancy comparing these healthy processes with the enrichment which comes to the landlord who happens to own a plot of land on the outskirts of a great city, who watches the busy population around him making the city larger, richer, more convenient, more famous every day, and all the while sits still and does nothing.

Roads are made, streets are made, services are improved, electric light turns night into day, water is brought from reservoirs a hundred miles off in the mountains – and all the while the landlord sits still. Every one of those improvements is effected by the labour and cost of other people and the taxpayers. To not one of those improvements does the land monopolist, as a land monopolist, contribute, and yet by every one of them the value of his land is enhanced.

Some years ago in London there was a toll bar on a bridge across the Thames, and all the working people who lived on the south side of the river had to pay a daily toll of one penny for going and returning from their work. The spectacle of these poor people thus mulcted of so large a proportion of their earnings offended the public conscience, and agitation was set on foot, municipal authorities were roused, and at the cost of the taxpayers, the bridge was freed and the toll removed. All those people who used the bridge were saved sixpence a week, but within a very short time rents on the south side of the river were found to have risen about sixpence a week, or the amount of the toll which had been remitted!

I hope you will understand that, when I speak of the land monopolist, I am dealing more with the process than with the individual land owner who, in most cases, is a worthy person utterly unconscious of the character of the methods by which he is enriched. I have no wish to hold any class up to public disapprobation. I do not think that the man who makes money by unearned increment in land is morally worse than anyone else who gathers his profit where he finds it in this hard world under the law and according to common usage. It is not the individual I attack; it is the system. It is not the man who is bad; it is the law which is bad. It is not the man who is blameworthy for doing what the law allows and what other men do; it is the State which would be blameworthy if it were not to endeavour to reform the law and correct the practice. We do not want to punish the landlord. We want to alter the law.[1]

This speech was made in the heat of the great debate about land taxes referred to earlier (Chapter 11). Two weeks later, Lloyd George gave his famous Limehouse speech on the same topic in one of the poorest parts of East London. His aim was to show the difference between the rewards of hard work and the rewards of owning land.

If the value goes up not owing to your efforts, if you spend money on improving it, we will give you credit for it but, if it goes up owing to the industry and the energy of the people living in that locality, one-fifth of that increment shall in future be taken as a toll by the State. They say: Why should you tax this increment on landlords and not on other classes of the community? They say: You are taxing the landlord because the value of his property is going up through the growth of population, through the increased prosperity for the community. Does not the value of a doctor's business go up in the same way?

The landlord is a gentleman – I have not a word to say about him in his personal capacity – the landlord is a gentleman who does not earn his wealth. He does not even take the trouble to receive his wealth. He has a host of agents and clerks to receive it for him. He does not even take the trouble to spend his wealth. He has a host of people around him to do the actual spending for him. He never sees it until he comes to enjoy it. His sole function, his chief pride, is stately consumption of wealth produced by others. What about the doctor's income? How does the doctor earn his income? The doctor is a man who visits our homes when they are darkened with the shadow of death: who, by his skill, his trained courage, his genius, wrings hope out of the grip of despair, wins life out of the fangs of the Great Destroyer. All blessings upon him and his divine art of healing that mends bruised bodies and anxious hearts. To compare the reward which he gets for that labour with the wealth which pours into the pockets of the landlord purely owing to the possession of his monopoly is a piece, if they will forgive me for saying so, of insolence which no intelligent man would tolerate.[2]

The philosophy behind land value taxation (LVT) is based on the idea that land, in its unimproved state, is a gift of nature and, unlike capital and labour, has no cost of production. Furthermore, since land is fixed in supply – again, unlike capital and labour – its value is purely a scarcity value reflecting the competing needs of the community for work, leisure and housing. Thus the value of land, excluding the value of investment in improvements, owes nothing to the owner or to individual effort and everything to the community at large and the value of land properly belongs to the community. This should be self-evident from cases such as the Jubilee Line Extension. More recently, a study carried out on the new Channel Tunnel Rail Link in 2009 concluded that the value of housing stock – in reality, the value of land – in north Kent may increase by around £1.3 billion 'representing a capitalised value of . . . benefits to current residents'.[3] So skewed has our understanding of land and property become that this was presented in the report as being one of the economic benefits of the new railway when, in fact, it is merely a transfer of wealth from the taxpayer who funded much of the project to homeowners in Kent – they get a £1.3 billion windfall paid for by the rest of us! Moreover, it is not a benefit to residents as claimed but to landowners. Many tenants may not be able to afford the increased levels of rent that may be demanded in this already overheated land market.[4]

It is the land element of house prices that has been responsible for the hugely inflated housing market in recent years. Prior to 1983, the land component in the cost of a house was around 10 per cent. It is now around 50 per cent. Again, this should come as no surprise since demand for houses in popular areas has consistently outstripped supply and, since the supply of land is finite, it is land values that are responsible for the rise in prices. Just as one pays higher prices for city-centre parking or the best seats in the concert hall, so the owners of land should pay a levy based on the land values that others have created but which have, historically, been captured and capitalised into private gains.

The folly of our obsession with ever-rising land prices is evident in the Granton Waterfront Project in Edinburgh where plans to regenerate 350 hectares of land have ground to a halt in the face of the bursting of the land speculation bubble. The plan was to build 8,000 new houses, '15% of which will be affordable'.[5] Presumably the remaining 85 per cent will be unaffordable? In the good times, landowners pocket the enormous profits from rising land values. In the bad times, lending institutions collapse, taxpayers foot the bill and ordinary people lose their homes.

The way to prevent such periods of boom and bust, to prevent the owners of land accruing windfall capital gains at the expense of the taxpayer, to allow the non-property-owning citizens of the country to share the wealth their labours create and to reduce taxes on personal incomes and business profits is to exact a levy on land values. Sometimes called land value taxation or site value rating, it is an idea that is attracting growing support from across the political spectrum.

Current Support for LVT

LVT was adopted by the Co-operative Party in its manifesto for the 2010 General Election.

> There is significant evidence to suggest that the shortage of homes in the UK has been artificially created by a poorly functioning property market. This has had the effect of substantial growth in house prices, with the market rewarding those with property assets at the expense of people seeking places to live.
>
> In order to prevent similar problems emerging in the upturn, the Government should use taxation to change incentives within the property market, ensuring that it incentivises the productive use of land rather than expected capital gains in an upward market. The Government should replace council tax and national non-domestic rates with a land value tax.[6]

In addition to this party political support, there is increasing interest in the idea from policy makers, academics and think tanks.[7]

Compass recently published a pamphlet on the housing crisis in which the author concluded that:

> [s]ocial justice demands that the gains in land value be shared more equitably with the community than at present, and a tax system that could stabilise the housing market and reduce the chances of booms and busts is in everyone's interest. Possibly, the most effective fiscal policy means of achieving this would be to replace the unpopular and regressive council tax and the system of business rates with an annual land value tax (LVT). All land would face an annual charge for the benefits received as a consequence of being a landowner on the basis of the unimproved site value of the land, which would be revalued for tax purposes annually. This could be structured so that it eventually provided a similar level of overall public revenue to council tax and business rates (currently £25.6 billion and £19.6 billion respectively). It is important to be clear here – we are not talking about a tax on property values. If people improve or develop

their home then the benefits would still accrue to them. We are just talking about the value of the land their home sits on, which is therefore the most public and social asset there can be.[8]

In academic circles, LVT is undergoing something of a renaissance. As Iain McLean, Professor of Politics at Oxford University, comments in an Institute for Public Policy Research (IPPR) paper:

> The present tax regime suppresses economic activity (S.106 agreements) and encourages bubbles (Council Tax). Land tax could yield more while costing less. Policymakers have an opportunity to implement Tom Paine's dream. Which is also the dream of David Ricardo, Henry George, and Lloyd George. What better way than that could there be to mark the centenary of the People's Budget in 2009?[9]

And John Muellbauer, Professor of Economics at Oxford University argued in the same volume that:

> The tax falls ultimately upon ownership, and not on development nor on business activity. It captures part of the benefits accruing to land owners from public investment or the private investment of others. It thus underwrites the funding of public investment, since the rise in land values that a worthwhile project engenders will automatically generate a rise in tax revenue to fund the project. This should encourage better public investment decisions not only regarding individual projects, but the scale of such investment.[10]

Even the Governor of the Bank of England, Mervyn King, in the standard textbook on the British tax system is persuaded that the 'underlying intellectual argument for seeking to tax economic rents retains its force'.[11]

In December 2009, Adam Posen, an external member of the Monetary Policy Committee of the Bank of England advocated property taxes as a tool for dampening asset bubbles:

> So what could be done to limit or pre-empt real estate price booms? We should think in terms of automatic stabilisers – not

least because economies that have had deeper automatic stabilisers have done better in responding to the crisis without increasing structural deficits, since they are contractionary during booms. We also should think in terms of automatic stabilisers because that means a rule rather than discretion, and thus would be more credible in deterring unrealistic price movements by home owners and speculators.[12]

LVT in Scotland

Land value taxation has the potential to deliver huge benefits to the Scottish economy. Increasingly, young families cannot afford to buy a house, young farmers cannot afford a farm and communities lack the means to secure land and property that would be useful to them. Meanwhile, the middle-aged and middle classes hang on to their dream of ever-increasing property prices, blissfully unaware of the social time bomb ticking away beneath them.

Traditionally, farmers and landowners don't like land taxes. But let's take a look, for example, at dairy farmers who continue to face serious financial problems. The cost of production of a litre of milk in 2008–09 was 29.64p but they received just 25p for each litre they sold. Milk cooperatives have been going bust and the industry is in real crisis. In the normal business world, there would not be many investors buying dairy farms when faced with such dire prospects.[13] And yet 2009 research by the residential and commercial real estate agents, Knight Frank, showed that UK farmland prices outperformed the FTSE 1000, prime country houses and prime London property, nearly doubling in value since 1995. Andrew Shirley, head of rural property at Knight Frank, claimed that, as a long-term investment, farmland provided a return akin to gold.[14]

What's going on? Well, land is now an investment for a wide range of wealthy individuals from the UK and abroad and for institutions and investment funds. Their motives include capital appreciation, tax relief and safe havens for capital in troubled times. So the price of dairy farms and many other kinds of property, including buy-to-let houses, rises out of all proportion to the financial return that can be made from the asset.

LVT exacts a levy at anything from a few per cent to 100 per cent on the annual rental value of the land alone. Say, for example, a house is worth £150,000. This value is made up of £60,000 land value and £90,000 building value. In other words, if the house was demolished, the site would be worth £60,000. This can be converted into an annual rental value by the application of what's known as the discount rate which is basically a benchmark rate of return on capital. If this is, say, 10 per cent, then the annual rental value of the land, in this case, is £6,000. A rate of LVT at, say, 5 per cent of the capital value (or 50 per cent of the rental value) will thus cost this homeowner £3,000 per year.

The beauty of LVT is that it forces the purchasers of land to think long and hard about what land is actually worth to them. Faced with an annual charge, people will stop paying inflated prices and house prices will drift back down to an affordable and sensible level that reflects the true value of the location and the true value of the building upon it. It rewards those who invest in improvements – since these are not taxed – and penalises speculators – those who land-bank or sit on derelict and empty property. Unlike the council tax, if you improve your house by investing in insulation, an extra bedroom or a garage, you will be rewarded by a higher capital value and no rise in tax liability. LVT kills unearned capital appreciation and the hyper-inflated property market stone dead.

It does not take much effort to speculate that a good deal of existing or proposed public investment which is causing so much political difficulty – Borders Railway, Glasgow Airport Rail Link (GARL), the building of a second road bridge over the Firth of Forth, the staging of the 2014 Commonwealth Games and such like – could be financed, at least in part, by recovering the financial benefits that flow to landowners by way of increased land values. Indeed, even existing initiatives, such as the Cairngorms National Park, could potentially meet a significant portion of their running costs from the enhanced land values that property owners enjoy due to National Park status.

The rationale is that it is fair that the principal source of public revenue should come from unearned windfalls and from the land values that are generated by the efforts and demands of the community. Taxes on hard work (income tax), investment (capital gains tax) and consumption (post-tax income) should be relegated to the bottom of the list of revenue sources when such a substantial revenue can be obtained by returning to the community the value it creates through public infrastructure, development permissions and rising land values.

A new form of finance for Scotland

Historically, land taxes were commonplace. Indeed, they were virtually the sole source of government revenue up until the nineteenth century and remained an important source until the middle of the twentieth century. Since then, property interests have ensured their elimination and the only place they remain is in the form of the council tax and business rates levied by local government.

The only property owners who pay tax on land are homeowners and businesses and the owners of over 90 per cent of the land in the country pay nothing towards the provision of local services. Moreover, the council tax is highly regressive with the owners of low-value properties paying proportionately more in relation to the value and capital gains of their property compared to those living in high-value properties. In Edinburgh, for example, the 45,638 properties in Band B pay 14.77 per cent of the total council tax yield but, in terms of the value, these properties represent only 9.94 per cent of the total property value. At the other end of the scale, the 19,294 properties in Band G contribute 13.38 per cent of the council tax revenue but represent 21.55 per cent of the stock value.

The introduction of LVT would allow four injustices in current taxation policy to be resolved. It would:

- spread the burden across all property owners
- remove the regressive effects of the council tax
- provide an equitable source of revenue for public infra-structure projects and
- provide affordable housing.

Let's look at each of these in turn.

SPREADING THE BURDEN

The total value of land in Scotland, excluding all improvements – buildings, drainage, roads, etc. – is around £120 billion and this is made up of the elements outlined in Table 16. The table shows the total value, the current tax take, percentage of current contribution, the future take under a 3.2p rate of LVT and the percentage of future contribution. The 3.2p figure is designed to yield a total tax take that equates to the existing council tax and business rates yield.

Homeowners appear to pay a greater share of the proposed future total but, in fact, this is due solely to the extension of LVT to cover second homes, vacant property and the abolition of the council tax relief. Business will gain with a 60 per cent reduction in business rates for industry and business and retail. Agriculture is a significant loser but primarily as a consequence of the current inflated values of farmland which, itself, is largely a result of the capitalisation of public grants and subsidies over the years. As LVT is applied and public subsidy reduces, these values will drop. This will make it easier for new entrants to get into farming and, in turn, will reduce the burden of debt on existing farmers and allow higher levels of investment in productive agriculture as opposed to land.

REMOVING UNFAIRNESS

An important consequence of switching to a system of LVT is greater fairness in the burden of tax between those living in low-value properties and those in high-value properties. Since the council tax was introduced in 1991, for example, a typical Band-A property worth £25,000 in 1991 would have been worth £67,000 in 2009 and would have made a capital gain of £42,000. During those years, the owner will have paid £9,598 in council tax – equivalent to 23 per cent of the capital gain. A property in Band H, on the other hand, will have risen in value from £300,000 in 1991 to £804,000 in 2009 – a gain of £504,000. The total tax paid is £28,794 equivalent to only 5.71 per cent of the capital gain. Not only do owners of high-value properties pay proportionately less on an annual basis, they also accrue significantly greater capital gains relative to the tax they pay.

Scottish land values and the Land Value Tax proposal

Land Use	Land value £	Current Council Tax or Business Rates	Current £ contribution %	Land Value Tax at 3.2p per £1 land value	Future £ contribution %
Agriculture	£18,200,000,000	£0	0.0%	£582,400,000	15.30%
Sporting Estates	£200,000,000	£0	0.0%	£6,400,000	0.17%
Forestry	£1,300,000,000	£0	0.0%	£41,600,000	1.08%
Vacant Land	£1,600,000,000	£0	0.0%	£51,200,000	1.33%
Residential Land	£76,700,000,000	£1,800,000,000	50.0%	£2,454,400,000	63.74%
Industrial	£5,200,000,000	£450,000,000	12.5%	£166,400,000	4.32%
Business & Retail	£17,100,000,000	£1,350,000,000	37.5%	£547,200,000	14.21%
Total	£120,300,000,000	£3,600,000,000	100%	£3,849,600,000	100%

Table 16

Source: 'Land Value Taxation: Making it Happen', author's report for the Scottish Green Party MSPs[1]

The introduction of LVT across Scotland would reduce the bills for 75 per cent of properties in Bands A–D whilst increasing the bills for the 25 per cent in Bands E–H as indicated in Table 17 below where the figures for Bands A–H represent the average council tax for Scotland in 2009.

Council Tax v Land Value Tax

Band	Current council tax	Percentage of contribution of band	LVT at 3.2p per £ land value	Percentage of contribution of band	Percentage +/-
A	£766	15.55%	£519.00	11.07%	−32.05%
B	£894	19.62%	£644.00	14.81%	−27.91%
C	£1,021	14.80%	£831.00	12.55%	−18.96%
D	£1,149	13.35%	£1,070.00	13.01%	−6.93%
E	£1,404	16.71%	£1,433.00	17.88%	+2.17%
F	£1,660	10.87%	£1,932.00	13.25%	+16.46%
G	£1,915	8.07%	£3,303.00	15.43%	+71.9%
H	£2,298	1.03%	£6,231.00	2.91%	+168.82%

Table 17

Source: 'Land Value Taxation: Making it Happen', author's report for the Scottish Green Party MSPs[15]

Column 1 represents the existing council tax bands. Column 2 is the current council tax payable in each band. Column 3 is the percentage of the total council tax take contributed by that band. Column 4 is LVT at 3.2p with the percentage contribution in column 5 and the increase or decrease in column 6.[16] Under LVT, contributions are made in direct proportion to the value of the land and thus are fairer than the current system of council tax which hits those in lower-value properties hardest.

PUBLIC INFRASTRUCTURE

In the last few years, a number of high-profile public infrastructure projects have been proposed in Scotland, including the Waverley Line, the GARL and the second Forth road crossing. The Waverley Line is the new railway to be constructed between Edinburgh and the Central Borders. In the Outline Business Case presented in support of the Waverley Railway (Scotland) Bill, an undertaking was given that Scottish Borders Council would contribute £7.4 million of the then £129.6 million capital cost of the project. This would be done by way of a flat-rate contribution of £1,500 from each of the anticipated 7,500 houses to be built over a thirty-year period in a defined catchment area of the new railway line. The sum raised as a result would be £11.25 million.

Such a contribution, however, reflects only a small proportion of the uplift in land values that can be expected to be attributed to the development of the railway because the levy applies only to new build. Since any uplift will, by and large, affect all properties within the Central Borders, a much fairer way to finance the railway would be to exact a levy on the increase in land values attributable to the railway across the region.

CHEAPER HOUSING

Take a look at the property pages of any newspaper or on the internet and find out how much you need to pay for a site on which to build a house. You will normally have to pay anything from £40,000 to £150,000 for a site with planning permission. You then need to install water and electricity and build the house. Such land would have been worth around a tenth of this before planning permission was granted. Across Scotland, volume builders like Mactaggart and Mickel own land they acquired decades ago – so-called land banks. Once planning permission is granted this land multiplies in value tenfold or more. When you come to buy a house, the land is around 40 per cent of the cost. So, if you buy a house for £200,000, the land is costing you £80,000. The bulk of this is pure profit for the housebuilder. To pay for your house, you have to borrow money from the bank – in effect, you're paying for the windfall profits of land speculation and you go on paying interest for decades to come. LVT eliminates this speculation and provides everyone with more affordable housing.

Land value taxation offers huge benefits for society by removing land speculation from the costs that families have to pay to own a house. Its adoption would transform the land market and the housing market by making land available at affordable prices.

A Public Park and Recreation Ground for the Public Behoof

Finding out more about community land rights

Interest in land issues has grown since the 1990s and intensified since Scotland's land reform laws were enacted. In particular, there has been growing interest in the question of community land rights such as common good land. As a result, more and more people are beginning to try to find out more about land law and to locate and research land records. Historically, this has been the exclusive domain of the lawyer and legal academic but we should all be better informed about such matters.

As mentioned previously, a report from the Scottish Law Commission referred to land registration law as being rather like plumbing – 'useful but unexciting and seldom thought about except when it goes wrong'.[1] Much the same could be said of land law as a whole. The problem is that the plumbing was designed years ago and in such a way that only qualified plumbers can understand it. When we go to inspect the water supply, we find that all the water is being diverted to the wealthy neighbours and we can't switch it off.

It is worth remembering here that, whilst landowners own the land, land law belongs to everyone. The next time anyone challenges you by claiming 'this is my land', ask them by virtue of whose laws is this the case. Before we can effectively tackle any of the issues raised in this book, we need to be better equipped to find out more for ourselves and this chapter, therefore, provides a brief introduction to the key sources for doing this. For years, people have approached me for advice on how to find out more about who owns land and the rights involved and, for years, I happily gave such advice as best I could. In 2009, I published *Community Land Rights: A Citizen's Guide* to provide this information in a comprehensive and user-friendly format. Anyone wishing to learn more is advised to get hold of a copy.[2] What follows is a brief summary of the key sources of information about land rights in Scotland. Familiarity with these sources is essential to anyone trying to understand and resolve matters relating to landownership in Scotland.

Registers of Scotland

The principal source of definitive information on landownership is held by the Keeper of the Registers of Scotland in two main registers – the Register of Sasines and the Land Register. These are described in further detail in Chapter 11. Whenever land is transferred, a deed is drawn up containing details of the land, the parties to the transfer, the price and any conditions attached to the sale. This deed is submitted to the Keeper for recording in either of the two Registers. Prior to the introduction of the Land Register, this deed was copied and transferred to the National Archives of Scotland for preservation. Any property sold in recent years will be on the Land Register and an enquiry to the Keeper will determine whether any property is recorded. The Register of Sasines however, will need to be consulted for historical information prior to 1981–2003, depending on the county.

The Sasines Register is basically a chronological series of short extracts of deeds called Minutes showing key information, such as seller, buyer, property and price, organised by county and year and bound together in a Minute Book. They are indexed by persons and places. But the Minute Book contains all sorts of deeds for all sorts of properties across a whole county and so is of limited value. What is far more useful is the Search Sheet. This was introduced in 1876 and presents the Minutes in a chronological sequence for each distinct property thus enabling its history to be scanned with ease. To investigate the deeds recorded for a local estate or your own house for example, it is necessary simply to get hold of a copy of this Search Sheet which costs £2.12 from the Registers of Scotland. An example is provided in Figure 11. From it, one can identify relevant deeds and these, in turn, can be examined and photocopies made in the National Archives of Scotland. There are also other Search Sheets – so-called General Search Sheets – which contain all the deeds relating to a particular organisation such as the Town Council of a burgh, the Crown Estate Commissioners, Lighthouse Board etc.

To complement information from the Registers of Scotland, the Inland Revenue Survey of 1910, referred to in Chapter 11, is useful.[3] Given the lack of plans associated with historic deeds in the Register of Sasines, the IRS is invaluable since it shows the boundaries, ownership and tenancy of every parcel of land in Scotland from the extensive estates of the Duke of Sutherland to the flats and offices in the centre of Edinburgh. Never before or since has such a comprehensive and detailed survey of landownership in Great Britain and Ireland ever been published. It is a vital tool for researchers as, with great ease, one can find out the ownership of land complete with boundaries in 1910. That may be a hundred years ago but the information acts as an anchor in an otherwise featureless sea from which one can work both backwards and forwards on the basis of that rare commodity – a map with ownership boundaries.

Other Useful Records

The IRS Survey and the Registers of Scotland form the main sources of reliable and authoritative information on landownership in Scotland. Other evidence, however, can also be useful. The National Archives of Scotland and the National Library of Scotland together with local archives, libraries and museums are vital for any research. The Scottish Archive Network provides a portal to many of these collections and, thanks to the Internet, a considerable amount of research can be carried out from home. Key websites are:

Scottish Archive Network	www.scan.org.uk
National Archives of Scotland	www.nas.gov.uk
National Library of Scotland	www.nls.uk
Scotland's Places	www.scotlandsplaces.gov.uk
Scran	www.scran.ac.uk
Pastmap	www.rcahms.gov.uk/pastmap.html

All sorts of records can be found using the above resources including court records, plans, estate records, burgh records, photographs, architectural drawings and government records.

To get an idea of the potential for local enquiry into land rights, it might be useful to look at two cases. Both concern burghs in Scotland. Neither represents anything like the fruits of systematic research – indeed quite the opposite for they are merely titbits – but they illustrate the kinds of information that can be uncovered with a little effort.

BLAIRGOWRIE

Blairgowrie is a burgh in Perthshire. In actual fact, it is part of the joint burgh of Blairgowrie and Rattray. My granny lived in Blairgowrie and my mother was brought up there. I have a passing familiarity with the town and so when, in recent years, small pieces of information dropped into my lap, I put them in a pile, so to speak. Here's what's in it.

As part of my survey of common good land in Scotland in 2005, I asked Perth and Kinross Council what common good land there was in the former burghs in Perth and Kinross. They reported none for Aberfeldy, Blairgowrie or Kinross and so I asked them specifically to confirm whether this was indeed the case. An email of 14 September 2005 from the council advised that 'there is no knowledge of any landed property held by the respective common good committees for the above areas'. Now this would be unusual since most town councils handed over property to their successor district councils in 1975 and Blairgowrie and Rattray is a sizeable settlement. In 2009, in a follow-up survey, the council did reveal some common good property which is encouraging.

Was the Council correct in this assertion? Let's find a local history of Blairgowrie. Remember, we are looking, in the first instance, at market squares, parks, civic buildings, common muirs and the like, and so a local history can give us some clues. Whilst I was visiting my mother in the summer of 2007, I noticed a book she had entitled *A Social History of Blairgowrie and Rattray: the Market Town, the Mill Town, the Berry Town* which was edited and compiled by Margaret Laing. I dipped into it. The opening

A FICTIONAL SEARCH SHEET

134 -   66

Search Sheet County of Selkirk

SS 4356

03456 (No.36) 2 November 1972   626.12 PLAN
LEASE by TRUSTEES OF THE 1954 MARRIAGE SETTLEMENT of JAMES WILLIAM PEWHURST
- to BRITISH BROADCASTING CORPORATION for 25 years from 4 April 1973 - of
ground extending to 68 metres square delineated black and coloured pink on
plan, part of lands and estate of THE HAINING in Parish of Selkirk
extending to 5500 acres referred to in Disp to Archibald Gordon Pewhurst,
recorded 12 March 1951 from whom the Granter obtained title by Impl of
Will. Dated 13 Oct 1972.
- UHF/UVF Transmitting Station at Tom Hill, THE HAINING, SELKIRK
- Rent - £250 per annum   To SS 32454

04350 (No. 3) 4 December 1972   632.766
NOTICE OF PAYMENT OF IMPROVEMENT GRANT of £4000 by SECRETARY OF STATE FOR
SCOTLAND to AGNES WILSON, Broomhouse Cottages, Selkirk in respect of No. 2
Broomhouse Cottage, ESTATE OF THE HAINING, the present landlord thereof
being the TRUSTEES OF THE 1954 MARRIAGE SETTLEMENT of JAMES WILLIAM
PEWHURST, containing conditions to be observed for 5 years from 5 May 1972.
Dated 16 October 1972.

0531 (No. 20) 5 February 1973   645.2
FEU DISP by TRUSTEES OF THE 1954 MARRIAGE SETTLEMENT of JAMES WILLIAM
PEWHURST - to Trustees for SELKIRK MEMORIAL HALL - of 6,577 square metres,
formerly part of the farm and lands of Wester Bolton, part of lands known
as THE HAINING, Parish of Selkirk, referred to in Disp to Archibald Gordon
Pewhurst, recorded 12 March 1951 from whom the Granter obtained title by
Impl of Will. Dated 22 December 1973
 - reserving minerals.
- £1 PLAN   To SS 34333

0722 (No. 12) 18 March 1973   660.210
CONVEY by TRUSTEES OF THE 1954 MARRIAGE SETTLEMENT of JAMES WILLIAM
PEWHURST - to COUNTY COUNCIL OF SELKIRK of 123/1000 acre of ground, bounded
on east by the A465 road from Selkirk to Kelso, part of the Farm and Lands
of Easter Bolton, part of lands and estate known as THE HAINING Parish of
Selkirk, referred to in Disp to Archibald Gordon Pewhurst, recorded 12
March 1951 from whom the Granter obtained title by Impl of Will
- reserving minerals. Dated 21 February 1973. (with DUPLICATE PLAN)
Stenhouse Corner Works
£1360.00   To SS 32

Interpreting a search sheet

Refer to the one page extract of a fictional Search Sheet opposite. The volume and page number of the Search Sheet volume (Volume 134, pg 66 in the County of Selkirk) is shown at the top. The Search Sheet number of Haining Estate is Selkirk 4356. This Search Sheet runs over many pages from 12 March 1951 when the estate was created. You will see a reference to this date in the first Minute:-

........5500 acres referred to in Disp to Archibald Gordon Pewhurst, recorded 12 March 1951....

This extract shows just one page from 1972 -1973. The Minutes show examples of a lease, the payment of a housing improvement grant, a feudal disposition (sale by feu charter), and a statutory acquisition by the roads authority. Using the first Minute as an example:-

03456   is the yearly running number of the Register of Sasines for Selkirk for 1972. This deed is number 3456 in 1972.

(No. 36)   is the daily running number. This deed is the 36th to be recorded in Selkirk on 2 November 1972.

2 Nov 1972 is the date of recording.

626.12   is the Volume and page number of the Sasine volume containing the full title deeds obtainable from the National Archives of Scotland or from the Copy Deeds service of the Registers of Scotland.

PLAN   A handwritten note indicating that the deed contains a plan.
Dated
13 Oct 1972 The date the deed was signed.

To SS 32454 The number of the new Search Sheet which the land is "carried out" to and where subsequent legal transactions affecting the "new" estate or interest are recorded.

Figure 11: Example of a Search Sheet

Source: The information contained in this example of a Search Sheet is fictitious and is provided for educational purposes only

chapter deals with the history of the burgh. Blairgowrie was created a burgh of barony in 1634 and was united with the Burgh of Rattray to become the Burgh of Blairgowrie and Rattray in 1929. The first mention of the common good is on page seventeen where the chain of office of the newly merged burgh is discussed. In 1953, it was decided to commission a new chain at a cost of no more than £400. Not more than £200 was to be taken from the Common

Good Fund and local businesses were invited to subscribe to the cost of the chain, each link of which was to cost £12. Page seven lists the subscribers who, I was delighted to read, included my grandfather, Mr Robert W. Lowe, who contributed £12.

Other interesting information from this local history included the fact that, in the mid 1960s, the Town Council bought the former Clydesdale Bank in Leslie Street and turned this into their new Council Chambers, selling off the old Mechanics Institute which they had hitherto been using. This building should probably form part of the Common Good Fund.

Mention is also made of the Well Meadow, an area of green space in the heart of the town. This land was conveyed by a feu disposition from William Macpherson to the Bailies and Council of Blairgowrie on 26 June 1824. The deed stated that it should always be used for holding the public markets and fairs of Blairgowrie and that it shall not be in the power of the said Bailies' Council 'to convert the same into arable or garden ground or to build upon the same or feu the same to others'.

Davie Park is another local park. An area close to the former bleaching green on the Loon Braes – more common good? – was gifted to the town by the Davie family to mark the Golden Jubilee of Queen Victoria in 1887. In handing over the land, William Davie and his sister stipulated that it was 'for the use of the inhabitants of Rattray and Blairgowrie' and Chief Magistrate Bridie, later to become Provost, accepted the 11.5-acre site on behalf of the Council. In 1946, an additional 4 acres was bought and developed into two football pitches, a cricket pitch, a hockey pitch and a putting green. From this useful information, the next stage would be to obtain the Search Sheet for the burgh and to examine the relevant deeds to establish whether or not such areas and others form part of the common good of the joint burgh.

Also in the pile are press reports about the Rattray Arrow, an archery prize forged by Thomas Ramsay of Perth in 1612. In 2006, Robert Mercer-Nairne, the owner of Meikleour Estate, asked Sotheby's to auction the arrow. Residents of Rattray claim it was presented to the people of the town in the seventeenth century and, therefore, it belongs to them. If so, it would form part of the common good of the town.

Finally, I had a quick look at the question of commonties and the first place to look is the *Directory of Former Scottish Commonties* by Ian Adams. On page 198, we find the entry for the Parish of Rattray as follows:

COMMONTY OF BROAD MOSS

The commonty of Broad Moss, consisting of nearly 300 acres, occupied a hill of the same name north of Rattray (NO1947). A summons of division of commonty was raised in 1826 by Alexander Whitson of Parkhill against Thomas, Earl of Kinnoul (Whitson v Kinnoul – CS238 W/11/32). Commission was granted to Charles Husband, sheriff-substitute of Perthshire. Few documents remain in this process which appears to have been abandoned in 1828. In 1837 it was still undivided and the only commonty in the parish (NSA x, 244).

This is interesting. There may be an extant commonty as well as common good land! Does it still exist? A quick search in the catalogue of the National Archives reveals a 'Plan of Broad Moss Common'[4] dated 1863. Was it ever finally divided?

The above is typical of many Scottish burghs. In the countryside and smaller villages, there may be less to uncover but who knows?

DUNBLANE

In 2006, I went to a conference in Dunblane. Months previously, my survey of common good land had been published. Stirling Council denied there was a Common Good Fund for Dunblane and continues to deny the existence of any common good assets. However, Dunblane is a burgh and had a Town Council up until 1975. It is extremely unlikely that there is no property defined as common good in Dunblane. While chatting with a local resident of Dunblane, the subject of the common good came up. He had an allotment at the Laighills, a large area of parkland to the north-west of the town, and was currently trying to persuade the Council to expand the site. My brother also has an allotment there and so I was curious to find out more. Was the park common good? We decided to make some initial enquiries. To begin with, the man with the allotment at Laighills uncovered a local history volume which reported:

The Laighills were the site of the town's first golf course, laid out as a nine hole course in 1892, and in use until the present course was built in 1923. The club house was at the foot of Laighill Loan.

In 1909 Mr RH Martin of New York, a native of Dunblane, bought the Laighills for £1,000 from Cromlix Estate, and presented them as a gift to the people of Dunblane. There had been earlier plans to build houses here.

This extract demonstrates the usefulness of local history sources since it provided a name – Mr RH Martin – a year – 1909 – and a property – Cromlix Estate – that could be used to conduct further research in the Register of Sasines.

I then located the Search Sheet for the Burgh of Dunblane in the Register of Sasines (Search Sheet number 2122 in the County of Perthshire). On page three of the Search Sheet, there is a Minute referring to the subjects of 'Laighills', part of the 'lands and estate of Cromlix' accompanied by a detailed description of the boundaries. The Minute begins thus:

> 2, *Disp.* by ARTHUR WILLIAM HENRY HAY DRUMMOND of Cromlix, with consent of and by (1) Trustees of the deceased JOHN WILLISON, Farmer, Acharn, Parish of Killin and Parishholm, Parish of Douglas (in right to the extent of £9900, of Bond, dated 3rd, and recorded in this Register 13th Apr. 1883, for £15,000, by the Hon. Arthur Drummond of Cromlix, with consent, to Dugald Stuart), (2) AGNES

Following this is the Minute of the disposition or sale, from Arthur William Henry Hay Drummond of Cromlix, with consent of various third parties with an interest in the property, to the Provost, Magistrates and Councillors of the Burgh of Dunblane. It begins thus:

> recorded in this Register 11th Mar. 1905 [for £1500], by said Arthur William Henry Hay Drummond), to the effect of disburdening the lands and others after mentioned of said respective securities—To The Provost, Magistrates and Councillors of the Burgh of Dunblane,—of said US-5 Dated Jun. 20, 25 and 28 and Jul. 1, 3, 4, 6, 7, 13, 18, 24 and 27, 1911; with Warrant of Registration thereon, on behalf of said Provost, Magistrates and Councillors.

And continues . . .

> (L.) parts of the lands and Estate of CROMLIX, known as LICHELL or the LAIGHHILLS, which lands of Laighhills are divided into 2 parts, viz, (1) a portion to the east of the line of the Caledonian Railway Company, (2) a portion to the west of said line of said Railway Company, and bounded on the north, north west, west and south west by the River Allan following the curve thereof until the point where the Laighhill Burn joins said River, and again on the east by said Burn until it

This Minute contains the evidence we were looking for – namely, that the land was disponed to the Provost, Magistrates and Councillors of the Burgh of Dunblane.

Now we needed to locate the relevant deed. This, we hoped, would explain what had happened to Mr Martin who, according to the local history source, had been the seller of the land. This is contradicted by the Minute that shows that it was, in fact, Mr William Drummond.

The deed is twenty-eight pages long and the first twelve pages are concerned with outlining the legal and financial positions of the seller. The juicy bit – the dispositive clause – is at the foot of the reverse of Folio 44 – pages of deeds of this antiquity are numbered as physical pages with each page having a front and a reverse, a recto and a verso.

> In consideration of the sum of Nine hundred and forty pounds Sterling instantly paid to me the said Honourable Arthur William Henry Hay Drummond by the Provost Magistrates and Councillors of the Burgh of Dunblane said sum being provided to the latter by Robert Hay Martin Asbestos Mine Owner New York United States of America a native of Dunblane as a gift for the purpose of enabling the said Provost Magistrates and Councillors to acquire the said lands and others for the public behoof as the price of the said lands and others and of . . .

This provided the explanation we were looking for – namely, that the role of Robert Hay Martin was to have provided a gift of money to the Burgh to acquire the land. We also found the following burdens in the title:

under the special condition that the said lands hereby disponed shall be used as a Public Park and Recreation Ground for the public behoof and shall not be used for building dwelling houses thereon or for any other purposes than of a Public Park and Recreation Ground.

It is clear that Laighills is unambiguously part of the common good of Dunblane. What's more, it was acquired using a gift of money from a wealthy benefactor who stipulated that it was for public benefit and should be used as 'a Public Park'.

It is common good land!

The Poor Still Have No Lawyers

The way forward for land reform

Land is about power. It is about how power is derived, defined, distributed and exercised. It always has been and it still is thanks to a legal system that has historically been constructed and adapted to protect the interests of private property. The few counterbalances to this, such as the defence of public rights to the foreshore or to burgh commons, have been significant but limited in scope. Ultimately, the dispensation of land we have today is the product of centuries of vested interests organising things to their own advantage. We are thus living with both a legacy and a culture that have become so ingrained as to be almost invisible and have been subject to only the most cursory and short-term critique. If we want real land reform, we need to raise our game in terms of what we do and how we organise. In this concluding chapter, I want to map out some of the way ahead.

Before examining in more detail what this means for the future, it is important to get one thing out of the way. Engaging in any debate about land often leads to assertions about the sanctity of property rights. This is usually only raised by those who oppose land reform but it is pervasive nevertheless. There is no sanctity to property rights any more than any other aspect of the law. Landowners own land certainly but they don't own the law and the rights that underpin it. Property rights are defined by Parliament and they can be amended, adapted and reformed as society sees fit. The one constraint on this is the need to ensure that human rights are respected.

Article 1 of the European Convention on Human Rights states that:

Every natural or legal person is entitled to the peaceful enjoyment of his possessions. No one shall be deprived of his possessions except in the public interest and subject to the conditions provided for by law and by the general principles of international law. The preceding provisions shall not, however, in any way impair the right of a State to enforce such laws as it deems necessary to control the use of property in accordance with the general interest or to secure the payment of taxes or other contributions or penalties.

The key phrase is 'the general interest' and it has already been tested in the English courts. In 1986, the Trustees of the second Duke of Westminster argued that the Leasehold Reform Act of 1967, which enabled tenants under long leases to purchase their freehold interest at what were regarded as favourable rates, breached this article. Although the court recognised that the act did indeed deprive the applicants of their possessions, it also recognised that 'the compulsory transfer of property from one individual to another may, in principle, be considered to be "in the public interest", if the taking is effected in pursuance of legitimate social policies'.

The abolition of the feudal system in Scotland was compatible with human rights on the same grounds even though it deprived superiors of their property. And, in England, the European Court of Human Rights recently upheld adverse possession (squatters' rights) over valuable building land.[1]

In practice the history of land reform is littered with examples of the redefinition of property rights from the Crofting Act of 1886 to the Town and Country Planning Act of 1947 and the Land Tenure Reform (Scotland) Act of 1974. Since the restriction of individual private property rights usually involves the expansion of everyone else's, land reform measures will justifiably continue to redefine property rights in the public interest.

This final chapter maps out a vision of the future and where further land reform might take us. It will argue positively for further reform in community ownership, community land rights, inheritance law, taxation regimes, land information and democratic control of public land.

What is land for?

A key question is what is land for? Ultimately it should be for people and nature (though not necessarily in that order). But that's not how we have organised things. Instead, in a country of over 19 million acres and 5 million people, families are still homeless, the housed are burdened by record levels of debt, the young can't begin to imagine what it must be like to own their own home and young farmers have no prospect of getting hold of a farm. The Scottish Government is currently preparing a land use strategy but it has little to say about such questions. Whilst public and community ownership are dis-cussed, private landownership is subject to no critical analysis and landowners are referred to as land managers.

Yet all across the country, the division of land is one of the fundamental determinants of land use and of the future for individuals and communities. As Professor Bryan MacGregor noted in the first McEwen Memorial Lecture:

> The impact of the land tenure system goes far beyond land use. It influences the size and distribution of an area's population; the labour skills and the entrepreneurial experiences of the popula-tion; access to employment and thus migration; access to hous-ing; access to land to build new houses; the social structure; and the distribution of power and influence. In many areas of rural Scotland, large landowners play a crucial role in local develop-ment: they are the rural planners.[2]

Remember the respondent who told the Land Reform Policy Group that they:

> should not underestimate the profound influence in many parts of rural Scotland still, of the need to avoid your views 'offending' estate owners, their factors, lawyers and other agents.
>
> The inhibiting influence of this 'estate culture' can perhaps be imagined in the area where I live . . . [where] circa 95% of the entire area is held by 15 estates covering more than 500 square miles . . . [and] should add to a sense of their influence on both the development of the area and the lives of individuals in the area (see pp. 319–20).

This influence is so deep-seated and so all-encompassing that it is easy to miss it. Its manifestations are ubiquitous and it even pervades the planning system. For decades, the owner of the Lunga Estate in Argyll has allowed a community to develop on his land and the people live there in a variety of attractive cabins. Despite the cabins having been there for many years, Argyll and Bute Council has served enforcement notices on residents who now face eviction.[3] Meanwhile, landowners such as Lisbet Rausing are given planning permission to build vast modern hunting lodges in the middle of the wilderness of Corrour, near Fort William.[4] As I write, an advert arrives by email offering me 'a well-located, sizeable commercial forest (261.5 hectares) in the south of Scotland. Suitable for an investor requiring an asset backed capital accumulator in a tax free environment with 100% relief from Inheritance Tax.' Is this what land is for? Should it not be for local people to live and work and play in and on?

Underlying this is a discourse from landed interests who seek to portray themselves as so uniquely worthy to hold so much of Scotland that they often fail to see the contradictions. Crofting, for example, is regulated. Assignations of tenancy, de-crofting, amalgamations and even the competence of an occupier are subject, at least in theory, to the interventionist powers of the Crofters Commission. Such regulation is deemed to be appropriate for a few acres of bog and rock above Newtonmore when, at the same time, the transfer of thousands of acres of land outside the crofting areas can be traded in the VIP lounge of Heathrow Airport with no scrutiny whatsoever.

The biggest contradiction is, perhaps, over the question of whether landed estates are businesses or not. Responses to the consultation on succession law reform by the Scottish Estates Business Group and the Scottish Rural Property and Business Association made much of the fact that any changes to inheritance law would have a damaging impact on farms and rural estates, describing such holdings as landed businesses. This is a frequent assertion in relation to any changes in the law or taxation and serves to disguise the true motivation of landowners which has nothing to do with the management of a business and everything to do with the preservation of landed power. But, if landed estates are businesses, why don't they pay business rates like every other business? Why were sporting rates abolished in 1995? Why do landed estates qualify for business property relief and inheritance tax relief?

The purpose in reforming Scotland's land laws is to bring some equity, fair play and social justice to a situation which, as has been described in this book, still works to perpetuate landed hegemony at the expense of the public interest. So what changes should those who want to see land reform be looking for? I have split them into two broad categories of law and policy. Let's look at the law first.

Land law

It is an old joke among lawyers that there is no law relating to land reform. Most radical change in the world occurs through revolution. The lawyers simply come in to tidy up afterwards. I have faith in lawyers and I have faith in and respect for the law but we need to reform our laws and we need to remove from the law all those statutes, conventions and cases which legitimise the theft of land and which disadvantage the public interest. First of all, we need to end the situation whereby an ordinary member of the public caught in possession of stolen goods would be prosecuted for reset but could quite legally get away with it if it were land.

Much of what I have argued in this book highlights the role that prescription has played in the appropriation of land that was never legitimately owned by those who claimed to do so. It is a useful device to cure defective titles where past mistakes have been made or to resolve disputes between owners. But its extensive use over the centuries to legitimise titles of doubtful provenance means that we should be rightly suspicious of the role it plays in landownership today. Prescription is little more than a device to apply a veneer of legality to what is essentially theft. It is a principle that was introduced to Scots law in 1617 to legitimise the theft of Church property and, 450 years after the Reformation, it can still be used to obtain title to land that has never been granted to the claimant and may even belong to someone else.

The key provisions of the Prescription and Limitation (Scotland) Act 1973 should be repealed with immediate

effect and a wholesale review of the principle and application of prescription should be undertaken by the Scottish Law Commission.

Land registration changes everything with respect to the record of ownership. It provides a state-guaranteed title to land and, in the process of drafting titles, the Keeper of the Registers of Scotland has to decide whether or not some or all of the land being registered can truly be shown to be owned by the historic deeds. Prior to this, the Register of Sasines was an imprecise record of ownership often with no plan with which to relate the property – the Cuillin is a good example of this. Now, however, there is a very detailed computerised plan and land not indemnified by the Keeper is land that, after a diligent search of the records, she is not satisfied is owned by the person claiming to own it. If no ownership can be proven she can and does withhold indemnity. This is the best indication of land that has a doubtful provenance but, as the law stands at the moment, such defects are cured by ten years' possession following the recording of the title. If someone cannot prove their ownership of land from evidence in the Register of Sasines to the standard demanded by the Keeper, they should not be entitled to ownership.

All land and property rights over which indemnity has been withheld should, instead, be ineligible for registration and be put up for public auction under the arrangements for *a non domino* titles (see next point).

Earlier, I highlighted the issue of *a non domino* titles and the bizarre situations that can arise where a number of people each try to claim ownership. It is wrong that anyone from anywhere in the world can simply claim part of Scotland for themselves by such a device. The Land Registration etc. (Scotland) Act 2012 tightened up the rules very slightly, but this land grabbing should really come to an end.

***A non domino* dispositions should cease to be lawful. All such land should be registered in the name of the Crown to be administered by the Crown Office in the same way as it manages *bona vacantia* and *ultimus haeres* and put up for public auction.**

At the time of writing in 2013, succession law is under discussion within the Land Reform Review Group. As discussed in Chapter 28, there is much need for reform but this is and will be strongly opposed by vested interests. What is important to stress is that there is a public and a private aspect to inheritance law. The private element relates to the legitimate interests of families to maintain some sense of continuity across the generations. The public element relates to the need to ensure that wealth does not become unduly concentrated in the hands of the few, that each succeeding generation has a fair start in life and that the resources of the country can be used according to the needs of the current gen-eration and not constrained by those who are no longer around. Succession law has been responsible for perpetuating landed privilege by denying children and spouses a legal right to inherit land. This needs to change. The objection from landed interests that businesses need to be handed down to individuals has no merit. Plenty of businesses are managed by multiple owners. Indeed, it is the very basis for the company with share capital.

All children and spouses should be given legal rights to inherit land and no exceptions should be made for mansion houses, landed estates or agricultural businesses.

A recurring theme of this book has been the consequences of the poor having no lawyers and how common land has been appro-priated by powerful interests at the expense of the community. It is time to reverse this process. The dispossession of Scotland's commons has been an insidious and subversive process aided and abetted by the Scots law of property. In the process, much of our heritage and culture and many of our rights have been eroded. It is time to recover them.

The Scottish Parliament should enact a Land Restitution Act to enable the recovery of common land that has been appropriated by means other than due judicial process.

Crown land in Scotland is public land and areas such as the seabed are of increasing value. Currently, the Scottish Government is responsible for the vast majority of planning, regulation and administration of the seabed but has no right to the revenues which flow south to the Crown Estate Commission – even though it is Scottish public land. These revenues could be used to revitalise coastal communities and to provide a Scottish Land Fund to finance community acquisition of land. The Scottish Parliament has the power to legislate over the property rights of the Crown in Scotland.

The Scottish Parliament should abolish all Crown rights over Crown land. The revenues should be used to create a Scottish Land Fund, a Scottish Sovereign Wealth Fund and to offset the administrative costs of managing the seabed and coast.

As outlined in Chapter 29, too much land is owned by secretive offshore companies and anonymous trusts and nominee companies. This lack of transparency is not in the public interest and everyone who owns land of any sort should be willing to have that fact made public. To argue otherwise is to undermine the very principle of a public register which was established back in 1617 when there were no companies or other sorts of impersonal entities.

All titles recorded in the Land Register should be in the name of a natural person or a legal entity registered within the EU. The ultimate ownership of all corporate owners should be declared.

Land policy

Despite the lack of enthusiasm shown by the SNP government for land reform, it is still very much unfinished business and there is plenty that could be done to make landownership more diverse and democratic. But the challenges don't stop there. Perhaps the biggest challenge is to sort out the dysfunctional housing market where a generation have grown rich by the tax-free escalation in land values whilst the young stare into the abyss of a future with massive debts and nowhere to live. Arguably the best thing that public policy could deliver would be an overhaul to the taxation and planning system so that everyone who wants a piece of land can obtain one at a reasonable price. The following are some ideas about how public policy could be changed to promote land reform.

Community ownership has been one of the most prominent features of land reform over the past fifteen years. It has been an undoubted success but the potential is yet to be fully realised. This is due to the fact that it has been largely restricted to rural areas and, in particular, the Highlands and Islands, that the community right to buy is fiendishly complex and bureaucratic, and that the funding structures devised have been primitive and unsustainable. As I have argued, community ownership is not a new idea – it is a very old idea. Indeed, it should be the normal state of affairs for a lot of land as it would allow a greater degree of independence, responsibility and income generation for urban and rural communities.

Community ownership of all types should be more widely promoted in urban and rural Scotland, the community right to buy should be reviewed and simplified and detailed investigations should be undertaken into all remaining common land.

The one striking feature of agricultural holdings in Scotland is the high proportion of farms that are tenanted. The rest of Western Europe abolished tenant farming centuries ago and has seen no reason to return to it. Giving tenant farmers a statutory right to buy the farm on which generations of a family may have lived and worked is a modest but vital measure. No farmer would be obliged to buy their holding and, if landowners are correct and the system is so beneficial to all concerned, none will want to. But those who feel that such a move might offer them a better future would be entitled to exercise the same right that, for example, crofters and council house tenants now enjoy. Such a move should be allied to new arrangements to make existing tenancies more flexible. At the same time, the ownership of farms has become more concentrated and the public funds available to support agriculture have ended up lining the pockets of the wealthiest farmers. Farm ownership should be more diverse so as to encourage more people into agriculture and sustain rural populations.

All tenants of farms holding a protected agricultural tenancy should be given the right to acquire their farms. A policy of one farm per farmer, as exists in Denmark, should be introduced together with a cap on public subsidy.

Perhaps the most significant signal that government was serious about reforming land policy would be to recognise the fact that the massively inflated land market is an economic problem rather than a symptom of prosperity. Over the past thirty years, the whole British economy has increasingly been founded on property-based debt and the accompanying industries such as construction, estate agency, retailing and financial services. The current economic malaise was caused by the fact that land values spiralled out of control, having been backed by cheap credit which, in turn, was backed by exotic and toxic financial products. It is time to get land values back to sensible levels and to release the speculative gains on land so that it can be invested in infrastructure, a new carbon-free economy and public services. The way to do this is to return land values to the community that creates them by an annual levy on land values. This would reduce house prices, reduce the price of commercial and industrial property and encourage investment in buildings and improvements. Young people would be able to afford houses and wealthier individuals would be able to invest in their homes without being penalised since only the land component of a house's value would be assessed for the levy.

The Scottish Parliament should abolish Council Tax and Business Rates and introduce land value taxation to finance local government services.

The vast majority of Scotland's population live in towns and cities. Prior to 1975, Scotland's 196 burghs enjoyed substantial autonomy and civic pride in their affairs. The abolition of Town Councils has made local government more remote and unaccountable whilst eroding local distinctiveness and character. Common Good Funds have disappeared and communities have lost control of vital land and property that had been theirs for hundreds of years. Returning power to Scotland's burghs would promote democracy and enhance community well-being.

The Scottish Parliament should restore Town Councils and pass a new Common Good Act to return all common land and property to the communities to whom they belong.

Public land is, in theory, managed on behalf of the public by organisations accountable to ministers and, through them, to Parliament. One only needs to examine some of the problems with Scottish Natural Heritage, the Forestry Commission and the Crown Estate Commissioners to see that there has been almost as much disillusionment with public landowners as with private ones. The problem is not public landownership itself any more than the problem with private ownership is because it is private. The problem lies in the way such bodies are structured and managed. The Forestry Commission, for example, is still governed by Commissioners appointed by the Queen – just as it was in 1919 when it was dealing with a national emergency. Reforming the structures of such bodies to make them more accountable, diverse and responsive to local views will transform the way they do business.

Decision-making and management of all public land should be placed in the hands of elected regional land boards.

Concluding thoughts

It is easy to be impressed by the heady rhetoric of politicians spouting forth on the land question and how they are going to solve it, particularly since it has been so bleak a prospect for so long. Most land reform programmes around the world have taken place in response to political upheaval – be that a revolution, decolonisation or the overthrow of a dictator. The establishment of the Scottish Parliament was none of these things but it was a dramatic event that changed the political landscape forever. In the wake of its formation, it was possible to achieve things that generations beforehand had found impossible and, within the term of the first Parliament, National Parks were established, feudal tenure was abolished, the right to roam was enshrined in law, crofting communities could buy out their landlord against his or her will, tenant farmers could aspire to own their farms and communities could register an interest in land they would like to buy. This was truly significant and, although I have been accused of not having been as supportive of these reforms as some would have liked (for good reasons as it transpired), I do regard them as historic. But, once they were achieved, the political class has sat back and done very little almost as though land reform were some sort of rite of passage or some cathartic process that had to be undertaken to show something had been done.

The truth is that there is a significant gulf between the ideas I have articulated in this book and the instincts and views of most politicians, civil servants, lawyers and property professionals. This gulf is illustrated, for example, by the very different responses to rising house prices. Almost without exception, it is regarded as a good thing by this group of people. I, on the other hand, think it is manifestly unjust, socially divisive, economically stupid and morally repugnant. Most of this group of people are wholly relaxed about the fact that so few people own so much land. I am not. Land reforms of the sort outlined here may thus be difficult to achieve.

What has happened over the past fourteen years of devolution represents a beginning in tackling the manifest iniquities in Scotland's landownership structures. It is only a beginning, however, and already there are signs that those who stand to gain most from nothing further being done are winning important concessions. On the other hand, there is evidence that many more people understand that something more fundamental has to be done. Underlying the banking collapse and the housing bubble is an economic outlook that is out of date and redundant. Underlying Scotland's land laws is an equally redundant set of assumptions about who owns what and how they are entitled to hold on to it.

If some of what has been related in this book helps to awaken more people to take an interest in land issues, it will have done its job. If more people take the time to understand Scotland's history and Scotland's land laws, then perhaps we can look forward to a better future where the poor, at last, have some lawyers.

Notes

ACKNOWLEDGEMENTS

1. www.data-archive.ac.uk/sharing/faq.asp

CHAPTER 1: *Show the People That Our Old Nobility Is Not Noble*

1. Johnston, T., *Our Scots Noble Families*, p. x.
2. Gronemeyer, M., 'Helping', in Wolfgang Sachs (ed.), *The Development Dictionary*, p. 53.
3. Johnston, *Our Scots Noble Families*, p. vii.
4. Wightman, A., *Who owns Scotland*, p. 205.
5. Land grab might be thought of as an emotive term but it was used by Professor Keith Brown of the University of St Andrews in describing the appropriation of land accompanying the Reformation. See Houston, R. and Knox, W. (eds), *The New Penguin History of Scotland*, p. 212.

CHAPTER 2: *Superiors and Vassals*

1. Her Majesty's Revenue and Customs website provides a useful directory of land law terms. Go to www.hmrc.gov.uk and type 'Scottish land law' in the search box. See also www.scottishlaw.org.uk/lawscotland/abscotslawland.html. The Registers of Title (RoT) book is also useful www.ros.gov.uk/rotbook/
2. A useful summary of the feudal system is provided by the Scottish Parliament in 'Abolition of Feudal Tenure'.

CHAPTER 3: *Robert the Bruce – a Murdering Medieval Warlord*

1. Grant, A., 'Franchises North of the Border', quoting Strayer.
2. Houston and Knox, *The New Penguin History*, pp. 132–33.
3. McNeill, P. and MacQueen, H., *Atlas of Scottish History to 1707*, pp. 199–200.
4. Mackintosh, J., *The History of Civilisation in Scotland*, p. 236.
5. A good example of the latter was the Thane of Fife who was granted a crown charter c.1136.

6. Johnston, T., *The History of the Working Classes in Scotland*, p. 161.
7. Innes, C. *Lectures in Scotch Legal Antiquities*, p. 39.
8. McNeill and MacQueen, *Atlas of Scottish History to 1707*, pp. 412–13.
9. Barrow, G., cited by Sellar, D., 'Farewell to Feudalism', in Dewar, P. B. (ed.), *Burke's Landed Gentry: The Kingdom in Scotland*.
10. Grant, 'Franchises North of the Border'. A useful list of the locations of surviving moot hills where barons dispensed justice can be found at www.en.wikipedia.org/wiki/Moot_hill
11. Grant, A., 'The Death of John Comyn: What Was Going On?', *Scottish Historical Review*, vol. LXXXVI, 2:222, October 2007, pp. 176–224.
12. Johnston, *The History of the Working Classes in Scotland*, pp. 23–4.
13. Nusbacher, A. *1314 Bannockburn*, pp. 46–7.
14. Rodger, R., *The Transformation of Edinburgh*, p. 59. The story of Edinburgh's role in the revival of the feudal title is outlined in Chapter 2 of this book.
15. Reid, K., *The Law of Property in Scotland*, p. 377.
16. The case of Young v Deuar, Court of Session 17 November 1814, cited in Rodger, *The Transformation of Edinburgh*, p. 64.
17. The case of Gordon v Marjoribanks, 1818, 6 Dow 87, HL, 1415, cited in Rodger, *The Transformation of Edinburgh*, p. 66.
18. The case of Corporation of Tailors of Aberdeen v Coutts 1840 1 Rob. App 296 which affirmed the validity of feudal burdens.

CHAPTER 4: *To Spoil the Kirk of Christ of Her Patrimony*

1. Lynch, M. (ed.), *The Oxford Companion to Scottish History*, p. 366.
2. Ibid., p. 366.
3. Johnston, *Our Scots Noble Families*, p. xxxiii.
4. Johnston, *The History of the Working Classes in Scotland*, p. 40.
5. Teinds were a tax on certain produce of land appropriated for the main-tenance of the church. In England they are know as tithes. Teinds were abolished by Section 56 of the Abolition of Feudal Tenure etc. (Scotland) Act 2000.
6. Knox, J., *The First Book of Discipline*, 'Sixth Head', available at www.swrb.com/newslett/actualNLs/bod_ch03.htm#SEC06
7. Mackintosh, *History of Civilisation in Scotland*, vol. II, p. 61.
8. Meikle, M. M., *A British Frontier?*, p. 219.
9. Callander, R. F., *A Pattern of Landownership in Scotland*, p. 30.
10. For details of these and other changes in the Scottish Borders, see Meikle, *A British Frontier?*.
11. Houston and Knox, *The New Penguin History*, p. 211.
12. Lynch, *The Oxford Companion to Scottish History*, p. 502.
13. Mackintosh, *History of Civilisation in Scotland*, vol. II, p. 116.
14. Robertson, *Historical Tales and Legends of Ayrshire*, p. 30. A pictorial story is available at Dunure Community Council website, www.dunure.info/castle/castle.html. A gruesome transcript of the original complaint of Allan Stewart

to the Privy Council can be read in *Charters of the Abbey of Crossraguel*, vol. II, published by Ayrshire and Galloway Archaeological Association in 1886, available at www.archive.org/stream/chartersabbeycr00abbegoog#page/n19/mode/1up

15. See J. Erskine's *An Institute of the Law of Scotland in Four Books*, pp. 479–85, for an explanation of the arrangements surrounding annexation of the Church lands. Ockrent's *Land Rights: An Enquiry into the History of Registration for Publication in Scotland*, pp. 49–50, has a description and McNeill and MacQueen's *Atlas of Scottish History to 1707* has a useful map of the Lords of Erection on page 221.

16. Quoted in Mackintosh, *History of Civilisation in Scotland*, vol. II, p. 433.

CHAPTER 5: *The Palladium of Our Land Proprietors*

1. Brown, K. M. et al. (eds), *The Records of the Parliaments of Scotland to 1707*, 1450/1/16. This searchable database is available at www.rps.ac.uk Date accessed: 28 March 2010.

2. Ockrent, L., *Land Rights: An Enquiry into the History of Registration for Publication in Scotland*, p. 49.

3. Brown et al., *The Records of the Parliaments of Scotland to 1707*, 1617/5/26. Date accessed: 11 January 2010.

4. Rankine, J., *The Law of Landownership in Scotland*, p. 32.

5. Ibid.

6. Ibid., p. 26, citing Stair, *Institutions of the Law of Scotland*, 4.35.15.

7. Kames, H. H., *Elucidations Respecting the Common and Statute Law of Scotland*, p. 262.

8. Rankine, *The Law of Landownership in Scotland*, p. 27.

9. Auld v Hay (1880) 7R 663.

10. Ibid.

11. Hansard *Parliamentary Debates*, 3rd series, vol. 192, col. 1815, 19 June 1868. The debate was concerned with a long-standing dispute between Scottish landowners and the Crown over ownership of the foreshore. See MacAskill, J., '"The most arbitrary, scandalous act of tyranny": the Crown, private proprietors and the ownership of the Scottish foreshore in the nineteenth century', *Scottish Historical Review*, 2006.

12. Brown et al., *The Records of the Parliaments of Scotland to 1707*, 1617/5/30. Date accessed: 5 May 2010.

13. Young v Leith (1847) 9D 937. Lord Fullerton gave the judgment of the majority.

14. Smith, A., *An Inquiry into the Nature and Causes of the Wealth of Nations*, Book III, Ch. 2.3.

15. Stair, *Institutions of the Law of Scotland*, vol. III, iv, 22.

16. Callander, *A Pattern of Landownership in Scotland*, p. 36.

17. Brown et al., *The Records of the Parliaments of Scotland to 1707*, 1685/4/49. Date accessed: 3 February 2010.

18. McCulloch, J. R., *A Treatise on the Succession to Property Vacant by Death*, p. 53.
19. Shaw, S., *An Accurate Alphabetical Index of the Registered Entails in Scotland*.
20. Scottish Law Commission, *Report on Conversion of Long Leases*, p. 3, citing Guthrie Report, para. 44.
21. Sinclair, J., *General Report of the Agricultural State and Political Circumstances of Scotland*, vol. 1, p. 105.
22. Ibid., Appendix, vol. II, Ch. XVI, Section VII, p. 256.
23. Smith, A., *Wealth of Nations*, Book III, Ch. 2.
24. *Hansard*, HL Deb, 13 May 1834, vol. 23, col. 886.
25. Ibid., col. 889.
26. Smith, *Wealth of Nations*, Book III, 2.2.
27. Innes, *Lectures in Scotch Legal Antiquities*, p. 108.
28. Brown et al., *The Records of the Parliaments of Scotland to 1707*, A1504/3/136. Date accessed: 20 January 2010.
29. Brown et al., *The Records of the Parliaments of Scotland to 1707*, A1504/3/137. Date accessed: 20 January 2010.
30. Innes, *Lectures in Scotch Legal Antiquities*, p. 155. This is the passage from which the title of this book is derived.
31. Horn, D. B., *A Short History of the University of Edinburgh 1556–1889*, p. 194.
32. Innes, *Lectures in Scotch Legal Antiquities*, p. 3.
33. Innes, *Lectures in Scotch Legal Antiquities*, pp. 3–4.
34. Innes, *Lectures in Scotch Legal Antiquities*, p. 6.
35. Innes, *Lectures in Scotch Legal Antiquities*, p. 7.
36. See www.rps.ac.uk
37. Sinclair, *General Report of the Agricultural State and Political Circumstances of Scotland*, vol. I, p. 115.
38. Houston and Knox, *The New Penguin History*, p. 242.
39. Johnston, *The History of the Working Classes in Scotland*, p. 88.

CHAPTER 6: *In Edinburgh They Hate Us*

1. For more on the background to the politics of the Highland land question, see T. M. Devine, *Clanship to Crofters' War*, J. Hunter, *Last of the Free*, and P. Hopkins, *Glencoe and the End of the Highland War*.
2. The Gaelic word *dùthaich* means 'land, native country or territory over which hereditary rights are exercised'. For a fuller discussion of the concept, see Chapter 9.
3. Foster, S., Macinnes, A. and MacInnes, R., *Scottish Power Centres from the Middle Ages to the Twentieth Century*, p. 163.
4. Murray, W. H., *Rob Roy MacGregor*, pp. 29–32.
5. MacLean, J. P., *History of the Island of Mull*, pp. 21–2.
6. Brown et al., *The Records of the Parliaments of Scotland to 1707*, 1587/7/70. Date accessed: 29 March 2010.
7. Ibid., 1597/11/40. Date accessed: 25 January 2010.
8. The Gentlemen Adventurers of Fife were a groups of Scots gentry who, with

500 armed mercenaries, were instructed by James VI and I in a contract agreed in the Convention of Estates meeting on 29 June 1598 to 'plant policy and civilisation in the hitherto most barbarous Isle of Lewis' (*The Register of the Privy Council*, Series 1, vol. V, AD 1592–1599, edited and abridged by David Masson, HM General Register House, 1882, p. 463). Their efforts were resisted by islanders who fought a guerrilla war against them. After a succession of failed attempts, the adventurers gave up and sold the island to Mackenzie of Kintail.

9. Skene, W. F., *Celtic Scotland: A History of Ancient Alban, Vol. III, Land and People*, pp. 348–49.
10. Innes, *Lectures in Scotch Legal Antiquities*, p. 157.
11. Johnston, *The History of the Working Classes in Scotland*, p. 161.
12. Maitland Club, *Miscellany of the Maitland Club*, pp. 22–3.
13. Grant, J. F., *The Macleods: The History of a Clan 1200–1956*, p. 241.
14. Grant, 'Franchises North of the Border', p. 5.
15. Devine, *Clanship to Crofters' War*, p. 67.

CHAPTER 7: *A State of Possession Already Subsisting Beyond the Memory of Man*

1. Callander, *A Pattern of Landownership in Scotland*, p. 103. For a detailed analysis of commonties, see I. H. Adams, 'The Legal Geography of Scotland's Common Lands'.
2. For more information on individual commonties, see I. H. Adams, *Directory of Former Scottish Commonties*.
3. Rankine, *The Law of Landownership in Scotland*, p. 600.
4. Callander, *A Pattern of Landownership in Scotland*, pp. 104–105.
5. Ibid., p. 109.
6. Ibid., p. 105.
7. Adams, *Directory of Former Scottish Commonties*, p. vii.
8. Rankine, *The Law of Landownership in Scotland*, p. 600.
9. Brown et al., *The Records of the Parliaments of Scotland to 1707*, 1695/5/204. Date accessed: 18 January 2010.
10. Adams, I. H., 'Economic Process and the Scottish Land Surveyor', *Imago Mundi*, vol. 27, 1975, pp. 13–18.
11. Adams, 'The Legal Geography of Scotland's Common Lands', p. 307.
12. Sinclair, J., *General View of the Agriculture of the Northern Counties and Islands of Scotland*.

CHAPTER 8: *Mere Miserable Starved Caricatures of Their Former Greatness*

1. Houston and Knox, *The New Penguin History*, p. 208. The earliest burghs date to William the Lion's reign but it was with David I that their rise to prominence is associated.

2. Brown et al., *The Records of the Parliaments of Scotland to 1707*, 1469/19. Date accessed: 19 January 2010.
3. Johnston, *The History of the Working Classes in Scotland*, pp. 163–4.
4. Brown et al., *The Records of the Parliaments of Scotland to 1707*, 1491/4/23. Date accessed: 20 January 2010. For the amended act currently on statute book, see www.opsi.gov.uk/RevisedStatutes/Acts/asp/1491/casp_14910019_enm_1
5. HMSO, 'Report of the Commissioners Appointed to Inquire into the State of Municipal Corporations in Scotland', *General Report* p. 23.
6. HMSO, 'Report of the Commissioners Appointed to Inquire into the State of Municipal Corporations in Scotland', Part I, p. 282.
7. HMSO, 'Report of the Commissioners Appointed to Inquire into the State of Municipal Corporations in Scotland', Part I, p. 286.
8. Johnston, *The History of the Working Classes in Scotland*, p. 165.
9. Hansard, HC Deb, 27 September 1831, vol. 7, cc663–6.
10. House of Commons, 'Report from the Select Committee to whom the Several Petitions from the Royal Burghs of Scotland were Referred', pp. 265–69.
11. House of Commons, 'Report from the Select Committee to whom the Several Petitions from the Royal Burghs of Scotland in the years 1818, 1819, and 1820 were Referred', p. 4.
12. These details are derived from HMSO, Municipal Corporations, 'Local Reports, Part I', pp. 455–63.
13. Johnston, *The History of the Working Classes in Scotland*, p. 174.
14. Ibid.
15. Details of this area of law are the subject of a forthcoming book by A. Jarman, *Custom, Community and Common Land*, to be published by Dundee University Press in 2013.
16. The case of Home v Young (1846) 9 D. 286. See A. Jarman, 'Customary Rights in Scots Law', *The Journal of Legal History*, 28:2, pp. 207–32 for discussion.
17. The case of Dempster v Cleghorn. See Loux, A. C., 'The Great Rabbit Massacre', *Liverpool Law Review*.
18. Callander, *A Pattern of Landownership in Scotland*, p. 59.

CHAPTER 9: *I Hereby Take Possession of This Island of Rockall*

1. For full details of the Rockall story from which I have derived much of this account, see F. MacDonald, 'The Last Outpost of Empire: Rockall and the Cold War', *Journal of Historical Geography*, 2006.
2. PRO FO 371/115454, letter from J. R. Grundon, General Department, Foreign Office, to the Secretary of the Admiralty, April 1955. Cited in MacDonald, F., 'The Last Outpost of Empire: Rockall and the Cold War', *Journal of Historical Geography*, 32, 2006, fn 49.
3. Ibid., fn 60, which reads: 'See James Cooke's "Instructions from the Admiralty", quoted in Sorrenson, 'The ship as a scientific instrument', 225, 228.'

Macdonald has Sorrenson in fn 1 as follows: 'R. Sorrenson, 'The ship as a scientific instrument in the eighteenth century', *Osiris* 11 (1996) 221–236'.

4. For more on the background to Rockall, including the conveyancing matters, see *Scots Law Times*, 1968, p. 125, 1976, pp. 257–62, 1985 and 321–25.

5. The full details of these negotiations are discussed in Symmons, C. R., 'Ireland and the Rockall Dispute: An Analysis of Recent Developments', *IBRU Boundary and Security Bulletin*, spring 1998.

6. For a full discussion of these issues, see C. F. Roth, 'Without Treaty, without Conquest: Indigenous Sovereignty in Post-Delgamuuk v British Columbia', *Wicazo Sa Review*, vol. 17, no. 2, 'Sovereignty and Governance, II', autumn, 2002, pp. 143–65.

7. Office of the Auditor General of British Columbia, *Treaty Negotiations in British Columbia*, p. 1.

8. *Mabo and Others v Queensland (No. 2)*, 3 June 1992, High Court of Australia.

9. *Mabo and Others v Queensland (No. 2)*, Brennan at 28.

10. *Mabo and Others v Queensland (No. 2)*, Brennan at 28 and 29.

11. *Mabo and Others v Queensland (No. 2)*, Decision at 2.

12. *Mabo and Others v Queensland (No. 2)*, Order at 1.

13. Scottish Parliamentary Petition PE1297. Mr MacDonald's website (www.macdonaldofkeppoch.org) also makes interesting reading and includes an address to the clans at Homecoming 2009. He is also much concerned with the fiction of clans and chieftainship, vesting himself as Chief of the Honourable Clan Ranald of Lochaber Mac Mhic Raonuill and proud of his place on the Council of Clan Macdonald.

14. *Mabo and Others v Queensland (No. 2)*, Bennan at 83

15. Allodial land is land held absolutely with no other hierarchical interest. Following the abolition of feudal tenure, all land in Scotland is now allodial. See paragraph 188 of Explanatory Notes to Abolition of Feudal Tenure etc. (Scotland) Act 2000.

16. *Mabo and Others v Queensland (No. 2)*, Bennan at 83(7).

17. See www.macdonaldofkeppoch.org/membership.php

18. MacKinnon, I., *Crofters: indigenous people of the Highlands and Islands*, Scottish Crofting Foundation.

CHAPTER 10: *Look Here, Boy, Steady On. Let's Get This Thing Straight*

1. Gash N., *Politics in the Age of Peel: a Study in the Technique of Parliamentary Representation 1830–1850*, p. 36.

2. Johnston, *The History of the Working Classes in Scotland*, p. 211.

3. This may sound counterintuitive but it was the introduction of a system of representation that allowed it to be less unwieldy. All freeholders could still attend if they wished but it was now possible for the counties to be represented by a minimum of two delegates, thus saving all the freeholders from having to attend.

4. Brown, D. J., ' "Nothing but Strugalls and Coruption": the Commons' Elections for Scotland in 1774', *Parliamentary History*, p. 2.

5. Hutchison, I. G. C., 'The Electorate and the Electoral System in Scotland, c1800–c1950', in Romanelli, R., *How Did They Become Voters?: The History of Franchise in Modern European Representation*, pp. 418–19.

6. Ibid., p. 420.

7. Hume, J., *Remarks on the First Report of the Select Committee on Fictitious Votes in Scotland with Extracts from the Evidence*, p. 3.

8. Ibid., p. 19.

9. Ibid., pp. 43–4.

10. Date given by Houston and Knox, *The New Penguin History*, p. 378.

11. Morton and Morris, in Houston and Knox, *The New Penguin History*, p. 378.

12. Devine, T. M., *The Scottish Nation 1700–2000*, pp. 457–8.

13. Boyd, G., 'To Restore the Land to the People and the People to the Land'.

14. Carter, I., *Farm Life in North-East Scotland 1840–1914: the Poor Man's Country*, p. 171.

15. Rodger, *The Transformation of Edinburgh*, p. 52. The details of this property empire and those of the other Edinburgh schools are derived from Chapter 2 of Rodger's *The Transformation of Edinburgh*.

16. Ibid., p. 48.

17. Ibid., p. 49.

18. E. A. Cameron's *Land for the People?* provides a good overview of this period.

19. Devine, *Scottish Nation*, p. 459. Andrew Samuel argues that landowners' power is a consequence of cultural forces as much as legal doctrines, see A. M. M. Samuel, 'Cultural Symbols and Landowners' Power', *Sociology*, vol. 34:4, pp. 691–706.

20. *Glasgow Herald*, 15 December 1986.

21. Wightman, *Who Owns Scotland*, p. 153.

22. See www.alastairmcintosh.com/articles/1998_slf.htm

23. NAS AF45/801

24. See www.sebg.org

25. For relevant documents, see www.andywightman.com/poor

26. Turcan Connell played a critical role in opposing community right-to-buy applications and submitted several responses on behalf of different members of the Fforde family to proposals to extend crofting to Arran. They have also played an influential role in the developing law of succession (see Chapter 28).

CHAPTER 11: *Lord Derby, Lloyd George and John McEwen*

1. See www.ros.gov.uk for further information. See also Wightman, A., *Community Land Rights* for guidance on how to use the Registers of Scotland for research.

2. Scottish Law Commission, *Report on Land Registration*.

3. Cannadine, D., *The Decline and Fall of the British Aristocracy*, p. 19.

4. HL Deb, 19 February 1872, vol. 209, col. 639.
5. HMSO, *Return of Owners of Lands and Heritages Scotland 1872–1873*, Prefatory Remarks.
6. Ibid.
7. Figures derived from Callander, *A Pattern of Landownership in Scotland*, Fig. 5.7, p. 69, with the addition of figures for Orkney and Shetland from HMSO, *Return*.
8. The return can be viewed online at www.scotlandsplaces.gov.uk/digital_volumes/book.php?book_id = 553
9. Cannadine, *The Decline and Fall of the British Aristocracy*, p. 69.
10. George, H., *Progress and Poverty*, p. 364.
11. Ibid., p. 364.
12. Short, B., *Land and Society in Edwardian Britain*, p. 25.
13. Finance (1909–1910) Act, 26 (1).
14. Cannadine, *The Decline and Fall of the British Aristocracy*, p. 69.
15. Short, *Land and Society*, p. 80.
16. Mather, A. S., 'Rural Land Occupancy in Scotland: resources for research', *Scottish Geographical Magazine*, vol. 111:2, 1995, pp. 127–31.
17. The National Archives of Scotland reference for the collection is RHP 20000.
18. Millman, R., 'The Marches of the Highland Estates', *Scottish Geographical Magazine*, vol. 85:3, pp.174 and 177.
19. McEwen, J., *Who Owns Scotland*, 1st edition, p. 14.
20. *Scottish Forestry*, 32, 1978, p. 67.
21. Highland Council, Highland Council Landownership Database, 1998.
22. The basis of this decision was a commissioned research report, Environmental Resources Management (ERM), 'Ownership of Land Holdings in Rural Scotland'. The leaflet was published by Registers of Scotland and is available at www.ros.gov.uk/pdfs/land_ownership.pdf. Note that it fails to mention the www.whoownsscotland.org.uk website.
23. See www.whoownsscotland.org.uk
24. See www.whoownsscotland.org.uk/os.php for full details.
25. In fact, we were better informed following the 1910 Inland Revenue survey which was a comprehensive survey of the whole of urban and rural Britain and Ireland. However, since it was never made public until recently, it cannot be claimed to have ever informed us about anything other than history.

CHAPTER 12: *Who Owns Scotland?*

1. Figures are current as of 31 December 2012.
2. 1872 figures are based upon the Return of Owners of Lands and Heritages. The 1970 figures are McEwen's figures edited as described in *Who Owns Scotland* (1996) Table 2, p. 158, and further edited to remove Crown Land, the Stornoway Trust and the National Trust for Scotland in order to bring all years on to the same basis for analysis as 2012. The 2012 figures are based on the latest data available, some of which dates back to 2002 and is thus not a

snapshot but more an integrated series of snapshots taken over the period 2002 to 2012. It serves well enough, however, as a comparator with the 1995 data.

3. Sources for these figures are as follows:

Scottish Ministers (forestry estate) – *Forestry Commission Scotland Annual Review 2008–09*, p. 26

Scottish Ministers (agricultural estate) – Scottish Government, *Asset Management Review* minus the West Harris estate which has since been sold

Scottish Ministers (crown land) – Crown Estate Commission website, www.thecrownestate.co.uk/tce_faqs/scottish_faqs.htm

Scottish Ministers (other) – Scottish Government, *Asset Management Review*

Local authorities – no aggregate information is available on land owned by local authorities and this figure is an estimate based on *Who Owns Scotland* (1996), Table 1 minus land now owned by Scottish Water

Scottish Natural Heritage – Scottish Natural Heritage, *SNH Heritage Land*, Board Paper June 2009

Scottish Water email – this is a 'management' figure and not a precise computation

Secretary of State for Defence – figure is derived from Annex A of the Defence Estates, *Defence Estates Development Plan (DEDP)*, 2009, which can be found at www.mod.uk/DefenceInternet/MicroSite/DE/OurPublications/DEPublications/DefenceEstatesDevelopment-Plan.htmAnnex A includes owned and leased land. Defence Estates never replied to my emails requesting a breakdown between the two and the figure I provide is based on my own knowledge of the estate.

Highlands and Islands Enterprise – figure consists of HIE's Cairngorm and Orbost estates

4. See www.balmoralcastle.com
5. Land Reform Policy Group, 'Identifying the Solutions', September 1998, p. 23.
6. See number 13 of 'Key facts about Royal finances', available at www.royal.gov.uk/LatestNewsandDiary/Factfiles/Royalfinances.aspx
7. Scottish Government, *Asset Management Review*.
8. Devine, *Clanship to Crofters' War*, p. 64.
9. Callander, *A Pattern of Landownership in Scotland*, p. 11.

CHAPTER 13: *A Considerable Ridge of Very High and Lofty Hills*

1. *The Herald*, 23 March 2000.
2. Scottish Parliament, Official Report, 23 March 2000, Col 952.
3. *West Highland Free Press*, 31 March 2000.
4. Scottish Parliamentary Written Answer S10–1528, 6 April 2000.
5. Crown Estate Commissioners press release, 18 May 2000.
6. Speech to Scottish Landowners' Federation, 20 April 2000.

7. *Guardian*, 1 June 2000.

8. 'Advice Memorandum' by Alan Menzies, June 2000, and 'Opinion of Counsel' by James Drummond Young, July 2000. Mr Drummond Young has since been appointed a judge in the Court of Session (2001) and Chairman of the Scottish Law Commission (2007).

9. 'Advice Memorandum', paras. 4.5 and 4.6.

10. This test reflects the principles most recently set out in the case of Hamilton v McIntosh Donald 1994, cited by 'Opinion of Counsel' by Drummond Young on page 2. The required period to obtain prescriptive possession is ten years or twenty years against the Crown. (Prescription and Limitation (Scotland) (Act) 1973 (1).)

11. First Statistical Account, Volume 3, No. XXXII, p. 246.

12. Innes, C., *Origines Parochiales Scotiae*, p. 343.

13. Lord McLaren in Cooper's Trustees v Stark's Trustees 1898, 25R 1160 at 1168.

14. Innes, *Lectures in Scotch Legal Antiquities*, p. 155.

15. Skene, *Celtic Scotland: A History of Ancient Alban, Vol. III, Land and People*, p. 371. The forests he refers to are the royal forests rather than the sporting estates that developed in the nineteenth century.

16. Rankine, *The Law of Landownership in Scotland*, p. 101.

17. As Rankine, *The Law of Landownership in Scotland*, states on p. 101, 'The peculiarity of a bounding charter is, that no amount of possession under it of a corporeal subject beyond the limits can enable the possessor to vindicate the ownership thereof. He owns so much as his charter gives him: to acquire in that way property in anything beyond would be to fly in the face of his title. For this purpose, any specification of a limit is good so far as it goes; as, for instance, that the subject is within a parish or county named.'

    Further discussion of the importance of boundaries is explored by Alan Blackshaw in his article in the *West Highland Free Press*, 9 February 2001.

    The following extract from Rennie, 'Land Registration and the Decline of Property Law', p. 71, is also instructive. '[W]hat is required as to title is a recorded deed which contains either a description of the land which it is sought to acquire or, rather more flexibly, a description habile to include such land. Provided, therefore, the description is not obviously bounding, possession apparently outwith the description can be used to explain the description and thus make it habile. It is sufficient if the description might be interpreted as including the disputed land.'

18. Brown v North British Railway Company, 1905, 8F 123.

19. Brown v North British Railway Company, 1906, 8F 534.

20. Brown v North British Railway Company, 1906, 8F 534.

21. Officers of State v Smith, SC, 1846, 710, per Lord Cockburn at 723, quoting Robertson's Reports, sec 3, at 182.

22. Letter to the author from Anne Laird, Head of Legal Services, Registers of Scotland, 19 February 2010.

23. Letter from Michael Cunliffe to Alan Blackshaw, 7 April 2000.

24. Crown Estate Act 1961 1(1).

25. For more details, see Chapter 14. A former senior official in the Crown Office in Edinburgh privately confirmed to me that the Crown Estate Commissioners were a source of 'endless aggravation' in their lack of understanding of the respective roles of each body.

26. See Chapter 14. The CEC were to admit five years later that they had no locus in the case of the Cuillin and that the QLTR would administer the mountains if they didn't. See para 12 in Annex 4 of Crown Estate Review Working Group (CERWG), *The Crown Estate in Scotland: new opportunities for public benefits.*

27. MacLeod Estate Office press release, 18 July 2000.

28. Scotland Office press release, 18 July 2000.

CHAPTER 14: *Simple Fraudulent Misrepresentation*

1. For a very thorough description and analysis of the Crown Estate in Scotland, you are well advised to read the report of the Crown Estate Review Working Group (CERWG), *The Crown Estate in Scotland: new opportunities for public benefits.*

2. Crown Estate Act 1961 1(1).

3. See CERWG, *The Crown Estate: new opportunities for public benefits*, Annex 6, for further details on this interesting story.

4. Crown Estate Commission, 'The Crown Estate Scotland, Report 2009', p. 5, available at www.thecrownestate.co.uk/scotland_report_2009-2.pdf

5. www.thecrownestate.co.uk/tce_faqs/scottish_faqs.htm

6. House of Commons, 'The management of the Crown Estate', Treasury Committee Eighth Report 2009–10, p. Ev19.

7. Opinion of Lord Uist in the Petition of the Crown Estate Commissioners for Declarator. [2010] COSH 70, 4 June 2010.

8. See 'The Right Future for the King's Park' at www.andywightman.com/docs/KP_draft1.pdf

9. Crown Estate Act 1961, Section 1(5).

10. CERWG, *The Crown Estate*.

11. Scottish Law Commission, *Law of the Foreshore and Sea Bed*, para 1.14. This statement is merely a reflection of Schedule 5 of the Scotland Act 1998.

12. See House of Commons, 2012. The Crown Estate in Scotland. Seventh Report 2010–2012, HC 1117. Other material and reports are collated at www.andywightman.com.

13. www.thecrownestate.co.uk/financial-information.htm

CHAPTER 15: *From Lord Leverhulme to Lord Sewel*

1. For an insight into commons globally, a good place to start is the website of the International Association for the Study of the Commons – www.indiana.edu/~iascp. A number of useful papers are also available at the *International Journal of the Commons* – www.thecommonsjournal.org

2. Boyd, 'To Restore the Land to the People and the People to the Land'.
3. Boyd,' To Restore the Land to the People and the People to the Land'.
4. Sourced from the website of the Feuars of Letham which is now unavailable.
5. See http://alnwickhillpa.org
6. See www.assyntcrofters.co.uk
7. See MacAskill, *We Have Won the Land*.
8. HC, 4 June 1992, col. 1020.
9. A. McIntosh's *Soil and Soul* covers these developments in an insightful way.
10. HC, 4 June 1992, col. 1024.
11. *Scotsman*, 26 September 1996.
12. See Lorna Campbell at www.caledonia.org.uk/socialland/clu.htm for a dis-cussion of the early years of the CLU.
13. See *Scottish Land Fund Evaluation, Final Report*, 2007.
14. For discussion of the wider significance of this movement see, for example, the many papers by Fiona Mackenzie, including 'Contesting land, creating community, in the Highlands and Islands, Scotland', *Scottish Geographical Magazine*, 2004, Chenevix-Trench, H. and Philip, L. J., 'Community and Conservation Land Ownership in Highland Scotland: a common focus in a changing context', *Scottish Geographical Journal*, 2001 and Bryden, J. and Geisler, C., 'Community-based land reform: lessons from Scotland', *Land Use Policy*, 2007.
15. Wightman, A., *Scotland: Land and Power – The agenda for Land Reform*, p. 73.
16. Hunter, *From the Low Tide of the Sea to the Highest Mountain Tops*.

CHAPTER 16: *Those Who for Our Sake Went Down to the Dark River*

1. For further information on the scale of the sector in the Highlands and Islands including community groups see www.caledonia.org.uk/socialland/nfp06.htm
2. HC Deb, 04 March 1892, vol. 2, cols 91–128.
3. See www.hmrc.gov.uk/heritage/index.htm and click on Land, Buildings and their Contents. All the examples cited here can be found by exploring the website. Full details of the access terms can be seen at www.hmrc.gov.uk/manuals/ihtmanual/annex.htm
4. See Altyre Estate (no. 1) undertakings under Scotland (North) at www.hmrc.gov.uk/heritage/lbsearch.htm
5. See The Doune of Rothiemurchus (no. 33) undertakings under Scotland (North) at www.hmrc.gov.uk/heritage/lbsearch.htm
6. See Lochdochart Estate (no. 24) undertakings under Scotland (North) at www.hmrc.gov.uk/heritage/lbsearch.htm
7. See South Ben Chonzie (no. 29) undertakings under Scotland (North) at www.hmrc.gov.uk/heritage/lbsearch.htm
8. See Arran Estate (no. 3) undertakings under Scotland (South) at www.hmrc.gov.uk/heritage/lbsearch.htm

9. Email from John Kerr, SNH, 6 April 2010.

10. HC Deb, 09 April 1946, vol. 421, col. 1838.

11. For a review of its relative failure, see P. W. Rickwood, 'The National Land Fund 1946–80: the failure of a policy initiative' *Leisure Studies*, vol. 6:1, January 1987, pp. 15–23.

12. For a general review, see T. A. Croft, 'Conservation charity land ownership in Scotland', *Scottish Geographical Journal*, vol. 120:1, 2004, pp. 71–82.

13. The expansion of conservation landownership has been controversial. See F. MacDonald, 'Viewing Highland Scotland', *Area*, vol. 30:3, 1998, pp. 237–244, and Mather, A. S., 'Protected Areas in the Periphery', *Journal of Rural Studies*, 1993.

14. Wightman, *Scotland on Sunday*, 23 February 1997; available at www.caledonia.org.uk/land/awightma.htm

CHAPTER 17: *Tartanry, Royalty and Balmorality*

1. Lorimer, H., 'Guns, Game and the Grandee', *Ecumene*, vol. 7:4, 2000, p. 405.

2. Data from Higgins, P. et al., 'Sporting Estates and the Recreational Economy in the Highlands and Islands of Scotland', *Scottish Affairs*, vol. 31, 2000, pp. 18–36. For further insight into the cultural politics of the hunting estate, Lorimer's 'Guns, Game and the Grandee' is excellent.

3. For a historical perspective, see W. Orr, *Deer Forests, Landlords and Crofters*.

4. Deer forest is the term given to a large tract of land devoted to deer stalking. The term 'forest' is used in its archaic sense of a hunting ground. Most sporting estates in Scotland today are devoid of woodland cover.

5. Lister-Kaye, J., *Ill Fares the Land*.

6. Figures from Orr, *Deer Forests, Landlords and Crofters*, Scottish Land Enquiry and Higgins et al., 'Sporting Estates and the Recreational Economy in the Highlands and Islands of Scotland'. The apparent rapid increase between 1957 and 2002 is a result of including all hunting estates and not simply those designated as deer forests.

7. See Orr, *Deer Forests, Landlords and Crofters*. Afforestation is the term used by writers in the nineteenth century to describe the creation of a deer forest and must have seemed the obvious term to use. It had nothing to do with planting trees.

8. See Hunter, J., *On the Other Side of Sorrow*.

9. Hastings, M., 'Animal Rights and Wrongs', *The Field* (June 1995), np.

10. Vlissingen died on 21 August 2006. The majority of Letterewe Estate is owned by a company and the ownership was therefore unaffected.

11. Letterewe Estate, 'Letterewe Management Plan 1999–2009'.

12. Higgins et al., 'Sporting Estates and the Recreational Economy in the Highlands and Islands of Scotland'.

13. Bound, J., 'Found, the perfect sporting estate', *Broughton's online magazine*, 2003.

14. James Hunter speaking on *Eorpa*, BBC Scotland, 19 October 1995.

15. *The Herald*, 'Sporting Estates to Escape Rates Burden', 9 June 94.
16. Higgins et al., 'Sporting Estates and the Recreational Economy in the Highlands and Islands of Scotland'.
17. Crowe, L. and Reid, P., 'The increasing commercialisation of countryside recreation facilities', *Managing Leisure*, vol. 3, 1998, pp. 204–212.
18. These ideas were floated in a paper by Wightman and Higgins in 2000.
19. See, for example, R. F. Callander and N. MacKenzie, *The Management of Wild Red Deer in Scotland*, D. Macmillan, 'The Economic Case for Land Reform', and Lister-Kaye, *Ill Fares the Land*.

CHAPTER 18: *I Want the Assurance That I Will Not Be Evicted*

1. See Section 72(5) of the Agricultural Holdings (Scotland) Act 2003.
2. Scottish Parliament, 'Official Report', 12 March 2003, George Lyon, at col. 16386.
3. Napier Commission, *Report of the Commissioners of Inquiry*, 'Evidence', vol. I, 8 May 1883, paras 10 and 23.
4. Napier Commission, *Report of the Commissioners of Inquiry*, 'Report with Appendices', p. 7.
5. Ibid., p. 109.
6. Hunter, J., *The Making of the Crofting Community*, p. 162.
7. Carter, I., *Farm Life in North-East Scotland 1840–1914*, p. 169.
8. Ibid., pp. 171–72. The Pentland Act was the popular name for the Small Landholders (Scotland) Act 1911 which came into force on 1 April 1912. It allowed for state acquisition of land for settling landless farmers and set up the Scottish Land Court. Lord Pentland was Secretary of State for Scotland.
9. Scottish Land Enquiry Committee, 'Report of Scottish Land Enquiry, 1914', p. 157.
10. Ibid., p. 158.
11. See Scottish Parliament, 'Official Report', and 'Papers of Rural Development Committee', 29 Oct 2002, for a flavour of the debate.
12. See http://rcil.ros.gov.uk/RCIL/default.asp?Category = RCILAT Unfortunately, some of the interests that are marked as registered are not since they have expired (they last five years). The number of registered interests is certainly in excess of 1,000. The extent of registered interests was calculated by deriving the average acreage for the 356 registrations out of the 743 examined that stated an area and applying this as an average for the total 1,071 registered interests.
13. See www.scotland.gov.uk/Topics/farmingrural/Agriculture/grants/Latest-Payments/Background
14. Scottish Parliament Official Report, 10 June 2009, col. 18151.
15. Pack, B., Inquiry into Future Agricultural Support for Scotland, 'Interim Report'; available at www.scotland.gov.uk/Topics/farmingrural/Agriculture/inquiry
16. Of these, Rob Edwards has been most persistent and, in 2007, he succeeded

in securing the release of five years' worth of payments. See www.robed-wards.com/2007/09/115-million-han.html

17. See   www.scotland.gov.uk/Topics/farmingrural/Agriculture/grants/Latest-Payments/Introduction

18. Data for 2000–2004 is derived from a Freedom of Information request by the journalist, Rob Edwards (see endnote 16, just above). Data for 2005–2009 was downloaded on 28 April 2010 from the Scottish Government website.

19. See www.pressandjournal.co.uk/Article.aspx/1635315?UserKey=

20. NFUS submission to Pack Enquiry, 5 March 2010, para 40.

21. Pack, 'Interim Report', pp. 29–30.

22. Pack, 'Interim Report', Figure 4, p. 31.

23. Pack, 'Interim Report', p. 39.

24. Scottish Crofting Foundation comments on the Pack Inquiry, March 2010.

CHAPTER 19: *A Highly Unsatisfactory Guddle*

1. Scottish Parliament, Crofting Reform (Scotland) Bill, SPICE Briefing SB10/01.

2. The extent of common grazings is derived from Reid, D., Crofters' Common Grazings, Commonweal Working Paper 2. One of the problems associated with understanding crofting tenure is the lack of good quality statistics. No one, for example, knows for sure how much land is under crofting tenure.

3. In order to exercise the crofting community right to buy, a map has to be prepared of the land under crofting tenure. No such maps exist and they thus have to be generated from scratch using historic records in the Scottish Land Court, Crofters Commission, Registers of Scotland and elsewhere. It is a time-consuming affair and even one mistake can render the whole process void.

4. Brian Wilson, *West Highland Free Press*, 19 February 2010.

5. Shucksmith, M., Committee of Inquiry on Crofting, 'Final Report', 2008.

6. Shucksmith, 'Final Report', at 2.1.5.

7. Extract from written evidence of James Hunter to Rural Affairs Committee, 20 January 2010. His oral testimony is worth reading for an insight into the contemporary issues around crofting and can be obtained from Scottish Parliament Rural Affairs Committee, 'Official Report', 20 January 2010, col. 2303.

8. MacKinnon, I. and Walker, S., 'The State of Crofting in Camuscross', p. 33.

CHAPTER 20: *Planting Forests Is a Sure Way To Grow Rich*

1. See Wightman, *Who Owns Scotland*, p. 178.

2. Julia Hands and Kronospan are two examples. Hands is Chairman and Chief Executive of Hand Picked Hotels and has built up a portfolio of at least seven forestry estates covering 17,500 acres across Scotland. Kronospan is a timber processing company based in North Wales and owns at least eleven forestry holdings covering 16,500 acres.

3. Mather, A. S., 'The Structure of Forest Ownership in Scotland: a first approximation', *Journal of Rural Studies*, vol. 3:2, 1987, pp. 175–82.
4. See Wightman, 2012. *Forest Ownership in Scotland*.
5. See www.communitywoods.org and also a useful short essay at www.eh-resources.org/community_forest.html
6. Land Reform Policy Group, 'Recommendations for Action', p. 12.
7. Agricultural Holdings (Scotland) Act 2003, Section 42.
8. See, for example. www.breadalbanefarmforestry.co.uk

CHAPTER 21: *I Will Not Allow House Prices To Get Out of Control*

1. Dorling, D., et al, *Poverty, Wealth and Place in Britain, 1968 to 2005*.
2. National Statistics News Release, 10 Dec 2009.
3. See www.creditaction.org.uk/assets/PDF/statistics/2013/january-2013-summary.pdf
4. Office of National Statistics, Public Sector Finances, December 2012.
5. See, for example, www.pricedout.org.uk, www.housepricecrash.co.uk and, rather more provocatively, www.itsalltheirfault.com
6. Wiletts, D, *The Pinch*.
7. See Chart 3, median net financial wealth, in Benito et al., 'The role of household debt and balance sheets in the monetary transmission mechanism', *Bank of England Quarterly Bulletin*, 2007, Q1.
8. HC Deb, 2 July 1997, vol. 297, col. 313.
9. Skerratt, S., et al., *Rural Scotland in Focus*, '2010 Report', Figure 1, p. 31.
10. For interesting discussion of this, see T. Crawshaw, 'Rethinking housing taxation' (Shelter) and T. Lloyd, 'Don't bet the house on it' (Compass).
11. As argued by Lloyd, 'Don't bet the house on it', p. 31.
12. In this respect, the Scottish Parliament's Register of Interests of Members is significantly more transparent, detailed and informative than the Register of Members' Financial Interests of the House of Commons. It discloses, for example, that Jim Hume, the Liberal Democrat MSP for the South of Scotland owns not only a farm in the Borders but no fewer than five houses in Edinburgh, one in Fife and one in East Lothian all rented out at between £5000 and £10,000 per year. It's rather important to know such details when politicians vote on matters to do with the affordability of housing.
13. Charles Moore, *Daily Telegraph*, 26 March 2010.

CHAPTER 22: *Three Score Men with Clubs and Staves*

1. This is in stark contrast to England where commons remain extensive. See, for example, Short, C., 'The traditional commons of England and Wales in the twenty-first century: meeting new and old challenges', *International Journal of the Commons*, vol. 2:2, 2008, pp. 192–221.
2. Adams, *Directory of Former Scottish Commonties*. It is perhaps indicative of the lack of interest in the topic that Ian Adams' key academic paper was

published, not in Scotland, but in a Belgian sociology journal: Adams, 'The Legal Geography of Scotland's Common Lands', *2 Revue de l'Institut de Sociologie*, 1973, pp. 259–323.

3. Innes, *Lectures in Scotch Legal Antiquities*, p.155.
4. Johnston, *The History of the Working Classes in Scotland*, p. 164.
5. Adams, 'The Legal Geography of Scotland's Common Lands', and Callander, *A Pattern of Landownership in Scotland*, ch. 8.
6. See http://commons.wikimedia.org/wiki/Category:Village_greens_in_Scotland for images of some of the village greens in Scotland.
7. Open Spaces Society – see www.oss.org.uk/village-greens
8. Knox, S., 'The Scattalds of Shetland'.
9. Brown et al., *The Records of the Parliaments of Scotland to 1707*, 1695/5/204. Date accessed: 2 March 2010.
10. See SWT reserve details at www.swt.org.uk/visit/reserves/REM RedMossofBalerno
11. Callander, *A Pattern of Landownership in Scotland*, p. 117.
12. This figure is based on the number of commonties for which no record of division could be located by Adams (1971) or where a commonty was extant in 1845.
13. Adams, *Directory of Former Scottish Commonties*, p. 142.
14. At the time of going to press the title had yet to be granted by the Keeper of the Register of Scotland. See www.andywightman/poor for latest information.
15. Sources of information on the Alyth Commonty include miscellaneous papers, deeds and correspondence in the possession of the author. Full details of the case with history and maps can be seen at www.andywightman.com/poor
16. Reid and Gretton, *Conveyancing*, paras 7–25.
17. He cannot have tried too hard since the deed was clearly recorded in the Register of Sasines. His claim was reported in *The Herald*, 15 February 2006.
18. *The Herald*, 15 February 2006.
19. In 2005 Historic Scotland designated the castle a scheduled monument. In the Schedule the Squires are noted as the owners. Interestingly, the schedule was signed by the then Director of Heritage Policy at Historic Scotland, Sheenagh Adams. She is now the Keeper of the Registers of Scotland and may one day have to revisit this case to sort out the competing claims.
20. Section 43 of the Land Registration etc. (Scotland) Act 2012 now regulates the use of *a non domino* dispositions.
21. See, for example, Tesco Stores Ltd v The Keeper of the Registers of Scotland and Safeway Stores plc at www.lands-tribunal-scotland.org.uk/decisions/LTS.LR.1999. 2,3.html
22. Deed recorded 1 Feb 1923, GRS Perth, 1147.141.
23. Gordon, W. M., *Scottish Land Law*, 1999, paras 15–55, p. 439. He cites in support of this view Macandrew v Crerar, 1929, SC 699. This was a case in

Perth Sheriff Court involving the division of a 99-acre commonty known as Cow Park.

24. Letter from Keith S. Black to Provost Sim, 13 May 1949.
25. Letter to Arthur Woodburn MP reprinted in *Alyth Voice*, October 2007).
26. Disposition by Trustees of the Earl of Airlie to Sir Neis A. Ramsay and Richmond M. H. Haddo recorded in the General Register of Sasines in the County of Perth 15 September 1977.
27. Reid, K., and Gretton, G. L., *Conveyancing*, 3rd edition, pp. 7–25.
28. As quoted in Opinion of Lord Menzies in Board of Management of Aberdeen College v Youngson, 2005, CSOH 31.
29. Letter from Peter D. Clark, Area Land Agent, Forestry Commission to Mr R. Price, Toutie Street, Alyth, 6 May 2008.
30. See www.birsecommunitytrust.org.uk
31. Simpson, J. H., *The Feuars of Gifford*.
32. For further information on Travellers and their customs, see www.scottish-travellered.net and www.showmensguild.com

CHAPTER 23: *All Property of a Burgh*

1. Callander, *A Pattern of Landownership in Scotland*, p. 120.
2. Bogle, K. R., *Scotland's Common Ridings*.
3. Wightman, A. and Perman, J., 'Common Good Land in Scotland: a Review and Critique', Commonweal Working Paper No. 5, 2005, Caledonia Centre for Social Development, Inverness.
4. Bob Shields, *Daily Record*, 14 June 2003.
5. The state of knowledge has improved considerably in recent years with the publication of the Wightman and Perman report (see endnote 3 just above) and Andrew Ferguson's *Common Good Law*.
6. Magistrates of Banff v Ruthin Castle Ltd, 1944, SC 35, 1944 SLT 373, at p. 37.
7. Magistrates of Banff v Ruthin Castle Ltd 1944, SC 35, 1944 SLT 373, at p. 60.
8. Wilson v Inverclyde Council 2003, SC 366, 2004 SLT 265.
9. Scottish Parliamentary written answer S2W-29685 17 November 2006.
10. Letter from Mr Archibald Strang.
11. See Scottish Parliamentary Petitions PE875, PE896 and PE961.
12. Letter from David Milne, head of Best Value and Performance Team, Scottish Executive to Local Authority Directors of Finance, 16 March 2007.
13. Local Authority (Scotland) Accounts Advisory Committee, 'Accounting for the Common Good Fund: A Guidance Note for Practitioners'.
14. Data from A. Wightman, 'Common Good Funds 2009'. Note that the figure for the total value of Common Good Funds in 2005 (£1.42 billion) is derived from Wightman and Perman, 2005, in which the total figure is erroneously given as £1.8 billion on page 44.
15. See Bort et al., *The Silent Crisis*.

CHAPTER 24: *Let for a Penny a Year*

1. See www.scottishcommons.org/burghs/edinburgh.htm for further details and links to various papers relating to Edinburgh's common good.
2. *The Herald*, 25 November 1989.
3. Report of 9 November 1979 by R. McIntosh, Director of Estates and presented to the Policy Sub-Committee of the Policy and Resources Committee on 15 November 1979.
4. The council retains an interest in the Tourist Information Office, which sits on top of the Princes Mall, the lease of which was not sold in 1989. It is not known whether it pays any rent to the Common Good Fund.
5. Review of Common Good in Edinburgh. Report to Finance and Resources Committee, 28 January 2008, Item No. 14.
6. See Wightman, Common Good Funds 2005–2012.
7. Scottish Law Commission, *Report on Conversion of Long Leases*.

CHAPTER 25: *Problems Rarely Arise with Land in Private Ownership*

1. Ewan Cameron's 2001 paper 'Unfinished Business: the land question and the Scottish Parliament' provides an excellent overview of land reform in the twentieth century and the debates in the 1990s leading up to and including the establishment of the Scottish Parliament.
2. Hunter, J., *The Making of the Crofting Community*; Carter, I., *Farm Life in North-East Scotland 1840–1914*, and Prebble, J., *The Highland Clearances*.
3. The people who delivered the McEwen lectures were:
   1993 Professor Bryan MacGregor
   1995 Dr James Hunter
   1996 Professor John Bryden
   1997 Professor David McCrone
   1998 Rt Hon. Donald Dewar MP
   1999 Andy Wightman
   The texts of all the McEwen lectures are available at www.caledonia.org.uk/land/lectures.htm
4. A flavour of this is provided by the debate on landownership in the House of Commons on 6 November 1996 – see www.publications.parliament.uk/pa/cm199697/cmhansrd/vo961106/debtext/61106-01.htm
5. The Land Reform Policy Group was chaired by Lord Sewel. The Deputy Chair was Isabelle Low, Head of Land Use Division in the Scottish Office. The other members were Professor John Bryden (external assessor); Murray Elder, Special Adviser to the Secretary of State for Scotland; Alan Fraser, Head of Enterprise and Tourism Division, Scottish Office; Douglas Greig, Chief Economist, Agriculture, Environment and Fisheries Department, Scottish Office; David Henderson-Howat, Chief Conservator, Forestry Commission; Joyce Lugton, Civil Law Division, Scottish Office; Hugh MacDiarmid, Solicitor's Office, Scottish Office; John Randall, Head of Countryside and Natural Heritage Unit, Scottish Office; and Philip Rycroft,

Head of Agricultural Policy Co-ordination and Rural Development Division, Scottish Office.

6. See for example *The Herald* and the *Scotsman* on 27 April, 1998.
7. Respondents to Government consultations are informed that, unless they clearly state otherwise, their response will be made available to the public to look at.
8. Detailed analysis conducted by Peter Gibb of Land Reform Scotland.
9. Dewar, D., 'Land Reform for the 21st Century', John McEwen Memorial Lecture, 1998.
10. These figures are derived from an analysis I conducted in the Scottish office library on 23 December 1998. It differs from the official analysis because, for example, many responses were categorised as 'individuals' by civil servants where no declaration was made that they were landowners. Knowing that they were landowners, I categorised them as such. I have not attributed names to the selected quotes from the submissions although these are on the public record.
11. *Scotland on Sunday*, 3 January 1999.
12. My bumping into the Duke of Buccleuch was an uncanny parallel to events of six months earlier when Alastair McIntosh had bumped into him whilst *he* was being ejected from a meeting of the Scottish Landowners' Federation – see Chapter 10.
13. Cameron, 'Unfinished Business'.
14. *The Scotsman*, 12 Feb 1999.
15. 'Scottish Parliament Official Report', vol. 3, no. 924, col. 857, November 1999.
16. Magnus Linklater commented unfavourably on the way in which the Justice 2 Committee had treated witnesses in an article in *Scotland on Sunday*, 1 Dec 2002. Links to the written and oral evidence on the Land Reform Act can be found at www.scottish.parliament.uk/business/committees/historic/justice2/reports-02/j2r02-02-vol02-01.htm
17. Copies of all the Action Plans are available at www.andywightman.com/poor
18. Introduction to 'Recommendations for Action'.
19. Scottish Land Commission, 'Public Policy Toward Land in Scotland'.
20. Wightman, A., 'Land Reform: An agenda for 2007–11 Scottish Parliament'.
21. CERWG, 'The Crown Estate'.
22. Wightman, A., 'Land Reform (Scotland) Act 2003 (Part 2, the community right to buy) a Two-Year Review'.
23. Scottish Parliamentary Written Answer S3W-24967.
24. A reliable source informed me that Scottish Ministers told the Scottish Rural and Environment Directorate in 2007 that 'enough has been done on land reform'.
25. See www.landreformreview.org. The members of the Review Group are Dr Alison Elliot (Chair), Professor Jim Hunter (Vice-Chair) and Dr Sarah Skerrat (Vice-Chair). The names of the thirteen advisers can be found on the Group's website.

CHAPTER 26: *Little More Than an Instrument for Extracting Money*

1. Scottish Law Commission, *Report on Land Registration*.
2. For an analysis of the most important legal reforms of this period, see Steven, A. J. M., 'Revolution in Scottish Land Law', *Electronic Journal of Comparative Law*, vol. 8:3, October 2004. For an overview of Scotland's land tenure system, see Callander, *How Scotland is Owned*. A good textbook on the topic (designed for law students) is *Property, Trusts and Succession* by G. Gretton and A. Steven.
3. Scottish Law Commission, *Report on Land Registration*, para. 3.5.
4. Scottish Law Commission, *Property Law – Abolition of the Feudal System* (1991) and *Property Law – Abolition of the Feudal System* (1999).
5. See HMSO, *Land Tenure in Scotland: A Plan for Reform* (1969) and HMSO, *Land Tenure Reform in Scotland* (1972).
6. Scottish Law Commission, *Property Law – Abolition of the Feudal System*, para. 1.14.
7. Abolition of Feudal Tenure etc. (Scotland) Act 2000, Section 1.
8. 'Feudalism No More', *Scots Law News*, 16 March 2003; available at www.law.ed.ac.uk/sln/blogentry.aspx?blogentryref=7069
9. Scottish Law Commission, 'Report on Law of the Foreshore and Sea Bed', para 1.10.
10. Ibid., para 5.4.
11. HC Deb, 06 November 1996, vol. 284, col. 1157.
12. HC Deb, 06 November 1996, vol. 284, col. 1162.
13. HC Deb, 06 November 1996, vol. 284, col. 1170.
14. Leasehold Casualties (Scotland) Act 2001
15. Scottish Law Commission, *Report on Conversion of Long Leases*.
16. Scottish Law Commission, *Report on Land Registration*.
17. See www.andywightman.com under category 'Land Registration' and, in particular, my evidence to the Economy, Energy and Tourism Committee at http://www.andywightman.com/docs/aw_20120113.pdf
18. See note 11, Chapter 5.
19. It is interesting to note that the Scottish Law Commission, in their 2010 *Report on Land Registration*, do, actually, refer to the fact that there are those who argue that prescription is theft (see *Report on Land Registration*, para. 16.5).

CHAPTER 27: *Bureaucratic Nit-Picking and Fine Legal Arguments*

1. See http://rcil.ros.gov.uk/RCIL/default.asp?category=rcil&service=home
2. For some insight into the issues raised during the passage of the legislation, see Caledonia Briefing Papers 1, 2, 3 and 5 at www.andywightman.com/briefings
3. The data that follows is derived from a survey undertaken by the Scottish Government in 2012 and published as *Overview of Evidence on Land Reform in Scotland*.

4. These figures were supplied by the Scottish government in response to a Freedom of Information request and cover the costs of staffing, travel and subsistence for the civil servants who administer the right-to-buy scheme.

5. See Land Reform Policy Group, 'Identifying the Solutions', p. 23.

6. Callander, *A Pattern of Landownership in Scotland*, p. 11.

7. Wightman, *Scotland: Land and Power*, p. 76.

8. See Marland, A., 'Seton Fields Case Study', and Wightman, *Land Reform (Scotland) Act 2003*.

9. Kermack, L., *Coping with Rights to Buy – Part 1*, p. 9.

10. For an excellent legal analysis of the Land Reform Act, see Combe, M. M., 'Parts 2 and 3 of the 'Land Reform (Scotland) Act 2003: a Definitive Answer to the Scottish Land Question', *Juridical Review*, 2006, Part 3, pp. 195–228. See also Combe, M. M., 'No Place Like *Holme*: Community Expectations and the Right to Buy', *Edinburgh Law Review*, vol. 11:1, 2007, pp. 109–116. Also Combe, M. M., 'Access to Land and Landownership', *Edinburgh Law Review*, vol. 14, pp. 106–13, 2010.

11. The *Scotsman*, 25 January 2003. See also *Sunday Times*, 3 February 2003.

12. Scottish Labour, 'On Your Side', Scottish Parliament Manifesto, 2003.

13. Scottish Statutory Instrument 2004 No. 296, *The Community Right to Buy (Definition of Excluded Land) (Scotland) Order 2004*.

14. Boyd, G., 'The Prince, the Merchant and the Citizen', May 1999; available at www.caledonia.org.uk/land/prince.htm

15. See Office of the Deputy Prime Minister (ODPM), 'Communities Taking Control: Final Report of the Cross-sector Work Group on Community Ownership and Management of Assets', p. 42; available at www.andywightman.com/poor

16. 'Call for new urban area "right to buy" ', the *Scotsman*, 25 January 2003.

17. 'Scottish Parliament Official Report' 25 February 2010, col. 24038.

18. At a meeting with Mark Ruskell MSP on 6 June 2006 to discuss concerns about the operation of the community right to buy, Rhona Brankin confirmed that a review would be carried out 'later this year'.

19. Scottish Parliament Written Answers 18 January 2007 S2O–11669.

20. 'Scottish Parliament Written Answers', 8 July 2009, S3W-24965.

21. 'Scottish Parliament Official Report', 23 Jan 2003, col. 14387.

22. Scottish Executive, Land Reform Action Plan August 2003. This stated, 'In accordance with Amendment 208 at Stage 3 of the Land Reform (Scotland) Bill's passage through the Scottish Parliament (Official Report Col. 17390–17391), future land reform updates will be presented to Parliament on a regular basis, and will include an update on the diversity of land ownership in Scotland.' This has never happened, despite the amendment being proposed by Roseanna Cunningham, the minister currently responsible for land reform, who, in a Written Answer on 30 April 2010 (S3W–33020), said that there were no plans to publish such a report.

23. Caledonia Centre for Social Development, 'Response to the Draft Land Reform Bill June 2001', available at www.caledonia.org.uk/land/response1.htm

CHAPTER 28: *Undermining the Whole Fabric of Scottish Family Life*

1. Stair, *The Institutions of the Law of Scotland*, III, 4.22.
2. For an official explanation, see the Scottish Government's 'Rights of Succession: a brief guide to the Succession (Scotland) Act 1964: Revised 2005', available at www.scotland.gov.uk/Publications/2005/12/05115128/51285 If you are a real sucker for punishment, try the Scottish Law Commission's reports of 1990, 2007 and 2009.
3. For discussion, see J-P. Platteau and J-M. Baland, 'Impartible Inheritance Versus Equal Division: a Comparative Perspective Centred on Europe and Sub-Saharan Africa'.
4. Smith, A., *Wealth of Nations*, Book 3, Ch. 2.3.
5. Scottish Land Enquiry Committee, 'Report of Scottish Land Enquiry, 1914', p. 543.
6. Mackintosh Committee, 'Law of Succession in Scotland', p. 9.
7. HL Deb, 12 March 1964, vol. 256, col. 571.
8. HL Deb, 12 March 1964, vol. 256, col. 585.
9. HL Deb, 12 March 1964, vol. 256, cols 551, 552 and 555.
10. This is particularly the case in farming families.
11. Scottish Law Commission, 'Report on Succession', *Scot Law Com*, No. 124, p. 20.
12. Scottish Law Commission, 'Report on Succession', *Scot Law Com*, No. 124, p. 21.
13. Scottish Law Commission, 'Discussion Paper on Succession DP136' and 'Report on Succession', *Scot Law Com*, No. 215.
14. Responses from SRPBA, SEBG and Turcan Connell referred to in *Scot Law Com*, No. 215, para 3.63, p. 53, footnote 65.
15. Scottish Law Commission, 'Discussion Paper on Succession DP136', *Scot Law Com*, paras 3.120 and 3.121.
16. Scottish Law Commission, 'Discussion Paper on Succession DP136', *Scot Law Com*, para. 1.5.
17. 'Scottish Parliament Official Report', 21 January 2010, col. 23017.
18. Fergus Ewing, letter to Scottish Law Commission, 13 July 2009.

CHAPTER 29: *Their Unjust Concealing of Some Private Right*

1. Land in Granton forms part of the Waterfront development, some which was sold to Edinburgh City Council in November 2004 for a sum to date of £13,450,173. Interestingly, the title to this is registered as MID2 and was only the second title to be recorded in the new Land Register. The first was MID1 – Edinburgh Castle.
2. Edwards, A., 'Towards a Clean World', *Journal of Money Laundering Control*, vol. 5:4, pp. 279–86.
3. Edwards, A., 'Quinquennial Review', pp. 104–105.
4. Land Registry, '10-Year Strategic Plan, 2003–4 to 2012–13', p. 45–46.

5. The work involves searching Companies House records for which a fee is charged.

6. Al Fayed v Commissioners of Inland Revenue, Court of Session, 31 May 2002.

7. Al Fayed v Commissioners of Inland Revenue, Court of Session, 31 May 2002, at 61.

8. *Sunday Herald*, 5 October 2003.

9. Scottish Law Commission, *Report on Land Registration*.

10. For discussion of the issues surrounding the Land Registration Act 2012, see www.andywightman.com under category – 'Land Registration'.

CHAPTER 30: *We Do Not Want To Punish the Landlord*

1. Speech delivered by Churchill in the King's Theatre, Edinburgh, on 17 July 1909.

2. For a convenient version of this speech see the Liberal history website at www.liberalhistory.org.uk/item_single.php?item_id = 47&item = history

3. Buchanan, P., *Economic Impact of High Speed 1*, p. 22.

4. Buchanan, *Economic Impact of High Speed 1*. Figure S1 on page 3 shows the increase in house prices.

5. www.waterfront-ed.com/info/The-Master-Plan.aspx

6. 'Co-operative Party Manifesto', 2010.

7. In addition to the ones quoted here, see M. Wadsworth, *Tax, Benefits, Pensions* which advocates LVT as a replacement tax whilst scrapping Council Tax, Stamp Duty, Land Tax, Capital Gains Tax on disposals of land and buildings, Inheritance Tax and the TV licence fee.

8. Lloyd, 'Don't bet the house on it', pp. 36–7.

9. McLean, I., 'The politics of land tax – then and now', in Maxwell, D. and Vigor, A. (eds), *Time for Land Value Tax?*

10. Muellbauer, J., 'Property Taxation and the economy', in Maxwell, D. and Vigor, A. (eds), *Time for Land Value Tax?*

11. Kay, J., and King, M., *The British Tax System*, p. 179.

12. Posen, A. S., 'Finding the Right Tool for Dealing with Asset Price Booms', speech to the MPR Monetary Policy and Markets Conference, London, 1 December 2009.

13. See website www.dfos.co.uk for details of the complaints of producers.

14. Shirley, A., quoted by Wilkinson, T. L., 'Buying farmland is as good as gold', *eFinancialNews Ltd*, 2009; available at www.andywightman/poor

15. Wightman, A., 'A Land Value Tax for Scotland', available at www.andy-wightman.com/docs/LVTREPORT.pdf.

16. Ibid.

17. The property values underlying this are derived from the median of 1991 values (the baseline for the current council tax bands) updated using house price inflation data to 2009 values.

CHAPTER 31: *A Public Park and Recreation Ground for the Public Behoof*

1. Scottish Law Commission, *Report on Land Registration*, p. 1.
2. The book is available at www.andywightman.com/shop.htm
3. The Inland Revenue Survey maps are held by the National Archives of Scotland. Detailed instructions for how to locate maps in the collection are provided in Wightman, *Community Land Rights*, pp. 42–51.
4. National Archives of Scotland, RHP 43998.

CHAPTER 32: *The Poor Still Have No Lawyers*

1. A useful summary of this case can be found at www.propertylawuk.net/adversepossessionpyegraham.html
2. MacGregor, B., 'Land Tenure in Scotland'.
3. www.lungaclearances.org
4. www.corrour.co.uk

Bibliography and Further Reading

A number of the publications listed below are available to download at www.andywightman.com/poor

Adams, I. H., *Directory of Former Scottish Commonties* (Scottish Record Society, Edinburgh, 1971)

Adams, I. H., 'The Legal Geography of Scotland's Common Lands', *2 Revue de l'Institut de Sociologie*, Université Libre de Bruxelles, 1973

Adams, I. H., 'Economic Process and the Scottish Land Surveyor', *Imago Mundi*, vol. 27, 1975.

Benito, A. et al., 'The role of household debt and balance sheets in the monetary transmission mechanism', *Bank of England Quarterly Bulletin*, 2007, Q1

Besley, T., 'Consumption and Interest Rates', speech by Tim Besley, Member of the Monetary Policy Committee, Bank of England. (Centre for Economic Policy Research, 19 July 2007)

Bogle, K. R., *Scotland's Common Ridings* (Tempus, Stroud, 2004)

Bort, E., McAlpine, R., & Morgan, G. *The Silent Crisis. Failure and revival in local democracy in Scotland* (The Jimmy Reid Foundation, 2012)

Bound, J., 'Found, the perfect sporting estate', *Broughton's online magazine*, 2003

Boyd, G., 'To Restore the Land to the People and the People to the Land: the emergence of the not-for-private-profit landownership sector in the Highlands and Islands of Scotland', *Journal for Community Work and Development*, vol. 3, spring 1998

Boyd, G., 'The Prince, the Merchant and the Citizen' (Caledonia Centre for Social Development, Inverness, 1999)

Brown, D. J., ' "Nothing but Strugalls and Coruption": the Commons' Elections for Scotland in 1774', *Parliamentary History*, vol. 15:1 (1996), 100–119

Brown, K. M. et al. (eds), *The Records of the Parliaments of Scotland to 1707*, a searchable database available at www.rps.ac.uk

Bryden, J., 'Land Tenure and Rural Development', John McEwen Memorial Lecture, 1996

Bryden, J. and Geisler, C., 'Community-based land reform: lessons from Scotland', *Land Use Policy*, vol. 24 (2007), 24–34

Buchanan, P., *Economic Impact of High Speed 1* (London and Continental Railways, London, 2009)

Cahill, K., *Who Owns Britain* (Canongate, Edinburgh, 2001)

Callander, R. F., *A Pattern of Landownership in Scotland* (Haughend Publications, Finzean, 1987)

Callander, R. F. and MacKenzie, N., *The Management of Wild Red Deer in Scotland* (Rural Forum, Perth, 1991)

Callander, R. F., *How Scotland is Owned* (Canongate, Edinburgh, 1998)

Cameron, E. A., *Land for the People?: the British Government and the Scottish Highlands, c. 1880–1925* (Tuckwell Press, Edinburgh, 1996)

Cameron, E. A., 'Unfinished Business: the land question and the new Scottish Parliament', *Contemporary British History*, vol. 15 (2001), 83–114

Cannadine, D., *The Decline and Fall of the British Aristocracy* (Yale University Press, New Haven and London, 1990)

Carter, I., *Farm Life in North-East Scotland 1840–1914: the Poor Man's Country* (John Donald, Edinburgh, 1979)

Chenevix-Trench, H. and Philip, L. J., 'Community and Conservation Land Ownership in Highland Scotland: a common focus in a changing context', *Scottish Geographical Journal*, vol. 117 (2001), 139–156,

Combe, M. M., 'Parts 2 and 3 of the Land Reform (Scotland) Act 2003: a Definitive Answer to the Scottish Land Question?' *Juridical Review* 195 (2006), 196–200

Combe, M. M., 'No Place Like *Holme*: Community Expectations and the Right to Buy', *Edinburgh Law Review*, vol. 11:1 (2007), 109–116

Crawshaw, T., *Rethinking Housing Taxation: options for reform* (Shelter, London, 2009)

Croft, T. A., 'Conservation Charity Land Ownership in Scotland', *Scottish Geographical Journal*, vol. 120:1 (2004), 71–82

Crowe, L. and Reid, P, 'The Increasing Commercialisation of Countryside Recreation Facilities: the case of Scottish mountain bothies', *Managing Leisure*, vol. 3 (1998), 204–212

Crown Estate Review Working Group, *The Crown Estate in Scotland: new opportunities for public benefits* (Highland Council, Inverness, 2007)

Defence Estates, 'Defence Estates Development Plan'; available at www.mod.uk/DefenceInternet/MicroSite/DE/OurPublications/DEPublications/DefenceEstatesDevelopmentPlan.htm

Devine, T. M., *Clanship to Crofters' War: the social transformation of the Scottish Highlands* (Manchester University Press, Manchester, 1994)

Devine, T. M., *The Scottish Nation 1700–2000* (Penguin, London, 1999)

Dewar, D., 'Land Reform for the 21st Century', John McEwen Memorial Lecture, 1998

Dorling, D, et al., *Poverty, Wealth and Place in Britain, 1968 to 2005* (Joseph Rowntree Foundation, Bristol, 2007)

Edwards, A., 'Towards a Clean World', paper presented at Cambridge International Symposium, 13 September 2001, and subsequently published in *Journal of Money Laundering Control*, vol. 5:4, 279–86

Edwards, A., 'Quinquennial Review' (HM Land Registry, London, June 2001)

ERM, *Ownership of Land Holdings in Rural Scotland* (Scottish Executive Central Research Unit, Edinburgh, 2001)

Erskine, J., *An Institute of the Law of Scotland in Four Books* (Bell & Bradfute, Edinburgh, 1824)

Ferguson, A., *Common Good Law* (Avizandum, Edinburgh, 2006)

Foster, S., Macinnes, A. and MacInnes, R., *Scottish Power Centres from the Middle Ages to the Twentieth Century* (Cruithne Press, Glasgow, 1998)

Gash N., *Politics in the Age of Peel: a study in the technique of parliamentary representation 1830–1850* (Longmans, Green, London, 1953)

George, H., *Progress and Poverty* (Appleton & Company, New York, 1881)

Gordon, W. M., *Scottish Land Law*, 2nd Edition, (W. Green, Edinburgh, 1999)

Grant, A., 'The Death of John Comyn: What Was Going On?' *The Scottish Historical Review*, vol. 86:2, no. 222 (2007) 176–224

Grant, A., 'Franchises North of the Border: Baronies and Regalities in Medieval Scotland', in Prestwich, M. (ed.), *Liberties and Identities in the Medieval British Isles* (Boydwell and Brewer, Woodbridge, 2008)

Grant, J. F., *The Macleods: the History of a Clan 1200–1956* (Faber and Faber, London, 1959)

Gretton, G. L. and Steven, A. J. M., *Property, Trusts and Succession* (Tottel Publishing, Haywards Heath, 2009)

Gronemeyer, M., 'Helping', in Wolfgang Sachs (ed.), *The Development Dictionary* (Zed Books, London,1992)

Hastings, M., 'Animal Rights and Wrongs', *The Field* (June 1995)

Higgins, P., Wightman, A. and MacMillan, D., 'Sporting Estates and Recreational Land Use in the Highlands and Islands of Scotland', ESRC Report R000223163, 2002

Highland Council, Highland Council Landownership Database (Highland Council, Inverness, 1998)

HMSO, 'Report of the Commissioners Appointed to Inquire into the State of Municipal Corporations in Scotland' (HMSO, London, 1836)

HMSO, 'Return of Owners of Lands and Heritages Scotland 1872–1873 17 & 18 Vict., CAP. 91' (HMSO, Edinburgh, 1874)

HMSO, 'Land Tenure in Scotland: a Plan for Reform', Cmd 3099, 1969

HMSO, 'Land Tenure Reform in Scotland', Government Green Paper, 1972

Hopkins, P., *Glencoe and the End of the Highland War* (John Donald, Edinburgh, 1986)

Horn, D. B., *A Short History of the University of Edinburgh 1556–1889* (Edinburgh University Press, Edinburgh, 1967)

House of Commons, 'Report from the Select Committee to whom the Several Petitions from the Royal Burghs of Scotland were Referred' (London, HMSO, 1819)

House of Commons, 'Report from the Select Committee to whom the Several Petitions from the Royal Burghs of Scotland were Referred in the years 1818, 1819 and 1820' (HMSO, London, 1820)

House of Commons, 'The Management of the Crown Estate', Treasury Committee Eighth Report of Session 2009–10, HC 325–1, 2010

Houston, R. and Knox, W. (eds), *The New Penguin History of Scotland: from the earliest times to the present day* (Penguin, London, 2001)

Hume, J., *Remarks on the First Report of the Select Committee on Fictitious Votes in Scotland with Extracts from the Evidence* (Adam and Charles Black, Edinburgh, 1887)

Hunter, J., *The Making of the Crofting Community* (John Donald, Edinburgh, 1976)

Hunter, J., *On the Other Side of Sorrow: nature and people in the Scottish Highlands* (Mainstream, Edinburgh, 1995)

Hunter, J., 'Towards a Land Reform Agenda for a Scots Parliament', John McEwen Memorial Lecture, 1995

Hunter, J., *Last of the Free: a millennial history of the Highlands and Islands of Scotland* (Mainstream, Edinburgh, 2000)

Hunter, J., *From the Low Tide of the Sea to the Highest Mountain Tops. Community Ownership of Land in the Highlands and Islands of Scotland* (The Islands Book Trust, Kershader, 2012)

Hutchison, I. G. C., 'The Electorate and the Electoral System in Scotland, c1800–c1950', in Romanelli, R. (ed.), *How Did They Become Voters?: the History of Franchise in Modern European Representation*, (Kluwer Law International, The Hague, 1998), 418–419

Innes, C., *Origines Parochiales Scotiae: the antiquities ecclesiastical and territorial of the parishes of Scotland* (Lizars, Edinburgh, 1854)

Innes, C., *Lectures in Scotch Legal Antiquities* (Edmonston and Douglas, Edinburgh, 1872)

Jarman, A. L., 'Customary Rights in Scots Law: Test Cases on Access to Land in the Nineteenth Century', *The Journal of Legal History*, vol. 28:2 (2007), 207–32

Jarman, A. L., *Custom, Community and Common Land* (Dundee University Press, Dundee, forthcoming)

Johnston, T. *Our Scots Noble Families* (Forward Publishing, Glasgow, 1909 (republished by Argyll Publishing, Glendaruel, Argyll, 1999))

Johnston, T., *The History of the Working Classes in Scotland* (Forward Publishing, Glasgow, 1929)

Kames, H. H., *Elucidations Respecting the Common and Statute Law of Scotland* (William Creech, Edinburgh, 1777)

Kay, J. and King, M., *The British Tax System* (Oxford University Press, Oxford, 1990)

Kermack, L., *Coping with Rights to Buy – Part I*, Scottish Perspective, Turcan Connell

Knox, J., *The First Book of Discipline*, 'Sixth Head', available at www.swrb.com/newslett/actualNLs/bod_ch03.htm#SEC06

Knox, S., 'The Scattalds of Shetland' (PhD thesis, University of Edinburgh, 1980)

Land Reform Policy Group, 'Identifying the Problems' (The Scottish Office, Edinburgh, 1998)

Land Reform Policy Group, 'Identifying the Solutions' (The Scottish Office, Edinburgh, 1998)

Land Reform Policy Group, 'Recommendations for Action' (The Scottish Office, Edinburgh, 1999)

Land Registry, '10-Year Strategic Plan, 2003–4 to 2012–13', p. 45–46.

Letterewe Estate, 'Letterewe Management Plan 1999–2009' (Letterewe Estate, Letterewe, 1998)

Lister-Kaye, J., *Ill Fares the Land: a Sustainable Land Ethic for the Sporting Estates of the Highlands and Islands* (Scottish Natural Heritage, Edinburgh, 1994)

Lloyd, T., 'Don't Bet the House on It: No turning back to housing boom and bust' (Compass, London, 2009)

Local Authority (Scotland) Accounts Advisory Committee, 'Accounting for the Common Good Fund: A Guidance Note for Practitioners' (LASAAC, Edinburgh, 2007)

Lorimer, H., 'Guns, Game and the Grandee: the cultural politics of deer-stalking in the Scottish Highlands', *Ecumene*, vol. 7:4, 2000

Loux, A. C., The Great Rabbit Massacre – A 'Comedy of the Commons'? Custom, Community and Rights of Public Access to the Links of St Andrews. *Liverpool Law Review*, vol. 22, 2000, 123–55

Lynch, M. (ed.), *The Oxford Companion to Scottish History* (Oxford University Press, Oxford, 2001)

Mabo and Others v Queensland (No. 2), High Court of Australia, [1992] HCA 23; (1992) 175 CLR 1 F.C. 92/014, 3 June 1992

MacAskill, J., *We Have Won The Land: the story of the purchase by the Assynt Crofters' Trust of the North Lochinver Estate* (Acair, Stornoway, 1999)

MacAskill, J., ' "The most arbitrary, scandalous act of tyranny": the Crown, private proprietors and the ownership of the Scottish foreshore in the nineteenth century', *Scottish Historical Review*, Vol. 85:2, No. 220, October 2006, 277–304

McCrone, D., 'Land, Democracy and Culture in Scotland', John McEwen Memorial Lecture, 1997

McCulloch, J. R., *A Treatise on the Succession to Property Vacant by Death* (Longman, Brown, Green and Longmans, London, 1848)

MacDonald, F., 'Viewing Highland Scotland: ideology, representation and the "natural heritage"', *Area*, vol. 30:3, 1998, 237–244

MacDonald, F., 'The Last Outpost of Empire: Rockall and the Cold War', *Journal of Historical Geography*, 32, 2006, 627–47

McEwen, J., *Who Owns Scotland* (EUSPB, Edinburgh, 1977, 1st edition)

MacGregor, B., 'Land Tenure in Scotland', John McEwen Memorial Lecture, 1993

McIntosh, A., *Soil and Soul: People versus Corporate Power* (London, Aurum Press, 2001)

Mackenzie, A. F. D., 'Contesting land, creating community, in the Highlands and Islands, Scotland', *Scottish Geographical Journal*, vol. 120:3, 2004, 159–80

Mackenzie, A. F. D., 'A common claim: community land ownership in the Outer Hebrides, Scotland', *International Journal of the Commons*, vol. 4:1, 2010

Mackenzie, F., *Places of Possibility. Property, Nature and Community Land Ownership* (Wiley-Blackwell, London, 2012)

MacKinnon, I., *Crofters: indigenous people of the Highlands and Islands*, Scottish Crofting Foundation, 2008

MacKinnon, I. And Walker, S., 'The State of Crofting in Camuscross', 2009

Mackintosh, J., *The History of Civilisation in Scotland* (Aberdeen, 1877)

Mackintosh Committee, 'Law of Succession in Scotland', *Report of the Committee of Inquiry*, 1950–51 Cmd. 8144 (Scottish Home Department, Edinburgh, 1951)

McLean, I., 'The politics of land tax – then and now', in Maxwell, D. and Vigor, A., *Time for Land Value Tax?* (IPPR, London, 2005)

MacLean, J. P., *History of the Island of Mull* (Greenville, Ohio, 1923)

Macmillan, D., 'The Economic Case for Land Reform', University of Aberdeen, Department of Agriculture, Economics Group Research paper Ref 99/1

McNeill, P. and MacQueen, H., *Atlas of Scottish History to 1707* (University of Edinburgh, Edinburgh, 1996)

Maitland Club, *Miscellany of the Maitland Club Consisting of Original Papers and Other Documents Illustrative of the History and Literature of Scotland Vol. II* (Maitland Club, Edinburgh, 1840)

Marland, A., 'Seton Fields Case Study' (Caledonia Centre for Social Development, Inverness, 2007)

Mather, A. S., 'Protected Areas in the Periphery', *Journal of Rural Studies*, vol. 9:4, October 1993, pp. 371–84

Mather, A. S., 'The Structure of Forest Ownership in Scotland: a first approximation', *Journal of Rural Studies*, vol. 3:2, 1987, 175–82

Mather, A. S., 'Protected Areas in the Periphery: Conservation and Controversy in Northern Scotland', *Journal of Rural Studies*, vol. 9:4, 1993, 371–84

Meikle, M. M., *A British Frontier?: Lairds and Gentlemen in the Eastern Borders 1540–1603* (Tuckwell Press, Phantassie, 2004)

Millman, R., 'The Marches of the Highland Estates', *Scottish Geographical Magazine*, vol. 85:3, 1969, 172–81

Muellbauer, J., 'Property Taxation and the economy', in, Maxwell, D. and Vigor, A., *Time for Land Value Tax?* (IPPR, London, 2005)

Murray, W. H., *Rob Roy MacGregor: his life and times* (Canongate, Edinburgh, 1982)

Napier Commission, 'Report of the Commissioners of Inquiry into the Conditions of the Crofters and Cottars in the Highlands and Islands of Scotland', (House of Commons, London, 1884)

Nusbacher, A., *1314 Bannockburn* (Tempus, Stroud, 2005)

Ockrent, L., *Land Rights: An Enquiry into the History of Registration for Publication in Scotland* (William Hodge and Company, London, 1942)

ODPM, 'Communities Taking Control: Final Report of the Cross-sector Work Group on Community Ownership and Management of Assets' (Office of the Deputy Prime Minister, London, April 2006)

Office of the Auditor General of British Columbia, *Treaty Negotiations in British Columbia: An Assessment of the Effectiveness of British Columbia's Management and Administrative Processes* (Office of the Auditor General, Victoria, November 2006)

Old Statistical Account 1791–1799, vol. 3, no. XXXII, Bracadale

Orr, W., *Deer Forests, Landlords and Crofters* (John Donald, Edinburgh, 1982)

Platteau, J-P. and Baland, J-M., 'Impartible Inheritance Versus Equal Division: a Comparative Perspective Centred on Europe and Sub-Saharan Africa', in de Janvry, A., *Access to Land, Rural Poverty, and Public Action* (World Institute for Development Economics Research, Oxford University Press, Oxford, 2001)

Posen, A. S., 'Finding the Right Tool for Dealing with Asset Price Booms', speech to the MPR Monetary Policy and Markets Conference, London, 1 December 2009

Prebble, J., *The Highland Clearances* (Secker and Warburg, London, 1963)

Rankine, J., *The Law of Landownership in Scotland* (William Green & Sons, Edinburgh, 1909, 4th edition)

Reid, D., 'Crofters' Common Grazings', Commonweal Working Paper 2 (Caledonia Centre for Social Development, Inverness, January 2003)

Reid, K., *The Law of Property in Scotland* (Butterworths, Edinburgh, 1996)

Reid, K. and Gretton, G. L., *Conveyancing* (Thomson/W. Green, Edinburgh, 2004, 3rd edition)

Rennie, R., 'Land Registration and the Decline of Property Law', *Edinburgh Law Review*, vol. 14, 2010, 62–79

Rickwood, P. W., 'The National Land Fund 1946–1980: the failure of a policy initiative', *Leisure Studies*, vol. 6:1, January 1987, 15–23

Robertson, W., *Historical Tales and Legends of Ayrshire* (Hamilton, Adams and Co, London, 1889)

Rodger, R., *The Transformation of Edinburgh: Land, Property and Trust in the Nineteenth Century* (Cambridge University Press, Cambridge, 2001)

Roth, C. F., 'Without Treaty, without Conquest: Indigenous Sovereignty in Post-Delgamuuk v British Columbia', *Wicazo Sa Review*, vol. 17:2, 'Sovereignty and Governance, II' (autumn, 2002)

Samuel, A. M. M., 'Cultural Symbols and Landowners' Power: the Practice of Managing Scotland's Natural Resource', *Sociology*, vol. 34:4, 2000, 691–706

Scottish Government, *Asset Management Review of Rural Land*, Report to the Minister for the Environment' (Scottish Government, Edinburgh, 2009)

Scottish Government, *Overview of Evidence on Land Reform in Scotland* (Central Research Unit, 2012)

Scottish Land Commission, 'Public Policy Toward Land in Scotland' (Scottish Land Commission, 1997)

Scottish Land Enquiry Committee, *Scottish Land Rural and Urban*, The Report of the Scottish Land Enquiry Committee (Hodder and Stoughton, London, 1914)

Scottish Land Fund, *The Scottish Land Fund Evaluation, Final Report*, 4 May 2007, SQW Consulting

Scottish Law Commission, *Report on Succession*, Scot Law Com No 124 (Scottish Law Commission, Edinburgh, 1990

Scottish Law Commission, *Property Law – Abolition of the Feudal System*, Discussion Paper 93 (Scottish Law Commission, Edinburgh, 1991)

Scottish Law Commission, *Report on Abolition of the Feudal System*, Scot Law Com No 168 (Scottish Law Commission, Edinburgh, 1999)

Scottish Law Commission, *Report on Law of the Foreshore and Sea Bed*, Scot Law Com No 190 (Scottish Law Commission, Edinburgh, 2003)

Scottish Law Commission, *Report on Conversion of Long Leases*, Scot Law Com No 204 (Scottish Law Commission, Edinburgh, 2006)

Scottish Law Commission, *Discussion Paper on Succession*, Discussion Paper 136 (Scottish Law Commission, Edinburgh, 2007)

Scottish Law Commission, *Report on Succession*, Scot Law Com No 215 (Scottish Law Commission, Edinburgh, 2009)

Scottish Law Commission, *Report on Land Registration*, Scot Law Com No, 222 (Scottish Law Commission, Edinburgh, 2010)

Scottish Natural Heritage, *SNH Heritage Land: Towards a land ownership policy and rationalisation of SNH's land holding* SNH/09/3/2

Scottish Parliament, 'Abolition of Feudal Tenure 99/31' (Scottish Parliament, Edinburgh, 19 August 199)

Scottish Parliament, Crofting Reform (Scotland) Bill SPICe Briefing 10/01 (Scottish Parliament, Edinburgh, 8 January 2010)

Sellar, D., 'Farewell to Feudalism', in Dewar, P. B. (ed.), *Burke's Landed Gentry: The Kingdom in Scotland* (Burke's Peerage and Gentry, London, 2001)

Shaw, S., *An Accurate Alphabetical Index of the Registered Entails in Scotland* (Edinburgh, 1784)

Short, B., *Land and Society in Edwardian Britain* (Cambridge University Press, Cambridge, 1997)

Short, C., 'The traditional commons of England and Wales in the twenty-first century: meeting new and old challenges', *International Journal of the Commons*, vol. 2:2 (July 2008), 192–221.

Shucksmith, B., 'Committee of Inquiry on Crofting, Final Report 2008' (www.croftinginquiry.org)

Simpson, J. H., *The Feuars of Gifford* (Scotland's Cultural Heritage, Edinburgh, 1986)

Sinclair, J. *General View of the Agriculture of the Northern Counties and Islands of Scotland* (London, 1795)

Sinclair, J., *General Report of the Agricultural State and Political Circumstances of Scotland* (Abernethy & Walker, Edinburgh, 1814)

Skene, W. F., *Celtic Scotland: A History of Ancient Alban, Vol. III, Land and People* (David Douglas, Edinburgh, 1880)

Skerratt, S., et al., *Rural Scotland in Focus 2010* (Scottish Agricultural College, Edinburgh, 2010)

Smith, A., *An Inquiry into the Nature and Causes of the Wealth of Nations* (W. Strahan and T. Cadell, London, 1776)

Stair, Viscount, *The Institutions of the Law of Scotland* (Edinburgh, 1681)

Steven, A. J. M., 'Revolution in Scottish Land Law', *Electronic Journal of Comparative Law*, vol. 8:3 (October 2004)

Symmons, C. R., 'Ireland and the Rockall Dispute: An Analysis of Recent Developments', *IBRU Boundary and Security Bulletin* (spring 1998)

Wadsworth, M., *Tax, Benefits, Pensions: Keep It Simple Part 2: Ten steps to simplicity* (The Bow Group, London, 2006)

Wightman, A., *Who Owns Scotland* (Canongate, Edinburgh, 1996)

Wightman, A., *Scotland: Land and Power – The Agenda for Land Reform* (Luath Press, Edinburgh, 1999)

Wightman, A., 'Land Reform: Politics, Power and the Public Interest', John McEwen Memorial Lecture, 1999

Wightman, A. and Higgins, P., 'Sporting Estates and the Recreational Economy in the Highlands and Islands of Scotland', *Scottish Affairs*, vol. 31 (2000), 18–36

Wightman, A. and Perman, J., 'Common Good Land in Scotland: A Review and Critique', 'Commonweal Working Paper Number 5' (Caledonia Centre for Social Development, Inverness, 2005)

Wightman, A., 'Land Reform: An agenda for the 2007–2011 Scottish Parliament' (Wightman, 2007)

Wightman, A., 'Land Reform (Scotland) Act 2003: (Part 2, the community right to buy) a Two-Year Review' (Caledonia Centre for Social Development, Inverness, 2007)

Wightman, A., *Community Land Rights: A Citizen's Guide* (Ballallan House, Portree, 2009)

Wightman, A., 'Common Good Funds 2005–2012' (forthcoming in 2013)

Wightman, A., 'A Land Value Tax for Scotland' (Scottish Green Party MSPs, 2010)

Wightman, A., *Forest Ownership in Scotland. A Scoping Study* (Forest Policy Group, Aberfeldy, 2012)

Wightman, A., *Scotland needs radical land reform.* Evidence to the Land Reform Review Group, January 2013

Wiletts, D., *The Pinch: How the Baby Boomers Took Their Children's Future – And How They Can Give it Back* (Atlantic Books, London, 2010)

Wilkinson, T. L., 'Buying farmland is as good as gold', *eFinancialNews Ltd*, London, 2009

Appendix

List of Burghs in First Schedule to the Local Government (Scotland) Act 1947

Counties of Cities
Aberdeen
Dundee
Edinburgh
Glasgow

Large Burghs
Airdrie
Arbroath
Ayr
Clydebank
Coatbridge
Dumbarton
Dumfries
Dunfermline
Falkirk
Greenock
Hamilton
Inverness
Kilmarnock
Kirkcaldy
Motherwell and Wishaw
Paisley
Perth
Port Glasgow
Rutherglen
Stirling

Small Burghs
Aberchirder
Aberfeldy
Aberlour
Abernethy
Alloa
Alva
Alyth
Annan
Ardrossan
Armadale
Auchterarder
Auchtermuchty
Ballater
Banchory
Banff
Barrhead
Bathgate
Biggar
Blairgowrie and Rattray
Bo'ness
Bonnyrigg and Lasswade
Brechin
Bridge of Allan
Buckhaven and Methil
Buckie
Burghead
Burntisland

Callander
Campbeltown
Carnoustie
Castle Douglas
Cockenzie and Port Seton
Coldstream
Coupar Angus
Cove and Kilcreggan
Cowdenbeath
Crail
Crieff
Cromarty
Cullen
Culross
Cumnock and Holmhead
Cupar
Dalbeattie
Dalkeith
Darvel
Denny and Dunipace
Dingwall
Dollar
Dornoch
Doune
Dufftown
Dunbar
Dunblane
Dunoon

Small Burghs—contd

Duns
East Linton
Elgin
Elie and Earlsferry
Ellon
Eyemouth
Falkland
Findochty
Forfar
Forres
Fortrose
Fort William
Fraserburgh
Galashiels
Galston
Gatehouse
Girvan
Gourock
Grangemouth
Grantown-on-Spey
Haddington
Hawick
Helensburgh
Huntly
Innerleithen
Inveraray
Inverbervie
Invergordon
Inverkeithing
Inverurie
Irvine
Jedburgh
Johnstone
Keith
Kelso
Kilrenny, Anstruther
   Easter and Wester
Kilsyth
Kilwinning
Kinghorn

Kingussie
Kinross
Kintore
Kirkcudbright
Kirkintilloch
Kirkwall
Kirriemuir
Ladybank
Lanark
Langholm
Largs
Lauder
Laurencekirk
Lerwick
Leslie
Leven
Linlithgow
Loanhead
Lochgelly
Lochgilphead
Lochmaben
Lockerbie
Lossiemouth and
   Branderburgh
Macduff
Markinch
Maybole
Melrose
Millport
Milngavie
Moffat
Monifieth
Montrose
Musselburgh
Nairn
Newburgh
New Galloway
Newmilns and
   Greenholm
Newport

Newton-Stewart
North Berwick
Oban
Oldmeldrum
Peebles
Penicuik
Peterhead
Pitlochry
Pittenweem
Portknockie
Portsoy
Prestonpans
Prestwick
Queensferry
Renfrew
Rosehearty
Rothes
Rothesay
St. Andrews
St. Monance
Saltcoats
Sanquhar
Selkirk
Stewarton
Stonehaven
Stornoway
Stranraer
Stromness
Tain
Tayport
Thurso
Tillicoultry
Tobermory
Tranent
Troon
Turriff
Whitburn
Whithorn
Wick
Wigtown

Index

Italics = entry in Table or Figure
34n n = footnote

a non domino 278–280
  and Hill of Alyth 283
  and reform 406
  and Rockall 91
  and Thornhill 288–289
Aberdeen
  bishopric of 26
  Board of Management of College
    of 431n
  Corporation of Tailors of 414n
  University of 133, 136
Aberdeenshire 26
  and Highlands 110
  and land reform 65, 110, 236
Abolition of Feudal Tenure etc.
  (Scotland) Act 2000 *see under*
  feudalism
Access to Mountains (Scotland) bill
  206
Adams, Ian 268, 270, 272, 274, 397
  and Legal Geography paper xiv
Adams, Sheenagh *see under* Registers
  of Scotland, Keeper
Agricultural Holdings (Scotland) Act
  1883 234
  1949 111, 238, 312
  1991 233, 238
  2003 232, 238, 239, 262, 313, 326,
    352

agricultural subsidies 240–248, 409
Aikman, Logan 208
Airlie, Earl of 107
  and Balmoral 152
  and heritage tax exemption 209
  and Hill of Alyth commonty 277,
    281–285
Aitken, Bill 355
Alexander III 16
allodial tenure 99, 181, 419n
Alnwickhill Proprietors' Association
  195
Altyre Estate 209
Alyth
  Hill of 276–277, 281–285
  Market Muir 201
Anderson Strathern Nominees Ltd.
  369
Arbuthnott, Lord 114
Argyll and Bute Council
  and Crown Estate 188 –189
  and landownership database 138 –
    139
  and Lunga Estate 404
Argyll, Duke of 27, 32, 34, 118, 137,
    255, 365
  and prescription 36, 341
Association for the Protection of
  Rural Scotland 208

Assynt Crofters' Trust 150, 195–198, *200*, 202, 204, 250, 314–315
Atholl, Duke of 118, 137, 154, 255, 365
Auld v Hay, 1880 35
Australia, terra nullius 14, 93–95
Austria 126, 260
Ayr *see under* common good

Bachnagairn 152
Baird, John 109
Balerno Common 271, 290
Balfour, Robert 209
Balmoral 151–154, 220
Banff *see under* common good
Bannockburn *see* Bruce, Robert
Belgium 260, 303
Ben Nevis 170, 217
Berlin Conference of 1884–85 12, 17, 87
Birse 26
Birse Community Trust *201*, 285–286
Blairgowrie *see under* common good
Bocardo Société Anonyme *158, 163*, 373–375
Boghead 338
Bona vacantia 182, 185, 406
Book of Discipline 24–25, 28
Borve and Annishader 197
Boyack, Sarah 171, 356
Bracadale *see* Cuillin
Braeriach 209
Brankin, Rhona 356
British Columbia 92
Brown, Gordon 209, 266
Bruce, Robert the 12–19, 74, 88, 184
Bryce, James 206
Bryden, John 316
Buccleuch, Duke of 4, 84, 104, 107, 116, 118, 137, *154*, 243, 324–325, 361, 365, 368–370
Buccleuch Estates Ltd. 368–370, 375
burgage tenure 71, 74–80
burghs

commons *see under* common good
and commonty division 71
origins of 75, 290
elections in 74–76, 102–105
and land reform 410
list of *Appendix*
sale of superiorities in 80–82
Burgh Police (Scotland) Act of 1833 80
Burntisland *see under* common good
business rates 107, 381, 385–386

Cairngorms 114, 136, 209, 213, 214–217, 230, 384
Caledonia Centre for Social Development 357
Callander, Robin xiii, 2, 26, 68–69, 86, 270, 272, 286, 293
Cameron, Dr Ewen 325
Campbell of Glenorchy, Sir John 58
Cannadine, David 106, 128, 130, 137, 161
Capital Transfer Act 1984 211
Carluke *see under* commonty
Carluke Development Trust 275
Carluke Parish Historical Society 275
Carter, Ian 236, 313
Cassillis, 4th Earl of 28
Castle Douglas *see under* common good
Cayman Islands 215, 372
Channel Tunnel Rail Link 379
Charles I 32, 55–56
Charles II 55
Chartist Land Plan 110, 193
Chris Brasher Trust 204
Christie of Lochdochart, John 135, 210
Churchill, Winston 212, 338, 377–378
Claim of Right 108
clan
    Campbell 58
    Chattan 59

Gregor 58
lands of 57–64, 96–97, 161
MacLeod and Cuillin 170, 177
MacFarlane 278–279
Coldstream *see under* common good
Commendator 26, 28, 29
Commercial Land Company 110, 193
Committee of the Articles 32
Committee of Inquiry on Crofting 251
Common Agricultural Policy 240
Common chest of Wittenberg 303
common good 74–87, 291–304
Act of 1491 76–77, 292–312
Ayr 294–296
Banff 298
Blairgowrie 393–396
Burntisland 294
Castle Douglas 85
Coldstream 85
Crieff 85
Dalkeith 85
definition of 298–299
Dunblane 397–400
Dunkeld 85
Edinburgh 20, 77–82, 305–310
Eyemouth 85
Forfar 297
Fortrose 83–84
Fraserburgh 85
Galston 85
Gatehouse-of-Fleet 85
Girvan 85
Hamilton 300–301
historical loss of 74–87
Kinghorn 347
Kinross 293
and land reform 328, 339, 410
Letham 195
Musselburgh 294
Port Seton 294
Rattray *see* Blairgowrie
Rothesay 187
St Andrews 86

Selkirk 187
and superiorities 79–82
value of 302
common mosses 71, 271–272, 293
commonty
Aberdeenshire 286–288
Carluke 274–276
division of 70–71, 271–276
Forest of Birse 285–286
Hill of Alyth 276–277, 281–285
Thornhill 288–290
uses of 69
Community Land Rights 390–400
Community Land Unit 198–199, 320, 350
community ownership 192–205, 291, 314, 345, 409
and commons 270
of woodlands 262
in urban Scotland 351–352
Comrie 210, 345
conditional tax exemption 208–211
Connolly, Billy 306
Co-operative Party 381
Corrour 404
cottars 51, 65, 249
Council Tax 381–388, 410
Countryside Commission for Scotland 133
Craig, James 20
Creag Meagaidh 148, 258
Crieff *see under* common good
Criminal Law (Consolidation) (Scotland) Act 1995 36
Crofters Commission 146, 252–253, 404
Crofters' Holdings (Scotland) Act 1886 65, 109–110, 194, 235–236, 250, 311–312, 402
crofting 99, 146, 194, 234–236, 249–254
Cromlix Estate 398–399
Crossgates 345
Crossraguel Abbey 28–29
crown commons 71, 270

Crown Estate Commission 184–191,
    335, 407–408, 411
Crown Estate Review Working
    Group 189, 328
Crown Estates Act 1961 186
crown land and rights 24, 27, 43, 55–
    56, 98, 184–191, 280, 328, 407–
    408
  in Australia 92–95, 98–99
  and Balmoral 151–154
  and colonialism 88–92
  and Cuillin 171–173, 179–183, 188
  extent of 146–148
  and feudalism 9, 12–17, 31–32, 39,
    48–50, 56, 57–63, 77–78, 97–99,
    103, 333
  and foreshore and seabed 335
  history of 12–16, 184
  and ownerless property 406
  and Rockall 88–91
Crown Office 91, 182, 185, 334,
    406
Crown Private Estates Act 1862 152
Cuillin 36, 167–183, 188–189, 217,
    342, 406
Cunliffe, Michael 171
Cunningham, Roseanna 327, 328,
    355–356
Cunningham, Tom 289
Cyprus 369

Dalkeith *see under* common good
Dalkeith, Earl of 105, 370
Dalton, Hugh 212
David I 13–16, 74
davoch 176
Delnadamph Estate 152
Denmark, 88, 90,91, 107, 108, 109,
    267, 409
Derby, Lord 126–127
Dewar Donald 182, 315, 320–325,
    338, 343, 349
Dingwall-Fordyce, Andrew 116
Drummond, Arthur William Henry
    Hay 398–399

Drummond Young, James, Lord
    172–180, 299, 423n
Duchy of Cornwall 153
Duff House 298
Dulverton, Lord 114, 215
Dunblane *see under* common good
dùthaich 58, 95–98

Easterhouse 3, 355
Edinburgh *see under* common good
    and feudalism
Edinburgh Merchant Company 113
Edward IV 58
Edwards, Andrew 370, 372
Eigg, Isle of 196, 198, 202–204,
    217, 291, 314–315, 320, 344,
    350
Eilean I Vow 278
elegant power 4
England 13, 15–18, 25, 39, 58–59, 62,
    79, 80, 103, 108, 114, 115, 126,
    185, 227, 270, 324, 339, 354,
    371, 382, 402
entail, law of 39, 42–48, 51, 110, 236,
    339, 363, 366, 416n
Equal Franchise Act of 1928 331
European Convention on Human
    Rights 401–402
Ewing, Fergus 366
Eyemouth *see under* common good

Faculty of Advocates 361
Falkirk Tryst 271
Family Law (Scotland) Act 2006 364
Fayed, Mohammed al 373
Fettes Trust 11
feudalism
  abolition of 41, 47, 97, 316, 331–
    334
  and Arran 333, 337
  and common good 77–78
  and commonties 68, 269
  and the crown 184
  and the Cuillin 176
  definitions of 8–11

and Edinburgh New Town 10–11, 20–22
in Europe 108
and the Highlands 57–65
history and development of 12–22, 48–51, 69, 96–98, *313*
and human rights 402
and land reform 312, 323–326
and Raider of the Lost Titles 334, 336–338
and Robert the Bruce 16–19
Fforde, Charles 210, 420n
Fictitious Votes in Scotland 103–104
Fife, Duke of 151, 298
Finance Act of 1910 131
Finland 260
Forbes, James 26
foreshore 146, 179, 185, 187, 190, 316, 334–335, 401
Forest Policy Group 260
forestry 255–262, 411
   ownership of 259–261
   and tax breaks 257
   and tenant farmers 262
   and Wightman, Andy 136, 257
Forestry Commission 145–146, 150, 193, 222, 256, 258, 259, 285, 316, 411
Forfar *see under* common good
Forsyth, Michael 198, 250
Fortrose *see under* common good
France 18, 39, 41, 108, 109, 260
Fraser, Murdo 284
Fraserburgh *see under* common good
Friends of the People Society 109

Galbraith, Guy 168
Galbraith, Sam 315
Galston *see under* common good
Gardner, Daniel 91
Gatehouse-of-Fleet *see under* common good
General Band Act, 1587 59
Gentlemen Adventurers of Fife 61, 416n

George, Henry 129, 382
George Watson's College, Edinburgh 113
Germany 108, 303, 369, 370
Gigha 196, *201*, 202, 204, 314, 344
Girvan *see under* common good
Gladstone, William 110
Glasgow City Council 355
Glen Doll 152
Glenfeshie 114, 214–215
Glendale 194
Glenmore Properties Ltd 243, 245–246
Gordon, Sir Alexander 26
Grampian Regional Council 336
Grant of Rothiemurchus, John *160*, 209
Granton 369, 380, 436n
Gray of Contin, Lord 117

Haddington, Duke and Earl of 27, 362
Hamilton, Duke of 47, 106
Hamilton, Brian 289, 336–338
Hamilton, Duncan 171
Hamilton, Neil 373
Hamilton *see under* common good
Hankey, Maurice 318
Hardie, Andrew 109
Hastings, Max 223
Heriot's Trust 11, 22, 112–113, 306
Heritage Lottery Fund 215
Highlands and Islands Enterprise 146, 150, 197, 198, 320, 328, 350
Highland Council 138–140, 189, 204
Highland Land League 109
Highland Land Law Reform Association 236
HMRC *see under* Inland Revenue
Hope, Dennis M 95
house prices 263–265
Hungary 260
Hunter, James 58, 205, 226, 235, 252, 313, 317
hunting estates 219–231

Huntly, Earl of 26
hypothec 110, 236

Iceland 88, 90, 91
Inchcape, Lord 106, 243
Inland Revenue 162, 372–374
    1910 survey 127–133, 131, 392,
    421n
Innes, Cosmo 1, 15, 50, 51–54, 61,
    83, 175, 176, 269, 283, 349
Invergeldie Estate 210
Ireland 12, 17, 88, 90, 91, 127, 128,
    373, 389, 392

James IV 23, 58, 63, 77
James V 24, 59
James VI 29, 32, 59, 62, 170
John Muir Trust 170, 204, 213–214,
    216, 217
Johnston, Tom 3, 4, 18, 24, 55, 62,
    76, 78, 84, 102, 128, 269, 283,
    311
Jubilee Line 377, 379
Juridical Society 52

Kames, Lord 35, 53
Kidd, Bill 355
King, Mervyn 382
King's Park, Stirling 188
Kinghorn *see under* common good
Kinghorn Community Land
    Association 257
Kinross *see under* common good
Knoydart 148, 151–153, 159, 232–
    233

Laighills, Dunblane 397–400
land reform 1–7, 115–116, 118, 140,
    192–205, 231, 233, 236, 240,
    311–329, 344–358
    and crofting 249–252
    and Finland 260
    history of 107–119, 236
    and land tenure 330–342
    proposals for 401–412

and succession 366
    see also community ownership
Land Reform Review Group xvii,
    313, 329, 356, 375
Land Reform (Scotland) Act 2003
    204, 210, 313, 326–329, 343–
    358
    and Scottish Land Fund 200
Land Reform Policy Group 262, 313,
    316, 324, 336, 346, 350, 352,
    353, 432n
Land Register 39, 121–122, *123–125*,
    137–142, 180, 183, 274, 280,
    340, 372, 391, 408
Land Registration (Scotland) Act
    1979 312
    reform of 39–340, 375, 405
Land Registration etc. (Scotland)
    Act 2012 279–280, 375
Land Registry 371–372
Land Restitution Act 407
Land Settlement (Scotland) Act 1919
    111
land tenure 330–342
Land Tenure Reform (Scotland) Act
    1974 11, 312, 402
land value taxation 376–389
landowners
    aristocracy 161–162
    community 143, 192–205
    heritage 143, 206–218
    offshore 162–165
    private 143, 150–161
    public 143, 145–150
    secret 368–375
    top 100 landowners *154–161*
landownership
    and the franchise 16, 19, 80–83,
    102–105
    statistics 142–166
Latvia 260
Lawson, Nigel 257
Lean, Geoffrey 257
leasehold 11, 308, 313, 326, 334, 338–
    339, 402

leasehold casualties 334, 338
Leases Act 1449 31
Litchfield, Leon 243
Letham *see under* common good
Letterewe Estate 224–225
letters of fire and sword 58
Leverhulme, Lord 193
Lithuania 260
Lloyd George, David 105, 128–131, 193, 212, 378, 382
loans 270–273, 293
Local Authority (Scotland) Accounts Advisory Committee 302
Lochhead, Richard 242, 245
Long Leases (Scotland) Act 2012 310, 339
Lord of the Isles 57–58, 170
Lords of the Congregation 27
Lunga Estate 404
Luther, Martin 23, 303
Luxembourg 369
Lyon, George 232

Mabo, Eddie 14, 93–100
McCabe, Tom 300
MacDonald, Calum 168, 315
MacDonald of Keppoch, Ranald Alasdair 96–100
McEwen, John 134–137, 311, 313–315
McEwen Memorial Lecture 320, 343, 403, 432n
McGrath, John 191
MacGregor, Professor Bryan 403
Mackenzie George 52
Mackintosh Report on succession 361–362
McLean, Iain 382
MacLeod, John *see* Cuillin
Macpherson, John 194
MacPherson, Malcolm 296
MacQueen, Professor Hector 333
Mactaggart and Mickel 389
Malcolm III 13
Mar Lodge Estate 136, 214–216
Martin, Campbell 299

Mather, Sandy 132–133, 259
Menzies, Alan 172, 177
Mercer-Nairne, Robert 396
Merriam people *see* Mabo, Eddie
Metsäliito 260
Michie, Ray 196
Millman, Roger 133–136
Minginish *see* Cuillin
Monro, Sir Hector 337
Moray, Earl of 22, 243
Morrison, Alasdair 170, 181
Morrison, James 162
Mountainous Country Fund 208
Muellbauer, John 382
Muir, Thomas 109
Murray, David 307–308
Musselburgh *see under* common good

Napier Commission 110, 234–236, 323
Napoleonic Code 41
National Farmers Union Scotland 118, 238, 240, 246, 363, 364
National Land Company 110, 193
National Land Fund 212–213
National League and Covenant 55
national parks 116, 208, 211–212, 316, 326, 411
National Trust for Scotland 111, 170, 208, 212, *216*
Nature Conservancy Council 114, 148, 215
Neilston 345
Netherlands 43, 107, 109, 225, 303
Nobleman's Covenant *see* National League and Covenant
North British Railway Company 178
North East Mountain Trust 136
Norway 39, 229, 260

Office of the Deputy Prime Minister 354
oighreachd 58
Ordnance Survey 121, 139–140, 274, 276

Ostrom, Professor Elinor 192
ounceland 176
Our Scots Noble Families 128, 311
Outer Space Treaty 1967 95
Overseas landownership *see under*
    landowners

Pack, Brian 242, 246–247
Paine, Tom 382
Parliament Act 1911 111, 130
Perman, James 294
Perth & Kinross Council 329, 393
Perth, Treaty of 16
Poland 260
Pont
    Robert 29
    Timothy 29
Port Seton *see under* common good
Porter, Shirley 257
Posen, Adam 382
Potier, Malcolm 196
Pottinger, George 215
Poulson, John 215
Prebble, John 313
prescription 32–37, 63–64, 174, 291,
    312, 330, 340–342
    and *a non domino* 278–280
    and Alyth 283–284
    and Cuillin 174–183
    and public rights 339
    and reform 405–406
primogeniture 40–48, 106, 110, 153,
    236, 359–367
Privy Council 29, 58, 60, 62, 78, 170,
    414n

Queen's and Lord Treasurer's
    Remembrancer 182, 185–186,
    334

Radical War 1820 109
Raider of the Lost Titles 334, 336–
    338
Ramsay of Bamff, Sir James 277,
    283

Rankine, John 34–35, 68, 70, 177–
    178
Rattray *see under* common good
Rausing, Lisbet 404
Reform Act (Scotland) 1832 80, 312
Reformation 23–30
    and burgh reform 303–304
    and Luther *see* Luther
    and nobility 55
    and prescription 33–35
    and Register of Sasines 32
Register of Sasines
    Act 31–32, 37–39, 121–122, 375
    and Highlands 63
    and Inland Revenue Survey 132
    and Land Register 121–122, 137–
    138, 142, 180
    reform 406
    using 150, 391–392, 394–396
Registers of Scotland
    and agricultural tenant right to
    buy 239–240
    Keeper of 91, 121–122, 138, 180,
    239, 279–280, 391, 406
    and Cuillin 180
Registration Act, 1617 *see under*
    Register of Sasines
Return of Owners of Lands and
    Heritages Scotland 127–128
revocation, acts of 48, 55
Ricardo, David 382
Richard, Cliff 257
Ritchie, Bill 315
Rockall 88–92
Rosebery, Lord 47, 243
Rosie, George 257
Ross, Willie 294–296
Rothesay *see under* common good
Rothiemurchus 209
Rowardennan Estate 213
Roxburghe, Duke and Earl of 34,
    104, 107, 137, 243, 365
Royal Botanic Garden Edinburgh 54,
    146
Royal Scottish Forestry Society 135

Royal Society for the Protection of Birds 114, 166, 213–215, 217, *216, 244*
runrig 272, 276, 293
Russia 369
Ruthin Castle Ltd 298
Rynacra Commonty 272–273

St Andrews *see under* common good
Salmond, Alex 190, 285, 329, 336
Sauchieburn, Battle of 23
scattalds 271
Schiehallion 272
Scottish Crofting Foundation 99, 247
Scottish Estates Business Group 118, 364, 365, 404
Scottish Farms Alliance 236
Scottish Government 96, 150, 189, 200, 241–242, 245, 256, 301, 310, 328, 340, 354, 355, 366, 374, 375, 403, 407
    see also Scottish Ministers
Scottish Labour Party 134, 312, 351
Scottish Land and Estates *see* Scottish Landowners' Federation
Scottish Land and Property Federation *see* Scottish Landowners' Federation
Scottish Land Enquiry Committee 222, 237, 361
Scottish Land Fund 199–200, 202, *313*, 408
Scottish Land Reform Alliance 109
Scottish Land Reform Association 236
Scottish Land Restoration League 109
Scottish Landowners' Federation (SLF) 111, 114–118, 133, 171, 183, 209, 226, 317–318, 322, 324, 327, 337, 361, 363, 364, 404
Scottish Law Commission 122, 189–190, 280, 309–310, 325, 328, 330–342, 363–364, 375, 390, 406

Scottish Ministers
    and Alyth 285
    and community right to buy 343–350
    and crown property 182, 185–191
    and Forestry Commission 256
    landholdings 145–150
Scottish Mountaineering Club 208
Scottish National Party 134, 190, 252, 312, 327–329, 356, 366, 408
Scottish Natural Heritage 139, 148, 210–211, 215, 411
Scottish Parliament
    Acts of 54
    agricultural holdings 232
    crofting 65, 252–254
    and crown property 190–191
    and Cuillin 170
    feudalism 96, 333
    land reform 137–138, 192, 197, 262, 311–317, 328, 350–352, 355–358, 367, 407–410
    land tenure reform 331, 342
    landowners 105, 115–116, 118–119
    leasehold 310
    parliamentary answers 171, 299–300, 355
    petitions 96
Scottish Rural Property and Business Association *see* Scottish Landowners' Federation
Scottish Tenant Farmers Association 238
Scottish Water 145, *146*, 150
Scottish Wildlife Trust 204, 214, *216*, 217, 272
Seafield, Earl of 107, 118, 137, 243, 337
Secretary of State for Defence (MoD) 145–146, *149*
Selkirk *see under* common good
Seton Fields Community Company 349
Sewel, John *313*, 315–316, 322, 327

Shucksmith, Mark 251–252
Silverburn 345
Sinclair, Sir John 44, 54, 72
single farm payments 240–248
Skouboe, Flemming 215
Slovakia 260
Small Landholders Act 1911 111,
    311, 312
Smith, Adam 40, 45, 48, 360
Soames, Sir Nicholas 208–209
Södra 260
South Uist 89, 199, 204, 252–254
Southesk, Earl of 243
sporting estates 219–231, 387
sporting rates 226–227, 405
Stair, Lord 35, 41, 43, 52, 53, 107,
    360
Stewart, Allan 28, 36
Stirling Council 188, 397
Stormonth-Darling, Lord 178
Stornoway 193–194
succession 153, 318, 328, 331, 334,
    360–367, 404, 407
Sweden 259–260

tenant farmers 3, 5, 10, 25, 27, 32, 33,
    38, 65, 72, 74, 106, 110–111,
    127, 131–132, 232–248, 256,
    262, 275, 276–277, 281, 316,
    318, 323, 328, 352, 380, 409, 411
Tenements (Scotland) Act 2004 326
Thomson, Thomas 51, 54
Thornhill 288–290
Title Conditions (Scotland) Act 2003
    334
Titles to Land Consolidation
    (Scotland) Act 1868 359
Town and Country Planning Act
    1947 402
Town Councils 20, 75, 76, 81, 86,
    112, 193, 281–283, 292–302,
    306, 347, 393, 396–397, 410
Transfer of Crofting Estates
    (Scotland) Act 1997 146, 198, 250

Treasury 117, 185, 187–191, 267,
    369–370, 374, 275
Trotter, Alexander 117
Turcan Connell 118, 349, 364

Udal law 97, 271
ultimus haeres 182, 186, 406
Ulva 209
unciate 131–133
United Nations Economic
    Commission for Europe 259
University of Aberdeen Department
    of Forestry 133, 136
Unna, Percy 208

Victoria, Queen 12, 151–152, 220,
    396,
van Vlissingen 224
Vidal, HMS 89–91, 95

Wales 103, 128, 170, 270, 371
Wallace, Jim 140, 171, 183, 250
Wallace, William 16
Wark, Lord 298–299
Watson, Adam 136
Watson, Drennan 136
Waverley Market 305–310
Waverley Railway (Scotland) Bill
    389
West Highland Free Press 170,
    312
Westminster Ardtornish, Treaty of
    58
Westminster, Duke of 365, 402
Who Owns Scotland 4, 126, 128, 134,
    137–141, 142–166, 311, 340,
    373–374
Will Woodlands 215
Wilson, Allan 350–351, 357
Wilson, Brian 171–172, 181–182,
    198–199, 250–251, 315, 317,
    320, 337, 350
Wittenberg 303
Wogan, Terry 257